SYMBOLIC EXCHANGE A

Theory, Culture & Society

Theory, Culture & Society caters for the resurgence of interest in culture within contemporary social science and the humanities. Building on the heritage of classical social theory, the book series examines ways in which this tradition has been reshaped by a new generation of theorists. It will also publish theoretically informed analyses of everyday life, popular culture, and new intellectual movements.

EDITOR: Mike Featherstone, *University of Teesside*

Recent volumes include:

Changing Cultures
Feminism, Youth and Consumerism
Mica Nava

Globalization
Social Theory and Global Culture
Roland Robertson

Risk Society
Towards a New Modernity
Ulrich Beck

Max Weber and the Sociology of Culture
Ralph Schroeder

Postmodernity USA
The Crisis of Social Modernism in Postwar America
Anthony Woodiwiss

The Body and Social Theory
Chris Shilling

Sociology in Question
Pierre Bourdieu

Economies of Signs and Space
Scott Lash and John Urry

Religion and Globalization
Peter Beyer

Baroque Reason
The Aesthetics of Modernity
Christine Buci-Gluckmann

SYMBOLIC EXCHANGE AND DEATH

Jean Baudrillard

Translated by
Iain Hamilton Grant

with an Introduction by
Mike Gane

SAGE Publications
London • Thousand Oaks • New Delhi

English translation © Sage Publications 1993
Introduction and Bibliography © Mike Gane 1993

First published in English 1993, Reprinted 1995

Originally published as *L'échange symbolique et la mort*, © Editions
Gallimard 1976

This translation is published with financial support from the French
Ministry of Culture.

Published in association with *Theory, Culture & Society*, School of
Health, Social and Policy Studies, University of Teesside

SAGE Publications Ltd
6 Bonhill Street
London EC2A 4PU

SAGE Publications Inc
2455 Teller Road
Thousand Oaks, California 91320

SAGE Publications India Pvt Ltd
32, M-Block Market
Greater Kailash – I
New Delhi 110 048

British Library Cataloguing in Publication data

Baudrillard, Jean
  Symbolic Exchange and Death. – (Theory,
  Culture & Society Series)
  I. Title   II. Grant, Iain Hamilton   III. Series
  301.01

  ISBN 0–8039–8398–0
  ISBN 0–8039–8399–9 pbk

Library of Congress catalog card number 93–85813

Typeset by Photoprint, Torquay, Devon
Printed in Great Britain by The Cromwell Press Ltd,
Broughton Gifford, Melksham, Wiltshire

CONTENTS

INTRODUCTION

MIKE GANE

Symbolic Exchange and Death, published in France in 1976, is without doubt Jean Baudrillard's most important book. It appeared alongside works by Claude Lévi-Strauss and Michel Foucault in Gallimard's prestigious series Bibliothèque des Sciences Humaines. It is remarkable in many respects that it has taken some years for the full impact of Baudrillard's work to be felt in English-speaking cultures, and then under something of a misunderstanding. For various complex reasons Baudrillard's name is associated with postmodernism, indeed he has often been called the 'high priest of postmodernism', yet it is clear that Baudrillard's own relationship with postmodernism is hardly positive. The interest in postmodernism has certainly served Baudrillard for there is enormous curiosity in establishing just what Baudrillard's position is if it is not postmodern. The translation and publication of *Symbolic Exchange and Death* will be decisive in this respect.

The great interest in Baudrillard's work in recent years has led to a sudden flood of translations, and this has not been without its own problems, for works written at many years distance have appeared in English as contemporaneous publications. The first work to appear in translation was *The Mirror of Production* in 1975 (French original 1973) followed in 1981 by *For a Critique of the Political Economy of the Sign* (originally 1972). Parts of *Symbolic Exchange and Death* became available in 1981 in journal article form, and in 1983 in the collection *Simulations* by Semiotext(e) in New York, a publishing house which subsequently published *In the Shadow of the Silent Majorities* (1983, originally 1978), *Forget Foucault* (1987, originally 1977), and *The Ecstasy of Communication* (1988, originally 1987). Two books of selected writings, *Jean Baudrillard: Selected Writings* (1988) and *Revenge of the Crystal* (1990), are now available in English, as are *Seduction* (1990, originally 1979), *Fatal Strategies* (1990, originally 1983), *Cool Memories* (1990, originally 1987) and *Transparency of Evil* (1993, originally 1990). The year 1993 will also see the publication of *Baudrillard Live*, a selection of interviews. The question arises therefore of how to make sense of this corpus and how does *Symbolic Exchange and Death* figure in it?

First of all some background on Jean Baudrillard himself. He was born in Reims in 1929. His formation and early teaching experience was as a Germanist. He wrote an early thesis on Nietzsche and Luther, and was particularly interested in the work of Hölderlin. His first publications were literary critical essays in *Les temps modernes* (1962–3). He was also interested in photography (an edited book of photographs was published in 1963), an interest he still maintains (in December 1992 there was an exhibition of his photographs in a gallery on the Champs-Élysées). In the 1960s he was the principal translator of the works of Peter Weiss into French, but he also translated Brecht and a sociological work on Third World millenarian movements by Wilhelm Mülhmann. In the 1960s he converted to sociology under the influence of Henri Lefebvre and Roland Barthes. Most of his university teaching career was at Nanterre in Paris. In the late 1960s he was associated with *Utopie* and later with *Traverses*, both radical journals outside the orthodox organisation of the left. He was deeply influenced by situationism but was never attached in any formal manner. In the 1970s he began to travel, to the USA, about which he wrote the book *America* (1988, originally 1986), but also more widely, as is partially documented in his *Cool Memories*. Initially, his main axis of travel in Europe was Paris–Milan–Barcelona, which today has become Paris–Berlin–Madrid. He has recently spent time in Berlin as well as Argentina and Brazil, and has made a rare visit to Britain: he reckons to spend about half of his time out of France. It comes as no surprise that Baudrillard has a growing world reputation, indeed he was the subject of a recent conference (in Montana in 1990, published as *Jean Baudrillard*, Stearns and Chaloupka, 1992), and that in recent surveys he ranks in the leading half-dozen French intellectuals in terms of citations and translations.

The flood of translations of Baudrillard's works has been accompanied by commentaries from writers such as Fredric Jameson, Douglas Kellner and Arthur and Marilouise Kroker. By and large these writers have tried to link Baudrillard's ideas with postmodernism. Jameson used Baudrillard to fill out a conception of postmodernism as the cultural formation of 'late capitalism'. In effect this line was taken a great deal further by Arthur and Marilouise Kroker. Douglas Kellner first presented Baudrillard as the major postmodern theorist but later altered the thesis, admitting that in reality Baudrillard's writings were generally extremely hostile to post-modernism. Kellner's book on Baudrillard (1989) is an attempt to argue that he is a dangerous writer whose position needs to be entirely rejected. Yet there is still a sense in which the relation to Baudrillard is one of repulsion and attraction. Even Kellner points to the 'insightful' and 'brilliant' analyses in *Symbolic Exchange and Death* (Kellner, 1989: 102).

Baudrillard's position in *The System of Objects* (1968), but even more so in *The Consumer Society* (1970), seems influenced by a Marxist point of view. But there is a violent reaction to Marxism in *The Mirror of Production* (1973) that leads to the new synthesis that is explored in *Symbolic Exchange and Death* (1976). A formula in *For a Critique of the Political Economy of the Sign* (1981, originally 1972), the 'semiological reduction of the symbolic properly constitutes the ideological process' (p. 98), can be taken as a key statement of Baudrillard's object. It was at that time very clearly considered an analysis of crucial processes within capitalist society: an 'ideological reduction to the (capitalist) system of order and social values' (p. 100). Certainly in the years leading up to 1972 Baudrillard seemed to be working within a Marxist framework: he referred to the capitalist mode of production as the basis of the social formation. In 1970, with his book *The Consumer Society*, it was clear that unlike more orthodox Marxists he saw that affluence and consumption has profound consequences for social structure and cultural integration. Marxists like Althusser talked of the key role of social class reproduction in the family and the school ('ideological apparatuses of the State'), Baudrillard talked of the power of consumption and repressive ambience in a line of thought influenced by Barthes, Marcuse and McLuhan.

It became clear, however, that the critical base, the theoretical position, from which Baudrillard undertook his analyses was somewhat ambivalent. On the one hand there is in this period a gesture to the importance of the proletarian position. There is also increasing reference to the significance of an order higher than that of the semiotic culture. He called this the 'symbolic order', a more radical if more primordial basis. At first the symbolic order is discussed with reference to the famous analysis of gift-exchange by Marcel Mauss (see Baudrillard, 1981, originally 1972: 64ff.). This is an initial study, the first of a long series of oppositions between the symbolic and the semiotic order. Thus it is essential to clarify the nature of these two concepts. Of course this cannot be done definitively since many of the concepts have been modified through the course of Baudrillard's subsequent evolution. It is Baudrillard's own account of the sacred culture defined by Durkheim in *The Elementary Forms of the Religious Life* (1915), it is that defined by Max Weber as the enchanted world of traditional societies, it is the fatalistic culture of peasants. For Baudrillard Marx was not sufficiently radical in his analysis, it was not use-value which should have been contrasted with exchange-value, but symbolic exchange which should have been contrasted with commodity exchange. Baudrillard's reading of Marx suggests that his conception of communism was trapped within the matrix of the cultural order of rationalisation and therefore could not be other than its (bad) mirror-image. Like Mauss, Baudrillard suggests the superiority of the symbolic order over the semiotic order (the obligation of gift over the cash nexus) while witnessing the apparent destruction of the former by the latter. Against the Marxists, Baudrillard appears more radical, and more primitive. But there are surprises. Baudrillard does not simply document the course of the destruction of the symbolic order but analyses the ironic evolution of the semiotic order itself.

If we turn to *Symbolic Exchange and Death* we can follow the analyses of the *ideological process*. Chapter 1, on capitalism and production, is perhaps a crucial analysis. It is curious in many respects. It is written in a highly rhetorical style, playful, wilfully malicious. Although the analyses of simulation, fashion, sexuality, death, are likely to be more celebrated, this first chapter in a sense is more fundamental – yet the text is both assertive, dogmatic and at the same time illusive. The writing is in the main unsupported by any burden of evidence or any attempt at systematic argument, as if a highly perverse dialectical mania had grasped the writer. First of all Baudrillard presents the thesis that in order to grasp the nature of modern capitalism it must be thought of not as a mode of production but as a code dominated by the 'structural law of value'. This term is obviously developed from Marx's own law of value, but here it detaches itself from economics and becomes a mechanism which invades all cultural spheres. In other words all spheres can be analysed as the process of the political economy of the sign. Baudrillard insists in fact that the development of modern society is uneven, and like Weber argues that the process first attacks art, politics and culture and then the economy itself. The economy, after having passed through a specific phase of simulation known as the capitalist mode of production (the phase of the factory, etc.), undergoes an ironic logic since the mode of production inverts itself and begins to destroy the very separations it was built upon. Capital itself proceeds to destroy the hierarchy of base and superstructure, of production and reproduction, of labour and capital.

There are two steps in the argument which must be examined. The first is the argument concerning the nature of the change of the terms within the capitalist mode of production. The second is the argument concerning the relation between the symbolic order and capitalism. The character of the former argument is perhaps best grasped as process occurring at an already advanced stage of the destruction of the natural economy of primitive symbolic exchange (the argument follows on from that presented in *The Mirror of Production*). For Baudrillard the primitive society has no 'mode of production', indeed perhaps industrial factory capitalism is the only 'mode of production' that has existed as such. However, once the structural law of value attacks the elements of the system the code becomes determinant, ending any order of causation between the spheres of production and consumption. Hence the historical dialectic between them comes to an end. Baudrillard produces the irony of the Althusserian version of Marx which suggested that reproduction (class struggle) was determinant in history, for Baudrillard suggests that when reproduction becomes dominant labour and production change their sense, they lose their finality, that is, they lose their rationality as purposeful work as they become reproduced for the sake of the reproduction of work itself. This idea reflects the great change that has occurred in Western societies in relation to the meaning of the term alienation. When this happens all elements in the system are affected as the proletariat is incorporated into the social order; trade unions, strikes, revolts such as May '68 lose their claim to justice and radicality. Indeed the organisations and theoreticians who mark time with insistence on the centrality of 'production' and 'labour' – and those who believe in 'the use-value of their labour power – the proletariat – are virtually the most mystified and the least susceptible to this revolt' (p. 30 below). Baudrillard reorganises the theory of resistance and revolt from one based on internal system contradiction (Marx) to that of exclusion and excommunication (Durkheim and Mauss).

The second element in the argument is the scope and role Baudrillard gives to the symbolic order within the capitalist system. It almost appears as a replacement for the notion of a social infrastructure, and on occasions Baudrillard has formulations which approach this image. It is a mistake, then, to think that *Symbolic Exchange and Death* is simply about the 'ideological process' of the reduction of the symbolic by the semiotic. It is also about the irruption of the symbolic within the semiotic. The challenge, the stake is, he says, a dimension 'immanent in the code' (p. 39 below). In an analysis which at first sight appears slightly facile, the terms Baudrillard uses to analyse capitalism reverse all previous conceptions. The capitalist presents the gift of work to the proletarian. Because the proletarian cannot return this gift and cannot cancel it he cannot cancel the power of the capitalist. But the position and order of the capitalist is vulnerable none the less, since Baudrillard claims nothing can evade symbolic obligation, indeed not even the system itself: terrorism, the taking of hostages, sacrificial martyrdom, are challenges to the system which pass into the symbolic order. If there is a strategy in Baudrillard's work perhaps this is where it is discussed: the fundamental challenge to the semiotic system will be in the form of a gift which it will not be able to return (pp. 36–43 below).

The chapters which follow study themes directly related to the apparent destruction of the symbolic by the semiotic order. The chapter on simulation discusses the genealogy of the orders of simulation from the counterfeit, through production proper to the hyperreal order itself. Chapter 3 examines the case of fashion and the fashion cycle which is crucial to the analysis of consumer society and the commutation of all cultural elements, even the most apparently critical, to the code of fashion and its temporality. Chapter 4 examines the body and sexuality. Here the 'phallus exchange standard' operates as a cultural parallel with the law of value determining a specific destruction of the radical difference between the sexes and the symbolic exchanges based on it. In the next chapter, on death, Baudrillard presents a genealogy of the dead, the destruction of the original unities of life and death and the rituals which integrated the relations between generations in traditional societies. In the final chapter Baudrillard uses Saussure against Saussure. The great analyst of the sign, the originator of structural linguistics and semiology, Saussure also wrote voluminous notebooks on the hidden anagrams in classical literature. Baudrillard argues that this provides a clue to reading such poetry not as accumulation but as sacrificial, cyclical, as prestation and cancellation (extermination). This chapter also includes a critique of the Freudian analysis of jokes seen as complicit with the order of accumulation and repression.

After *Symbolic Exchange and Death* was published in 1976 Baudrillard published a number of brilliant short articles and reviews – a critical review of Foucault, a critique of the architecture of the Pompidou Centre, etc., as well as a set of poems called *L'ange de stuc* (*The Stucco Angel*). His next major work was *Seduction*, published in 1979. This developed the theme of the opposition of seduction to the semiotic and masculine principle of production; it suggested a return of the principle of seduction in consumer society, but in a changed form, that of the ludic, a cool seduction. In 1983 Baudrillard published *Fatal Strategies*, which charted the collapse of agency in a society dominated by the code and the phenomena which accompanied the disappearance of the constraints of the dialectic. It became clear that a crucial influence on Baudrillard, apart from Marx, Freud, Saussure and Mauss, was Nietzsche. The latter's anti-modernist aphoristic style was evident in Baudrillard's *Cool Memories*, published in 1987, one of Baudrillard's most successful works. In recent years Baudrillard has published *Transparency of Evil*, *The Illusion of the End* and a collection of articles on the Gulf War. These works continue the analysis of the apparent destruction of the symbolic by the semiotic and the subsequent ironic evolution of the semiotic order; they still draw on the theory and analyses of *Symbolic Exchange and Death*, in fact at points are almost unintelligible without a knowledge of that text. Indeed, in a recent interview (1991), Baudrillard drew attention to the fact that in France *Symbolic Exchange and Death* was

> the last book that inspired any confidence . . . Everything is deemed brilliant, intelligent, but not serious. There has never been any real discussion about it. I don't claim to be tremendously serious, but there are nevertheless some philosophically serious things in my work! In the fine arts milieu I was received fairly well, but with such misunderstanding! (Baudrillard, 1993: 189)

Certainly with this English translation it is evident that many of the misunderstandings that have surrounded the writings of Baudrillard, perhaps far beyond the fine arts milieu, will find they have no textual basis. More than that of course, the publication of this translation brings to the English-speaking public a document which has already had enormous indirect influence. For those who have wished that Baudrillard would express his argument in more orthodox terms, this is undoubtedly the text where he attempted to do precisely that.

References

Baudrillard, J. (1968) *Le système des objets*. Paris: Denoël.
Baudrillard, J. (1970) *La société de consommation*. Paris: Gallimard.
Baudrillard, J. (1975, originally 1973) *The Mirror of Production*. St Louis, MO: Telos.
Baudrillard, J. (1976) *L'échange symbolique et la mort*. Paris: Gallimard.
Baudrillard, J. (1981, originally 1972) *For a Critique of the Political Economy of the Sign*, tr. Charles Lewin. St Louis, MO: Telos.
Baudrillard, J. (1983, originally 1978) *In the Shadow of the Silent Majorities: Or, the End of the Social and Other Essays*. New York: Semiotext(e).

Baudrillard, J. (1983) *Simulations*, tr. Paul Foss et al. New York: Semiotcxt(e).

Baudrillard, J. (1987) *Forget Faucault*, tr. H. Beitchmann and M. Polizzoti. New York: Semiotext(e).

Baudrillard, J. (1988, originally 1986) *America*, tr. C. Turner. London: Verso.

Baudrillard, J. (1988, originally 1987) *The Ecstasy of Communication*, ed. Sylvère Lotringer, tr. B. and C. Schutze. New York: Semiotext(e).

Baudrillard, J. (1988) *Jean Baudrillard: Selected Writings*, ed. Mark Poster, tr. J. Mourrain. Cambridge: Polity.

Baudrillard, J. (1990, originally 1979) *Seduction*, tr. B. Singer. London: Macmillan.

Baudrillard, J. (1990, originally 1983) *Fatal Strategies*. London: Pluto.

Baudrillard, J. (1990, originally 1987) *Cool Memories*, tr. C. Turner. London: Verso.

Baudrillard, J. (1990) *Revenge of the Crystal: Selected Writings on the Modern Object and its Destiny*. London: Pluto.

Baudrillard, J. (1993, originally 1990) *Transparency of Evil: Essays on Extreme Phenomena*, tr. J. Benedict. London: Verso.

Baudrillard, J. (1993) *Baudrillard Live: Selected Interviews*, ed. M. Gane. London: Routledge.

Durkheim, E. (1915, originally 1912) *The Elementary Forms of the Religious Life*, tr. J.W. Swain. London: Allen and Unwin.

Gane, M. (1991a) *Jean Baudrillard: Critical and Fatal Theory*. London: Routledge.

Gane, M. (1991b) *Baudrillard's Bestiary: Baudrillard and Culture*. London: Routledge.

Kellner, D. (1989) *Jean Baudrillard: From Marxism to Post-Modernism and Beyond*. Cambridge: Polity.

Kroker, A. (1992) *The Possessed Individual: Technology and Postmodernity*. London: Macmillan.

Pefanis, J. (1991) *Heterology and the Postmodern: Bataille, Baudrillard and Lyotard*. London: Duke University Press.

Stearns, W. and Chaloupka, W. eds (1992) *Jean Baudrillard*. London: Macmillan.

PREFACE

Symbolic exchange is no longer the organising principle of modern society. Of course, the symbolic haunts modern social institutions in the form of their own death. Indeed, since the symbolic no longer rules these social forms, they experience it only as this haunting, and as a demand forever blocked by the law of value. Even though a certain idea of revolution has, since Marx, attempted to find a way past the law of value, it long since became a revolution in accordance with the Law. Even psychoanalysis gravitates around this haunting, which it fends off while at the same time circumscribing it within an individualised unconscious, thus reducing it, under the Law of the Father, to the obsessional fear of castration and the Signifier. Always the Law. However, beyond the topologies and economics, both libidinal and political, gravitating around a materialist or desiring-production on the stage of value, an outline of social relations emerges, based on the extermination of value. For us, the model of this relation harks back to primitive formations, but this radical utopia is slowly beginning to intrude at every level of contemporary society; this intoxicating revolt no longer has anything to do with the laws of history, nor even – but we will have to wait for a later stage for this to appear, since it is a recent phantasy – with the 'liberation' of a 'desire'.

In this light, other theoretical events, such as Saussure's anagrams and Mauss's gift-exchange, assume cardinal importance. In the long run, these hypotheses are more radical than Marx's or Freud's, whose interpretations are censored by precisely their imperialism. The anagrams or gift-exchanges are not merely transitory phases within the disciplines of linguistics and anthropology, nor are they inferior forms compared to the vast machinations of the unconscious and the revolution. Here one predominant form emerges, from which Marxism and psychoanalysis, though they may not be aware of it, derive. This form is equally dismissive of political and libidinal economy, outlining instead a beyond of value, a beyond of the law, a beyond of repression and a beyond of the unconscious. This is taking place here and now.

When Freud proposes the theory of the death drive, this is the one theoretical event of the same order as the anagram and the gift, provided we radicalise it against Freud himself. Indeed we must switch the targets of each of these three theories, and turn Mauss against Mauss, Saussure against Saussure and Freud against Freud. The principle of reversibility (the counter-gift) must be imposed against all the economistic, psychologistic and structuralist interpretations for which Mauss paved the way. The Saussure of the *Anagrams* must be set against Saussurian linguistics, against even his own restricted hypotheses concerning the anagram. The Freud of the death drive must be pitched against every previous psychoanalytic edifice, and even against Freud's version of the death drive.

At the price of paradox and theoretical violence, we witness that the three hypotheses describe, in their own respective fields (but this propriety is precisely what the general form of the symbolic annihilates), a functional principle sovereignly outside and antagonistic to our economic 'reality principle'.

Everywhere, in every domain, a single form predominates: reversibility, cyclical reversal and annulment put an end to the linearity of time, language, economic exchange, accumulation and power. Hence the reversibility of the gift in the counter-gift, the reversibility of exchange in the sacrifice, the reversibility of time in the cycle, the reversibility of production in destruction, the reversibility of life in death, and the reversibility of every term and value of the *langue* in the anagram. In every domain it assumes the form of extermination and death, for it is the form of the symbolic itself. Neither mystical nor structural, the symbolic is inevitable.

The reality principle corresponded to a certain stage of the law of value. Today the whole system is swamped by indeterminacy, and every reality is absorbed by the hyperreality of the code and simulation. The principle of simulation governs us now, rather than the outdated reality principle. We *feed* on those forms whose finalities have disappeared. No more ideology, only simulacra. We must therefore reconstruct the entire genealogy of the law of value and its simulacra in order to grasp the hegemony and the enchantment of the current system. A structural revolution of value. This genealogy must cover political economy, where it will appear as a second-order simulacrum, just like all those that stake everything on the real: the real of production, the real of signification, whether conscious or unconscious.

Capital no longer belongs to the order of political economy: it operates with political economy as its simulated model. The entire apparatus of the commodity law of value is absorbed and recycled in the larger apparatus of the structural law of value, thus becoming part of the third order of simulacra (see below). Political economy is thus assured a *second life*, an eternity, within the confines of an apparatus in which it has lost all its strict determinacy, but maintains an effective presence as a system of reference for simulation. It was exactly the same for the previous apparatus – the natural law of value – which the system of political economy and the market law of value also appropriated as their imaginary system of reference ('Nature'): 'nature' leads a ghostly existence as use-value at the core of exchange-value. But on the next twist of the spiral, use-value is seized as an alibi within the dominant order of the code. Each configuration of value is seized by the next in a higher order of simulacra. And each phase of value integrates the prior apparatus into its own as a phantom reference, a puppet reference, a simulated reference.

A revolution separates each order from its successor: these are the only genuine revolutions. We are in the third order, which is the order no longer of the real, but of the hyperreal. It is only here that theories and practices, themselves floating and indeterminate, can reach the real and beat it to death.

Contemporary revolutions are indexed on the immediately prior state of the system. They are all buttressed by a nostalgia for the resurrection of the real in all its forms, that is, as second-order simulacra: dialectics, use-value, the transparency and finality of production, the 'liberation' of the unconscious, of repressed meaning (the signifier, or the signified named 'desire'), and so on. All these liberations provide the ideal content for the system to devour in its successive revolutions, and which it brings subtly back to life as mere phantasmas of revolution. These revolutions are only transitions towards generalised manipulation. At the stage of the aleatory processes of control, even revolution becomes meaningless.

The rational, referential, historical and functional machines of consciousness correspond to industrial machines. The aleatory, non-referential, transferential, indeterminate and floating machines of the unconscious respond to the aleatory machines of the code. But even the unconscious is reabsorbed by this operation, and it has long since lost its own reality principle to become an operational simulacrum. At the precise point that its *psychical* reality principle merges into its *psychoanalytic* reality principle, the unconscious, like political economy, also becomes a model of simulation.

The systemic strategy is merely to invoke a number of floating values in this hyperreality. This is as true of the unconscious as it is of money and theories. Value rules according to the indiscernible order of generation by means of models, according to the infinite chains of simulation.

Cybernetic operativity, the genetic code, the aleatory order of mutation, the uncertainty principle, etc., succeed determinate, objectivist science, and the dialectical view of history and consciousness. Even critical theory, along with the revolution, turns into a second-order simulacrum, as do all determinate processes. The deployment of third-order simulacra sweeps all this away, and to attempt to reinstate dialectics, 'objective' contradictions, and so on, against them would be a futile political regression. You can't fight the aleatory by imposing finalities, you can't fight against programmed and molecular dispersion with *prises de conscience* and dialectical sublation, you can't fight the code with political economy, nor with 'revolution'. All these outdated weapons (including those we find in first-order simulacra, in the ethics and metaphysics of man and nature, use-value, and other liberatory systems of reference) are gradually neutralised by a higher-order general system. Everything that filters into the non-finality of the space-time of the code, or that attempts to intervene in it, is disconnected from its own ends, disintegrated and absorbed. This is the well known effect of recuperation, manipulation, of circulating and recycling at every level. 'All dissent must be of a higher logical type than that to which it is opposed' (Anthony Wilden, *System and Structure* [London: Tavistock, 1977], p. xxvii). Is it at least possible to find an even match to oppose third-order simulacra? Is there a theory or a practice which is subversive because it is more aleatory than the system itself, an indeterminate subversion which would be to the order of the code what the revolution was to the order of political economy? Can we fight DNA? Certainly not by means of the class struggle. Perhaps simulacra of a higher logical (or illogical) order could be invented: beyond the current third order, beyond determinacy and indeterminacy. But would they still be simulacra? Perhaps death and death alone, the reversibility of death, belongs to a higher order than the code. Only symbolic disorder can bring about an interruption in the code.

Every system that approaches perfect operativity simultaneously approaches its downfall. When the system says 'A is A', or 'two times two equals four', it approaches absolute power and total absurdity; that is, immediate and probable subversion. A gentle push in the right place is enough to bring it crashing down. We know the potential of tautology when it reinforces the system's claim to perfect sphericity (Ubu Roi's belly).

Identity is untenable: it *is* death, since it fails to inscribe its own death. Every closed or metastable, functional or cybernetic system is shadowed by mockery and instantaneous subversion (which no longer takes the detour through long dialectical labour), because all the system's inertia acts against it. Ambivalence awaits the most advanced systems, that, like Leibniz's binary God, have deified their functional principle. The fascination they exert, because it derives from a profound denial such as we find in fetishism, can be instantaneously reversed. Hence their fragility increases in proportion to their ideal coherence. These systems, even when they are based on radical indeterminacy (the loss of meaning), fall prey, once more, to meaning. They collapse under the weight of their own monstrosity, like fossilised dinosaurs, and immediately decompose. This is the fatality of every system committed by its own logic to total perfection and therefore to a total defectiveness, to absolute infallibility and therefore irrevocable breakdown: the aim of all bound energies is their own death. This is why the only strategy is *catastrophic*, and not dialectical at all. Things must be pushed to the limit, where quite naturally they collapse and are inverted. At the peak of value we are closest to ambivalence, at the pinnacle of coherence we are closest to the abyss of corruption which haunts the reduplicated signs of the code. Simulation must go further than the system. Death must be played against death: a radical tautology that makes the system's own logic the ultimate weapon. The only strategy against the hyperrealist system is some form of pataphysics, 'a science of imaginary solutions'; that is, a science-fiction of the system's reversal against itself at the extreme limit of simulation, a reversible simulation in a hyperlogic of death and destruction.[1]

The symbolic demands meticulous reversibility. *Ex-terminate* every *term*, abolish value in the term's revolution against itself: that is the only symbolic violence equivalent to and triumphant over the structural violence of the code.

A revolutionary dialectic corresponded to the commodity law of value and its equivalents; only the scrupulous reversion of death corresponds to the code's indeterminacy and the structural law of value.[2]

Strictly speaking, nothing remains for us to base anything on. All that remains for us is theoretical violence – speculation to the death, whose only method is the radicalisation of hypotheses. Even the code and the symbolic remain terms of simulation: it must be possible to extract them, one by one, from discourse.

Notes

1. Death is always equally what waits at the *term* of the system, and the symbolic *extermination* that stalks the system itself. It is not that there are two words to designate the finality of death internal to the system, the one in-scribed everywhere in its operational logic, and the other a radical counter-finality ex-scribed on the system as such, but which haunts it everywhere: only the term of death, and it alone, figures on both sides. This ambiguity can already be discerned in the Freudian death-drive. Rather than an ambiguity, however, it simply translates the proximity of complete perfection and immediate defectiveness.

2. Death ought never to be understood as the real event that affects a subject or a body, but as a *form* in which the determinacy of the subject and of value is lost. The demand of reversibility puts an end to determinacy and indeterminacy at the same time. It puts an end to bound energies in stable oppositions, and is therefore in substantial agreement with theories of flows and intensities, whether libidinal or schizo. The unbinding of energies is, however, the very form of the current system, which consists in a strategic drift of value. The system can be connected and disconnected, but all the freed energies will one day return to it: this is how the concepts of energy and intensity come about. Capital is an energetic and intense system. Hence the impossibility of distinguishing the libidinal economy from the political economy (see Jean-François Lyotard, *Libidinal Economy* [tr. I.H. Grant, London: Athlone, 1992]) of the system of value; and the impossibility of distinguishing capitalist schizzes from revolutionary schizzes (see Gilles Deleuze and Félix Guattari, *Anti-Oedipus: Capitalism and Schizophrenia I* [tr. R. Hurley, M. Seem and H.R. Lane, London: Athlone, 1984]). For the system is master: like God it can bind or unbind energies; what it is incapable of (and what it can no longer avoid) is reversibility. Reversibility alone therefore, rather than unbinding or drifting, is fatal to it. This is exactly what the term symbolic 'exchange' means.

1

THE END OF PRODUCTION

The Structural Revolution of Value

Saussure located two dimensions to the exchange of terms of the *langue*, which he assimilated to money. A given coin must be exchangeable against a real good of some value, while on the other hand it must be possible to relate it to all the other terms in the monetary system. More and more, Saussure reserves the term *value* for this second aspect of the system: every term can be related to every other, their *relativity*, internal to the system and constituted by binary oppositions. This definition is opposed to the other possible definition of value: the relation of every term to what it designates, of each signifier to its signified, like the relation of every coin with what it can be exchanged against. The first aspect corresponds to the structural dimension of language, the second to its functional dimension. Each dimension is separate but linked, which is to say that they mesh and cohere. This coherence is characteristic of the 'classical' configuration of the linguistic sign, under the rule of the commodity law of value, where designation always appears as the finality of the structural operation of the *langue*. The parallel between this 'classical' stage of signification and the mechanics of value in material production is absolute, as in Marx's analysis: use-value plays the role of the horizon and finality of the system of exchange-values. The first qualifies the concrete operation of the commodity in consumption (a moment parallel to designation in the sign), the second relates to the exchangeability of any commodity for any other under the law of equivalence (a moment parallel to the structural organisation of the sign). Both are dialectically linked throughout Marx's analyses and define a rational configuration of production, governed by political economy.

A revolution has put an end to this 'classical' economics of value, a revolution of value itself, which carries value beyond its commodity form into its radical form.

This revolution consists in the dislocation of the two aspects of the law of value, which were thought to be coherent and eternally bound as if by a natural law. *Referential value is annihilated, giving the structural play of value the upper hand.* The structural dimension becomes autonomous by excluding the referential dimension, and is instituted upon the death of reference. The systems of reference for production, signification, the affect, substance and history, all this equivalence to a 'real' content, loading the sign with the burden of 'utility', with gravity – its form of representative equivalence – all this is over with. Now the other stage of value has the upper hand, a total relativity, general commutation, combination and simulation – simulation, in the sense that, from now on, signs are exchanged against each other rather than against the real (it is not that they just happen to be exchanged against each other, they do so *on condition* that they are no longer exchanged against the real). The emancipation of the sign: remove this 'archaic' obligation to designate something and it finally becomes free, indifferent and totally indeterminate, in the structural or combinatory play which succeeds the previous rule of determinate equivalence. The same operation takes place at the level of labour power and the production process: the annihilation of any goal as regards the contents of production allows the latter to function as a code, and the monetary sign, for example, to escape into infinite speculation, beyond all reference to a real of production, or even to a gold-standard. The flotation of money and signs, the flotation of 'needs' and ends of production, the flotation of labour itself – the commutability of every term is accompanied by speculation and a limitless inflation (and we really have *total liberty* – no duties, disaffection and general disenchantment; but this remains a magic, a sort of magical obligation which keeps the sign chained up to the real, capital has freed signs from this 'naïvety' in order to deliver them into pure circulation). Neither Saussure nor Marx had any presentiment of all this: they were still in the golden age of the dialectic of the sign and the real, which is at the same time the 'classical' period of capital and value. Their dialectic is in shreds, and the real has died of the shock of value acquiring this fantastic autonomy. Determinacy is dead, indeterminacy holds sway. There has been an extermination (in the literal sense of the word) of the real of production and the real of signification.[1]

I indicated this structural revolution of the law of value in the term 'political economy of the sign'.[2] This term, however, can only be regarded as makeshift, for the following reasons:

1. Does this remain a political-economic question? Yes, in that it is always a question of value and the law of value. However, the mutation that affects it is so profound and so decisive, the content of political economy so thoroughly changed, indeed annihilated, that the term is nothing more than an allusion. Moreover, it is precisely *political* to the extent that it is always the *destruction* of social relations governed by the relevant value. For a long time, however, it has been a matter of something entirely different from economics.

2. The term 'sign' has itself only an allusive value. Since the structural law of value affects signification as much as it does everything else, its form is not that of the sign in general, but that of a certain organisation which is that of the code. The code only governs certain signs however. Just as the commodity law of value does not, at a given moment, signify just any determinant instance of material production, neither, conversely, does the

structural law of value signify any pre-eminence of the sign whatever. This illusion derives from the fact that Marx developed the one in the shadow of the commodity, while Saussure developed the other in the shadow of the linguistic sign. But this illusion must be shattered. The commodity law of value is a law of equivalences, and this law operates throughout every sphere: it equally designates the equivalence in the configuration of the sign, where one signifier and one signified facilitate the regulated exchange of a referential content (the other parallel modality being the linearity of the signifier, contemporaneous with the linear and cumulative time of production).

The classical law of value then operates simultaneously in every instance (language, production, etc.), despite these latter remaining distinct according to their sphere of reference.

Conversely, the structural law of value signifies the indeterminacy of every sphere in relation to every other, and to their proper content (also therefore the passage from the *determinant* sphere of signs to the *indeterminacy* of the code). To say that the sphere of material production and that of signs exchange their respective contents is still too wide of the mark: they literally disappear as such and lose their specificity along with their determinacy, to the benefit of a form of value, of a much more general assemblage, where designation and production are annihilated.

The 'political economy of the sign' was also consequent upon an extension of the commodity law of value and its confirmation at the level of signs, whereas the structural configuration of value simply and simultaneously puts an end to the regimes of production, political economy, representation and signs. With the code, all this collapses into simulation. Strictly speaking, neither the 'classical' economy nor the political economy of the sign ceases to exist: they lead a secondary existence, becoming a sort of phantom principle of dissuasion.

The end of labour. The end of production. The end of political economy. The end of the signifier/signified dialectic which facilitates the accumulation of knowledge and meaning, the linear syntagma of cumulative discourse. And at the same time, the end of the exchange-value/use-value dialectic which is the only thing that makes accumulation and social production possible. The end of the linear dimension of discourse. The end of the linear dimension of the commodity. The end of the classical era of the sign. The end of the era of production.

It is not *the* revolution which puts an end to all this, it is *capital itself* which abolishes the determination of the social according to the means of production, substitutes the structural form for the commodity form of value, and currently controls every aspect of the system's strategy.

This historical and social mutation is legible at every level. In this way the era of simulation is announced everywhere by the commutability of formerly contradictory or dialectically opposed terms. Everywhere we see the same 'genesis of simulacra': the commutability of the beautiful and the ugly in fashion, of the left and the right in politics, of the true and the false in every media message, the useful and the useless at the level of objects, nature and culture at every level of signification. All the great humanist criteria of value, the whole civilisation of moral, aesthetic and practical judgement are effaced in our system of images and signs. Everything becomes undecidable, the characteristic effect of the domination of the code, which everywhere rests on the principle of neutralisation, of indifference.[3] This is the generalised brothel of capital, a brothel not for prostitution, but for substitution and commutation.

This process, which has for a long time been at work in culture, art, politics, and even in sexuality (in the so-called 'superstructural' domains), today affects the economy itself, the whole so-called 'infrastructural' field. Here the same indeterminacy holds sway. And, of course, with the loss of determination of the economic, we also lose any possibility of conceiving it as the determinant agency.

Since for two centuries historical determination has been built up around the economic (since Marx in any case), it is there that it is important to grasp the interruption of the code.

The End of Production

We are at the end of production. In the West, this form coincides with the proclamation of the commodity law of value, that is to say, with the reign of political economy. First, nothing is *produced*, strictly speaking: everything is *deduced*, from the grace (God) or beneficence (nature) of an agency which releases or withholds its riches. Value emanates from the reign of divine or natural qualities (which for us have become retrospectively confused). The Physiocrats still saw the cycles of land and labour in this way, as having no value of their own. We may wonder, then, whether there is a genuine *law* of value, since this law is *dispatch* without attaining rational expression. Its form cannot be separated from the inexhaustible referential substance to which it is bound. If there is a law here, it is, in contrast to the commodity law, a *natural* law of value.

A mutation shakes this edifice of a natural distribution or dispensing of wealth as soon as value is *produced*, as its reference becomes labour, and its law of equivalence is generalised to every type of labour. Value is now assigned to the distinct and rational operation of human (social) labour. It is measurable, and, in consequence, so is surplus-value.

The critique of political economy begins with social production or the mode of production as its reference. The concept of production alone allows us, by means of an analysis of that unique commodity called labour power, to extract a *surplus* (a surplus-value) which controls the rational dynamics of capital as well as its beyond, the revolution.

Today everything has changed again. Production, the commodity form, labour power, equivalence and surplus-value, which together formed the outline of a quantitative, material and measurable configuration, are now things of the past. Productive forces outlined another reference which, although in contradiction with the relations of production, remained a reference, that of social wealth. An aspect of production still supports both a social form called capital and its internal critique called Marxism. Now, revolutionary demands are based on the abolition of the *commodity* law of value.

Now we have passed from the commodity law of value to the structural law of value, and this coincides with the obliteration of the social form known as production. Given this, are we still within a capitalist mode? It may be that we are in a hyper-capitalist mode, or in a very different order. Is the form of capital bound to the law of value in general, or to some specific form of the law of value (perhaps we are really already within a socialist mode? Perhaps this metamorphosis of capital under the sign of the structural law of value is merely its socialist outcome? Oh dear . . .)? If the life and death of capital are staked on the *commodity* law of value, if the revolution is staked on the mode of production, then we are within neither capital nor revolution. If this latter consists in a liberation of the social and generic production of man, then there is no longer any prospect of a revolution since there is no more production. If, on the other hand, capital is a *mode of domination*, then we are always in its midst. This is because the structural law of value is the purest, most illegible form of social domination, like surplus-value. It no longer has any references within a dominant class or a relation of forces, it works without violence, entirely reabsorbed without any trace of bloodshed into the signs which surround us, operative everywhere in the code in which capital finally holds its purest discourses, beyond the dialects of industry, trade and finance, beyond the dialects of class which it held in its 'productive' phase – a symbolic violence inscribed everywhere in signs, even in the signs of the revolution.

The structural revolution of value eliminated the basis of the 'Revolution'. The loss of reference fatally affected first the revolutionary systems of reference, which can no longer be found in any social substance of production, nor in the certainty of a reversal in any truth of labour power. This is because labour is not a *power*, it has become one *sign* amongst many. Like every other sign, it produces and consumes itself. It is exchanged against non-labour, leisure, in accordance with a total equivalence, it is commutable with every other sector of everyday life. No more or less 'alienated', it is no longer a unique, historical 'praxis' giving rise to unique social relations. Like most practices, it is now only a set of signing operations. It becomes part of contemporary life in general, that is, it is framed by signs. It is no longer even the suffering of historical prostitution which used to play the role of the contrary promise of final emancipation (or, as in Lyotard, as the space of the workers' enjoyment [*jouissance*] which fulfils an unremitting desire in the abjection of value and the rule of capital).[4] None of this remains true. Sign-form seizes labour and rids it of every historical or libidinal significance, and absorbs it in the process of its own reproduction: the operation of the *sign*, behind the empty allusion to what it designates, is to replicate itself. In the past, labour was used to designate the reality of a social production and a social objective of accumulating wealth. Even capital and surplus-value exploited it – precisely where it retained a use-value for the expanded reproduction of capital and its final destruction. It was shot through with finality anyway – if the worker is absorbed in the pure and simple reproduction of his labour power, it is not true that the process of production is experienced as senseless repetition. Labour revolutionises society through its very abjection, as a commodity whose potential always exceeds pure and simple reproduction of value.

Today this is no longer the case since labour is no longer productive but has become reproductive of the *assignation to labour* which is the general habit of a society which no longer knows whether or not it wishes to produce. No more myths of production and no more contents of production: national balance sheets now merely retrace a numerical and statistical growth devoid of meaning, an inflation of the signs of accountancy over which we can no longer even project the phantasy of the collective will. The pathos of growth itself is dead, since no-one believes any longer in the pathos of production, whose final, paranoid and panic-stricken tumescence it was. Today these codes are detumescent. It remains, however, more necessary than ever to reproduce labour as a social ritual [*affectation*], as a reflex, as morality, as consensus, as regulation, as the reality principle. The reality principle *of the code*, that is: an immense *ritual of the signs of labour* extends over society in general – since it *reproduces* itself, it matters little whether or not it *produces*. It is much more effective to socialise by means of rituals and signs than by the bound energies of production. You are asked only to become socialised, not to produce or to excel yourself (this classical ethic now arouses suspicion instead). You are asked only to consider value, according to the structural definition which here takes on its full social significance, as one term in relation to others, to function as a sign in the general scenario of production, just as labour and production now function only as signs, as terms commutable with non-labour, consumption, communication, etc. – a multiple, incessant, twisting relation across the entire network of other signs. Labour, once voided of its energy and substance (and generally disinvested), is given a new role as the model of social simulation, bringing all the other categories along with it into the aleatory sphere of the code.

An unnervingly strange state of affairs: this sudden plunge into a sort of secondary existence, separated from you by all the opacity of a previous life, where there was a familiarity and an intimacy in the traditional process of labour. Even the concrete reality of exploitation, the violent sociality of labour, is familiar. This has all gone now, and is due not so much to the *operative* abstraction of the *process* of labour, so often described, as to the passage of every *signification* of labour into an *operational* field where it becomes a floating variable, dragging the whole imaginary of a previous life along with it.

Beyond the autonomisation of production as *mode* (beyond the convulsions, contradictions and revolutions inherent in the mode), the *code* of production must re-emerge. This is the dimension things are taking on today, at the end of a 'materialist' history which has succeeded in authenticating it as the real movement of society. (Art, religion and duty have no real history for Marx – only production has a history, or, rather, it *is* history, it grounds history. An incredible fabrication of labour and production as historical reason and the generic model of fulfilment.)

The end of this religious autonomisation of production allows us to see that all of this could equally have been *produced* (this time in the sense of a stage-production and a scenario) fairly recently, with totally different goals than the internal finalities (that is, the revolution) secreted away within production.

To analyse production as a code cuts across both the material evidence of machines, factories, labour time, the product, salaries and money, and the more formal, but equally 'objective', evidence of surplus-value, the market, capital, to discover the rule of the game which is to destroy the logical network of the agencies of capital, and even the critical network of the Marxian categories which analyse it (which categories are again only an appearance at the second degree of capital, its *critical* appearance), in order to discover the elementary signifiers of production, the social relations it establishes, buried away forever beneath the historical illusion of the producers (and the theoreticians).

Labour

Labour power is not a 'power', it is a definition, an axiom, and its 'real' operation in the labour process, its 'use-value', is only the reduplication of this definition in the operation of the code. It is at the level of the sign, never at the level of energy, that violence is fundamental. The *mechanism* of capital (and not its law) plays on surplus-value – the non-equivalence of the salary and labour power. Even if the two were equivalent, even if salaries were abolished (for the sale of labour power), man would still be marked by this axiom, by this destiny of production, by this sacrament of labour which sets him apart like a sex. The worker is no longer a man, nor even a woman: it has its own sex, it is assigned this labour power as an end, and marked by it as a woman is marked by her sex (her sexual definition), as a Black is by the colour of his or her skin – all signs and nothing but signs.

We must distinguish what belongs to the *mode* and what belongs to the *code* of production. Before becoming an element of the commodity law of value, labour power is initially a status, a structure of obedience to a code. Before becoming exchange-value or use-value, it is already, like any other commodity, the *sign* of the operation of nature as value, which defines production and is the basic axiom of our culture and no other. This message, much more profoundly than quantitative equivalences, runs beneath commodities from the outset: to remove indeterminacy from nature (and man) in order to submit it to the determinacy of value. This is confirmed in the constructionist mania for bulldozers, motorways, 'infra-structures', and in the civilising mania of the era of production, a mania for leaving no fragment unproduced, for countersigning everything with production, without even the hope of an excess of wealth. Producing in order to mark, producing in order to reproduce the marked man. What is production today apart from this terrorism of the code? This is as clear for us as it was for the first industrial generations, who dealt with machines as with an absolute enemy, harbingers of total destructuration, before the comforting dream of a historical dialectic of production developed. The Luddite practices which arose everywhere to some extent, the savagery of attacking the instrument of production (primarily attacking itself as the productive force), endemic sabotage and defection bear lengthy testimony to the fragility of the productive order. Smashing machines is an aberrant act if they are the *means* of production, if any ambiguity remains over their future use-value. If, however, the *ends* of this production collapse, then the respect due to the means of production also collapses, and the machines appear as their true end, as direct and immediate operational signs of the social relation to death on which capital is nourished. Nothing then stands in the way of their destruction. In this sense, the Luddites were much clearer than Marx on the impact of the irruption of the industrial order, and today, at the *catastrophic* end of this process, to which Marx himself has misled us in the *dialectical* euphoria of productive forces, they have in some sense exacted their revenge.

We do not mean to invoke the prestige that may attach to a particular type of labour when we say that labour is a sign, nor even the sens2 of improvement signified by wage labour for the Algerian immigrant in relation to his tribal community, or for the Moroccan kid from the High Atlas Mountains whose only dream is to work for Simca, or for women in our own society. In this case, labour refers to a strict value: betterment or a different status. On the contemporary stage, labour no longer emerges from this referential definition of the sign. There is no longer any proper signification of a particular type of labour or of labour in general, but a system of labour where jobs are exchanged. No more 'right man in the right place',[5] an old adage of the scientific idealism of production. There are no more interchangeable but indispensable individuals in a determinate labour process, since the labour process itself has become interchangeable: mobile, polyvalent and intermittent structures of absorption, indifferent to every object and even to labour itself, when understood according to its classical operation and applied solely to localise each individual within a social nexus where nothing converges except perhaps within the imma-nence of this operational matrix, an indifferent paradigm which identifies every individual according to a shared radical, or a syntagma which links them into an indefinite combinatory mode.

Labour (even in the guise of leisure), like a primary repression, pervades every aspect of life in the form of a control, a permanent occupation of spaces and times regulated according to an omnipresent code. Wherever there are people, they must be *fixed*, whether in schools, factories, on the beach, in front of the TV, or being retrained. Generalised and permanent mobilisation. Such labour is not, however, productive in the sense of 'original': it is nothing more than the mirror of society, its imaginary, its fantastic reality principle. Perhaps its death drive.

This is the tendency of every current strategy that turns around labour: 'job enrichment,'[6] flexitime, mobility, retraining, continuing education, autonomy, worker-management, decentralisation of the labour process, even the Californian utopia of domestic cybernetics. Your quotidian roots are no longer savagely ripped up in order to hand you over to the machine – you, your childhood, your habits, your relationships, your unconscious drives, and even your refusal to work are integrated into it. You will easily find a place for yourself amongst all of this, a personalised job, or, failing that, there is a welfare provision calculated according to your personal needs. In any case, you will no longer be abandoned, since it is essential that everyone be a terminal for the entire system, an insignificant terminal, but a term none the less – not an inarticulate cry, but a term of the *langue* and at the terminus of the entire structural network of the language. The very choice of work, the utopia of a tailor-made job, signifies that the *die is cast*, that the structure of absorption is total. Labour power is no longer brutally bought and sold, it is designed, marketed and turned into a commodity – production re-enters the sign system of consumption.

An initial step of this analysis was to conceive the sphere of consumption as an extension of the sphere of the forces of production. We must now do the reverse. The entire sphere of production, labour and the forces of production must be conceived as collapsing into the sphere of 'consumption', understood as the sphere of a generalised axiomatic, a coded exchange of signs, a general lifestyle. In this way knowledge, the sciences, attitudes (D. Verres, *Le discours du capitalisme* [Paris: L'herne, 1971], p. 36: 'Why not consider the attitudes of the workforce as one of the resources to be managed by the boss?'), but also sexuality and the body, the imagination (ibid., p. 74: 'The imagination is all that remains bound to the pleasure principle, whereas the psychical apparatus is subordinated to the reality principle' (Freud). We must put a stop to this waste. The imagination should be realised as a force of production, it should be invested. The slogan of technocracy is: 'Power to the Imagination!'). The same goes for the unconscious, the revolution, and so on. True, all this is in the process of being 'invested' and absorbed into the sphere of value, but not so much market value as accountable value; that is, it is not mobilised for the sake of production, but indexed, allocated, summoned to play the part of a functional variable. It has become not so much a force of production as several pieces on the chessboard of the code, caught in the same game-rules. The axiom of production now tends to be reduced to *factors*, the axiom of the code reduces everything to a *variable*. One leads to equations and balance sheets of forces, and the other tends towards mobile and aleatory sets, which neutralise whatever escapes or resists them by *connection* and not by annexation.

This goes much further than Taylorism, or the Scientific Organisation of Labour (SOL), but its spectre marks an essential milestone of investment by the code. Two phases can be distinguished.

The 'pre-scientific' phase of the industrial system, characterised by maximum exploitation of labour power, is succeeded by the phase of machinery and the preponderance of fixed capital, where 'objectified labour appears not only in the form of product, or of the product employed as the means of labour, but in the form of the force of production itself' (Marx, *Grundrisse* [tr. Martin Nicolaus, Harmondsworth: Penguin, 1973], p. 694). This accumulation of objectified labour which supplants living labour as a force of production is subsequently multiplied to infinity by the accumulation of knowledge: 'The accumulation of knowledge and of skill, of the general productive forces of the social brain, is thus absorbed into capital, as opposed to labour, and hence appears as an attribute of capital, and more specifically of *fixed capital*' (ibid., p. 694).

In the phase of machinery, the scientific apparatus, the collective labourer and the SOL, the 'production process has ceased to be a labour process in the sense of a process dominated by labour as its governing unity' (ibid., p. 693). There is no longer any 'original' force of production, only a general machinery transforming the forces of production into capital; or, rather, a machinery which *manufactures both the force of production and labour power*. The whole social apparatus of labour is forestalled by this operation. The collective machinery has begun to produce social goals directly, and this is what produces production.

The hegemony of dead labour over living labour. Primitive accumulation merely accumulates dead labour to the point that it can reabsorb living labour. Or, in other words, it becomes capable of controlling the production of living labour for its own ends. This is why the end of primitive accumulation marks the decisive turning point of political economy: the transition to the preponderance of dead labour, to crystal-lised social relations incarnated in dead labour, weighing down on society in its entirety as the code of domination itself. Marx's greatest error was to have retained a belief in the innocence of machines, the technical process and science – all of which were supposedly capable of becoming living social labour once the system of capital was liquidated, despite the fact that this is precisely what the system is based on. This pious hope springs from having underestimated death in dead labour, and from thinking that death is overcome in the living, beyond a certain crucial point, by a sort of historical somersault of production.

Marx had, however, sensed this while noting that 'objectified labour confronts living labour within the process itself as the power which *rules* it; a power which, as the appropriation of living labour, is the form of capital' (*Grundrisse*, p. 693 [J.B.'s emphasis]). This also becomes apparent in the formula according to which, at a certain stage of capital, man '*steps to the side of the production process*, instead of being its chief actor' (ibid., p. 705). This formula goes well beyond political economy and its critique, since it literally signifies that it is a matter no longer of a production process, but of a process of exclusion and relegation.

We must again draw out all the consequences of this. When production attains this circularity and turns in on itself, it loses every objective determination. It incants itself as myth while its own terms have become signs. Simultaneously, when this sphere of signs (including the media, information, etc.) ceases to be a specific sphere for representing the unity of the global process of capital, then we must not only say with Marx that 'the production process has ceased to be a labour process' (ibid., p. 693), but that 'the process of capital itself has ceased to be a production process'.

With the hegemony of dead labour over living labour, the whole dialectic of production collapses. Following the same basic schema as the central oppositions of rationalist thought (truth and falsity, appearance and reality, nature and culture), all the oppositions according to which Marxism operates (use-value/exchange-value, forces of production/ relations of production) are also neutralised, and in the same way. Everything within production and the economy becomes commutable, reversible and exchangeable according to the same indeterminate specularity as we find in politics, fashion or the media. The indeterminate specularity of the forces and relations of production, of capital and labour, use-value and exchange-value, constitutes the dissolution of production into the code. Today the law of value no longer lies so much in the exchangeability of every commodity under the sign of a general equivalent, as it does in a much more radical exchangeability of all the categories of political economy (and its critique) in accordance with the code. All the determinations of 'bourgeois' thought were neutralised and abolished by the materialist thought of production, which has brought everything down to a single great historical determination. In its turn, however, this too is neutralised and absorbed by a revolution of the terms of the system. Just as other generations were able to dream of pre-capitalist society, we have begun to dream of political economy as a lost object. Now, even its discourse carries some referential force only because it is a lost object.

Marx:

> On the whole, types of work that are consumed as services and not as products separable from the worker hence not capable of existing as commodities independently of him . . . are of microscopic significance when compared with the mass of capitalist production. They may be entirely neglected, therefore, and can be dealt with under the category of wage-labour. (*Capital* [tr. Ben Fowkes, Harmondsworth: Penguin, 1976], Vol. 1, pp. 1044–5)

This chapter of *Capital* was never written: the problem posed by this disjunction, which confirms that between productive and unproductive labour, is utterly insoluble. Every Marxist definition of labour is split, but this was happening from the outset. In the *Grundrisse*, Marx says: 'Labour becomes productive only by producing its own opposite [that is, capital]' (p. 305n), from which we may logically conclude that if labour comes to reproduce itself, as is the case today within the compass of the 'collective labourer', it ceases to be productive. This is the unforeseen consequence of a definition which did not even consider that capital might take root in something other than the 'productive', precisely, perhaps, in labour voided of its productivity, in 'unproductive' labour, somehow neutralised, where capital simply eludes the dangerous determinacy of 'productive' labour and can begin to establish its total domination. By misunderstanding '*un*productive labour', Marx concedes the real undefined character of labour on which the strategy of capital is based.

'Production for unproductive consumption is quite as productive as that for productive consumption; always assuming that it produces or reproduces capital' (*Grundrisse*, p. 306n). According to Marx's own definition, there is a paradox here which results from an increasing sector of human labour becoming unproductive without apparently preventing capital from consolidating its dominance. In fact, however, this is all rigged in advance – there are not two or three types of labour,[7] capital itself whispered these pedantic distinctions to Marx, while never being stupid enough to believe in them itself, always merely 'naïvely' overlooking them. There is only one sort of labour (a fundamental definition in fact), and as luck would have it this is the one that Marx let slip through his fingers. Today all labour falls under a single definition, that bastard, archaic and unanalysed category of service-labour, and not the supposedly universal classical definition of 'proletarian' wage-labour.

This is not service-labour in the feudal sense, since labour has lost the sense of obligation and reciprocity that it had in the feudal context, but in the sense that Marx indicates: in service, prestation is inseparable from the prestator – an archaic aspect in the *productivist* vision of capital, but one that's fundamental if capital is grasped as a system of domination, as a system of 'infeudation' to a labouring society, that is, to a certain type of political society for which labour is the rule of the game. This is where we are (if we weren't already there in Marx's time): the reduction of every labour to a service, labour as pure and simple presence/occupation, consumption of time, *prestation* of time. We make an 'act' of labour as we make an act of presence or an act of allegiance. In this sense, prestation is in fact inseparable from the prestator. The service rendered conjoins the body, time, space and grey matter. Whether this produces or not is a matter of indifference as regards this personal indexation. Surplus-value disappears, of course, and the meaning of wages changes (we will come back to this later). It is not, however, a 'regression' of capital towards feudalism, but rather the dawn of its *real* domination, solicitation and total conscription of the 'person'. This is the tendency of every effort to 'retotalise' labour, making it into a total service where the prestator may be more or less absent, but increasingly personally involved.

In this sense labour can no longer be distinguished from other activities, particularly from its opposing term of free time, which, because it implies the same mobilisation and the same investment (or the same productive disinvestment), is today just as much a *service rendered*,[8] which, in accordance with any standard of justice, should merit a wage (this is not absolutely impossible).[9] In short, it is not only the imaginary distinction between productive and unproductive labour which is shaken up, but also the distinction between work and rest itself. There is quite simply no more labour in the specific sense of the term, so Marx ultimately did well not to write his chapter of *Capital*: it was condemned from the outset.

It is at precisely this moment that workers become 'agents of produc-tion'. This slippage of terminology – such things have their own importance – ironically signifies the status of one who produces nothing. The semi-skilled worker was no longer a labourer, but merely a worker facing the total indifferentiation of labour, no longer struggling over the content of labour nor over specific wages, but struggling over the generalised form of labour and the political wage. The formation of the 'agent of production' is accompanied by his liberation from the most abstract form – much more abstract than the old semi-skilled worker, exploited to death: the *manne-quin of labour* appeared, the lowest common denominator, the dumb waiter of labour's unreality principle. A pleasant euphemism: we no longer work, but merely perform 'acts of production'. This is the end of production-culture, hence the *a contrario* appearance of the term 'pro-ductive'. This 'productive agent' is no longer characterised by its exploi-tation, nor by its being raw material in a labour process; it is characterised by its mobility and interchangeability, by being an insignificant inflection of fixed capital. The 'agent of production' designates the ultimate status of Marx's worker who, as he said, 'steps to the side of the production process'.

The current phase, where 'the process of capital itself ceases to be a process of production', is simultaneously the phase of the disappearance of the factory: society as a whole takes on the appearance of a factory. The factory must disappear as such, and labour must lose its specificity in order that capital can ensure the extensive metamorphosis of its form throughout society as a whole. We must therefore formally recognise the disappear-ance of the determinate sites of labour, a determinate subject of labour, a determinate time of social labour, we must formally recognise the disap-pearance of the factory, labour and the proletariat if we want to analyse capital's current and real dominance.[10] The chain-store stage of society or the factory superstructure, the virtual reserve army of capital, is at an end. The principle of the factory and labour explodes and scatters over every aspect of society in such a way that the distinction between the two becomes 'ideological'. It becomes one of capital's traps for maintaining the factory's specific and privileged presence in the revolutionary imaginary. Labour is everywhere, because there is no more labour. Labour now reaches its definitive, completed form, its *principle*, which supports and confirms the principles elaborated in the course of history in those other social spaces that preceded manufacturing industry and served as a model for it: the asylum, the ghetto, the general hospital, the prison – all the sites of enclosure and concentration that our culture has hidden in its march to civilisation. Today, all these determinate sites are themselves losing even their own limits, they are spread throughout global society since the asylum form, carceral form and discrimination have begun to invest the whole social space, every moment of real life.[11] All these things – factories, asylums, prisons, schools – still exist, and will no doubt continue to exist for an indefinite period, as warning signs, to divert the reality of the domination of capital into an imaginary materiality. There have always been churches to hide the death of God, or to hide the fact that God was everywhere, which amounts to the same thing.

There will always be animal reserves and Indian reservations to hide the fact that they are dead, and that we are all Indians. There will always be factories to hide the death of labour, the death of production, or the fact that they are everywhere and nowhere at once. For there is nothing with which to fight capital today in *determinate* forms. On the contrary, should it become clear that capital is no longer determined by something or other, and that its secret weapon is the reproduction of labour as imaginary, then capital itself would be close to exhaustion.

Wages

Labour, which in its completed form has no relation to any determinate production, is also without any equivalent in wages. Wages are equivalent to labour power only from the perspective of the quantitative reproduction of labour power. When they become the sanction of the status of labour power, the sign of obedience to the rule of the game of capital, wages no longer possess any such meaning. They are no longer in any proportional or equivalence relation at all,[12] they are a sacrament, like a baptism (or the Extreme Unction), which turns you into a genuine citizen of the political society of capital. Beyond the economic investment which constitutes the worker's wage-revenue for capital (end of the salariat as exploitation, beginning of the salariat as the 'actionariat' of capitalist society – the worker's strategic function slides towards consumption as obligatory social service), it is the other sense of the term 'investment' which brings it into the current phase of wage-status: capital invested the worker with a wage just as one used to be invested with a charge or a responsibility. But capital also invested the worker as one might 'invest' a town, totally occupying it and controlling all access.[13]

It is not solely by means of wage-revenue that capital charges producers to keep money in circulation and thus to become real reproducers of capital, but more fundamentally by means of the wage-status by which they are turned into purchasers of goods in the same way that capital itself is the purchaser of labour. Every user uses consumer objects reduced to the functional status of the production of services, just as capital uses labour power. Everyone is thus invested with the fundamental mentality of capital.

On the other hand, as soon as wages are detached from labour power, nothing (not even the unions) stands in the way of an unlimited and maximal wage demand. If there is a 'right price' for a certain *quantity* of labour force, a price can no longer be fixed on consensus and global participation. The traditional wage demand is only a negotiation over the *producer's conditions*. The maximalist demand is an offensive form of the wage-earner's reversal of his status as a reproducer, a *status* to which he is condemned by means of the wage. It is a challenge. The wage-earner wants everything. His method is not only to aggravate the economic crisis of the system but to turn every political constraint that the system imposes against it.

The maximalist slogan runs: 'maximum wage for minimum labour'. The political result of this escalating reversal might indeed be to send the system into orbit, in accordance with its own logic of labour as enforced presence. For wage-earners operate no longer as producers, but rather in terms of non-production, a role assigned them by capital. Neither do they operate dialectically, their interventions are *catastrophic*.

The less there is to do, the more wage increases must be demanded, since the minimal job is a more obvious sign of an absurdity than that of enforced presence. This is the 'class' that capital transforms in its own image: even robbed of its exploitation, the use of its labour power, it couldn't pay capital too much for this *denial of production*, this loss of identity, this debauchery. The exploited can demand only the minimum, but lower their status and they are free to demand everything.[14] The striking thing about this is that capital can follow into these fields with relative ease. It is not too much for the unions to make those wage-earners without consciousness aware of the wage–labour equivalence which capital itself has abolished. It is not too much for the unions to channel this unlimited wage-blackmail into the wholesome straits of negotiation. Without the unions, the workers would immediately demand 50 per cent, 100 per cent or 200 per cent increases – and perhaps get them! There are examples of this in the United States and Japan.[15]

Money

The homology Saussure established between labour and the signified on the one hand, and wages and the signifier on the other, is a kind of matrix which can be used as a base from which to survey political economy in its entirety. Today, however, the contrary proves to be the case: signifiers are severed from signifieds and wages are severed from labour. The escalating play of the signifier parallels the escalation of wages. Saussure was right: political economy is a language [*langue*], and the same mutation that affects linguistic signs when they lose their referential status also affects the categories of political economy. The same process ramifies in two other directions.

1. Production is severed from every reference or social finality. It then enters a growth phase. We must not interpret this growth as an acceleration, but in another sense, as something which marks and brings about the end of production. This is characterised by a significant divergence between production, on the one hand, and a relatively contingent and autonomous consumption, on the other. When, after the crisis of 1929, and especially after the Second World War, consumption began to be literally 'planned', that is, took on the force at once of a myth and of a controlled variable, we enter a phase where neither production nor consumption retains any proper determinations nor respective ends. Both become caught in a cycle or spiral, they are overcome by a confusion propagated by growth which leaves the traditional social objectives of production and consumption well behind. This process has only itself as an end. It no longer targets needs or profits. It is not an acceleration of productivity, but a structural inflation of the signs of production, an oscillation and proliferation of every sign, including monetary signs. It is the era of rocket launching programmes, Concorde, and total war strategies, of the proliferation of industrial estates, social or individual infrastructural facilities, training programmes and recycling, etc. – production for production's sake in accordance with a constraint of reinvestment at any cost (reinvestment no longer operating as the rate of surplus-value). The crowning achievement of this reproductive planning promises to be anti-pollution measures, where the entire 'productive' system will recycle and therefore eliminate its own waste products. This huge equation adds up to zero; not nothing, however, because the dialectic of pollution and anti-pollution 'produces' inchoate aspirations to growth without end.

2. The monetary sign is severed from every social production and then enters a phase of speculation and limitless inflation. Inflation is to money what the escalation of wages is to the sale of labour power, and what growth is to production. In each case, the same split releases the same burst of frantic activity and the same virtual crisis: the splitting of wages and the 'right price' of labour power, and the splitting of money and real production, both result in the loss of a system of reference. Abstract social labour time on the one hand and the gold-standard on the other lose their function as indices and criteria of equivalence. Wage inflation and monetary inflation (as well as growth) are therefore of the same type and are inseparable.[16]

Purged of finalities and the *affects* of production, money becomes speculative. From the gold-standard, which had already ceased to be the representative equivalent of a real production but still retains traces of this in a certain equilibrium (little inflation, the convertibility of money into gold, etc.), to hot money and generalised flotation, money is transformed from a referential sign into its structural form – the 'floating' signifier's own logic, not in Lévi-Strauss's sense, where it has not yet discovered its signified, but in the sense that it is well rid of every signified (every 'real' equivalent) as a brake to its proliferation and its unlimited play. Money can thus be reproduced according to a simple play of transfers and writings, according to an incessant splitting and increase of its own abstract substance.

Hot money: a name given to Euro-dollars, doubtless in order to characterise the senseless circulations of the monetary sign. Now, however, we should more accurately say that money has become 'cool', this term designating, following McLuhan and Riesman, an intense but non-affective relativity of terms, a play sustained purely by the rules of the game, the commutation of terms and the exhaustion of these commutations. By contrast, 'hot' characterises the referential phase of the sign, with its singularity and the opacity of its signified in the real, its very powerful affect and its minimal commutability. We are right in the middle of the sign's cool phase. The current system of labour is cool, every structural assemblage is, generally speaking, cool, while both 'classical' production and labour, hot processes *par excellence*, have been replaced by unlimited growth bound to a disinvestment of the contents and process of labour, which are cool processes.

Coolness is the pure play of the values of discourse and the commutations of writing. It is the ease and aloofness of what now only really plays with codes, signs and words, the omnipotence of operational simulation. To whatever extent affects or systems of reference remain, they remain hot. Any 'message' keeps us in the hot. We enter the cool era when the medium becomes the message. And this is precisely what has taken place with money. Once a certain phase of disconnection has been reached, money is no longer a medium or a means to circulate commodities, it is *circulation itself*, that is to say, it is the realised form of the system in its twisting abstraction.

Money is the first 'commodity' to assume the status of a sign and to *escape use-value*. Henceforth, it intensifies the system of exchange-value, turning it into a visible sign, and in this way makes the transparency of the market (and therefore of rarity too) visible. Today, however, money sanctions a further step: *it also escapes exchange-value*. Freed from the market itself, it becomes an autonomous simulacrum, relieved of every message and every signification of exchange, becoming a message itself and exchanging amongst itself. Money is then no longer a commodity since it no longer contains any use-value or exchange-value, nor is it any longer a general equivalent, that is, it is no longer a mediating abstraction of the market. Money circulates at a greater rate than everything else, and has no common measure with anything else.

We could of course say that this has always been the case that since the first light shone on the market economy, money circulated at the highest rate and drew every other sector into this acceleration. And throughout the history of capital there is a distortion of all the different levels (financial, industrial, agricultural, but also consumer goods, etc.) according to the speed at which it circulates. These distortions still persist today, as the resistance of national currencies (bound up with a market, a production and a local equilibrium) to international speculative currencies testifies. It is, however, the latter that is leading the offensive, because it is what circulates at the highest rate, it is what drifts and floats: a simple play of flotation can ruin any national economy. In accordance with a differential rate of rotation, every sector is thus directed by this high intensity flotation which, far from being a baroque, epiphenomenal process ('What is the Stock Market for?'), is the purest expression of the system. We discover this scenario everywhere: in the inconvertibility of currencies into gold, or in the inconvertibility of signs into their systems of reference; in the floating and generalised convertibility of currencies amongst themselves, or in the mobility and the endless structural play of signs. But we also discover this in the flotation of all the categories of political economy once they lose their gold-reference, labour power and social production: labour and non-labour, labour and capital, become commutable, all logic has dissolved; and we discover this in the flotation of all the categories of consciousness where the *mental equivalent of the gold-standard*, the subject, has been lost. There are no more authorities to which to refer, under whose jurisdiction producers could exchange their values in accordance with controlled equivalents: the end of the gold-standard. There are no more authorities to which to refer, under whose aegis a subject could exchange objects dialectically, or exchange their determinations around a stable identity in accordance with definite rules: the end of the conscious subject. (We are tempted to say that this is the reign of the unconscious.) The logical consequence of this is, if the conscious subject is the mental equivalent of the gold-standard, then the *unconscious is the mental equivalent of speculative currency and hot money*. Today, individuals, disinvested as subjects and robbed of their fixed relations, are drifting, in relation to one another, into an incessant mode of transferential fluctuations: flows, connections, disconnections, transference/counter-transference. Society as a whole could easily be described in terms of the Deleuzian unconscious,[17] or of monetary mechanics (or indeed in the Riesmanian terms of 'other-directedness', which is already, unfortunately in Anglo-Saxon and therefore barely schizophrenic terms, the flotation of identities). Why privilege the unconscious here (even if it is orphan and schizophrenic)? The unconscious is that mental structure contemporaneous with the most radical, current phase of dominant exchange; it is contemporaneous with the structural revolution of value.

Strikes

Within a system of production, strikes were historically justified as organised violence for purposes of snatching a fraction of surplus-value, or else power, from the opposing violence of capital. Today this form of the strike is dead:

1. It is dead because capital is in a position to leave every strike to continue until it rots, precisely because we are no longer in a system of production (maximalisation of surplus-value). Profits be damned so long as the reproduction of *the form of social relations* is saved!
2. It is dead because such strikes change nothing fundamental: contemporary capital merely redistributes itself, a matter of life or death for it. At best, strikes merely snatch only what, in the end, capital would have conceded anyway.

So if relations of production, and with them the class struggle, fall into orchestrated social and political relations, then clearly all that can intervene in this cycle is what escapes the organisation and definition of class as:

– a *representative* historical agency;
– a *productive* historical agency.

Only those who escape the swings and roundabouts of production and representation can disrupt these mechanisms and provoke, from the depths of their blinded state, a return to the 'class struggle', which might indeed mark the end of this struggle as a locus within the 'political'. It is here that the intervention of immigrants in recent strikes[18] takes on meaning.

Because millions of workers find themselves, by means of the mechanics of discrimination, deprived of all representative authority, their appearance on the Western stage of the class struggle carries the crisis of representation to a crucial level. Kept classless by society as a whole, including the unions (and, on this point, with the economic-racial complicity of their 'rank and file': for the organised proletarian 'class', centred on its relations with political-economic forces with the bourgeois capitalist class, the immigrant is 'objectively' an enemy of the class), the immigrants play, through the action of this social exclusion, the role of analysts of the relation between workers and the unions, and, more generally, of the relation between the 'class' and every representative authority of the 'class'. They are deviant as regards the system of political representation and of every authority who claims to speak in their name.

This situation will not last: unions and bosses have sensed the danger and have begun to reintegrate the immigrants as 'temporary full citizens', full-time extras on the stage of the 'class struggle'.

The Autopsy of the Unions The Renault strike of March–April 1973 constituted a general repetition of this crisis. Apparently confused, uncoordinated, manipulated and, in the final analysis, a failure (except for the extraordinary terminological victory that consisted in the replacement of the once taboo term 'semi-skilled worker' with the term 'agent of production'!), this strike was in reality the beautiful swan song of the unions, caught between their rank and file and the bosses. From the outset it was a 'savage' strike, unleashed by semi-skilled immigrant workers. The CGT,[19] however, had a weapon ready to counter this accidental war:

namely spreading the strike to other factories or to other sectors of the workforce, thus taking advantage of the now ritual spring mass demonstrations. Yet even this mechanism of control, which had been repeatedly tested ever since 1968, which the unions counted they could rely on for generations to come, let them down this time. Even the non-savage rank and file (at Seguin, Flins and Sandouville) were sometimes on strike and sometimes back at work (which is also important), without paying heed to the 'advice' from their unions. The unions were constantly being caught off-guard. The workers wanted nothing to do with whatever the unions won from management and put before them. Those concessions they drew from the workers in order to relaunch negotiations with management were rejected by the management, who then closed down the factories. Management appealed to the workers while ignoring the unions, and in fact deliberately forced the crisis in order to force the unions to retreat: couldn't they control *all* the workers? The unions' social legitimacy, and even their existence, was at issue. Hence the bosses' (and all levels of government) adoption of a 'hard line'. It was no longer a question of a test of strength between the organised (unionised) proletariat and the bosses, but of a *test of representativity* for the unions, under pressure from both the rank and file *and* management. Such tests result from every savage strike over the last few years sparked off by non-union personnel, rebellious youth, immigrants: the classless.

The stakes at this level are extraordinary. The entire edifice of society threatens to collapse with the unions' legitimacy and representativity. Adjudicators and other mediating bodies no longer count for much. Even the police are useless without the unions if the latter cannot police the factories and elsewhere. In May '68, it was the unions who saved the regime, but now their knell is being sounded. The import of the stakes is profoundly expressed in the utter confusion of events such as the Renault strike and May '68 (and this holds good for student demonstrations just as it does for the Renault strikes). To strike or not to strike. Where do we stand on this? No-one can decide any more. What are the objectives? Where are the enemy? What are we talking about? The Geiger counters that the unions, parties and micro-groups used to measure the masses' readiness for combat are thrown into turmoil. The student movement is too fluid for the hands of those who would like to structure it according to their own objectives: don't they have any objectives? In any case, it did not want to *become objectified behind its back*. The workers went back to work without gaining a thing, while eight days beforehand they had refused when they were offered palpable benefits. In fact, this confusion is similar to what happens in dreams: it betrays a resistance or a censorship acting on the dream-content itself. Here it betrays something of vital importance, something difficult, however, for the proletarians themselves to accept: the social struggle has been *displaced* from the traditional, external enemy of the class, management and capital, onto the internal class enemy, the proper representative authority for the class, the party or the union. These are the authorities to which the workers delegate their power, which is turned against them under the form of management or government delegations of power. Capital itself only alienates labour power and its product, its only monopoly is *production*. Parties and unions alienate social power from the exploited and have a monopoly on *representation*. Calling them into question is a revolutionary historical development. But this development is paid for by a loss of clarity, a loss of resolution, an apparent regression, the absence of continuity, logic and objectives, etc. This is because everything becomes uncertain when it is a matter of confronting one's own repressive agency, of driving the unionist, shop steward, official or spokesperson *from one's own head*. But the confusing character of spring '73 indicates precisely that we have fundamentally located the problem: the unions and parties are dead, all that remains for them to do is die.

The Corrupted Proletariat The crisis of representation is the crucial *political* aspect of the latest social movements. In itself, this crisis may prove fatal to the system, and already we can see the emerging outline (in the unions themselves) of its formal overcoming (its recuperation) in a generalised schema of *self-management*. No more delegation of power – everyone will be fully responsible for production! The new ideological generation is coming! But it will have a great deal to do, because this crisis is intricately bound up with another crisis, deeper still, which touches production itself, the very system of productivity. And there again, indirectly of course, the immigrants are in the position of analysts. Just as they analyse the 'proletariat's' relation to its representative agencies, they analyse the *workers' relation to their own labour power*, their relation to themselves as a productive force (and not only to a few of them, selected as representative authorities). This is because they have recently been extracted from a non-productivist tradition; because they had to be socially destructured in order to be thrown into the process of Western labour, and because, in return, it is they who thoroughly destructure the general process and morality of production which dominates Western societies.

It is just as if their forced recruitment into the European market provoked an increasing corruption of the European proletariat as regards labour and production. It is no longer simply a matter of 'clandestine' practices of resistance to labour (go-slows, wastage, absenteeism, etc.), which have never stopped. This time the workers downed tools openly, collectively and spontaneously, just like that, suddenly, asking for nothing, negotiating nothing, to the great despair of both unions and management, and started work again just as spontaneously, *as a group*, the following Monday. Neither failure nor victory, it was not a strike, it was just a '*stoppage*', a euphemism which says far more than the term 'strike'. The whole discipline of labour collapses, all the moral norms and practices that industrial colonisation has imposed on Europe for two centuries disintegrate and are forgotten with apparent ease, without the 'class struggle' strictly speaking. Discontinuity, latitudinarianism, indiscipline as regards working hours, indifference with regard to wage pressure, to surplus, promotion, accumulation, forecasting. You do only what you have to, then stop and go back to it later. This is exactly the behaviour that inhabitants of 'developing countries' were reproached for by the colonists, who found it impossible to train the inhabitants to obey value and labour, rational and continuous time, the concept of saving wages, and so on. It is only by sending them abroad that the inhabitants were finally integrated into the labour process. And it is at precisely this point that Western workers start to 'regress' more and more into the behaviour of 'underdeveloped' inhabitants. It is not that seeing the Western proletariat in the grip of corruption constitutes a revenge for colonisation in its most advanced form (importing manual labour), although one day it might have to be the turn of the proletariat to be exported to the developing countries in order to relearn the historical and revolutionary values of labour.

There is a direct relation between the ultra-colonisation of immigrant workers (since the colonies were not profitable where they were, they had to be imported) and the industrial de-colonisation which affects every sector of society (everywhere, in schools and in factories, we move from the *hot* phase of the investment of labour to *the cynical and cool execution of tasks*). Because they have most recently left their 'savage' indifference for 'rational' labour, these immigrants (and the young or rural semi-skilled workers) are in a position to analyse Western society with the recent, fragile, superficial and arbitrary collectivisation enforced by labour, this collective paranoia, which has spawned a morality, a culture and a myth. We have forgotten that it was only two centuries ago that this industrial discipline was imposed, at unprecedented cost, on the West itself, that it has never quite succeeded and is beginning to crack dangerously (it will barely have lasted as long, indeed, as overseas colonisation).

Strike for Strike's Sake   Strike for strike's sake is the true condition of the contemporary struggle. Unmotivated, with neither objective nor political referent, it is the oppositional response adopted against a production which is also unmotivated, with neither a referent, nor a social use-value, nor any other finality than its own – *production for production's sake*, in short, a system which has become only a system of *reproduction*, revolving around itself in a gigantic tautology of the labour process. Strike for strike's sake is the complementary tautology, but, since it unveils a new form of capital corresponding to the final stage of the law of value, it is also subversive.

Strikes have at last ceased to be a means, and only a means, of putting pressure on the relation of *political* forces and the power game. It becomes an end. Even on their own ground they negate, by means of a radical parody, the sort of finality without end that production has become.

In production for production's sake, there is no more waste. We have no use for this term, which means something only in a restricted utilitarian economy. It relies on a pious critique of the system. Concorde, the space programme, etc., are not a waste of resources; on the contrary, since the system, having reached this high point of 'objective' futility, produces and reproduces *labour itself*. Besides, this is precisely what everyone (including the workers and the unions) demands of it. Everything revolves around jobs (the social is just a matter of job creation), and in order to keep their jobs, the British unions are prepared to transform Concorde into a supersonic bomber. Inflation or unemployment? Long live inflation! Labour, like social security, has come to be just another consumer good to be distributed throughout society. The enormous paradox is that the less labour becomes a productive force, the more it becomes a *product*. This is not the least important characteristic of the current mutations of the capitalist system, the revolution from the specific stage of production to the stage of reproduction. It has less and less need of labour power in order to function and grow, while there are increasing demands on it to produce more and more labour.

Corresponding to the absurd circularity of a system where one labours only to produce more labour is the demand for strikes for strikes' sake (at any rate, this is the point at which the majority of 'protest' strikes have today come to an end). 'Pay us for the days we are on strike' basically means 'pay us in order that we may *reproduce* strikes for strikes' sake'. This is the reversal of the absurdity of the system in general.

Today, *all* products, labour included, are beyond both use and futility. There is no more productive labour, only reproductive labour. In the same way there is no more 'productive' or 'unproductive' consumption, only a *reproductive* consumption. Leisure is as productive as labour, factory labour as 'unproductive' as leisure or the service industries, it is irrelevant what formula we use. *This indifference precisely marks the phase of the completion of political economy. Everyone is reproductive*; that is, everyone has lost the concrete finality which once marked them out from one another. Nobody produces any more. Production is dead, long live reproduction!

The Genealogy of Production The system currently reproduces capital according to its most rigorous definition, as the *form of social relations*, rather than in its vulgar sense as money, profits and the economic system. Reproduction has always been understood as, and determined by, an 'increasing' reproduction of the mode of production, even though it became necessary to conceive of the mode of production as *a* modality (and not the only one) of the *mode of reproduction*. Productive forces and the relations of production, the sphere of material productivity in other words, are perhaps only one of many possible, and therefore historically relative, conjunctions of the process of reproduction. Reproduction is a form which far outstrips economic exploitation, and so the play of productive forces is not its necessary condition.

The historical status of the 'proletariat' (the industrial wage-earners) is primarily one of incarceration, concentration and exclusion. The seventeenth-century incarceration described by Foucault[20] expands grotesquely in the age of industrial manufacture. Didn't 'industrial' labour (which, unlike cottage industries, is collective, controlled, and stripped of the means of production) evolve within the first great *hôpitaux généraux*? In the beginning, society, in the process of rationalisation, incarcerated its idle, its wanderers, its deviants, gave them an 'occupation' and fixed them, imposed its rational principle of labour on them. But these outcasts contaminated the process of rationalisation in turn, and the rupture produced when society instituted its principle of rationality spilled over the whole of the society of labour: the Great Confinement is a model in miniature, later generalised in the industrial system of every society that, under the sign of labour and productivist finality, became a concentration camp, a detention centre or a prison.

Instead of extending the concepts of the proletariat and exploitation to racial or sexual oppression and such like, we should ask ourselves if it is not the other way round. What if the fundamental status of the worker, like the mad, the dead, nature, beasts, children, Blacks and women, was initially to be not *exploited* but *excommunicated*? What if he was initially not deprived and exploited but discriminated against and branded?

My hypothesis is that there has never been a genuine class struggle except on the grounds of this discrimination: sub-humans struggle against their status as beasts, against the abjection of the caste division that condemns them to the sub-humanity of labour. This lies behind every strike and every revolt, and today it is still behind the most 'wage-related' demonstrations. Hence their virulence. Having said that, today the proletarian is a 'normal' being, the worker has been promised the dignity of a full 'human being', and, moreover, in accordance with this category, he seizes onto every dominant discrimination: he is racist, sexist and repressive. As regards today's deviants and whoever is discriminated against, no matter what their social standing, he has sided with the bourgeoisie and the normal human being. How true: the fundamental law of this society is not the law of exploitation, but the *code of normality*.

May '68: The Illusion of Production   The first shockwaves of this transition from production to pure and simple reproduction took place in May '68. They struck the universities first, and the faculty of human sciences first of all, because that was where it became most evident (even without a clear 'political' consciousness) that *we were no longer productive*, only reproductive (and that lecturers, science and culture were themselves only relays in the general reproduction of the system). All this was experienced as total futility, irresponsibility ('What are sociologists for?'), as a relegation, and provoked the student movement of '68 (rather than the absence of prospects, since there are always plenty of prospects *in reproduction* – it was rather the places, the spaces where something actually *happens* that had ceased to exist).

These shockwaves are still being felt. They cannot but reach the very limits of the system, as soon as entire sectors of society topple from the rank of *productive forces* to the pure and simple status of *reproductive forces*. Although this process was first felt in the cultural sectors of science, justice and the family – the so-called 'superstructural' sectors – it is clear today that it is progressively affecting the entire so-called 'infrastructural' sector: a new generation of partial, savage and occasional strikes since '68 testify no longer to the 'class struggle' of a proletariat attached to production, but to the revolt of those who, even in the factories, are attached to reproduction.

Nevertheless, in this same sector there are marginal, anomic groups who are the first to register these effects: young semi-skilled workers brought directly from rural areas into the factories, immigrants, non-union members; and so on. For all the above mentioned reasons, the 'traditional', organised and unionised proletariat have looked likely to be the last to react, since it is they who can entertain the *illusion of 'productive' labour* for longest. The consciousness of being, in relation to everyone else, the true 'producers' and, albeit at the cost of the exploitation, nevertheless being at the very source of social wealth is a 'proletarian' consciousness which is reinforced and sanctioned by the organisation, constituting what is certainly the most solid *ideological* defence against the destructuration of the current system which, far from turning whole strata of the population into proletarians or, as Marxian theory proper has it, expanding the exploitation of 'productive' labour, aligns everybody under the same reproductive worker status.

'Productive' manual workers, more than anybody else, thrive on the *illusion of production* just as they experience their leisure under the illusion of freedom.

As long as these things are experienced as sources of wealth or satisfaction, as use-value, then the worst, most alienated and exploited labour is bearable. As long as we can still discover a 'production' corresponding (even if this is only in the imagination) to individual or social needs (this is why the concept of need is so fundamental and so mystifying), the worst individual or historical situations are bearable because *the illusion of production is always the illusory coincidence of production and use-value*. Those who today believe in the use-value of their labour power – the proletariat – are virtually the most mystified and the least susceptible to this revolt which grabs people from the depths of their total futility and the circular manipulation which turns them into pure markers of senseless reproduction.

The day that this process spreads to all of society, May '68 will assume the form of a general explosion, and the problem of the link between the students and the workers will no longer be posed: it merely betrays the gulf that separates those in the current system who still believe in their own labour force and those who no longer believe in it.

Political Economy as a Model of Simulation

From now on political economy is the *real* for us, which is to say precisely that it is the sign's referential, the horizon of a defunct order whose simulation preserves it in a 'dialectical' equilibrium. It is the real, *and therefore* the imaginary, since here again the two formerly distinct categories have fused and drifted together. The code (the structural law of value) uses the systematic reactivation of political economy (the restricted market law of value) as our society's imaginary-real. Furthermore, the appearance of the restricted form of value is an attempt to obscure its radical form.

Profit, surplus-value, the mechanics of capital and the class struggle: the entire critical discourse on political economy is staged as a referential discourse. The mystery of value is enacted on stage (of course, the mystery has simply acquired a new value: the structural law of value has become mysterious): everyone agrees as to the 'determining instance' of economics, and this has become 'obscene'.[21] This is a provocation. Capital no longer looks to nature, God or morality, but strictly to political economy and its *critique* for its alibis, and lives through its own denunciation from within itself – feedback or a dialectical stimulus. Hence the essential role played by Marxian analysis in designer capital.

The same scenario is played out in economics as Bourdieu and Passeron describe it, taking place in the academic system whose alleged autonomy enables it to reproduce the class structure of society very efficiently. Similarly, the alleged autonomy of political economy (or rather its value as a determining agency) enables it to reproduce, just as efficiently, capital's symbolic function, its real domination over life and death established by the code, and which is continually stirring up political economy as a medium, an alibi and a fig-leaf.

A machine has to function if it is to reproduce relations of production. A commodity must have a use-value in order to sustain the system of exchange-value. This was the first-level scenario. Simulation is today at the second level: a commodity must function as an exchange-value in order better to hide the fact that it circulates like a sign and reproduces the code.[22]

Society has to reproduce itself as class society, as class struggle, it must 'function' at the Marxian-critical level in order the better to mask the system's real law and the possibility of its symbolic destruction. Marcuse pointed out a long time ago that dialectical materialism was getting out of hand: far from being deconstructed by the forces of production, the relations of production from now on submit to the forces of production (science, technology, etc.) and find a new *legitimacy* in them. There again, we must pass on to the second level: the social relations of symbolic domination utterly submit to the mode of production (both the forces of production *and* the relations of production), where we find, in the apparent movement of political economy *and the revolution*, a new legitimacy and the most perfect alibi.

Hence the necessity of resurrecting and dramatising political economy in the form of a movie script, to screen out the threat of symbolic destruction. Hence the kind of crisis, the perpetual simulacrum of a crisis, we are dealing with today.

In the aesthetic stage of political economy, the finality–without–end of production, the ethical, ascetic myth of accumulation and labour collapses. Capital, to avoid the risk of bursting from these liquefied values, thus becomes nostalgic once more for its great *ethical* epoch when production had a meaning, the golden age of shortages and the development of the forces of production. In order to re-establish finalities and to reactivate the principle of economics, we must generate shortages once again. Hence ecology, where the danger of absolute scarcity reinstates an ethic of energy conservation.

Hence the crisis of energy and raw materials, a real blessing for a system which, in the mirror of production, only reflects a fluctuating, empty form. The crisis will enable the return of a lost referentiality to the economic code, and will give the principle of production a gravity that evaded it. We will rediscover a taste for ascesis, that pathetic investment born of lack and deprivation.

The whole recent ecological turn had already taken up this process of regeneration during the crisis – no longer a crisis of overproduction as in 1929 – of the involution of the system, recycling its lost identity.[23] A crisis no longer of *production*, but of *reproduction* (hence the impossibility of grasping how much truth and how much simulacrum there may be in this crisis). Ecology is production haunted by shortages and using itself as a resource, once more discovering a natural necessity where the law of value is tried out again. But ecology is too slow. A sudden crisis, as happened with oil, constitutes a more energetic therapy. The less oil there is, the more we will become aware of how much production there is. From the moment that the place of raw materials is noted again, labour power will also resume its rightful place, and the entire mechanism of production will become intelligible once more. Production has been given another chance.

So don't panic. On the eve of the intensive mobilisation of labour power, when the ethics of labour power threatened to collapse, the crisis of material energy came at the right time to mask the truly catastrophic destruction of the *finality* of production, and displaced it onto a simple *internal contradiction* (but we know that the system thrives on its contradictions).

There is still an illusion in thinking that the capitalist system, at a certain threshold of increased reproduction, passes irreversibly from a strategy of shortage to a strategy of abundance. The current crisis proves that this strategy is reversible. The illusion still comes from a naïve faith in a *reality* of shortage or a *reality* of abundance, and therefore from the illusion of a real opposition between these two terms. When these two terms are quite simply alternatives, the strategic definition of neo-capitalism is to pass into not a phase of abundance (consumption, repressive desublimation, sexual liberation, etc.) but a phase of *systematic alternation* between the two terms – shortage and abundance – because neither retains a reference, nor therefore an antagonistic reality, and therefore because the system is indifferent to which one it employs.

The indeterminacy affecting terms, the neutralisation of a *dialectical opposition into a pure and simple structural alternation*, produces the characteristic effect of an *uncertainty surrounding the reality of the crisis*. Everyone tries to stave off the unbearable simulacrum-effect – characteristic of everything that issues from the systematic operation of the code – as a conspiracy. It is comforting to think that it was 'great capital' that provoked the crisis, because it restores a *real* political-economic agency and the presence of a (hidden) *subject* of the crisis, and therefore an historical truth. The terror of the simulacrum is over. So much the better: it is better to have the omnipresent political-economic fatality of capital than not, so long as it is clearly true. Better the *economic* atrocities of capital – profit, exploitation – than to face up to the situation we are in, where everything operates or breaks down through effects of the code. Misconstrual [*méconnaissance*] of the 'truth' of this global domination (if there is a global domination) is proportional to the crisis itself, where it is revealed for the first time on a massive scale.

The 1929 crisis was still a crisis of capital, measured by its rates of reinvestment, surplus-value and profit, a crisis of (over)production measured by the social finalities of consumption. The crisis is resolved by regulating demand in an endless exchange of finalities between production and consumption. From now on (and conclusively after the Second World War), production and consumption cease to be opposed and possibly contradictory poles. At a stroke, the entire economic field loses all internal determinacy along with the very possibility of a crisis. It no longer survives except as a process of economic simulation at the fringes of a process of reproduction, into which it is entirely absorbed.[24]

Have there ever been real shortages to grant the economic principle a reality, so that today we could say that it is disappearing and no longer functions save as a myth, an alternative myth, moreover, to that of abundance? In the course of history, have shortages ever had a *use-value*, an irreducible economic finality, so that today we could say that it has disappeared in the cycle of reproduction, merely consolidating the code's hegemonic control over genuine matters of life and death? We are saying that in order for the economy to *produce itself* (and this is all it ever produces), it needs this dialectical tension between scarcity and abundance. For the system to reproduce itself, however, it now requires only the *mythical operation of the economy*.

It is because the entire economic sphere has been defused that everything can be expressed in terms of political economy and production. Economics, preferably in its Marxian variety, becomes the explicit discourse of a whole society, the vulgate of every analysis. Sociologists, human scientists, etc. (even Christians, especially Christians of course), turn to Marxism as *the* discourse to which they refer. A whole new Divine Left is rising. Everything has become 'political' and 'ideological' by the same endless drift of the operation of integration. The newsflash is political, sport is political, not to mention art: reason is everywhere on the side of the class struggle. The entire latent discourse of capital has become manifest, we notice a widespread jubilation secure in the assumption of this 'truth'.

May '68 marked the decisive step in the *naturalisation of political economy*. Because the shock of May '68 shook the system down to the depths of its symbolic organisation, it has given urgency to a vital transition from 'superstructural' (moral, cultural, etc.) ideologies to an ideologisation of the infrastructure itself. By giving official status to oppositional discourse, capital will consolidate its power under cover of economic and political legislation. Political economy, *Marxian* political economy, has sealed the rift of May '68, just as the unions and the left-wing parties 'negotiated' the crisis on the ground. The hidden referent of economics and politics has therefore been dug up only in order to retrieve a catastrophic situation, and today it continues to be circulated, generalised and desperately reproduced, since the catastrophic situation opened up by May '68 is not over.

If we dared, we would say that economics and its critique are only superstructural; we will not dare, however, since to do so would only be to twist this old image around – where would the infrastructure be then? Etc. It would also provide economics with a chance to reappear one day in accordance with the see-saw effect which itself belongs to the code. We have been tricked too often with the infrastructure to start this mask-play up again. The system itself has put an end to infra- and superstructural determinations. Today it pretends to take political economy as the infrastructure because Marx kindly whispered this alternative strategy to it, but actually capital has never really functioned on this imaginary distinction, it is not that naïve. Its potency comes directly from its simultaneous development at every level, and from never having *fundamentally* posed itself the question of determination, the cunning distinction of agencies, or 'ideology'. It has never confused itself with production, as did Marx and every subsequent revolutionary who believed and still believes in production, confusing their phantasies with their lunatic hopes. For its part, capital is content to extend its laws in a single movement, inexorably occupying all the interstices of life without confusing its priorities. If it has set men to work, capital has also impelled them to culture, needs, languages and functional idioms, information and communication; it directs them to rights, to liberty and sexuality, it forces the instinct of preservation and the death instinct upon them; it has set them up everywhere in accordance with myths that are simultaneously opposed and indifferent. This is its only law: indifference. To set up a hierarchy of agencies would be far too dangerous a game, and would run the risk of backfiring. No, better to level out, neutralise, cover over and indifferentiate, which is what it knows how to do; that's how it follows its law. But it also dissimulates this fundamental process under the 'determinant' mask of political economy.

In the immense polymorphous machine of contemporary capital, the symbolic (gift and counter-gift, reciprocity and reversal, expenditure and sacrifice) no longer counts for anything, nature (the great referential of the origin and substance, the subject/object dialectic, and so on) no longer counts, political economy itself only survives in a brain-dead state, but all these phantoms continue to plague the operational field of value. Perhaps here, on an immense scale, we can discern the echo of what Marx drew to our attention: every event first passes through an historical existence before being revived under a parodical form. In our day, however, these two phases telescope, since good old materialist history has itself become a process of simulation, no longer even offering the chance of a grotesque, theatrical parody: today the terror based on things voided of their substance exerts itself directly, and simulacra immediately anticipate every determination of our lives. Now, rather than theatre and the imaginary, there is a fierce strategy of neutralisation that no longer leaves any significant place for a Napoleon III-type slapstick, an historical farce which, to Marx's mind, is effortlessly overcome by *real* history. It is a different matter as regards the simulacra which eliminate both ourselves and history simultaneously. But perhaps all this arises from a general illusion in Marx concerning the possibilities for a *revolution* of the system. He had clearly seen the extent to which there already lurked in capital in his own time a capacity for it to undermine its own bases and go 'into overdrive'. He clearly saw that capital tended to reduce, if not totally eliminate, the labour power in its processes, and substitute a dead labour power for it. Since, however, he thought that living labour power was the objective, historical and necessary foundation of capital, he could only think that it was digging its own grave. The illusion is that capital buried labour power. More subtly, however, it turns labour power into the second term of a stable opposition with capital. It makes this rupturing *energy* which should shatter the relations of production into a *term* homogeneous with the relations of production, in a simulation of opposition under the sign of dead labour. From now on a single hegemonic agency (dead labour) divides into capital and living labour. The antagonism is resolved by a binary apparatus of coded operativity. But what, you might ask, of surplus-value and production? Alright, capital doesn't give a damn. Without lending capital a Marxist's intuition (even though Marx did everything he could to *alert* capital to what was waiting for it: if it persisted in playing on the terrain of production, it was heading for its death in the short term – the economy was a fatal trap for capital), everything happened as if it had clearly understood Marx on this point and had, in consequence, 'chosen' to liquidate production so as to go onto another kind of strategy. I am saying that everything happens *as if*, because it is not completely certain that capital ever had this productivist view of itself (Marx was basically the only one who had, and he projected this phantasy onto it as an historical truth); it is more likely that it only ever *played* at production, even if this meant that production had to be abandoned at a later stage, were it to draw capital into fatal contradictions. Has capital ever taken production seriously? Don't be so stupid: at the height of the seriousness of production, capital is doubtless only a simulation.

That is why the only acts that accompany capital's real domination are situated in the field of this radical indeterminacy and break with this dissuasive economic strategy.

We will not destroy the system by a direct, dialectical revolution of the economic or political infrastructure. Everything produced by contradiction, by the relation of forces, or by energy in general, will only feed back into the mechanism and give it impetus, following a circular distortion similar to a Moebius strip. We will never defeat it by following its own logic of energy, calculation, reason and revolution, history and power, or some finality or counter-finality. The worst violence at this level has no purchase, and will only backfire against itself. We will never defeat the system on the plane of the *real*: the worst error of all our revolutionary strategies is to believe that we will put an end to the system on the plane of the *real*: this is their imaginary, imposed on them by the system itself, living or surviving only by always leading those who attack the system to fight amongst each other on the terrain of reality, *which is always the reality of the system*. This is where they throw all their energies, their imaginary violence, where an implacable logic constantly turns back into the system. We have only to do it violence or counter-violence since it thrives on symbolic violence – not in the degraded sense in which this formula has found fortune, as a violence 'of signs', from which the system draws strength, or with which it 'masks' its material violence: symbolic violence is deduced from a logic of the symbolic (which has nothing to do with the sign or with energy): reversal, the incessant reversibility of the counter-gift and, conversely, the seizing of power by the unilateral exercise of the gift.[25]

We must therefore displace everything into the sphere of the symbolic, where challenge, reversal and overbidding are the law, *so that we can respond to death only by an equal or superior death*. There is no question here of real violence or force, the only question concerns the challenge and the logic of the symbolic. If domination comes from the system's retention of the exclusivity of the gift without counter-gift – the gift of work which can only be responded to by destruction or sacrifice, if not in consumption, which is only a spiral of the system of surplus-gratification without result, therefore a spiral of surplus-domination; a gift of media and messages to which, due to the monopoly of the code, nothing is allowed to retort; the gift, everywhere and at every instant, of the social, of the protection agency, security, gratification and the solicitation of the social from which nothing is any longer permitted to escape – then the only solution is to turn the principle of its power back against the system itself: the impossibility of responding or retorting. *To defy the system with a gift to which it cannot respond save by its own collapse and death.* Nothing, not even the system, can avoid the symbolic obligation, and it is in this trap that the only chance of a catastrophe for capital remains. The system turns on itself, as a scorpion does when encircled by the challenge of death. For it is summoned to answer, if it is not to lose face, to what can only be death. The system must *itself commit suicide in response to the multiplied challenge of death and suicide.*

So hostages are taken. On the symbolic or sacrificial plane, from which every moral consideration of the innocence of the victims is ruled out, the hostage is the substitute, the alter-ego of the 'terrorist' – the hostage's death for the terrorist's. Hostage and terrorist may thereafter become confused in the same sacrificial act. The stakes are death without any possibility of negotiation, and therefore return to an inevitable overbidding. Of course, they attempt to deploy the whole system of negotiation, and the terrorists themselves often enter into this exchange scenario in terms of this calculated equivalence (the hostages' lives against some ransom or liberation, or indeed for the prestige of the operation alone). From this perspective, taking hostages is not original at all, it simply creates an unforeseen and selective relation of forces which can be resolved either by traditional violence or by negotiation. It is a tactical action. There is something else at stake, however, as we clearly saw at The Hague over the course of ten days of incredible negotiations: no-one knew what could be negotiated, nor could they agree on terms, nor on the possible equivalences of the exchange. Or again, even if they were formulated, the 'terrorists' demands' amounted to a radical denial of negotiation. It is precisely here that everything is played out, for with the impossibility of all negotiation we pass into the symbolic order, which is ignorant of this type of calculation and exchange (the system itself lives solely by negotiation, even if this takes place in the equilibrium of violence). The system can only respond to this irruption of the symbolic (the most serious thing to befall it, basically the only 'revolution') by the real, physical death of the terrorists. This, however, is its defeat, since their death was their stake, so that by bringing about their deaths the system has merely impaled itself on its own violence *without really responding to the challenge that was thrown to it.* Because the system can easily compute every death, even war atrocities, but cannot compute the death-challenge or symbolic death, since this death has no calculable equivalent, it opens up an inexpiable overbidding by other means than a death in exchange. Nothing *corresponds* to death except death. Which is precisely what happens in this case: *the system itself is driven to suicide in return*, which suicide is manifest in its disarray and defeat. However infinitesimal in terms of relations of forces it might be, the colossal apparatus of power is eliminated in this situation where (the very excess of its) derision is turned back against itself. The police and the army, all the institutions and mobilised violence of power whether individually or massed together, can do nothing against this lowly but symbolic death. For this death draws it onto a plane where there is no longer any response possible for it (hence the sudden structural liquefaction of power in '68, not because it was less strong, but because of the simple symbolic displacement operated by the students' practices). The system can only die in exchange, defeat itself to lift the challenge. Its death at this instant is a symbolic response, but a death which wears it out.

The challenge has the efficiency of a murderer. Every society apart from ours knows that, or used to know it. Ours is in the process of rediscovering it. The routes of symbolic effectiveness are those of an alternative politics.

Thus the dying ascetic challenges God ever to give him the equivalent of this death. God does all he can to give him this equivalent 'a hundred times over', in the form of prestige, of spiritual power, indeed of global hegemony. But the ascetic's secret dream is to attain such an extent of mortification that even God would be unable either to take up the challenge, or to absorb the debt. He will then have triumphed over God, and become God himself. That is why the ascetic is always close to heresy and sacrilege, and as such condemned by the Church, whose function it is merely to preserve God from this symbolic face-to-face, to protect Him from this mortal challenge where He is summoned to die, to sacrifice Himself in order to take up the challenge of the mortified ascetic. The Church will have had this role for all time, avoiding this type of catastrophic confrontation (catastrophic primarily for the Church) and substituting a rule-bound exchange of penitences and gratifications, the impressario of a system of equivalences between God and men.

The same situation exists in our relation to the system of power. All these institutions, all these social, economic, political and psychological mediations, are there so that no-one ever has the opportunity to issue this symbolic challenge, this challenge to the death, the irreversible gift which, like the absolute mortification of the ascetic, brings about a victory over all power, however powerful its authority may be. It is no longer necessary that the possibility of this direct symbolic confrontation ever takes place. And this is the source of our profound boredom.

This is why taking hostages and other similar acts rekindle some fascination: they are at once an exorbitant mirror for the system of its own repressive violence, and the model of a symbolic violence which is always forbidden it, the only violence it cannot exert: its own death.

Labour and Death

Other societies have known multiple stakes: over birth and kinship, the soul and the body, the true and the false, reality and appearance. Political economy has reduced them to just one: production. But then the stakes were large, the violence extreme and hopes too high. Today this is over. The system has rid production of all real stakes. A more radical truth is dawning, however, and the system's victory allows us to glimpse this fundamental stake. It is even retrospectively becoming possible to analyse the whole of political economy as having nothing to do with production, as having stakes of life and death. A symbolic stake.

Every stake is symbolic. There have only ever been symbolic stakes. This dimension is etched everywhere into the structural law of value, everywhere immanent in the code.

Labour power is instituted on death. A man must die to become labour power. He converts this death into a wage. But the economic violence capital inflicted on him in the equivalence of the wage and labour power is nothing next to the symbolic violence inflicted on him by his definition as a productive force. Faking this equivalence is nothing next to the equivalence, *qua* signs, of wages and death.

The very possibility of quantitative equivalence presupposes death. The equivalence of wages and labour power presupposes the death of the worker, while that of any commodity and any other presupposes the symbolic extermination of objects. Death makes the calculation of equivalence, and regulation by indifference, possible in general. This death is not violent and physical, it is the indifferent consumption of life and death, the mutual neutralisation of life and death in sur-vival, or death *deferred*.

Labour is slow death. This is generally understood in the sense of physical exhaustion. But it must be understood in another sense. Labour is not opposed, like a sort of death, to the 'fulfilment of life', which is the idealist view; labour is opposed *as a slow death* to a violent death. That is the symbolic reality. Labour is opposed as deferred death to the immediate death of sacrifice. Against every pious and 'revolutionary' view of the 'labour (or culture) is the opposite of life' type, we must maintain that the only alternative to labour is not free time, or non-labour, it is sacrifice.

All this becomes clear in the genealogy of the slave. First, the prisoner of war is purely and simply put to death (one does him an honour in this way). Then he is *'spared'* [*épargné*] and *conserved* [*conservé*] (=*servus*), under the category of spoils of war and a prestige good: he becomes a slave and passes into sumptuary domesticity. It is only later that he passes into servile labour. However, he is no longer a 'labourer', since labour only appears in the phase of the serf or the *emancipated* slave, finally relieved of the mortgage of being put to death. Why is he freed? Precisely in order to work.

Labour therefore everywhere draws its inspiration from deferred death. It comes from deferred death. Slow or violent, immediate or deferred, the scansion of death is decisive: it is what radically distinguishes two types of organisation, the economic and the sacrificial. We live irreversibly in the first of these, which has inexorably taken root in the *différance* of death.

The scenario has never changed. Whoever works *has not been put to death*, he is refused this honour. And labour is first of all the sign of being judged worthy only of life. Does capital exploit the workers to death? Paradoxically, the worst it inflicts on them is refusing them death. It is by deferring their death that they are made into slaves and condemned to the indefinite abjection of a life of labour.

The substance of labour and exploitation is indifferent in this symbolic relation. The power of the master always primarily derives from this suspension of death. Power is therefore never, contrary to what we might imagine, the power of putting to death, but exactly the opposite, that of allowing to live – a life that the slave lacks the power to give. The master confiscates the death of the other while retaining the right to risk his own. The slave is refused this, and is condemned to a life without return, and therefore without possible expiation.

By removing death, the master removes the slave from the circulation of symbolic goods. This is the violence the master does to the slave, condemning him to labour power. There lies the secret of power (in the dialectic of the master and the slave, Hegel also derives the domination of the master from the deferred threat of death hanging over the slave). Labour, production and exploitation would only be one of the possible avatars of this power structure, which is a structure of death.

This changes every revolutionary perspective on the abolition of power. If power is death *deferred*, it will not be removed insofar as the *suspension* of this death will not be removed. And if power, of which this is always and everywhere the definition, resides in the act of giving without being given, it is clear that the power the master has to unilaterally grant life will only be abolished if this life can be given to him – *in a non-deferred death*. There is no other alternative; you will never abolish this power by staying alive, since there will have been no reversal of what has been given. Only the surrender of this life, retaliating against a deferred death with an immediate death, constitutes a radical response, and the only possibility of abolishing power. No revolutionary strategy can begin without the slave putting his own death back at stake, since this is what the master puts off in the *différance* from which he profits by securing his power. Refuse to be put to death, refuse to live in the mortal reprieve of power, refuse the duty of this life and never be quits with living, in effect be under obligation to settle this long-term credit through the slow death of labour, since this slow death does not alter the future of this abject dimension, in the fatality of power. Violent death changes everything, slow death changes nothing, for there is a rhythm, a scansion necessary to symbolic exchange: something has to be given in the same movement and following the same rhythm, otherwise there is no reciprocity and it is quite simply not given. The strategy of the system of power is to *displace* the time of the exchange, substituting continuity and mortal linearity for the immediate retaliation of death. It is thus futile for the slave (the worker) to give little by little, in infinitesimal doses, to the rope of labour on which he is hung to death, to give his life to the master or to capital, for this 'sacrifice' in small doses is no longer a sacrifice – it doesn't touch the most important thing, the *différance* of death, and merely distils a process whose structure remains the same.

We could in fact advance the hypothesis that in labour the exploited renders his life to the exploiter and thereby regains, by means of this very exploitation, a power of symbolic response. There was counter-power in the labour process as the exploited put their own (slow) death at stake. Here we agree with Lyotard's hypothesis on the level of libidinal economics: the intensity of the exploited's enjoyment [*jouissance*] in their very abjection. And Lyotard is right. Libidinal intensity, the charge of desire and the surrendering of death are always there in the exploited,[26] but no longer on the properly symbolic rhythm of the immediate retaliation, and therefore total resolution. The enjoyment of powerlessness (on sole condition that this is not a phantasy aimed at reinstating the triumph of desire at the level of the proletariat) will never abolish power.

The very modality of the response to the slow death of labour leaves the master the possibility of, once again, repeatedly, giving the slave life through labour. The accounts are never settled, it always profits power, the *dialectic* of power which plays on the splitting of the poles of death, the poles of exchange. The slave remains the prisoner of the master's dialectic, while his death, or his distilled life, serves the indefinite repetition of domination.

This domination increases as the system is charged with neutralising the symbolic retaliation *by buying it back through wages*. If, through labour, the exploited attempts to give his life to the exploiter, the latter wards off this restitution by means of wages. Here again we must take a symbolic radiograph. Contrary to all appearances and experience (capital buys its labour power from the worker and extorts surplus labour), capital *gives* labour to the worker (and the worker himself gives capital to the capitalist). In German this is *Arbeitgeber*: the entrepreneur is a 'provider of labour'; and *Arbeitnehmer*: it is the capitalist who gives, who has the initiative of the gift, which secures him, as in every social order, a preeminence and a power far beyond the economic. *The refusal of labour, in its radical form, is the refusal of this symbolic domination* and the humiliation of being bestowed upon. The gift and the taking of labour function directly as the code of the dominant social relation, as the code of discrimination. Wages are the mark of this poisonous gift, the sign which epitomises the whole code. They sanction this unilateral gift of labour, or rather *wages symbolically buy back the domination exercised by capital through the gift of labour*. At the same time, they furnish capital with the possibility of confining the operation to a contractual dimension, thus stabilising confrontation on economic ground. Furthermore, wages turn the wage-earner into a 'consumer of goods', reiterating his status as a 'consumer of labour' and reinforcing his symbolic deficit. To refuse labour, to dispute wages is thus to put the process of the gift, expiation and economic compensation back into question, and therefore to expose the fundamental symbolic process.

Wages are no longer 'grabbed' today. You too are given a wage, not in exchange for labour, but so that you spend it, which is itself another kind of labour. In the consumption or use of objects, the wage-consumer finds herself reproducing exactly *the same symbolic relation of slow death as she undergoes in labour*. The user experiences exactly the same *deferred* death in the object (she does not sacrifice it, she 'uses' it and 'uses' it functionally) as the worker does in capital. And just as wages buy back this unilateral gift of labour, the price paid for the object is only the user buying back the object's deferred death. The proof of this lies in the symbolic rule which states that what falls to you without charge (lotteries, presents, gambling wins) must not be devoted to use, but spent as pure loss.

Every domination must be bought back, redeemed. This was formerly done through sacrificial death (the ritual death of the king or the leader), or even by ritual inversion (feasts and other social rites: but these are still forms of sacrifice). This social game of reversal comes to an end with the dialectic of the master and the slave, where the reversibility of power cedes its place to a dialectic of the reproduction of power. The redemption of power must always, however, be simulated, and this is done by the apparatus of capital where formal redemption takes place throughout the immense machine of labour, wages and consumption. Economics is the sphere of redemption *par excellence*, where the domination of capital manages to redeem itself without ever really putting itself at stake. On the contrary, it diverts the process of redemption into its own infinite reproduction. This is perhaps where we find the necessity of economics and its historical appearance, at the level of societies so much more vast and mobile than primitive groups, where the urgency of a system of redemption which could be measured, controlled and infinitely extended (which rituals cannot be) all at the same time, and which above all would not put the exercise and heredity of power back into question. Production and consumption are an original and unprecedented solution to this problem. By simulating redemption in this new form, the slide from the symbolic into the economic allows the definitive hegemony of political force over society to be secured.

Economics miraculously succeeds in masking the real structure of power by reversing the terms of its definition. While power consists in unilateral giving (of life in particular, see above), a contrary interpretation has been successfully imposed: power would consist in a unilateral taking and appropriation. Under cover of this ingenious retraction, real symbolic domination can continue to do as it will, since all the efforts of those under this domination will rush into the trap of *taking back* from power what it has taken from them, even 'taking power' themselves, thus blindly pushing on along the lines of their domination.

In fact, labour, wages, power and revolution must all be read against the grain:

– labour is not exploitation, it is given by capital;
– wages are not grabbed, capital gives them too – it does not buy a labour power, it buys back the power of capital;[27]

- the slow death of labour is not endured, it is a desperate attempt, a challenge to capital's unilateral gift of labour;
- the only effective reply to power is to give it back what it gives you, and this is only symbolically possible by means of death.

However, if, as we have seen, the system itself deposes economics, removes its substance and its credibility, then, in this perspective, doesn't it put its own symbolic domination back into question? No, since the system brings about the overall reign of its power strategy, the gift without counter-gift, which becomes fused with deferred death. The same social relations are set up in the media and in consumption, where we have seen ('Requiem pour les Media' [*Utopie*, 4, 1971]) that there is no possible response or counter-gift to the unilateral delivery of messages. We were able to interpret (CERFI's project concerning automobile accidents) auto-slaughter as

the price that the collective pays to its institutions . . .: the State's gifts inscribe a 'debt' in the collective accounts book. Gratuitous death is then merely an attempt to absorb this deficit. The blood on the roads is a desperate form of compensation for the State's tarmac gifts. The accident thus takes its place in the space that institutes a symbolic debt towards the State. It is likely that the more this debt grows, the more marked will be the tendency towards the accident. Every 'rational' strategy for curbing this phenomenon (prevention, speed limits, rescue services, repression) is effectively negligible. They simulate the possibility of integrating the accident into a rational system, and are therefore incapable of grasping the root of the problem: balancing a symbolic debt which founds, legitimates and reinforces the collective dependency on the State. On the contrary, these 'rational' strategies accentuate the phenomenon. In order to avert the effects of accidents, they propose to institute more mechanisms, more state institutions, supplementary 'gifts', which are simply means of aggravating the symbolic debt.

In this way the struggle is everywhere opposed to a political authority (cf. Pierre Clastres, *Society against the State* [tr. R. Hurley and A. Stein, New York: Zone Books, 1990]), which sets all the power it can draw from its showers of gifts – the survival it maintains and the death it withdraws – above the struggle in order to stockpile and then distil it for its own ends. Nobody really accepts this bonus forever, you give what you can,[28] but power always gives more so as to serve better, and an entire society or a few individuals can go to great lengths, even their own destruction, to put an end to it. This is the only absolute weapon, and the mere collective threat of it can make power collapse. Power, faced with this symbolic 'blackmail' (the barricades of '68, hostage-taking), loses its footing: since it thrives on my slow death, I will oppose it with my violent death. And it is because we are living with slow death that we dream of a violent death. Even this dream is unbearable to power.

Notes

1. If it were only a question of the ascendancy of exchange-value over use-value (or the ascendancy of the structural over the functional dimension of language), then Marx and

Saussure have already signalled it. Marx almost turns use-value into the medium or the alibi, pure and simple, of exchange-value. His entire analysis is based on the principle of equivalence at the core of the system of exchange-value. But if *equivalence* is at the core of the system, there is no *indeterminacy* in the global system (there is always a dialectical determinacy and finality of the mode of production). The current system, however, is itself based on indeterminacy, and draws impetus from it. Conversely, it is haunted by the death of all determinacy.

2.   [See Jean Baudrillard, *For a Critique of the Political Economy of the Sign*, tr. Charles Levin, St Louis, MO: Telos, 1972 – tr.]

3.   Theoretical production, like material production, loses its determinacy and begins to turn around itself, slipping abysally [*en abyme*] towards a reality that cannot be found. This is where we are today: undecidability, the era of *floating theories*, as much as floating money. No matter what perspective they come from (the psychoanalytic included), no matter with what violence they struggle and claim to rediscover an immanence, or a movement without systems of reference (Deleuze, Lyotard, etc.), all contemporary theories are floating and have no meaning other than to serve as signs for one another. It is pointless to insist on their coherence with some 'reality', whatever that might be. The system has removed every secure reference from theory as it has from any other labour power. Theory no longer has any use-value, the theoretical mirror of production has also cracked. So much the better. What I mean is that the very undecidability of theory is an effect of the code. Let there be no illusions: there is no schizophrenic 'drift' about this flotation of theories, where flows pass freely over the body without organs (of what, capital?). It merely signifies that any theory can from now on be exchanged against any other according to variable exchange rates, but without any longer being invested anywhere, unless it is the mirror of their writing.

4.   [Cf. Jean-François Lyotard, *Libidinal Economy*, tr. I.H. Grant, London: Athlone, 1992 – tr.]

5.   [In English in the original – tr.]

6.   [In English in the original – tr.]

7.   Marx, that cunning Jesuit, was not far from recognising this with his concept of the collective labourer:

> The product is transformed from the direct product of the individual producer into a social product, the joint product of a collective labourer, i.e., a combination of workers, each of whom stands at a different distance from the actual manipulation of the object of labour. With the progressive accentuation of the co-operative character of the labour process, there necessarily occurs a progressive extension of the concept of *productive labour*, and of the concept of the bearer of that labour, the *productive worker*. In order to work productively, it is no longer necessary for the individual himself to put his hand to the object; it is sufficient for him to be an organ of the collective labourer, and to perform any one of its subordinate functions. The definition of productive labour given above, the original definition, is derived from the nature of material production itself, and it remains correct for the collective labourer, considered as a whole. But it no longer holds good for each member taken individually. (*Capital*, pp. 643–4 [J.B.'s emphases])

8.   Free time is, so to speak, a form of 'complex labour', in the sense that, as opposed to simple labour, it accords with the definition of service: solidarity of the prestation and the prestator, non-equivalence to a time of abstract social labour, non-equivalence to a wage which reproduces labour power. Marx would have been able to see this were he not myopically concerned with productive labour and the multiple distinctions which together tend to salvage the subject of history: the productive worker. 'The reification of labour power, driven to perfection, would shatter the reified form by cutting the chain that ties the individual to the machinery', writes Marcuse. '[Automation] would open the dimension of free time as the one in which man's private and societal existence would constitute itself' (Herbert Marcuse, *One Dimensional Man* [London: Routledge

& Kegan Paul, 1964], p. 37). Instead of phantasising over free time, Marcuse understood that the system, throughout the technical progress and automation, produces free time as the extreme reification of labour power, as the accomplished form of abstract social labour time, simply by being the inverted simulation of non-labour.

Job training, qualification and education, etc., are other forms of complex labour. There is also a temptation to analyse them in terms of surplus-value, of the reinvestment by capital of science, training and research, of a constant capital superadded to the ordinary worker. Adam Smith writes: 'A man educated at the expensè of much labour and time . . . may be compared to one of those expensive machines' (*The Wealth of Nations* [Oxford: Oxford University Press, 1976] Vol. 1, p. 118). This is an error. Instruction, education and training are not long-term investments. They are rather the direct social relation of domestication and control. Capital doesn't look for any complex labour in this, but indulges in absolute waste, sacrificing an enormous part of its 'surplus-value' in the reproduction of its hegemony.

9. Paid unemployment already provides an example of this (one year of severance pay in France at the time of writing). In certain other countries, however, it has been replaced by a 'negative taxation' scheme, which provides for a basic minimum wage for all, housewives, the handicapped, the young unemployed, to be deducted from *eventual* paid labour. Unemployment quite simply disappears here as a critical conjunction (with all the political implications it used to have). Labour becomes an *option*, while wages become a certificate of existence, an automatic inscription in the social apparatus. Capital still remains as wages, but this time in its pure form – freed from a labour (as the signifier, following Saussure's analogy, was freed from the signified) which was only an occasional content of capital.

10. Throughout the social evolution of housing, we can see how capital's strategy has displaced itself from an economic process to an extensive process.

    In the beginning, workers' housing was simply a 'dorm', a branch of the factory, a functional site for the reproduction of labour power, a strategic site for both manufacture and business. Housing was not invested with the form of capital.

    Gradually, housing is invested as a space-time marked by a direct and generalised process of the control of social space. It becomes a site of reproduction, not of labour, but *of the habitat itself as a specific function*, as a direct form of social relation; no longer the reproduction of the worker, but of the inhabitant herself, the *user*. After the proletariat, the 'user' has become the ideal type of the industrial slave. The user of goods, of words, the user of sex, the user of labour herself (the worker, or the 'agent of production', becomes the user of the factory and of her labour as individual and collective equipment, as a *social* service), the user of transport, but also the user of her life and death.

    This decentred, extensive strategy, this all-out attack, the use or appropriation of use-value is the ultimate form of the self-management of social control.

11. Thus the Californian utopia of the cybernetic disintegration of the 'tertiary metropolis': home-based computer labour. Labour is pulverised into every pore of society and everyday life. As well as labour power, the space-time of labour also ceases to exist: society constitutes nothing but a single continuum of the processes of value. Labour has become a way of life. Nothing can reinstate the factory walls, the golden age of the factory and class struggle against the ubiquity of capital, surplus-value and labour, against their inevitable disappearance as such. The worker merely nourishes the imaginary of the struggle, just as the cop nourishes the imaginary of repression.

12. The concept of surplus-value has simply lost any meaning as regards a system which, from reproducing labour power in order to generate profit and surplus-value, has now become reproductive of life in its entirety through advanced redistribution or reinjection of every equivalent of social surplus labour. From this point on, surplus-value is everywhere and nowhere. Capital no longer has any 'incidental expenses', nor on the other hand has it any 'profit' in the sense of a unilateral extortion. The law of the system requires that you give yourself up to its redistributions in order that it circulates and that

each and everyone, caught in the tightly woven net of this incessant redistribution, might become a manager, while the whole group becomes able to manage its own surplus-value, thus implicating oneself fundamentally within the everyday political order of capital. And just as, viewed from the point of view of capital, surplus-value has lost all meaning, it has also lost all meaning from the point of view of the exploited. The distinction between a fraction of labour returning as a wage and a remainder called surplus-value has lost all meaning from the point of view of the worker who used to reproduce her labour power as a wage, but now reproduces her entire life in a generalised process of labour.

13.   [Baudrillard is playing on the French term *investissement*, used to translate Freud's *Besetzung*, rendered in English as 'cathexis'. The French term covers the political and libidinal economic sense of 'investment' as well as the military sense of the 'occupation' of hostile territory – tr.]

14.   Other parallel forms of maximalist reversal: equal wages for all, the struggle against qualifications. All these forms seek the end of the division of labour (the end of labour as social relation) and the end of the law of equivalence in the field of wages and labour power, which is of fundamental importance for the system. Therefore they indirectly target the very form of political economy.

15.   This same phenomenon arises in the 'developing' countries. There is no upper limit to the cost of raw materials once they, outside the grasp of economics, become the sign and the gauge of the acceptance of a global political order, a peaceful planetary co-existence where the developing countries are forcibly socialised under the great powers. The escalation of prices then becomes a challenge, not only to the wealth of the Western countries, but also to the political system of peaceful co-existence in the face of a single predominant global political class. Whether this class is capitalist or communist is of minor importance.

    Before the oil crisis, the Arabs made traditional wage demands: petrol must be sold at the right price. Now, however, these demands have turned around and become unlimited and maximal.

16.   The energy crisis gave both 'types' of inflation an alibi and a perfect deterrent in one go. From this point on, inflation as a structural crisis internal to the system may be plausibly blamed on the 'overvaluation' of energy and raw materials by the countries that produce them. Disaffection with the productivist system, which, amongst other things, is expressed in the maximal wage challenge, may be counteracted by the threat of poverty, that is, by threatening *the use-value of the economic system* itself.

17.   [See Gilles Deleuze and Félix Guattari, *Anti-Oedipus: Capitalism and Schizophrenia I*, tr. R. Hurley, M. Seem and H.R. Lane, London: Athlone, 1984, for an exposition of the 'Deleuzian unconscious' – tr.]

18.   This intervention, however, is not exclusive of any other group *deprived of social representation*. When young women, high school students, homosexuals and even 'proles' become 'savages', or if we admit that basically the unions do not represent them at all, but only themselves, then we all in like manner become 'immigrants'. On the other hand, these groups might cease to be 'immigrants'. There are then no 'immigrants as such', and they do not constitute a new historical subject, a neo-proletariat who would take over as the other.

19.   [Confédération générale du travail, the French Trades Union Congress – tr.]

20.   [For an exposition of the Great Confinement, see Michel Foucault, *Madness and Civilisation*, tr. Richard Howard, London: Tavistock, 1967 – tr.]

21.   As an illustration of this, we might analyse an advert for the Banque Nationale de Paris (BNP), which reads: 'I am interested in your money – fair's fair – lend me your money and you may profit from my bank.'

    To begin with, this is the first time that capital (in its front line institution, namely international finance capital) has so clearly and openly stated the law of equivalence, and, surprisingly, in the form of an advertising slogan. These things are usually unstated;

commercial exchange is seen as immoral, and all publicity tries to cover this up as a matter of urgency. We may therefore be sure that this candour is a second-degree mask.

Secondly, its apparent aim is to convince people on economic grounds to do themselves a good turn and take their money to the BNP. Its real strategy remains unofficial, however: to convince people by this 'man to man' capitalist openness, saying 'let's not be sentimental about this', 'no more of the ideology of dependence', 'cards on the table', etc., and so to seduce people by means of the obscenity of revealing the hidden, immoral law of equivalence. This is a 'macho' complicity where men share the obscene truth of capital. Hence the smell of lechery about his advert, the salaciousness and smuttiness of the eyes glued to your money as if it were your genitals. The technique used by the advert is a perverse provocation which is much more subtle than the simplistic seduction of the smile (such as was the theme of the Société Générale's [a bank – tr.] counter-offensive: 'It is not the banker who should smile, but the client'). People are seduced by the obscenity of the economic, taken to the level of the perverse fascination that the very atrocity of capital exercises on them. From this perspective the slogan quite simply signifies: 'I am interested in your arse – fair's fair – lend me your buttocks and I'll bugger you', which is not to everyone's distaste.

Behind the humanist morality of exchange there is a profound desire for capital, a vertiginous desire for the law of value; and this complicity, both economic and non-economic, is what the advert, perhaps without knowing it, seeks to recover, testifying to an *intuition* for politics.

Thirdly, the advertising executives could not have been unaware that this advert, with its vampiric image, scared the middle classes, so that to emphasise their lecherous complicity with this direct attack would provoke negative reactions. Why did they take this risk? Here we have the strangest trap: the advert was made to consolidate the resistance to the law of profit and equivalence so as to be better able to impose the equivalence of capital, profit, and the economic in general (the 'fair's fair') *at a time when this is no longer true*, when capital has displaced its strategy and so is able to state its 'law' since it is no longer its truth. Announcing this law is nothing more than a supplementary mystification.

Capital no longer thrives on the rule of any economic law, which is why the law can be made into an advertising slogan, falling into the sphere of the sign and its manipulation. The economic is only the quantitative theatre of value. This, as well as the fact that the role of money in all this is only a pretext, is expressed by the advert in its own way.

Hence the commutability of the advert itself, which can operate at every level, for example:

– I am interested in your unconscious – fair's fair – lend me your phantasies and you may profit from my analysis;
– I am interested in your death – fair's fair – take out a life insurance policy and I will make your death into a fortune;
– I am interested in your productivity – fair's fair – lend me your labour power and you may profit from my capital;

and so on. This advert could serve as a 'general equivalent' for all real social relations.

Finally, if the advert's basic message is not equivalence, $a = a$, fair's fair (no-one is fooled, as the advertising executives *well know*), could it be surplus-value (the fact that the operation ends up, for the banker and for capital, showing the equation: $a = a + a'$)? The advert can barely conceal this truth, and everyone can sense it. Capital slips in and out of the shadows here, almost unmasking itself, but it is not serious since what the advert really says comes neither from the order of quantitative equivalence, nor from surplus-value, but from the order of the tautology:

not: $a = a$
nor: $a = a + a'$
but: A *is* A

That is: a bank is a bank, a banker is a banker, money is money, and you can have none of it. While pretending to state the economic law of equivalence, the advert actually states the tautological imperative, the fundamental rule of domination. For whether a bank is a bank, or indeed whether a table is a table, or whether $2 + 2 = 4$ (and not 5 as Dostoyevsky had it), is the real capitalist credence. When capital says 'I am interested in your money', it feigns profitability in order to secure credibility. This credibility comes from the economic order (creditability), while the *credence* attached to the tautology sums up in itself the identity of the capitalist order and comes from the symbolic order.

22. So just as there had been (for Marx as well) a naturalist phantasy of use-value, there is for us today an economistic phantasy of exchange-value.

For us, in the structural play of the code, exchange-value plays the same role as use-value used to play in the market law of value, the role of the simulacrum of reference.

23. The American Senate has gone to the extent of calculating what it would cost to bring water back to the purity it had before the European conquest of the Americas (the '1491 standard', Christopher Columbus having landed, as we know, in 1492): $350 million. These millions matter little, however, since what the Senators are in fact calculating is the cost of bringing the system itself back to the original purity of primitive accumulation, the golden age of labour power. The 1890, or indeed 1840, standard?

In like fashion, the current monetary system dreams of gold and a gold standard to stabilise and regenerate fiduciary values. The current state of affairs is that free and unlimited speculation on the grounds of the loss of the gold-referent edges closer every moment to catastrophe: an arbitrariness and an inflation of such proportions that the authority of money itself is toppled and loses all its credibility. Again we have a cyclical regeneration by means of reference; a 'critical' regeneration is necessary in order to prevent financial exchanges from reaching the limits of unreality, where they would be destroyed.

24. There are, of course, contradictions remaining between the structural and the market law of value, just as, in a previous phase, there were between the law of the market and resistant pre-capitalist values (which contradictions have not completely disappeared). In this way, the ultimate end of the system is the control of death: death is one of the structural markings of life, it also clashes with economic imperatives and a traditional logic of profit (the enormous cost of long-term care, hospitalisation, and so on). A compromise results from this, an absurd equilibrium (we can afford to keep 35 per cent of all leukaemia sufferers alive). Assessing the marginal costs of death. Anything above this level and we let them die. But this is not cynical economics, on the contrary, the economy prevents the system from following the conclusions of its own logic and barring people's access to death.

There is in fact a constant play between the two forms of value, controlled by a strategy aiming at intensifying the crisis. And although the crisis seems to require a solution, it is this solution *already*.

25. The gift, under the sign of gift-exchange, has been made into the distinguishing mark of primitive 'economies', and at the same time into the alternative principle to the law of value and political economy. There is no worse mystification. The gift is our myth, the idealist myth correlative to our materialist myth, and we bury the primitives under both myths at the same time. The primitive symbolic process knows nothing of the gratuity of the gift, it knows only the challenge and the reversibility of exchanges. When this reversibility is broken, precisely by the unilateral possibility of giving (which pre-supposes the possibility of stockpiling value and transferring it in one direction only), then the properly symbolic relation is dead and power makes an appearance: it will merely be deployed thereafter throughout the economic apparatus of the contract. It is our (operational) fiction, our metaphysics, the idea that it is possible to accumulate stock-value in its head (capital), to make it increase and multiply: this is the trap of the accumulation and capital. It is equally our fiction, however, to think that we may relinquish it absolutely (with the gift). The primitives know that this possibility does not

exist, that the arresting of value on one term, the very possibility of isolating a segment of exchange, one side of the exchange, is unthinkable, that everything has a compensation, not in the contractual sense, but in the sense that the process of exchange is unavoidably reversible. They base all their relations on this incessant backfire, ambivalence and death in exchange, whereas we base our order on the possibility of separating two distinct poles of exchange and making them autonomous. There follows either the equivalent exchange (the contract) or the inequivalent exchange that has no compensation (the gift). But both, as we shall see, obey the same dislocation of the process and the same autonomisation of value.

26. This is no doubt especially true in the phase of physical abjection and savage exploitation, in capitalist 'prostitution' under the market law of value. How much of this remains in our phase, the structural law of value?

27. This is particularly clear when wages are unilaterally bestowed, imposed in 'negative taxation' without any labour in return. The wage-earner without equivalence: in this trans-economic contract, we see a pure domination and pure subservience to the gift and the premium emerge.

28. That is *symbolic exchange*. We must emphasise that it stands opposed to the entire liberal or Christian humanist ideology of the gift. The gift is the source and even the essence of power. Only the counter-gift, the reversibility of symbolic exchange, abolishes power.

2

THE ORDER OF SIMULACRA

The Three Orders of Simulacra

There are three orders of simulacra, running parallel to the successive mutations of the law of value since the Renaissance:

- The *counterfeit* is the dominant schema in the 'classical' period, from the Renaissance to the Industrial Revolution.
- *Production* is the dominant schema in the industrial era.
- Simulation is the dominant schema in the current code-governed phase.

The first-order simulacrum operates on the natural law of value, the second-order simulacrum on the market law of value, and the third-order simulacrum on the structural law of value.

The Stucco Angel

The counterfeit (and, simultaneously, fashion) is born with the Renaissance, with the destructuration of the feudal order by the bourgeois order and the emergence of overt competition at the level of signs of distinction. There is no fashion in a caste society, nor in a society based on rank, since assignation is absolute and there is no class mobility. Signs are protected by a prohibition which ensures their total clarity and confers an unequivocal status on each. Counterfeit is not possible in the ceremonial, unless in the form of black magic and sacrilege, which is precisely what makes the mixing of signs punishable as a serious offence against the very order of things. If we take to dreaming once more – particularly today – of a world where signs are certain, of a strong 'symbolic order', let's be under no illusions. For this order has existed, and it was a brutal hierarchy, since the sign's transparency is indissociably also its cruelty. In feudal or archaic caste societies, in *cruel* societies, signs are limited in number and their circulation is restricted. Each retains its full value as a prohibition, and each carries with it a reciprocal obligation between castes, clans or persons, so signs are not arbitrary. The arbitrariness of the sign begins when, instead of bonding two persons in an inescapable reciprocity, the signifier starts to refer a disenchanted universe of the signified, the common denominator of the real world, towards which no-one any longer has the least obligation.

The end of the *obligatory* sign is succeeded by the reign of the *emancipated* sign, in which any and every class will be able to participate. Competitive democracy succeeds the endogamy of signs proper to status-based orders. With the transit of values or signs of prestige from one class to another, we simultaneously and necessarily enter into the age of the *counterfeit*. For from a limited order of signs, the 'free' production of which is prevented by a prohibition, we pass into a proliferation of signs according to demand. These multiple signs, however, no longer have anything to do with the restricted circulation of the obligatory sign, but counterfeit the latter. Counterfeiting does not take place by means of changing the nature of an 'original', but, by extension, through completely altering a material whose clarity is completely dependent upon a restriction. Non-discriminatory (the sign is nothing any longer if not competitive), relieved of every constraint, universally available, the modern sign nevertheless still simulates necessity by giving the appearance that it is bound to the world. The modern sign dreams of its predecessor, and would dearly love to rediscover an *obligation* in its reference to the real. It finds only a *reason*, a referential reason, a real and a 'natural' on which it will feed. This designatory bond, however, is only a simulacrum of symbolic obligation, producing nothing more than neutral values which are exchanged one for the other in an objective world. Here the sign suffers the same fate as labour, for just as the 'free' worker is only free to produce equivalents, the 'free and emancipated' sign is only free to produce equivalent signifieds.

The modern sign then finds its value as the simulacrum of a 'nature'. This problematic of the 'natural' and the metaphysics of reality was, for the bourgeoisie since the Renaissance, the mirror of both the bourgeois and the classical sign. Even today there is a thriving nostalgia for the natural referent of the sign, despite several revolutions which have begun to shatter this configuration (such as the revolution of production when signs ceased to refer to a nature and referred instead to the law of exchange, passing into the market law of value). We will come back to these second-order simulacra.

It is with the Renaissance, then, that the forgery is born along with the natural, ranging from the deceptive finery on people's backs to the prosthetic fork, from the stucco interiors to Baroque theatrical scenery. The entire classical era was the age of the theatre *par excellence*. The theatre is a form that gripped social life in its entirety as well as all architecture from the Renaissance on. From these incredible achievements with stucco and Baroque art we can unravel the metaphysics of the counterfeit, as well as the new ambitions of Renaissance man. These latter consist in an earthly *demiurgy*, the transubstantiation of all nature into a single substance, a theatrical sociality unified under the sign of bourgeois values, beyond differences of blood, rank or caste. Stucco is the triumphant democracy of all artificial signs, the apotheosis of the theatre and fashion, revealing the unlimited potential of the new class, as soon as it was able to end the sign's exclusivity. The way is clear for unheard of combinations, for every game, every counterfeit – the Promethean designs of the bourgeoisie are first engrossed in the *imitation of nature*, before it throws itself into *production*. In the churches and palaces, stucco embraces all forms, imitates all materials: velvet curtains, wooden cornices, and fleshy curves of the body. Stucco transfigures all this incredible material disorder into a single new substance, a sort of general equivalent for all the others, accruing a theatrical prestige, since it is itself a representative substance, a mirror of all the others.

But simulacra do not consist only of the play of signs, they involve social relations and a social power. Stucco may appear to be extolling the expansion of science and technology, but it is also and especially bound to the Baroque, which is in turn bound to the matter of the Counter-Reformation and to the hegemony of the political and mental world which, for the first time, the Jesuits tried to institute in accordance with a modern conception of power.

There is a direct relation between the Jesuits' mental obedience (*perinde ac cadaver*) and the demiurgic ambition to exorcise the natural substance of things in order to replace it with a synthetic substance. Just as man submits to organisation, so things take on the ideal functionality of the corpse. Technology and technocracy are already fully operative in the notion of an ideal counterfeit of the world, expressed in the invention of a universal substance and a universal combinatory of substances. To reunify the world, split asunder after the Reformation, under a homogeneous doctrine, to universalise the world under a single word (from New Spain to Japan: the Missions), to constitute a *State* political *élite* with one and the same centralised strategy: such are the Jesuits' objectives. To do this, they will need to create efficient simulacra, such as the organisation's apparatus, as well as bureaucratic, theatrical (the great theatre of the Cardinals and the Grey Eminences), training and educational machinery, which aims, for the first time in a systematic fashion, to fashion an ideal nature on the model of the child. The stucco cladding of Baroque architecture is a major apparatus of the same order. All this issues from the productivist rationality of capital, but it already bears witness, not in production but in the counterfeit, to the same project of universal control and hegemony, to a social schema in whose foundations the internal coherence of a system already operates.

In the Ardennes there used to live an old cook for whom the construction of tiered cakes and the science of *pâtisserie*-sculpture had given him the arrogance to attempt to capture the world as God had left it (that is, in its natural state), to eliminate all its organic spontaneity and replace it with a single polymorphous material: reinforced concrete. Concrete furniture, chairs, chests of drawers, concrete sewing machines; and outside, in the courtyard, an entire orchestra, including the violins, in concrete. Everything in concrete! Concrete trees planted out with genuine leaves, a reinforced concrete boar with a real boar's skull inside it, concrete sheep covered in real wool. At last Camille Renault discovered the original substance, the pastry from which the diversity of things are distinguished solely by 'realistic' nuances such as the boar's skull and the leaves on the trees. Doubtless, however, this was only a concession from the demiurge to his visitors, for it was with a delighted smile that this good eighty-year-old god welcomed them to his creation. He sought no quarrel with divine creation, he simply remodelled it in order to make it more intelligible. There was no Luciferian revolt, no will-to-parody, nor a partisan and retro affinity with 'naïve' art. The Ardennes cook simply reigned over a unified mental substance (for concrete is a *mental* substance: like the concept, it enables phenomena to be ordered and separated at will). His project was not so far removed from the stucco builders of Baroque art, nor very different from projecting an urban community on to the terrain of a large contemporary group. The counterfeit still only works on substance and form, not yet on relations and structures, but at this level, it is already aiming at control of a pacified society, cast in a synthetic substance which evades death, an indestructible artifact that will guarantee eternal power. Isn't it a miracle that with plastics, man has invented an undegradable matter, thus interrupting the cycle which through corruption and death reverses each and every substance on the earth into another? Even fire leaves an indestructible residue of this substance outside the cycle. Here is something we did not expect: a simulacrum in which the project of a universal semiotics is condensed. This has no longer anything to do with the 'progress' of technology or the rational aims of science. It is a project which aims at political and mental hegemony, the phantasy of a closed mental substance like the Baroque stucco angels whose wing-tips touch in a curved mirror.

The Automaton and the Robot

A world separates these two artificial beings. One is the theatrical, mechanical and clockwork counterfeit of man where the technique is to submit everything to *analogy* and to the simulacrum-effect. The other is dominated by a technical principle where the machine has the upper hand, and where, with the machine, *equivalence* is established. The automaton plays the man of the court, the socialite, it takes part in the social and theatrical drama of pre-Revolutionary France. As for the robot, as its name implies, it works; end of the theatre, beginning of human mechanics. The automaton is the *analogon* of man and remains responsive to him (even playing draughts with him!). The machine is the *equivalent* of man, appropriating him to itself as an equal in the unity of a functional process. This sums up the difference between first- and second-order simulacra.

We must not be fooled by 'figurative' resemblance. Like God, the automaton questions nature (if not the mystery of the soul), the dilemma of being and appearance: what underlies nature; what is within us; what is behind appearances? Only the counterfeit of man allows these questions to be asked. Every metaphysics of man as the protagonist in the *natural theatre* of creation is embodied in the automaton before disappearing with the French Revolution, and the automaton has no other destiny than to be compared with the living man – with the aim of being more natural than him – whose ideal image the automaton is. The automaton is man's perfect double, even down to the subtlety of its gestures, in the workings of its organs and intelligence, almost inducing anxiety when we perceive that there is no difference between them, and that therefore the automaton has no need of a soul since it possesses an ideally naturalised body. Because this would be sacrilege, the difference between them is still maintained, as in the case of an automaton so perfect that on stage the illusionist mimicked its staccato movements in order that at least, even if the roles were reversed, confusion would be impossible. Thus the automaton's questions remain open, making it an optimistic mechanics, even if the counterfeit always retains a diabolical connotation.[1]

There is nothing like this with the robot. The robot no longer questions appearances, its only truth is its mechanical efficiency. It no longer needs to resemble man, to whom it is inevitably compared. The infamous metaphysical difference which gives the automaton mystery and charm no longer exists: the robot emphasises this difference for its own benefit. Being and appearance are founded on a single substance of production and labour. The first-order simulacrum never abolishes the difference: it presupposes the dispute always in evidence between the simulacrum and the real (a particularly subtle game in *trompe-l'oeil* painting, but all art thrives on this difference). The second-order simulacrum simplifies the problem by the absorption of appearances, or by the liquidation of the real, whichever you prefer. In any case it erects a reality without images, without echo, without mirrors, without appearances: such indeed is labour, such is the machine, such is the entire industrial system of production in that it is radically opposed to the principle of theatrical illusion. No more semblance or dissemblance, no more God or Man, only an immanent logic of the principle of operativity.

After this, robots and machines can proliferate – this is even their law – as automata, being sublime and singular mechanisms, have never done. Men themselves only began to proliferate when, with the Industrial Revolution, they took on the status of machines: freed of all semblance, freed even from their double, they grew increasingly similar to the system of production of which they were nothing more than the miniaturised equivalent. The simulacrum's revenge, which gave rise to the myth of the sorcerer's apprentice, did not take place with the automaton; on the contrary, this is the law of the second order, from which there still proceeds a hegemony of the robot, of the machine, of dead labour over living labour. This hegemony is necessary to the cycle of production and reproduction. It is with this reversal that we leave the counterfeit in order to enter into (re)production. We are leaving natural law and its play of forms in order to enter the market law of value and its calculations of forces.

The Industrial Simulacrum

A new generation of signs and objects arises with the Industrial Revolution – signs with no caste tradition that will never have known restrictions on their status, and which will never have to be *counterfeits*, since from the outset they will be *products* on a gigantic scale. The problem of their specificity and their origin is no longer posed: technics is their origin, they have meaning only within the dimension of the industrial simulacrum.

That is, the series: the very possibility of two or *n* identical objects. The relation between them is no longer one of an original and its counterfeit, analogy or reflection, but is instead one of equivalence and indifference. In the series, objects become indistinct simulacra of one another and, along with objects, of the men that produce them. The extinction of the original reference alone facilitates the general law of equivalences, that is to say, *the very possibility of production*.

The entire analysis of production will be swept aside if we stop regarding it as an original process, as *the* process at the origin of all the others, but conversely as *a* process which reabsorbs every original being and introduces a series of identical beings. Up to this point, we have considered production and labour as potential, as force and historical process, as a generic activity: an energetic-economic myth proper to modernity. We must ask ourselves whether production is not rather an intervention, a *particular* phase, *in the order of signs* – whether it is basically only one episode in the line of simulacra, that episode of producing an infinite series of potentially identical beings (object-signs) by means of technics.

The fabulous energies at work in technics, industry and economics should not hide the fact that it is at bottom only a matter of attaining this indefinite reproducibility, which is a definite challenge to the 'natural' order, and ultimately only a 'second-order' simulacrum and a somewhat weak imaginary solution to the question of world mastery. In relation to the era of the counterfeit, the double, the mirror and the theatre, games of masks and appearances, the serial and technical era of reproduction is basically an era of less ambitious scope (the following era of simulation models and third-order simulacra is of much more considerable dimensions).

Walter Benjamin, in 'The Work of Art in the Age of Mechanical Reproduction' [in *Illuminations*, tr. Harry Zohn, ed. Hannah Arendt, London: Jonathan Cape, 1970], was the first to draw out the essential implications of the principle of reproduction. He shows that reproduction absorbs the process of production, changes its goals, and alters the status of the product and the producer. He shows this in the fields of art, cinema and photography, because it is there that new territories are opened up in the twentieth century, with no 'classical' tradition of productivity, placed from the outset under the sign of reproduction. Today, however, we know that all material production remains within the same sphere. Today we know that it is at the level of reproduction (fashion, the media, advertising, information and communications networks), at the level of what Marx rather carelessly used to call the *faux frais* of capital (immense historical irony!), that is, in the sphere of simulacra and the code, that the unity of the whole process of capital is formed. Benjamin was also the first (with McLuhan after him) to grasp technology as a medium rather than a 'productive force' (at which point the Marxian analysis retreats), as the form and principle of an entirely new generation of meaning. The mere fact that any given thing can simply be reproduced, as such, in an exemplary double is already a revolution: one need only think of the stupefaction of the Black boy seeing two identical books for the first time. That these two technical products are *equivalent* under the sign of necessary social labour is less important in the long term than the *serial* repetition of the same object (which is also the serial repetition of individuals as labour power). Technique as a medium gains the upper hand not only over the product's 'message' (its use-value) but also over labour power, which Marx wanted to turn into the revolutionary message of production. Benjamin and McLuhan saw more clearly than Marx, they saw that the real message, *the real ultimatum, lay in reproduction itself.* Production itself has no meaning: its social finality is lost in the series. Simulacra prevail over history.

Moreover, the stage of serial reproduction (that of the industrial mechanism, the production line, the growth of reproduction, etc.) is ephemeral. As soon as dead labour gains the upper hand over living labour (that is to say, since the end of primitive accumulation), serial production gives way to generation through models. In this case it is a matter of a reversal of origin and end, since all forms change from the moment that they are no longer mechanically reproduced, but *conceived according to their very reproducibility*, their diffraction from a generative core called a 'model'. We are dealing with third-order simulacra here. There is no more counterfeiting of an original, as there was in the first order, and no more pure series as there were in the second; there are models from which all forms proceed according to modulated differences. Only affiliation to the model has any meaning, since nothing proceeds in accordance with its end any more, but issues instead from the model, the 'signifier of reference', functioning as a foregone, and the only credible, conclusion. We are dealing with simulation in the modern sense of the term, where industrialisation is only its initial form. Modulation is ultimately more fundamental than serial reproducibility, distinct oppositions more than quantitative equivalences, and the commutation of terms more than the law of equivalences; the structural, not the market, law of value. Not only do we not need to search for the secrets of the code in technique or economics, it is on the contrary the very possibility of industrial production that we must seek in the genesis of the code and the simulacrum. Every order subsur the previous order. Just as the order of the counterfeit was captured by order of serial reproduction (look at how art passed entirely into 'machinality'), so the entire order of production is in the process of toppling into operational simulation.

The analyses of both Benjamin and McLuhan stand on the borders of reproduction and simulation, at the point where referential reason disappears and production is seized by vertigo. These analyses mark a decisive advance over Veblen and Goblot, who, describing, for example, the signs of fashion still refer to a classical configuration where signs constitute a distinct material having a finality and are used for prestige, status and social differentiation. The strategy they deploy is contemporaneous with Marx's strategy of profit and commodity, at a moment where they could still speak of a use-value of the sign, or quite simply of economics at all, because there was still a Reason of the sign and a Reason of production.

The Metaphysics of the Code

> The mathematically minded Leibniz saw in the mystical elegance of the binary system where only the zero and the one count, the very image of creation. The unity of the Supreme Being, operating by means of a binary function against the nothing, was sufficient ground, he thought, from which all things could be made.
>
> Marshall McLuhan

The great man-made simulacra pass from a universe of natural laws into a universe of forces and tensions, and today pass into a universe of structures and binary oppositions. After the metaphysics of being and appearance, after energy and determinacy, the metaphysics of indeterminacy and the code. Cybernetic control, generation through models, differential modulation, feedback, question/answer, etc.: this is the new *operational* configuration (industrial simulacra being *mere operations*). Digitality is its metaphysical principle (Leibniz's God), and DNA is its prophet. In fact, it is in the genetic code that the 'genesis of simulacra' today finds its completed form. At the limits of an ever more forceful extermination of references and finalities, of a loss of semblances and designators, we find the digital, programmatic sign, which has a purely *tactical* value, at the intersection of other signals ('bits' of information/tests) and which has the structure of a micro-molecular code of command and control.

At this level, the question of signs and their rational destinations, their 'real' and their 'imaginary', their repression, reversal, the illusions they form of what they silence or of their parallel significations, is completely effaced. We have already seen the signs of the first order, complex signs with a wealth of illusion, change with the advent of machines into crude, dull, industrial, repetitive, echoless, functional and efficient signs. There is a still more radical mutation as regards the code's signals, which become illegible, and for which no possible interpretation can be provided, buried like programmatic matrices, light years, ultimately, from the 'biological' body, black boxes where every command and response are in ferment. End of the theatre of representation, the space of the conflicts and silences of the sign: only the black box of the code remains, the molecule emitting signals which irradiate us, networking questions/answers through us as identifying signals, and continuously tested by the programme we have hardwired into our own cells. Whether it is prison cells, electronic cells, party cells or microbiological cells we are dealing with, we are always searching for the smallest indivisible element, the organic synthesis of which will follow in accordance with the givens of the code. The code itself is nothing other than a genetic, generative cell where the myriad intersections produce all the questions and all the possible solutions from which to select (for whom?). There is no finality to these 'questions' (informational signals, impulses) other than the response which is either genetic and immutable or inflected with minuscule and aleatory differences. Even space is no longer linear or unidimensional but *cellular*, indefinitely generating the same signals like the lonely and repetitive habits of a stir-crazy prisoner. The genetic code is the perpetual jump in a floppy disk, and we are nothing more than VDUs [*cellules de lecture*]. The whole aura of the sign and signification itself is determinately resolved: everything is resolved into inscription and decoding.

Such is our third-order simulacrum, such is the 'mystical elegance of the binary system of zero and one', from which all beings issue. Such also is the status of the sign at the end of signification: DNA or operational simulation.

This is all perfectly summed up by Thomas Sebeok in 'Genetics and Semiotics' (*Versus*):

> Innumerable observations confirm the hypothesis that the internal world of the organic descends directly from the primordial forms of life. The most remarkable fact is the omnipresence of the DNA molecule. The genetic material of all the earth's known organisms is in large part composed of the nucleic acids DNA and RNA, whose structure contains information transmitted through reproduction from one generation to the next, and furthermore endowed with the capacity to reproduce itself and to imitate. In short, the genetic code is universal, or almost. Decoding it was an immense discovery to the extent that it showed that 'the two languages of the great polymers, the languages of nucleic acid and protein, correlate directly' . . . The Soviet mathematician Liapunov demonstrated in 1963 that every living system transmits a small but precise quantity of energy or matter containing a great volume of information through channels laid down in advance. This information is responsible for the subsequent control of large quantities of energy and matter. From this perspective numerous biological and cultural phenomena (storing, feedback, channelling messages and so on) can be conceived as manifestations of information processing. In the final analysis, information appears in large part to be the repetition of information, but still another kind of information, a kind of control which seems to be a universal property of terrestrial life, irrespective of its form or substance.
>
> Five years ago I drew attention to the convergence of genetics and linguistics as autonomous but parallel disciplines in the larger field of the science of communication (which is also a part of zoosemiotics). The terminology of

genetics is full of expressions taken from linguistics and communication theory . . . , which emphasised both the principal similarities and the important differences in the structure and function of genetic and verbal codes . . . Today it is clear that the genetic code must be considered as the most basic semiotic network, and therefore as the prototype of all the other systems of signification used by the animals, including man. From this point of view, molecules, which are systems of quanta of, and which act as stable vehicles of physical information, zoosemiotic and cultural systems including language, constitute a continuous chain of stages, with ever more complex energy levels, in the context of a unique and universal evolution. It is therefore possible to describe both language or living systems from a unifying cybernetic point of view. For the moment, this is only a useful and provisional analogy. . . . A reciprocal rapprochement between genetics, animal communication and linguistics may lead to a complete science of the dynamics of semiosis, which science may turn out, in the final analysis, to be nothing other than a definition of life.

So the outline of the current strategic model emerges, everywhere taking over from the great ideological model which political economy was in its time.

We find this again, under the rigorous sign of 'science', in Jacques Monod's *Chance and Necessity* [tr. Austyn Wainhouse, London: Collins, 1970]. The end of dialectical evolution. Life is now ruled by the discontinuous indeterminacy of the genetic code, by the *teleonomic* principle. Finality is no longer at the end, there is no more finality, nor any determinacy. Finality is there in advance, inscribed in the code. We can see that nothing has changed – the order of ends has ceded its place to molecular play, as the order of signifieds has yielded to the play of infinitesimal signifiers, condensed into their aleatory commutation. All the transcendental finalities are reduced to an instrument panel. This is still to make recourse to nature however, to an inscription in a 'biological' nature; a phantasm of nature in fact, as it has always been, no longer a metaphysical sanctuary for the origin and substance, but this time, for the code. The code must have an 'objective' basis. What better than molecules and genetics? Monod is the strict theologian of this molecular transcendence, Edgar Morin its ecstatic supporter (DNA = ADoNaï!). In each of them, however, the phantasm of the code, which is equivalent to the reality of power, is confused with the idealism of the molecule.

Again we find the hallucination or illusion of a world reunited under a single principle – a homogeneous substance according to the Counter-Reformation Jesuits. With Leibniz and his binary deity as their precursor, the technocrats of the biological (as well as the linguistic) sciences opt for the genetic code, for their intended programme has nothing to do with genetics, but is a social and historical programme. Biochemistry hypostatises the ideal of a social order governed by a kind of genetic code, a macromolecular calculus by the PPBS (Planning Programming Budgeting System), its operational circuits radiating over the social body. Here techno-cybernetics finds its 'natural philosophy', as Monod said. The biological and the biochemical have always exerted a fascination, ever since the beginnings of science. In Spencer's organicism (bio-sociologism) it was operative at the level of second and third order structures (following Jacob's classification in *The Logic of Life* [Harmondsworth: Penguin, 1989]), while today, in modern biochemistry, this applies to the level of fourth-order structures.

Coded similarities and dissimilarities: the exact image of cyberneticised social exchange. We need only add the 'stereospecific complex' to reinject the intracellular communication that Morin will transform into a molecular Eros.

Practically and historically, this means that social control by means of the *end* (and the more or less dialectical *providence* that ministers to the fulfilment of this end) is replaced with social control by means of prediction, simulation, programmed anticipation and indeterminate mutation, all governed, however, by the code. Instead of a process finalised in accordance with its ideal development, we are dealing with generative *models*. Instead of prophecy, we fall subject to 'inscription'. There is no radical difference between the two. Only the schemata of control change and, it has to be said, reach a fantastic degree of perfection. From a capitalist productivist society to a neo-capitalist cybernetic order, aiming this time at absolute control: the biological theory of the code has taken up arms in the service of this mutation. Far from 'indeterminate', this mutation is the outcome of an entire history where God, Man, Progress and even History have successively passed away to the advantage of the code, where the death of transcendence benefits immanence, which corresponds to a far more advanced phase of the vertiginous manipulation of social relations.

In its infinite reproduction, the system puts an end to the myth of its origin and to all the referential values it has itself secreted in the course of its process. By putting an end to the myth of its origin, it puts an end to its internal contradictions (there is no longer a real or a referential to which to oppose them) and also puts an end to the myth of its end, the revolution itself. With the revolution you could still make out the outline of a victorious human and generic reference, the original potential of man. But what if capital wiped generic man himself off the map (in favour of genetic man)? The revolution's golden age was the age of capital, where myths of the origin and the end were still in circulation. Once these myths were short-circuited (the only threat that capital had ever faced historically came from this *mythical* demand for rationality which pervaded it from the start) in a *de facto* operationality, a non-discursive operationality – once it became its own myth, or rather an indeterminate, aleatory machine, something like a *social genetic code* – capital no longer left the slightest opportunity for a determinate reversal. This is the real violence of capital. However, it remains to be seen whether this operationality is itself a myth, whether DNA is itself a *myth*.

This effectively poses the problem of the discursive status of science once and for all. In Monod, this discourse is so candidly absolutised that it provides a perfect opportunity for posing the problem:

Plato, Heraclitus, Hegel, Marx . . .: these ideological edifices, represented as a priori, were in reality a posteriori constructions designed to justify preconceived ethico-political theories. . . . For science, objectivity is the only a priori postulate of objectivity, which spares, or rather forbids it from taking part in this debate. [*Chance and Necessity*, p. 98]

However, this postulate is itself a result of the never innocent decision to objectify the world and the 'real'. In fact, it postulates the coherence of a specific *discourse*, and scientificity is doubtless only the space of this discourse, never manifest as such, whose simulacrum of 'objectivity' covers over this political and strategic speech. Besides, Monod clearly expresses the arbitrariness of this discourse a little further on:

It may be asked, of course, whether all the invariants, conservations and symmetries that make up the texture of scientific discourse are not fictions substituted for reality in order to obtain a workable image. . . . A logic itself founded upon a purely abstract, perhaps 'conventional', principle of identity – a convention with which, however, human reason seems to be incapable of doing without. [ibid., p. 99]

We couldn't put it more clearly: science itself determines its generative formula and its discourse model on the basis of a faith in a conventional order (and moreover not just any order, but the order of a total reduction). But Monod quickly glosses over this dangerous hypothesis of 'conventional' identity. A rigid basis would serve science better, an 'objective' reality for example. Physics will testify that identity is not only a postulate, but that it is *in things*, since there is an 'absolute identity of two atoms when they are found to be in the same quantitative state'. So, is it convention or is it objective reality? The truth is that science, like any other discourse, is organised on the basis of a conventional logic, but, like any other ideological discourse, requires a real, 'objective' reference within the processes of substance in order to justify it. If the principle of identity is in any way 'true', even if this is at the infinitesimal level of two atoms, then the entire conventional edifice of science which draws its inspiration from it is also 'true'. The hypothesis of the genetic code DNA is also true and cannot be defeated. The same goes for metaphysics. Science explains things which have been defined and formalised in advance and which subsequently conform to these explanations, that's all that 'objectivity' is. The ethics that come to sanction this objective knowledge are just systems of defence and misconstrual [*méconnaissance*] that aim to preserve this vicious circle.[2]

As Nietzsche said: 'Down with all hypotheses that have allowed belief in a real world.'

The Tactile and the Digital

Regulation on the model of the genetic code is in no way limited to effects in the laboratory or the exalted visions of theoreticians: these models invest life at its most banal level. Digitality is among us. It haunts all the messages and signs of our society, and we can clearly locate its most concrete form in the test, the question/answer, the stimulus/response. All content is neutralised by a continuous process of orchestrated interrogations, verdicts and ultimatums to be decoded, which this time no longer come from the depths of the genetic code but still possess the same tactical indeterminacy – the cycles of meaning become infinitely shorter in the cycles of the question/answer, the bit or the return of a minuscule quantity of energy/information to its point of departure. This cycle merely describes the perpetual reactualisation of the same models. The equivalent of the total neutralisation of signifieds by the code is the instantaneous verdict of fashion or of every billboard or TV advertising message. Everywhere supply devours demand, the question devours the answer, either absorbing and regurgitating it in a decodable form, or inventing it and anticipating its predictable corroboration. Everywhere the same *'scenario'* of 'trials and errors' (the burden of which, in laboratory tests, is borne by guinea-pigs), the scenario of the spectrum of choices on offer or the multiple choice ('test your personality'). The test is everywhere the fundamental social form of control, which works by infinitely dividing practices and responses.

We live in a *referendum* mode precisely because there is no longer any *referential*. Every sign and every message (objects of 'functional' utility just as much as fashion features or any televised information, polls or discussions) is presented to us as a question/answer. The entire communications system has passed from a complex syntactic structure of language to a binary system of question/answer signals – perpetual testing. Tests and referenda are, as we know, perfect forms of simulation: the question induces the answer, it is *design-ated* in advance. The *referendum*, then, *is only an ultimatum*: the unilateral question is precisely not an interrogation any more, but the immediate imposition of a meaning which simultaneously completes the cycle. Every message is a verdict, delivered like the verdict of polling statistics. The simulacrum of distance (or indeed of contradiction) between the two poles is nothing but a tactical hallucination, like the reality effect on the interior of the sign itself.

Benjamin provides this test-function at the concrete level of the technical apparatus:

> The artistic performance of the screen actor is presented by a camera, with a twofold consequence. The camera that presents the performance of the film actor to the public need not respect the performance as an integral whole. Guided by the camera-man, the camera continually changes its position with respect to the performance. The sequence of positional views which the editor composes with the material supplied him constitutes the completed film . . . Hence, the performance of the actor is subjected to a series of optical tests. This is the first consequence of the fact that the actor's performance is presented by means of the camera. Also, the film actor lacks the opportunity of the stage actor to adjust to the audience during the performance, since he does not present his performance to the audience in person. This permits the audience to take the position of the critic, without experiencing any personal contact with the actor. The audience's identification with the actor is really an identification with the

camera. Consequently the audience takes the position of the camera; its approach is that of testing.

[Note:] The expansion of the field of the testable which mechanical equipment brings about for the actor corresponds to the extraordinary expansion of the field of the testable brought about for the individual through economic conditions. Thus, vocational aptitude tests become constantly more important. What matters in these tests are segmental performances of the individual. The film shot and the vocational aptitude test are taken before a committee of experts. The camera director in the studio occupies a place identical with that of the examiner during aptitude tests.

[T]he work of art of the Dadaists became an instrument of ballistics. It hit the spectator like a bullet, it happened to him, thus acquiring a tactile quality. It promoted a demand for the film, the distracting element of which is also primarily tactile, being based on changes of place and focus which periodically assail the spectator. ('The Work of Art', pp. 230, 240)

Contemplation is impossible, images fragment perception into successive sequences and stimuli to which the only response is an instantaneous yes or no – reaction time is maximally reduced. The film no longer allows you to contemplate it, it interrogates you directly. According to McLuhan, it is in this sense that the modern media demand greater immediate participation,[3] incessant response and total plasticity (Benjamin compares the camera-man's operation to the surgeon's: tactility and manipulation). Messages no longer have an informational role, they test and take polls, ultimately so as to control ('contra-role' in the sense that all your responses are already inscribed in the 'role', on the anticipated register of the code). Editing [*montage*] and encoding in fact demand that the recipient dismantle [*démonte*] and decode in accordance with the same process. Every reading of a message is thus nothing more than a perpetual test of the code.

Every image, every media message and also every surrounding functional object is a test. That is to say, in all the rigour of the term, it triggers response mechanisms in accordance with stereotypes or analytic models. The object today is no longer 'functional' in the traditional sense of the term; it doesn't serve you, it *tests* you. It no longer has anything to do with yesterday's object, any more than 'mediatised' information has with the 'reality' of facts. Both object and information already result from a selection, an edited sequence of camera angles, they have already tested 'reality' and have only asked those questions to which it has responded. Reality has been analysed into simple elements which have been recomposed into scenarios of stable oppositions, just as the photographer imposes his own contrasts, lighting and angles onto his subject (any photographer will tell you that no matter what you do it is enough to catch the original from a good angle at the moment or inflection that turns it into the *exact response* to the instantaneous test of the apparatus and its code); exactly like the test or referendum when they translate a given conflict or problem into a question/answer game. Thus tested, reality tests you in return according to the same score-card, and you decode it following the same code, inscribed in its every message and object like a miniature genetic code.

You already test the mere fact that everything is presented today according to a spectrum or range, since it imposes selectivity on you. This conforms to the global usage we have of the surrounding world of *reading* and selective decoding – we live less as users than as readers and selectors, reading cells. But beware, since by the same token you are yourself constantly selected and tested by the medium itself. Just as we select a sample for purposes of a survey, the media frame and cut sample receivers by means of beamed messages which are in fact a network of selected questions. By a circular operation of experimental modifications and incessant interference, like nervous, tactile and retractile impulses, probing an object by means of short perceptual sequences until it has been localised and controlled, the media localise and structure not real, autonomous groups, but samples, modelled socially and mentally by a barrage of messages. 'Public opinion' is evidently the finest of these samples – not an unreal but a hyperreal political substance, the fantastic hyperreality which survives only by editing and manipulation by the test.

The irruption of the binary question/answer schema is of incalculable importance. Dislocating all discourse in a now bygone golden age, this schema short-circuits every dialectic of the signifier and the signified, a representative and a represented. There are no longer any objects whose signifieds are their functions, with opinion that 'representative' representatives would vote for, and the real interrogation to which the answer responds (and there are especially no longer any questions to which there are no answers). This entire process is dislocated: the contradictory processes of the true and the false, the real and the imaginary are abolished in this hyperreal logic of the *montage*. Michel Tort provides a fine analysis of this in his book on the Intelligence Quotient:

> The question as such does not determine its response in the form in which it was posed, it is the meaning given to it by the person to whom it was posed and also the idea the interrogated subject forms of the most appropriate tactic to adopt in order to respond according to the idea he forms of the interrogation's expectations. [*Le quotient intellectual*, Paris: Maspéro, 1974]

Tort again:

> The artifact is something other than a controlled transformation of the object for purposes of knowledge: it is a savage intervention in reality, at the end of which it is impossible to distinguish what in this reality arises out of objective knowledge and what results from the technical intervention (the medium). The IQ is such an artifact.

No more true and false since we can no longer find any gap between question and answer. In the light of these tests, intelligence, like opinion and more generally every process of signification, is reduced to the 'capacity to produce contrasting reactions to an increasing range of appropriate stimuli'.

This whole analysis directly reflects McLuhan's formula 'The Medium is the Message'. It is in fact the medium, the very mode of editing, cutting, questioning, enticement, and demand by the medium that rules the process of signification. So we can understand why McLuhan saw an era of *tactile* communication in the era of electronic mass-media. In this we are closer in effect to the tactile than we are to the visual universe, where there is greater distance, and reflection is always possible. At the moment that touching loses its sensory, sensual value for us ('touching is an interaction of the senses rather than a simple contact between a skin and an object'), it is possible that it might once more become the schema of a universe of communication – but this time as a field of *tactile* and *tactical* simulation where the message becomes a 'message', a tentacular enticement, a test. In every field we are tested, probed and sampled; the method is 'tactical' and the sphere of communication 'tactile'. Not to mention the ideology of 'contact', which in all of its forms, seeks to replace the idea of social relations. A whole strategic configuration revolves around the test (the question/answer cell) as it does around a molecular command-code.

The entire political sphere loses its specificity as soon as it enters the media's polling game, that is to say, when it enters the integrated circuit of the question/answer. The electoral sphere is in any case the first large-scale institution where social exchange is reduced to getting a response. Thanks to these simplified signals, the electoral sphere is also the first institution to be universalised: universal suffrage is the first of the mass-media. Throughout the nineteenth and twentieth centuries, political and economic practice merge increasingly into the same type of discourse; propaganda and publicity were fused, marketing and merchandising both objects and powerful ideas. This linguistic convergence between the economic and the political is moreover what marks a society such as ours, where 'political economy' has been fully realised. By the same token, it is also its end, since the two spheres are abolished in another reality or media hyperreality. Here again, each term is elevated to a higher power, that of third-order simulacra.

> While many regret the media's 'corruption of politics' and deplore the fact that the TV switch and the public opinion polls have cheerfully replaced opinion formation, this merely testifies that they have not understood politics at all. (*Le Monde*)

This phase of political hyperrealism is characterised by the necessary conjunction of the two-party system and the emergence of opinion polls as the mirror of this alternating equivalence of the political game.

Opinion polls are situated beyond all social *production* of opinion. They now refer only to a simulacrum of public opinion. This mirror of opinion is analogous in its way to that of the Gross National Product: the imaginary mirror of productive forces without regard for their social finality or counter-finality, the essential thing being merely that 'it' [*ça*] is reproduced. The same goes for public opinion, where what matters most is that it grows incessantly in its own image: this is the secret of mass representation. Nobody need *produce* an opinion any more, but everyone must *reproduce* public opinion, in the sense that all opinions are swallowed up in this kind of general equivalent and proceed from it thereafter (reproduce it, or what they take it to be, at the level of individual choice). For opinion as for material goods, production is dead: Long Live Reproduction!

If McLuhan's formula becomes significant anywhere, it is certainly here.[4] Public opinion is *par excellence* both the medium and the message. The polls informing this opinion are the unceasing imposition of the medium as the message. They thereby belong to the same order as TV and the electronic media, which, as we have seen, are also a perpetual question/answer game, an instrument of perpetual polling.

Polls manipulate the *undecidable*. Do they affect votes? True or false? Do they yield exact photographs of reality, or of mere tendencies, or a refraction of this reality in a hyperspace of simulation whose curvature we do not even know? True or false? Undecidable. However sophisticated their analyses, they always leave room for the reversibility of hypotheses. Statistics is just casuistry. This undecidability is proper to every simulation process (see above for the undecidability of the crisis). The internal logic of these processes (statistics, probabilities, operational cybernetics) is certainly rigorous and 'scientific', yet it somehow doesn't get any purchase on anything, it is a fabulous fiction whose index of refraction in (true or false) reality is zero. This condition is all that gives these *models* any force, but the only truth it leaves them comes from paranoid projection tests of a caste or group, undecidability dreaming of a miraculous adequation between the real and their own models, and therefore an absolute manipulation.

What is true in the scenario of statistics is also true of the regulated partition of the political sphere: the alternation of the forces in power, minority/majority substitutions and so on. At the limit of pure representation, 'it' [*ça*] no longer represents anything. Politics dies from the over-regulated play of its distinct oppositions. The political sphere (more generally, the sphere of power) is emptied. In some ways this is the ransom for the fulfilment of the desire of the political class for a perfect manipulation of social representation. Smoothly and surreptitiously, all social substance vanishes from this machine at the very moment of its perfected reproduction.

The same goes for opinion polls: it is ultimately only members of the political classes who believe in them, just as it is only brokers and advertising executives who really believe in publicity and market analyses. This is not due to a particular stupidity (although we can't rule this out), but because the polls are homogeneous to the way contemporary politics operate. They therefore take on a 'real' tactical value, operating as a regulating factor of the political classes in accordance with their own game-rules. The political classes, then, have good reason to believe in polls, as in fact they do. Ultimately, though, who else does? It is the burlesque spectacle of the hyperrepresentative (that is, not representative at all) political sphere that people savour and sample through opinion polls and the media. There is a jubilation proper to this spectacular nullity, and the final form that it takes is that of *statistical contemplation*. Such contemplation, moreover, is always coupled, as we know, with a profound disappointment – the species of disillusion that the polls provoke by absorbing all public speaking, by short-circuiting every means of expression. They exert fascination in proportion to this neutralisation through emptiness, to the vertigo they create by anticipating every possible reality in the image.

The problem of opinion polls, then, is not their objective influence at all. As far as propaganda and advertising are concerned, such influence is, as we know, largely annulled by individual or collective resistance or inertia. Their problem is the operational simulation that they institute across the entire range of social practices, the leukaemia infecting all social substance, replacing blood with the white lymph of the media.

The question/answer circularity runs through every domain. We are slowly beginning to notice that the whole domain of surveys, polls and statistics must be revised according to the radical suspicion brought to bear on their methods. The same suspicion bears, however, on ethnology. Unless you admit that the natives are totally 'natural' and incapable of simulation, then the problem is the same with the above as it is here: it is impossible to obtain a *non-simulated response* to a direct question, apart from merely reproducing the question. It is not even certain that we can test plants, animals or inert matter in the exact sciences with any hope of an 'objective' response. As to how those polled respond to the pollsters, how natives respond to ethnologists, the analysand to the analyst, you may be sure that there is total circularity in every case: those questioned always behave as the questioner imagines they will and solicits them to. Even the psychoanalytic transference and counter-transference collapses today under the shock of this stimulated, simulated and anticipated response, which is simply a modality of the self-fulfilling prophecy.[5] So we come up against the strange paradox where whatever those polled, analysands and natives say, it is irremediably short-circuited and lost. Indeed, it is on the basis of this foreclosure that these disciplines – sociology, psychoanalysis and ethnology – will be able to develop in leaps and bounds. Such amazing development is just hot air, however, since the circular response of those polled, the analysands and the natives is nevertheless a challenge and a victorious revenge: when they turn the question back on itself, isolating it by holding the expected mirror-image response up to it, then there is no hope that the question can ever get out of what is in fact the vicious circle of power. It is exactly the same in the electoral system, where 'representatives' no longer represent anything, by dint of controlling the electoral body's responses so well: somewhere, everything has escaped them. That is why the controlled responses of the dominated are nevertheless somehow a genuine response, a desperate vengeance which lets power bury power.

The systems of the 'advanced democracies' become stable through the formula of the two-party system. The *de facto* monopoly remains in the hands of a homogeneous political class, from the left to the right, but must not be exercised in this way. This is because single party rule, totalitarianism, is an unstable form which drains the political stage and can no longer ensure the feedback of public opinion, the minimal current in the integrated circuit that constitutes the transistorised political machine. The two-party system, by contrast, is the end of the end of representation since solicitation reaches its highest degree, in the name of a simple formal constraint, when you approach the greatest perfect competitive equation between the two parties. This is only logical: democracy attains the law of equivalence in the political order, and this law is fulfilled by the see-sawing of the two terms, which thus maintains their equivalence but by means of this minuscule divergence allows for public consensus and the closure of the cycle of representation: a theatre of operations where only the smoky reflections of political Reason continue to function. Democracy's credo of the individual's 'free choice' effectively turns into its exact opposite: voting has become absolutely *obligatory*. If this is not the case *de jure*, then it is through the structural, statistical constraint of the two-party system, reinforced by the opinion polls.[6] Voting has become absolutely *aleatory*: when democracy reaches a formally advanced stage, it is distributed in equal quantities (50/50). Voting merges with the Brownian motion of particles or probability calculus, as if the whole world were voting according to chance, as if signs were voting.

At this point, it matters little what the parties in power express historically and socially – it is even *necessary* that they no longer represent anything: the fascination of the game and the polls, the formal and statistical compulsion, is so much greater.

'Classical' universal suffrage already implies a certain neutralisation of the political field, in the name of a consensus over the rules of the game. But we can still distinguish the representatives and the represented in this game, on the basis of a real social antagonism in opinions. The neutralisation of this contradictory referential, under the sign of a public opinion which from now on is equal to itself, mediatised and homogenised by means of anticipation (polls), will make possible an alternation, not of parties, but of their 'heads', creating a simulated opposition between the two parties, absorbing their respective objectives, and a reversibility of every discourse into any other. Beyond the representative and the represented, this is the pure form of representation; just as, beyond the signifier and the signified, simulation marks the pure form of the political economy of the sign; just as, beyond use-value and exchange-value, beyond every substance of production, the flotation of currencies and their accountable drift marks the pure form of value.

It may seem that the historical movement of capital carries it from open competition towards oligopoly and then towards monopoly, that democracy moves from a multi-party system to a two-party system and then towards single-party rule: oligopoly, or real duopoly, results from the *tactical division of the monopoly*. In every domain duopoly is the completed stage of monopoly. It is not that a political will (State intervention, anti-trust laws, etc.) shatters the market's monopoly: any unitary system, if it wants to survive, must find a *binary regulation*. This does not change anything as regards monopoly, on the contrary, power is only absolute if it is able to diffract into various equivalents, if it knows how to divide in order to become stronger. This goes for detergent brands as much as for a 'peaceful co-existence'. Two superpowers are necessary in order to keep the universe under control: a single empire would crumble by itself. The balance of terror merely allows regulated oppositions to be put in place, for strategy is structural, never atomic. Even if this regulated opposition can be ramified into a more complex scenario, the matrix remains binary. From now on, it will never again be a question of a duel or open competitive struggle, but one of couplets of simultaneous oppositions.

From the smallest disjunctive unit (the question/answer particle) up to the macroscopic level of the great 'two-party' systems that govern the economy, politics and global co-existence, the matrix never changes. It is always the 0/1, the binary scansion that is affirmed as the metastable or homeostatic form of contemporary systems. It is the core of the processes of simulation that dominate us. It can be organised into a game of unstable variations, from polyvalence to tautology, without putting the strategic form of the duopoly into question. It is the divine form of simulation.[7]

Why has the World Trade Center in New York got *two* towers? All Manhattan's great buildings are always content to confront each other in a *competitive* verticality, from which there results an architectural panorama that is the image of the capitalist system: a pyramidal jungle, every building on the offensive against every other. The system itself can be spotted in the famous image we have of New York on arriving by sea. This image has changed completely in a few years. The effigy of the capitalist system has passed from the pyramid to the punch card. The buildings are no longer obelisks, but trustingly stand next to one another like the columns of a statistical graph. This new architecture no longer embodies a competitive system, but a countable one where competition has disappeared in favour of correlation. (New York is the only city in the world to have retraced, throughout the entire length and breadth of its history, the contemporary form of the capitalist system in this way, instantaneously changing according to this system. No European city has ever done this.) This architectural graphism belongs to the monopoly: the World Trade Center's two towers are perfect parallelepipeds, four hundred metres high on a square base; they are perfectly balanced and blind communicating vessels. The fact that there are two identical towers *signifies* the end of all competition, the end of every original reference. Paradoxically, if there were only one, the WTC would not embody the monopoly, since we have seen that it becomes stable in a dual form. For the sign to remain pure it must become its own double: this doubling of the sign really put an end to what it designated. Every Andy Warhol does this: the multiple replicas of Marilyn Monroe's face are of course at the same time the death of the original and the end of representation. The two towers of the WTC are the visible sign of the closure of a system in the vertigo of doubling, while the other skyscrapers are each the original moment of a system continually surpassing itself in the crisis and the challenge.

This doubling, this replication, inspires a particular fascination. However high they are and however much higher than all the others, the two towers nevertheless signify an arrested verticality. They ignore the other buildings, they are not of the same race, they no longer challenge them nor compare themselves to them; the two towers reflect one another and reach their highest point in the prestige of similitude. They echo the idea of the model they are for one another, and their semi-detached altitude no longer has a transcendent value, but only signifies that the commutative strategy of the model will now historically prevail over the heart of the system itself (as New York truly is), over the traditional strategy of competition. The buildings of the Rockefeller Center also mirror their glass and steel façades in one another, in the city's infinite specularity. The towers are themselves blind and no longer have a façade. Every reference to habitat, to the façade as 'face', to the interior and exterior, that we still find even in the Chase Manhattan Bank or in the most daring mirror buildings from the sixties has been erased. At the same moment that the rhetoric of verticality is disappearing, so too is the rhetoric of the mirror. There now remains only a series based on the binary code, as if architecture, in the image of the system, proceeded only by means of an unchanging genetic code, a definitive model.

The Hyperrealism of Simulation

We have just defined a digital space, a magnetic field of the code with its modelled polarisations, diffractions and gravitations, with the insistent and perpetual flux of the smallest disjunctive units (the question/answer cell operates like the cybernetic atom of *signification*). We must now measure the disparity between this field of control and the traditional field of repression, the police-space which used to correspond to a violence of signification. This space was one of reactionary conditioning, inspired by the Pavlovian apparatus of programmed and repetitive aggression which we also saw scaled up in 'hard sell' advertising and the political propaganda of the thirties. A crafted but industrial violence that aimed to produce terrified behaviour and animal obedience. This no longer has any meaning. Totalitarian, bureaucratic concentration is a schema dating from the era of the market law of value. The schema of equivalences effectively imposes the form of a general equivalent, and hence the centralisation of a global process. This is an archaic rationality compared to simulation, in which it is no longer a single general equivalent but a diffraction of models that plays the regulative role: no longer the form of the general equivalent, but the form of distinct oppositions. We pass from injunction to disjunction through the code, from the ultimatum to solicitation, from obligatory passivity to models constructed from the outset on the basis of the subject's 'active response', and this subject's involvement and 'ludic' participation, towards a total environment model made up of incessant spontaneous responses, joyous feedback and irradiated contacts. According to Nicolas Schöffer, this is a 'concretisation of the general ambience': the great festival of Participation is made up of myriad stimuli, miniaturised tests, and infinitely divisible question/answers, all magnetised by several great models in the luminous field of the code.

Here comes the great Culture of tactile communication, under the sign of techno-lumino-kinetic space and total spatio-dynamic theatre!

A whole imaginary based on contact, a sensory mimicry and a tactile mysticism, basically ecology in its entirety, comes to be grafted on to this universe of operational simulation, multi-stimulation and multi-response. This incessant test of successful adaptation is naturalised by assimilating it to animal mimicry ('the phenomenon of animals' adaptation to the colours and forms of their habitat also holds for man' – Nicolas Schöffer), and even to the Indians with their 'innate sense of ecology'! Tropisms, mimicry and empathy: the ecological evangelism of open systems, with positive or negative feedback, will be engulfed in this breach, with an ideology of regulation through information that is only the avatar, in accordance with a more flexible rationality, of the Pavlov reflex. Hence electro-shock is replaced by body attitude as the condition of mental health. When notions of need, perception, desire, etc., become operational, then the apparatuses of force and forcing yield to ambient apparatuses. A generalised, mystical ecology of the 'niche' and the context, a simulated environment eventually including the 'Centres for Cultural and Aesthetic Re-animation' planned for the Left Bank (why not?) and the Centre for Sexual Leisure, which, built in the form of a breast, will offer 'a superlative euphoria thanks to a pulsating ambience. . . . Workers from all classes will be able to enter these stimulating centres.' A spatio-dynamic fascination, just like 'total theatre', set up 'according to a hyperbolic, circular apparatus turning around a cylindrical spindle'. No more scenes, no more cuts, no more 'gaze', the end of the spectacle and the spectacular, towards the total, fusional, tactile and aesthesic (and no longer the aesthetic) etc., environment. We can only think of Artaud's total theatre, his Theatre of Cruelty, of which this spatio-dynamic simulation is the abject, black-humour caricature. Here cruelty is replaced by minimum and maximum 'stimulus thresholds', by the invention of 'perceptual codes calculated on the basis of saturation thresholds'. Even the good old 'catharsis' of the classical theatre of the passions has today become a homeopathy by means of simulation.

The end of the spectacle brings with it the collapse of reality into hyperrealism, the meticulous reduplication of the real, preferably through another reproductive medium such as advertising or photography. Through reproduction from one medium into another the real becomes volatile, it becomes the allegory of death, but it also draws strength from its own destruction, becoming the real for its own sake, a fetishism of the lost object which is no longer the object of representation, but the ecstasy of denegation and its own ritual extermination: the hyperreal.

Realism had already inaugurated this tendency. The rhetoric of the real already signals that its status has been radically altered (the golden age of the innocence of language where what is said need not be doubled in an effect of reality). Surrealism was still in solidarity with the realism it contested, but which it doubled and ruptured in the imaginary. The hyperreal represents a much more advanced phase insofar as it effaces the contradiction of the real and the imaginary. Irreality no longer belongs to the dream or the phantasm, to a beyond or a hidden interiority, but to *the hallucinatory resemblance of the real to itself*. To gain exit from the crisis of representation, the real must be sealed off in a pure repetition. Before emerging in pop art and painterly neo-realism, this tendency can already be discerned in the *nouveau roman*. Here the project is to construct a void around the real, to eradicate all psychology and subjectivity from it in order to give it a pure objectivity. In fact, this is only the objectivity of the pure gaze, an objectivity finally free of the object, but which merely remains a blind relay of the gaze that scans it. It is easy to detect the unconscious trying to remain hidden in this circular seduction.

This is indeed the impression made by the *nouveau roman*, a wild elision of meaning in a meticulous but blind reality. Syntax and semantics have disappeared: the object now only appears in court, where its scattered fragments are subjected to unremitting cross-examination. There is neither metaphor nor metonymy, only a successive immanence under the law enforcing authority of the gaze. This 'objective' microscopy incites reality to vertiginous motion, the vertiginous death of representation within the confines of representation. The old illusions of relief, perspective and depth (both spatial and psychological) bound up with the perception of the object are over with: optics in its entirety, scopics, has begun to operate on the surface of things – the gaze has become the object's molecular code.

There are several possible modalities of this vertigo of realistic simulation:

1.   The detailed deconstruction of the real, the paradigmatic close 'reading' of the object: the flattening out, linearity and seriality of part-objects.

2.   Abyssal vision: all the games of splitting the object in two and duplicating it in every detail. This reduction is taken to be a depth, indeed a critical metalanguage, and doubtless this was true of a reflective configuration of the sign in a dialectics of the mirror. From now on this infinite refraction is nothing more than another type of seriality in which the real is no longer reflected, but folds in on itself to the point of exhaustion.

3.   The properly serial form (Andy Warhol). Here the paradigmatic dimension is abolished along with the syntagmatic dimension, since there is no longer a flexion of forms, nor even an internal reflexion, only a

contiguity of the same: zero degree flexion and reflexion. Take photograph of twin sisters where the fleshy reality of their bo annihilated by their similarity. How do you invest when the beauty of t one is immediately duplicated in the other? The gaze can only go from one to the other, and these poles enclose all vision. This is a subtle means of murdering the original, but it is also a singular seduction, where the total extent of the object is intercepted by its infinite diffraction into itself (this scenario reverses the Platonic myth of the reunion of two halves separated by a symbol. In the series, signs subdivide like protozoa). Perhaps this is the seduction of death, in the sense that, for we sexually differentiated beings, death is perhaps not nothingness, but quite simply the mode of reproduction prior to sexual differentiation. The models that generate in infinite chains effectively bring us closer to the generation of protozoa; sex, which for us is confused with life, being the only remaining difference.

4. This pure machinality is doubtless only a paradoxical limit, however. Binarity and digitality constitute the true generative formula which encompasses all the others and is, in a way, the stabilised form of the code. This does not mean pure repetition, but minimal difference, the minimal inflexion between two terms, that is, the 'smallest common paradigm' that can sustain the fiction of meaning. A combinatory of differentiation internal to the painterly object as well as to the consumer object, this simulation contracts, in contemporary art, to the point of being nothing more than the infinitesimal difference that still separates hyperreality from hyperpainting. Hyperpainting claims to exhaust itself to the point of its sacrificial eclipse in the face of the real, but we know how all painting's prestige is revived in this infinitesimal difference: painting retreats into the border that separates the painted surface and the wall. It also hides in the signature, the metaphysical sign of painting and the metaphysics of representation at the limit, where it takes itself as its own model (the 'pure gaze') and turns around itself in the compulsive repetition of the code.

The very definition of the real is *that of which it is possible to provide an equivalent reproduction*. It is a contemporary of science, which postulates that a process can be reproduced exactly within given conditions, with an industrial rationality which postulates a universal system of equivalences (classical representation is not equivalence but transcription, interpretation and commentary). At the end of this process of reproducibility, the real is not only that which can be reproduced, but *that which is always already reproduced*: the hyperreal.

So are we then at the end of the real and the end of art due to a total mutual reabsorption? No, since at the level of simulacra, hyperrealism is the apex of both art and the real, by means of a mutual exchange of the privileges and prejudices that found them. The hyperreal is beyond representation (cf. Jean-François Lyotard, 'Esquisse d'une économie de l'hyperréalisme', *L'Art vivant*, 36, 1973)[8] only because it is entirely within simulation, in which the barriers of representation rotate crazily, an implosive madness which, far from being ex-centric, keeps its gaze fixed on

abyssal repetition. Analogous to the effect of an
.he dream, allowing us to say that we are dreaming,
.he play of censorship and the perpetuation of the
integral part of a coded reality that it perpetuates and

alism must be interpreted in inverse manner: *today
perrealist*. The secret of surrealism was that the most
could become surreal, but only at privileged instants
which a~ ~e out of art and the imaginary. Today everyday, political,
social, historical, economic, etc., reality has already incorporated the
hyperrealist dimension of simulation so that we are now living entirely
within the 'aesthetic' hallucination of reality. The old slogan 'reality is
stranger than fiction', which still corresponded to the surrealist stage in the
aestheticisation of life, has been outrun, since there is no longer any fiction
that life can possibly confront, even as its conqueror. Reality has passed
completely into the game of reality. Radical disaffection, the cool and
cybernetic stage, replaces the hot, phantasmatic phase.

The consummate enjoyment [*jouissance*] of the signs of guilt, despair,
violence and death are replacing guilt, anxiety and even death in the total
euphoria of simulation. This euphoria aims to abolish cause and effect,
origin and end, and replace them with reduplication. Every closed system
protects itself in this way from the referential and the anxiety of the
referential, as well as from all metalanguage that the system wards off by
operating its own metalanguage, that is, by duplicating itself as its own
critique. In simulation, the metalinguistic illusion reduplicates and completes the referential illusion (the pathetic hallucination of the sign and the
pathetic hallucination of the real).

'It's a circus', 'it's a theatre', 'it's a movie'; all these old adages are
ancient naturalist denunciations. This is no longer what is at issue. What is
at issue this time is *turning the real into a satellite*, putting an undefinable
reality with no common measure into orbit with the phantasma that once
illustrated it. This satellisation has subsequently been materialised as the
two-room-kitchen-shower which we really have sent into orbit, to the
'spatial power' you could say, with the latest lunar module. The most
everyday aspect of the terrestrial environment raised to the rank of a
cosmic value, an absolute decor, hypostatised in space. This is the end of
metaphysics and the beginning of the era of hyperreality.[9] The spatial
transcendence of the banality of the two-room apartment by a cool,
machinic figuration in hyperrealism[10] tells us only one thing, however: this
module, such as it is, participates in a hyperspace of representation where
everyone is already in possession of the technical means for the instant
reproduction of his or her own life. Thus the *Tupolev*'s pilots who crashed
in Bourget were able, by means of their cameras, to see themselves dying
at first hand. This is nothing other than the short-circuit of the response by
the question in the test, a process of instant renewal whereby reality is
immediately contaminated by its simulacrum.

A specific class of allegorical and somewhat diabolical objects
exist, made up of mirrors, images, works of art (concepts?). Althou
simulacra, they were transparent and manifest (you could distinguish
craftsmanship [*façon*] from the counterfeit [*contrefaçon*]) with their own
characteristic style and *savoir-faire*. Pleasure, then, consisted in locating
what was 'natural' within what was artificial and counterfeit. Today, where
the real and the imaginary are intermixed in one and the same operational
totality, aesthetic fascination reigns supreme: with subliminal perception (a
sort of sixth sense) of special effects, editing and script, reality is over-
exposed to the glare of models. This is no longer a space of production, but
a reading strip, a coding and decoding strip, magnetised by signs. Aesthetic
reality is no longer achieved through art's premeditation and distancing,
but by its elevation to the second degree, to the power of two, by the
anticipation and immanence of the code. A kind of unintentional parody
hovers over everything, a tactical simulation, a consummate aesthetic
enjoyment [*jouissance*], is attached to the indefinable play of reading and
the rules of the game. Travelling signs, media, fashion and models, the
blind but brilliant ambience of simulacra.

Art has for a long time prefigured this turn, by veering towards what
today is a turn to everyday life. Very early on the work of art produced a
double of itself as the manipulation of the signs of art, bringing about an
oversignification of art, or, as Lévi-Strauss said, an 'academicisation of the
signifier', irreversibly introducing art to the form of the sign. At this point
art entered into infinite *reproduction*, with everything that doubles itself,
even the banal reality of the everyday, falling by the same token under the
sign of art and becoming aesthetic. The same goes for production, which
we might say has today entered into aesthetic reduplication, the phase
where, expelling all content and all finality, it becomes somehow abstract
and non-figurative. In this way it expresses the pure form of production,
taking upon itself, as art does, the value of the finality without end. Art and
industry may then exchange their signs: art can become a reproductive
machine (Andy Warhol) without ceasing to be art, since the machine is
now nothing but a sign. Production can also lose all its social finality as its
means of verification, and finally glorify in the prestigious, hyperbolic and
aesthetic signs that the great industrial complexes are, 400 m high towers
or the numerical mysteries of the Gross National Product.

So art is everywhere, since artifice lies at the heart of reality. So art is
dead, since not only is its critical transcendence dead, but reality itself,
entirely impregnated by an aesthetic that holds onto its very structurality,
has become inseparable from its own image. It no longer even has the time
to take on the effect of reality. Reality is no longer stranger than fiction: it
captures every dream before it can take on the dream effect. A schizophrenic vertigo of serial signs that have no counterfeit, no possible sublimation,
and are immanent to their own repetition – who will say where the reality
they simulate now lies? They no longer even repress anything (which, if
you like, keeps simulation from entering the sphere of psychosis): even the

ıve been annihilated. The cool universe of digitality
of metaphor and metonymy. The simulation principle
ty principle as well as the pleasure principle.

he Insurrection of Signs

In the ., f 1972 in New York a spate of graffiti broke out which, starting with ghetto walls and fences, finally overcame subways and buses, lorries and elevators, corridors and monuments, completely covering them in graphics ranging from the rudimentary to the sophisticated, whose content was neither political nor pornographic. These graphics consisted solely of names, surnames drawn from underground comics such as DUKE SPIRIT SUPERKOOL KOOLKILLER ACE VIPERE SPIDER EDDIE KOLA and so on, followed by their street number – EDDIE 135 WOODIE 110 SHADOW 137, etc. – or even by a number in Roman numerals, a dynastic or filiatory index – SNAKE I SNAKE II SNAKE III, etc. – up to L (50), depending on which name, which totemic designation is taken up by these new graffitists.

This was all done with Magic Markers or spray-paint, allowing the inscriptions to be a metre or more in height by the entire length of the subway car. At night, youths would work their way into bus depots or subways, even getting inside the cars, breaking out into an orgy of graphics. The following day all these subway trains cross Manhattan in both directions. The graphics are erased (but this is difficult), the graffitists are arrested and imprisoned, the sale of marker pens and spray cans is forbidden, but to no avail, since the youths manufacture them by hand and start again every night.

Today this movement has stopped, or at least is no longer so extraordinarily violent. It could only have been ephemeral, and, besides, in a single year of history it developed greatly. The graffitists became more expert, with incredible baroque graphics, and ramified into styles and schools connected to the different groups in operation. Young Blacks and Puerto Ricans originated the movement, and the graffitists were particular to New York. Several wall paintings are found in other cities with large ethnic minorities, improvised collective works with an ethno-political content, but very little graffiti.

One thing is certain: both the graffitists and the muralists sprang up after the repressions of the great urban riots of 1966–70. Like the riots, graffiti was a savage offensive, but of another kind, changing content and terrain. A new type of intervention in the city, no longer as a site of economic and political power, but as a space-time of the terrorist power of the media, signs and the dominant culture.

The urban city is also a neutralised, homogenised space, a space where indifference, the segregation of urban ghettos, and the downgrading of districts, races and certain age groups are on the increase. In short, it is the cut-up space of distinctive signs. Multiple codes assign a determinate space-time to every act and instant of everyday life. The racial ghettos on the outskirts or in the city centre are only the limit expression of this urban configuration: an immense centre for marshalling and enclosure where the system reproduces itself not only economically and spatially, but also in depth by the ramifications of signs and codes, by the symbolic destruction of social relations.

There is a horizontal and vertical expansion of the city in the image of the economic system itself. Political economy, however, has a third dimension where all sociality is invested, covered and dismantled by signs. Neither architecture nor urbanism can do anything about this, since they themselves result from this new turn taken by the general economy of the system: they are its operational semiology.

The city was first and foremost a site for the production and realisation of commodities, a site of industrial concentration and exploitation. Today the city is first and foremost the site of the sign's execution, as in its life or death sentence.

In the city's 'red belt' of factories, and in the working-class outskirts, this is no longer the case for us. In this city, in the same space, the historical dimension of the class struggle, the negativity of labour power, were still inscribed, an irreducible social specificity. The factory, as the model of socialisation through capital, has not disappeared today but, in line with the general strategy, has been replaced by the entire city as the space of the code. The urban matrix no longer realises a *power* (labour power) but a *difference* (the operation of the sign): metallurgy has become semiurgy.

We see this urban scenario materialised in the new cities which directly result from the operational analysis of needs and sign-functions, and in which everything is conceived, projected and realised on the basis of an analytic definition: environment, transport, labour, leisure, play and culture become so many commutable terms on the chessboard of the city, a homogeneous space defined as a total environment. Hence the connection between the urban landscape and racism: there is no difference between the act of packing people into one homogeneous space (which we call a ghetto) on the basis of a racial definition, and the act of making people homogeneous in a new city on the basis of a functional definition of their needs. It follows one and the same logic.

The city is no longer the politico-industrial zone that it was in the nineteenth century, it is the zone of signs, the media and the code. By the same token, its truth no longer lies in its geographical situation, as it did for the factory or even the traditional ghetto. Its truth, enclosure in the sign-form, lies all around us. It is the ghetto of television and advertising, the ghetto of consumers and the consumed, of readers read in advance, encoded decoders of every message, those circulating in, and circulated by, the subway, leisure-time entertainers and the entertained, etc. Every space-time of urban life is a ghetto, each of which is connected to every other. Today a multiplicity of codes submit socialisation, or rather desocialisation, to this structural breakdown. The era of production, commodities and labour power merely amounts to the interdependence of all social processes, including exploitation, and it was on this socialisation, realised in part by capital itself, that Marx based his revolutionary perspective. But this historical solidarity (whether factory, local or class solidarity) has disappeared. From now on they are separate and indifferent under the sign of television and the automobile, under the sign of behaviour models inscribed everywhere in the media or in the layout of the city. Everyone falls into line in their delirious identification with leading models, orchestrated models of simulation. Everyone is commutable, like the models themselves. This is the era of geometrically variable individuals. As for the geometry of the code, it remains fixed and centralised. The monopoly of this code, circulating throughout the urban fabric, is the genuine form of social relations.

It is possible to conceive of the decentralisation of the sphere of material production, even that the historical relation between the city and commodity production is coming to an end. The system can do without the industrial, productive city, the space-time of the commodity and market-based social relations. The signs of this development are evident. It cannot, however, do without the urban as the space-time of the code and reproduction, for the centrality of the code is the definition of power itself.

Whatever attacks contemporary semiocracy, this new form of value, is therefore politically essential: graffiti for example. According to this new form there is a total commutability of elements within a functional set, each taking on meaning only insofar as it is a term that is capable of structural variation in accordance with the code.

Under these conditions, radical revolt effectively consists in saying 'I exist, I am so and so, I live on such and such street, I am alive here and now.' This would still be an identitarian revolt however, combating anonymity by demanding a proper name and a reality. The graffitists went further in that they opposed pseudonyms rather than names to anonymity. They are seeking not to escape the combinatory in order to regain an identity (which is impossible in any case), but to turn indeterminacy against the system, to turn *indeterminacy* into *extermination*. Retaliation, reversion of the code according to its own logic, on its own terrain, gaining victory over it because it exceeds semiocracy's own non-referentiality.

SUPERBEE SPIX COLA 139 KOOL GUY CRAZY CROSS 136 means nothing, it is not even a proper name, but a symbolic matriculation number whose function it is to derail the common system of designations. Such terms are not at all original, they all come from comic strips where they were imprisoned in fiction. They blasted their way out however, so as to burst into reality like a scream, an interjection, an anti-discourse, as the waste of all syntactic, poetic and political development, as the smallest radical element that cannot be caught by any organised discourse. Invincible due to their own poverty, they resist every interpretation and every connotation, no longer denoting anyone or anything. In this way, with neither connotation nor denotation, they escape the principle of signification and, as *empty signifiers*, erupt into the sphere of the *full signs* of the city, dissolving it on contact.

Names without intimacy, just as the ghettos have no intimacy, no private life, but thrive on an intense collective exchange. These names make no claim to an identity or a personality, but claim the radical exclusivity of the clan, gang, age group, group or ethnicity which, as we know, passes through the devolution of the name, coupled with an absolute loyalty, to this totemic designation, even if it came directly from the pages of underground comics. This form of symbolic designation is annihilated by our social structure which imposes a *proper* name and a *private* individuality on everyone, shattering all solidarity in the name of an urban, abstract and universal sociality. These names or tribal appellations have, by contrast, a real symbolic charge: they are made to be given, exchanged, transmitted and relayed in a collective anonymity, where these names are exchanged as terms to introduce group members amongst each other, although they are no more private a property than language.

This is the real force of a symbolic ritual, and, in this sense, graffiti runs contrary to all media and advertising signs, although they might create the illusion, on our city walls, that they are the same incantation. Advertising has been spoken of as a 'festival', since, without it, the urban environment would be dismal. But in fact it is only a cold bustle, a simulacrum of appeal and warmth, it makes no contacts, it cannot be revived by an autonomous or collective reading, and it does not create a symbolic network. More so than the walls that support it, advertising is itself a wall of functional signs made to be decoded, and its effects are exhausted in this decoding.

All media signs issue from this space without qualities, from this surface of inscription set up between producers and consumers, transmitters and receivers of signs. The city is a 'body without organs', as Deleuze says,[11] an intersection of channelled flows. The graffitists themselves come from the territorial order. They territorialise decoded urban spaces – a particular street, wall or district comes to life through them, becoming a collective territory again. They do not confine themselves to the ghetto, they export the ghetto through all the arteries of the city, they invade the white city and reveal that it is the real ghetto of the Western world.

A linguistic ghetto erupts into the city with graffiti, a kind of riot of signs. In the becoming-sign of the sign, graffiti has until now always constituted the basest form (the sexual and pornographic base), the shameful, repressed inscriptions in pissoirs and waste grounds. Only political and propagandistic slogans have conquered the walls in a direct offensive, full signs for which the wall is still a support and language a traditional medium. They are not aiming at the wall itself, nor at the pure functionality of signs as such. Doubtless it was only in May '68 in France that the graffiti and posters swept through the city in a different manner, attacking the support itself, producing a savage mobility on the walls, an inscription so sudden that it amounted to annihilating them. The inscriptions and frescoes at Nanterre actually hijacked the wall as a signifier of terrorist, functional gridded space: an anti-media action. The proof is that the government has been careful enough neither to efface nor to repaint the walls: the mass political slogans and posters have taken responsibility for this. There is no need for repression since the media themselves, the far-left media, have given the walls back their blind function. Since then, we have met with the Stockholm 'protest wall' where one is at liberty to protest on a certain surface, but where it is forbidden to put graffiti on neighbouring surfaces.

There has also been the ephemeral onslaught of the advertising hijack, limited by its own support, but already utilising the avenues the media have themselves opened up: subways, stations and posters. Consider also the assault on television by Jerry Rubin and America's counter-culture. This is a political attempt to hijack a great mass-medium, but only at the level of content and without changing the media themselves.

New York graffiti utilised urban clearways and mobile supports for the first time in a free and wide-ranging offensive. Above all, however, the very form of the media themselves, that is, their mode of production and distribution, was attacked for the first time. This was precisely because graffiti has no content and no message: this emptiness gives it its strength. So it was no accident that the total offensive was accompanied by a recession in terms of content. This comes from a sort of revolutionary intuition, namely that deep ideology no longer functions at the level of political signifieds, but at the level of the signifier, and that this is where the system is vulnerable and must be dismantled.

Thus the political significance of graffiti becomes clear. It grew out of the repression of the urban riots in the ghettos. Struck by this repression, the revolt underwent a split into a doctrinal *pur et dur* Marxist-Leninist political organisation on the one hand, and, on the other, a savage cultural process with neither goal, ideology, nor content, at the level of signs. The first group called for a genuinely revolutionary practice and accused the graffitists of folklore, but it's the other way round: the defeat of 1970 brought about a regression into traditional political activism, but it also necessitated the radicalisation of revolt on the real strategic terrain of the total manipulation of codes and significations. This is not at all a flight into signs, but on the contrary an extraordinary development in theory and practice (these two terms now no longer being kept distinct by the party).

Insurrection and eruption in the urban landscape as the site of the reproduction of the code. At this level, relations of forces no longer count, since signs don't operate on the basis of force, but on the basis of difference. We must therefore attack by means of difference, dismantling the network of codes, attacking coded differences by means of an uncodeable absolute difference, over which the system will stumble and disintegrate. There is no need for organised masses, nor for a political consciousness to do this – a thousand youths armed with marker pens and cans of spray-paint are enough to scramble the signals of urbania and dismantle the order of signs. Graffiti covers every subway map in New York, just as the Czechs changed the names of the streets in Prague to disconcert the Russians: guerrilla action.

Despite appearances, the City Walls Project, the painted walls, have nothing to do with graffiti. Moreover, they are prior to graffiti and will survive it. The initiative for these painted walls comes from the top as an innovatory attempt to enliven urbania set up with municipal subsidies. The 'City Walls Incorporated' organisation was founded in 1969 'to promote the program and technical aspects of wall-painting'. Its budget was covered by the New York Department of Cultural Affairs along with various other foundations such as that of David Rockefeller. His artistic ideology: 'The natural alliance between buildings and monumental painting.' His goal: 'To make a gift of art to the people of New York.' Consider also the 'Billboard Art Project' in Los Angeles:

> This project was set up to promote artistic representations that use the billboard as a medium in the urban environment. Thanks to the collaboration of Foster and Kleiser [two large advertising agencies], public billposting spaces have thus become an art showcase for the painters of Los Angeles. They create a dynamic medium and take art out of the restricted circle of the galleries and museums.

Of course, these operations are confined to professionals, artists brought together in a consortium from New York. No possible ambiguity here: this is a question of a politics of the environment, of large-scale urban planning, where both the city and art gain. They gain because the city does not explode with the eruption of art 'out in the open', in the streets, nor does art explode on contact with the city. The entire city becomes an art gallery, art finds a whole new parading ground in the city. Neither undergoes any structural alteration, they merely exchange their privileges.

'To make a gift of art to the people of New York'! We need only compare this to SUPERKOOL's formula: 'There are those who don't like it, man, but whether they like it or not, we've become the strongest art movement to hit the city of New York.'

This makes all the difference. Some of the painted walls may be beautiful, but that has nothing to do with it. They will find a place in the history of art for having been able to create space on the blind, bare walls, by means of line and colour alone: the *trompe-l'oeil*s are always the most beautiful, those painted walls that create an illusion of space and depth, those that 'enhance architecture with imagination', according to one of the artists' formulas. But this is precisely where their limits lie. They *play at* architecture without breaking the rules of the game, they recycle architecture in the imaginary, but retain the sacrament of architecture (from the technical support to the monumental structure, including even its social, class aspect, since most of the City Walls of this kind are in the white, civilised areas of the cities).

So architecture and town planning, even if they are transfigured by the imagination, cannot change anything, since they are mass-media themselves and, even in their most daring conception, they reproduce mass social relations, which is to say that collectively they allow people no response. All they can do is enliven, and participate in urban recycling, design in the largest sense: the simulation of exchange and collective values, the simulation of play and non-functional spaces. Hence the adventure parks for the children, the green spaces, the houses of culture; hence the City Walls and the protest walls, the green spaces of language [parole].

The graffitists themselves care little for architecture; they defile it, forget about it and cross the street. The mural artist respects the wall as he used to respect the limitations of his easel. Graffiti runs from one house to the next, from one wall of a building to the next, from the wall onto the window or the door, or windows on subway trains, or the pavements. Graffiti overlaps, is thrown up, superimposes (superimposition amounting to the abolition of the support as a framework, just as it is abolished as frame when its limits are not respected). Its graphics resemble the child's polymorphous perversity, ignoring the boundaries between the sexes and the delimitation of erogenous zones. Curiously, moreover, graffiti turns the city's walls and corners, the subway's cars and the buses, into a *body*, a body without beginning or end, made erotogenic in its entirety by writing just as the body may be in the primitive inscription (tattooing). Tattooing takes place on the body. In primitive societies, along with other ritual signs, it makes the body what it is – material for symbolic exchange: without tattooing, as without masks, the body is only what it is, naked and expressionless. By tattooing walls, SUPERSEX and SUPERKOOL free them from architecture and turn them once again into living, social matter, into the moving body of the city before it has been branded with functions and institutions. The end of the 'four walls' when they are tattooed like archaic effigies. End of the repressive space-time of urban transport systems where the subway cars fly past like missiles or living hydras tattooed up to the eyes. Something about the city has become tribal, parietal, before writing, with these powerful emblems stripped of meaning. An incision into the flesh of empty signs that do not signify personal identity, but group initiation and affiliation: 'A biocybernetic self-fulfilling prophecy world orgy I.'[12]

It is nevertheless astonishing to see this unfold in a Quaternary cybernetic city dominated by the two glass and aluminium towers of the World Trade Center, invulnerable metasigns of the system's omnipotence.

There are also frescoes and murals in the ghettos, the spontaneous artworks of ethnic groups who paint their own walls. Socially and politically, the impulse is the same as with graffiti. These are savage painted walls, not financed by the urban administration. Moreover, they all focus on political themes, on a revolutionary message: the unity of the oppressed, world peace, the cultural promotion of ethnic communities, solidarity, and only rarely the violence of open struggle. In short, as opposed to graffiti, they have a meaning, a message. And, contrary to the City Walls project, which drew its inspiration from abstract, geometrical or surrealist art, they are always inspired by figurative and idealist forms. We can also see the difference between a scholarly and cultivated avant-garde art and the popular, realist forms with a strong ideological content but formally 'less advanced' (even though they have a variety of inspirations, from children's drawings to Mexican frescoes, from a scholarly art to Douannier Rousseau, or from Fernand Léger up to the simple images of Epinal, the sentimental illustrations of popular struggles). In any case, it is a matter of a counter-culture that, far from being underground, is reflexive and connected to the political and cultural consciousness of the oppressed group.

Here again, some of these walls are beautiful, others less so. That this aesthetic criterion can operate is in a certain way a sign of weakness. What I mean is that even though they are savages and anonymous collectives, they respect their support as well as the language of painting, even if this is in order to articulate a political act. In this sense, they can very easily be looked on as decorative works of art (some of them are even conceived as such), and have an eye turned towards their own value. Most of them are protected from this museum-culturalisation by the rapid destruction of the fences and the crumbling walls – here the municipal authorities do not patronise through art, and the negritude of the support is in the image of the ghetto. However, their mortality is not the same as the mortality of graffiti, which is systematically condemned to police repression (it is even forbidden to take photographs of it). This is because graffiti is more offensive and more radical, bursting into the white city; above all it is trans-ideological, trans-artistic. This is almost a paradox: whereas the Black and Puerto Rican walls, even if they have not been signed, always carry a virtual signature (a political or cultural, if not an artistic, reference), graffiti, composed of nothing but names, effectively avoids every reference and every origin. It alone is savage, in that its message is zero.

We will come to what it signifies elsewhere, by analysing the two types of recuperation of which it is the object (apart from police repression):

1. It is recuperated as art. Jay Jacobs: 'A primitive, millenial, communitarian form, not an elitist one like Abstract Expressionism.' Or again: 'The subway cars rumble past one after the other throughout the station, like so many Jackson Pollocks hurtling by, roaring through the corridors of the history of art.' We speak of 'graffiti artists' and 'an eruption of popular art' created by youth, which 'will remain one of the important and characteristic manifestations of the art of the '70s', and so on. Always the aesthetic reduction, the very form of our dominant culture.

2. It is interpreted (and I am talking about the most admiring interpretations here) in terms of a reclamation of identity and personal freedom, as non-conformism: 'The indestructible survival of the individual in an inhuman environment' (Mitzi Cunliffe in *The New York Times*). A bourgeois humanist interpretation that comes from *our* feelings of frustration in the anonymity of large cities. Cunliffe again: 'It says [the graffiti says]: I AM, I am real, I have lived here. It says: KIKI, OR DUKE, OR

MIKE, OR GINO is alive, he's doing well and he lives in New York.' OK, but 'it' does not speak like that, it is our bourgeois-existentialist romanticism that speaks like that, the unique and incomparable being that each of us is, but who gets ground down by the city. Black youths themselves have no personality to defend, from the outset they are defending the community. Their revolt challenges bourgeois identity and anonymity at the same time. COOL COKE SUPERSTRUT SNAKE SODA VIRGIN – this Sioux litany, this subversive litany of anonymity, the symbolic explosion of these war names in the heart of the white city, must be heard and understood.

Notes

1. Counterfeit and reproduction always imply an anxiety, a disquieting strangeness. There is unease in front of the photograph, which has been assimilated into a sorcerer's trickery, an unease, more generally, in front of any technical equipment. Benjamin relates this to the unease bound up with the appearance of a mirror-image. There is already a little sorcery at work in the mirror, but how much more there would be were the image to be detached from the mirror, transported, stockpiled and reproduced at whim (cf. *The Student of Prague*, where the Devil detaches the student's image from the mirror and then hunts him down through the intermediary of this image). In this way all reproduction implies maleficence, from the event of being seduced by one's own image in the water, like Narcissus, to being haunted by the double, and, who knows, even to the mortal reversal of the vast array of technical equipment that today man disguises in his own image (the narcissistic mirage of technology, as McLuhan says), and that sends back endless halting and distorted reproductions of himself and his power, to the ends of the earth. Reproduction is diabolical in its essence, sending tremors down to our roots. This has hardly changed for us: simulation (which we describe here as the operation of the code) remains and will always remain the site of an immense project of control and death, just as the simulacrum-object (the primitive statue, the image or the photo) has from the outset always had black magic as its objective.
2. Furthermore, there is a flagrant contradiction in Monod's book, reflecting the ambiguity of all contemporary science: its discourse is directed at the code, that is, at third-order simulacra, but it still follows second-order 'scientific' schemata such as objectivity, the scientific 'ethic' of knowledge, the truth-principle and the transcendence of science, and so on. These things are all incompatible with third-order models of indeterminacy.
3. 'The weak "definition" of TV condemns its viewer to rearrange the few points he retains into a kind of abstract work of art. He thereby participates in the creation of a reality which is only pointillistically presented: the televiewer is in the situation of an individual who is asked to project his own phantasma onto inkblots which are not supposed to represent anything.' TV as a perpetual Rorschach test. Again: 'The TV image obliges us to always be filling in the blanks on the screen in a convulsive, kinetic and tactile sensory participation.'
4. 'The Medium is the Message' is even the formula of the political economy of the sign when it leads on to third-order simulation. A distinction of the medium from the message remains characteristic of second-order signification.
5. The whole contemporary 'psychological' situation is characterised by this short-circuit.
    The emancipation of children and adolescents, after a first phase of revolt and once the *principle of the right* to emancipation has been established, appears to be the real emancipation of parents. Youth (students, high school pupils and adolescents) seem to sense this in their increasingly relentless (although also always unreconciled) demands that parents or educators be present and speak. Alone at last, free and responsible, it

suddenly occurs to them that in the process the others have pocketed the real freedom. Nor is there any question of simply leaving them in peace. Instead they will be plagued, not by affective or spontaneous material demands but by a demand revised and corrected by implicit Oedipal knowledge. A hyperdependency (far greater than the other) distorted by irony and rejection, a *parody of the original libidinal mechanisms*. A demand without content or reference, unfounded, but so much more ferocious for all that: a naked demand to which there is no possible response. The content of knowledge (education) or affective relations (family), the familial or pedagogic referential having been eliminated during the act of emancipation, remains nothing more than a demand bound up with the empty form of the institution, a perverse, but so much more obstinate, demand. A 'transferential' desire (that is non- or irreferential), a desire fuelled by lack, by the vacant place, a 'liberated' desire, desire caught in its own vertiginous image, a desire to desire thereby also abyssal [*en abyme*]: a hyperreal desire. Stripped of symbolic substance, desire flows ever more intensely into its double, drawing its energy from its own reflection and from its own disillusionment. That is literally what the 'demand' is today, and it is clear that as opposed to 'classical' object or transference relations, this demand is insoluble and interminable.

Simulated Oedipus.
François Richard writes:

> The students *demanded* to be seduced, bodily or verbally. But they are also aware of this and play their part ironically. 'Give your knowledge and your presence: you've got the floor, so speak, that's what you're there for.' While this is certainly a protest, that is not all it is: the more authority is contested, the more laughable it appears, the greater the demand for an authority in itself. They also play Oedipus, so as to be able to annihilate him absolutely. They say that 'the prof is Papa' for a laugh, they play at incest, discontented, untouchable, they play the tease, ultimately to be desexualised.

Does the analysand constantly demand Oedipus, recite 'Oedipal' tricks and have 'analytic' dreams in order to respond to the analyst's supposed demand or to resist him? What about the student doing his 'Oedipus' number, his seduction number, familiarly brushing up against the seductee, moving closer in order to dominate? This is not desire, however, but its simulation, a simulated Oedipal psychodrama (but no less real or dramatic for all that). It is quite different when there are real libidinal stakes such as knowledge and power, or even a real work of mourning over knowledge and power (as was able to take place in the universities after '68). Now is the stage of desperate reproduction, where the stakes are zero and the simulacrum at a maximum, a simulation at once aggravated and parodic, as interminable as psychoanalysis and for the same reasons.   ·

Interminable psychoanalysis
There is a whole chapter to be added to the history of the transference and the counter-transference concerning their elimination through simulation. This chapter would also deal with the insolubility of the transference and the impossibility of psychoanalysis, because it is now psychoanalysis that produces and reproduces the unconscious as its institutional substance. Psychoanalysis too dies from the exchange of unconscious signs, just as the revolution dies from the exchange of political-economic signs. This short-circuit was indeed glimpsed by Freud in the form of the gift of the analytic dream or, with a 'prepared' analysand, the gift of their analytic knowledge. This was still interpreted as resistance, however, as a detour, and did not fundamentally question the analytic process or the principle of the transference. It is quite different though when the unconscious itself, the discourse of the unconscious, becomes impossible to find in accordance with the same scenario of simulatory anticipation as we have seen at work at all levels in machines of the third order. Analysis then can no longer be resolved, it becomes logically and historically interminable, since it settles on a substance that is a puppet of reproduction, an unconscious programmed by the demand, an insurmoun-

table instance from which the entire analysis is redistributed. Here again the unconscious's 'messages' have been short-circuited by the 'medium' of psychoanalysis. This is a libidinal hyperrealism. We must add the 'hyperreal' to the celebrated categories of the real, the symbolic and the imaginary, since it captures and redirects, perverts, the play of the three others.

6. Athenian democracy, far more advanced than our own, logically came to pay for votes as a service, after having tried every other repressive solution to complete the quorum.

7. In this sense it is necessary to undertake a radical critique of Lévi-Strauss's extension of binary structures as 'anthropological' mental structures, and dualistic organisation as the basic structure of primitive societies. The dualistic form with which Lévi-Strauss would like to grace primitive societies is only ever *our* structural logic, our own code. Indeed, it is the very structure of our domination of 'archaic' societies. Lévi-Strauss is kind enough to slip this to them in the form of the mental structures common to the human race. So they will be all the better prepared to receive the baptism of the West.

8. [See also Jean-François Lyotard, *Des dispositifs pulsionels*, Paris: Christian Bourgeois, 1979, pp. 99–108 – tr.]

9. The coefficient of reality is proportionate to the reserve of the imaginary that gives it its specific weight. This is true of terrestrial as well as space exploration: when there is no more virgin, and hence available to the imaginary, territory, when the map covers the whole territory, something like the reality principle disappears. In this sense, the conquest of space constitutes an irreversible threshold on the way to the loss of terrestrial references. Reality haemorrhages to the precise extent that the limits of an internally coherent universe are infinitely pushed back. The conquest of space comes after the conquest of the planet, as the last phantasmatic attempt to extend the jurisdiction of the real (for example, when the flag, technology and two-room apartments are carried to the moon); it is even an attempt to substantiate concepts or territorialise the unconscious, which is equivalent to the derealisation of human space, or its reversal into a hyperreality of simulation.

10. What about the cool figuration of the metallic caravan and the supermarket so beloved of the hyperrealists, or the Campbell's soup cans dear to Andy Warhol, or even that of the Mona Lisa when it was satellited into planetary orbit as the absolute model of the earth's art. The Mona Lisa was not even sent as a work of art, but as a planetary simulacrum where a whole world bears testimony to its existence (testifying, in reality, to its own death) for the gaze of a future universe.

11. [See Gilles Deleuze and Félix Guattari, *Anti-Oedipus: Capitalism and Schizophrenia I*, tr. R. Hurley, M. Seem and H.R. Lane, London: Athlone, 1984, and *A Thousand Plateaux: Capitalism and Schizophrenia II*, tr. Brian Massumi, London: Athlone, 1988, for the BWO – tr.]

12. [In English in the original – tr.]

3

FASHION, OR THE ENCHANTING SPECTACLE OF THE CODE

The Frivolity of the *Déjà Vu*

The astonishing privilege accorded to fashion is due to a unanimous and definitive resolve. The acceleration of the simple play of signifiers in fashion becomes striking, to the point of enchanting us – the enchantment and vertigo of the loss of every system of reference. In this sense, it is the completed form of political economy, the cycle wherein the linearity of the commodity comes to be abolished.

There is no longer any determinacy internal to the signs of fashion, hence they become free to commute and permutate without limit. At the term of this unprecedented enfranchisement, they obey, as if logically, a mad and meticulous recurrence. This applies to fashion as regards clothes, the body and objects – the sphere of 'light' signs. In the sphere of 'heavy' signs – politics, morals, economics, science, culture, sexuality – the principle of commutation nowhere plays with the same abandon. We could classify these diverse domains according to a decreasing order of 'simulation', but it remains the case that every sphere tends, unequally but simultaneously, to merge with models of simulation, of differential and indifferent play, the structural play of value. In this sense, we could say that they are all haunted by fashion, since this can be understood as both the most superficial play and as the most profound social form – the inexorable investment of every domain by the code.

In fashion, as in the code, signifieds come unthreaded [*se défiler*], and the parades of the signifier [*les défilés du signifiant*] no longer lead anywhere. The signifier/signified distinction is erased, as in sexual difference (H.-P. Jeudy, 'Le signifiant est hermaphrodite' [in *La mort du sens: l'idéologie des mots*, Tours/Paris: Mame, 1973]), where gender becomes so many distinctive oppositions, and something like an immense fetishism, bound up with an intense pleasure [*jouissance*][1] and an exceptional desolation, takes hold – a pure and fascinating manipulation coupled with the despair of radical indeterminacy. Fundamentally, fashion imposes upon us the rupture of an imaginary order: that of referential Reason in all its guises, and if we are able to enjoy [*jouir*] the dismantling or stripping of reason [*démantèlement de la raison*], enjoy the *liquidation* of meaning (particularly at the level of our body – hence the affinity of clothing and fashion), enjoy this endless finality of fashion, we also suffer profoundly from the corruption of rationality it implies, as reason crumbles under the blow of the pure and simple alternation of signs.

There is vehement resistance in the face of the collapse of all sectors into the sphere of commodities, and a still more vehement resistance concerning their collapse into the sphere of fashion. This is because it is in this latter sphere that the liquidation of values is at its most radical. Under the sign of the commodity, all labour is exchanged and loses its specificity – under the sign of fashion, the signs of leisure and labour are exchanged. Under the sign of the commodity, culture is bought and sold – under the sign of fashion, all cultures play like simulacra in total promiscuity. Under the sign of the commodity, love becomes prostitution – under the sign of fashion it is the object-relation itself that disappears, blown to pieces by a cool and unconstrained sexuality. Under the sign of the commodity, time is accumulated like money – under the sign of fashion it is exhausted and discontinued in entangled cycles.

Today, every principle of identity is affected by fashion, precisely because of its potential to revert all forms to non-origin and recurrence. Fashion is always *rétro*, but always on the basis of the abolition of the *passé* (the past): the spectral death and resurrection of forms. Its proper *actuality* (its 'up-to-dateness', its 'relevance') is not a reference to the present, but an immediate and total recycling. Paradoxically, fashion is the *inactual* (the 'out-of-date', the 'irrelevant'). It always presupposes a dead time of forms, a kind of abstraction whereby they become, as if safe from time, effective signs which, as if by a twist of time, will return to haunt the present of their inactuality with all the charm of 'returning' as opposed to 'becoming' structures. The aesthetic of renewal: fashion draws triviality from the death and modernity of the *déjà vu*. This is the despair that nothing lasts, and the complementary enjoyment of knowing that, beyond this death, every form has always the chance of a second existence, which is never innocent since fashion consumes the world and the real in advance: *it is the weight of all the dead labour of signs bearing on living signification* – within a magnificent forgetting, a fantastic ignorance [*méconnaissance*]. But let's not forget that the fascination exerted by industrial machinery and technics is also due to its being dead labour watching over living labour, all the while devouring it. Our bedazzled misconstrual [*méconnaissance*] is proportionate to the progressive hold of the dead over the living. Dead labour alone is as strange and as perfect as the *déjà vu*. The enjoyment of fashion is therefore the enjoyment of a spectral and cyclical world of bygone forms endlessly revived as effective signs. As König says, it is as though fashion were eaten away by a suicidal desire which is fulfilled at the moment when fashion attains its apogee. This is true, but it is a question of a *contemplative* desire for death, bound to the spectacle of the incessant abolition of forms. What I mean is that the desire for death is itself recycled within fashion, emptying it of every subversive phantasm and involving it, along with everything else, in fashion's innocuous revolutions.

Having purged these phantasms which, in the depths of the imaginary, add the bewitchment and charm of a previous life to repetition, fashion dances vertiginously over the surface, on pure actuality. Does fashion recover the innocence that Nietzsche noted in the Greeks: 'They knew how to live . . . to stop . . . at the surface, the fold, the skin, to believe in forms, tones, words. . . . Those Greeks were superficial – out of *profundity*' (*The Gay Science*, Preface, 2nd edition, 1886 [tr. Walter Kaufmann, New York: Random House, 1974], p. 38)? Fashion is only a simulation of the innocence of becoming, the cycle of appearances is just its recycling. That the development of fashion is contemporary with that of the museum proves this. Paradoxically, the museum's demand for an eternal inscription of forms and for a pure actuality function simultaneously in our culture. This is because in modernity both are governed by the status of the sign.

Whereas styles mutually exclude each other, the museum is defined by the virtual co-existence of all styles, by their promiscuity within a single cultural super-institution, or, in other words, the commensurability of their values under the sign of the great gold-standard of culture. Fashion does the same thing in accordance with its cycle: it commutes all signs and causes an absolute play amongst them. The temporality of works in the museum is 'perfect', it is perfection and the past: it is the highly specific state of what has been and is never actual. But neither is fashion ever actual: it speculates on the recurrence of forms on the basis of their death and their stockpiling, like signs, in an a-temporal reserve. Fashion cobbles together, from one year to the next, what 'has been', exercising an enormous combinatory freedom. Hence its effect of 'instantaneous' perfection, just like the museum's perfection, but the forms of fashion are ephemeral. Conversely, there is a contemporary look to the museum, which causes the works to play amongst themselves like values in a set. Fashion and the museum are contemporary, complicitous. Together they are the opposite of all previous cultures, made of inequivalent signs and incompatible styles.

The 'Structure' of Fashion

Fashion exists only within the framework of modernity, that is to say, in a schema of rupture, progress and innovation. In any cultural context at all, the ancient and the 'modern' alternate in terms of their signification. For us however, since the Enlightenment and the Industrial Revolution, there exists only an historical and polemical structure of change and crisis. It seems that modernity sets up a linear time of technical progress, production and history, and, simultaneously, a cyclical time of fashion. This only *seems* to be a contradiction, since in fact modernity is never a radical rupture. Tradition is no longer the pre-eminence of the old over the new: it is unaware of either – modernity itself invents them both at once, at a single stroke, it is always and at the same time 'neo-' and 'rétro-', modern and anachronistic. The dialectic of rupture very quickly becomes the dynamics of the amalgam and recycling. In politics, in technics, in art and in culture it is defined by the exchange rate that the system can tolerate without alteration to its fundamental order. Consequently fashion doesn't contradict any of this: it very clearly and simultaneously announces the *myth* of change, maintaining it as the supreme value in the most everyday aspects, and as the structural law of change: since it is produced through the play of models and distinctive oppositions, and is therefore an order which gives no precedence to the code of the tradition. For binary logic is the essence of modernity, and it impels infinite differentiation and the 'dialectical' effects of rupture. Modernity is not the transmutation but the commutation of all values, their combination and their ambiguity. Modernity is a code, and fashion is its emblem.

This perspective allows us to trace only the limits of fashion, in order to conquer the two simultaneous prejudices which consist:

1. in extending its field up to the limits of anthropology, indeed of animal behaviour;
2. in restricting, on the other hand, its actual sphere to dress and external signs.

Fashion has nothing to do with the ritual order (nor *a fortiori* with animal finery), for the good reason that it knows neither the equivalence/alternation of the old and the new, nor the systems of distinctive oppositions, nor the models with their serial and combinatory diffraction. On the other hand, fashion is at the core of modernity, extending even into science and revolution, because the entire order of modernity, from sex to the media, from art to politics, is infiltrated by this logic. The very appearance of fashion bears the closest resemblance to ritual – fashion as spectacle, as festival, as squandering – it doesn't even affirm their differences: since it is precisely the *aesthetic* perspective that allows us to assimilate fashion to the ceremonial (just as it is precisely the concept of festival that allows us to assimilate certain contemporary processes to primitive structures). The aesthetic perspective is itself a concern of modernity (of a play of distinctive oppositions – utility/gratuity, etc.), one which we project onto archaic structures so as to be better able to annex them under our analogies. Spectacle is our fashion, an intensified and reduplicated sociality enjoying itself *aesthetically*, the drama of change in place of change. In the primitive order, the ostentation of signs never has this 'aesthetic' effect. In the same way, our festival is an *'aesthetics' of transgression*, which is not the primitive exchange in which it pleases us to find the reflection or the model of our festivals – to rewrite the 'aesthetics' of potlach is an ethnocentric rewriting.

It is as necessary to distinguish fashion from the ritual order as it is to radicalise the analysis of fashion within our own system. The minimal, superficial definition of fashion restricts itself to saying: 'Within language, the element subject to fashion is not the signification of discourse, but its mimetic support, that is, its rhythm, its tonality, its articulation . . . in gesture . . . This is equally true of intellectual fashions: existentialism or structuralism – it is the vocabulary and not the inquiry that is taken on' (Edmond Radar, *Diogène* [50, Summer, 1965]). Thus a deep structure, invulnerable to fashion, is preserved. Consequently it is in the very production of meaning [*sens*], in the most 'objective' structures, that it must be sought, in the sense that these latter also comply with the play of simulation and combinatory innovation. Even dress and the body grow deeper: now it is the body itself, its identity, its sex, its status, which has become the material of fashion – dress is only a particular case of this. Certainly scientific and cultural popularisations provide fertile soil for the 'effects' of fashion. However, along with the 'originality' of their procedures, science and culture themselves must be interrogated, to see if they are subject to the 'structure' of fashion. If indeed popularisation is possible – which is not the case in any other culture (the facsimile, the digest, the counterfeit, the simulation, the increased circulation of simplified material, is unthinkable at the level of ritual speech, of the sacred text or gesture) – it is because there is, at the very source of innovation in these matters, a manipulation of analytic models, of simple elements and stable oppositions which renders both levels, the 'original' and the 'popularisation', fundamentally homogeneous, and the distinction between the two purely tactical and moral. Hence Radar does not see that, beyond discourse's 'gestures', the very meaning [*sens*] of discourse falls beneath the blow of fashion as soon as in an entirely self-referential cultural field, concepts are engendered and made to correspond to each other through pure specularity. It may be the same for scientific hypotheses. Nor does psychoanalysis avoid the fate of fashion in the very core of its theoretical and clinical practice. It too goes through the stage of institutional reproduction, developing whatever simulation models it had in its basic concepts. If formerly there was a *work* of the unconscious, and therefore a determination of psychoanalysis by means of its object, today this has quietly become the determination of the *unconscious by means of psychoanalysis itself*. Henceforth psychoanalysis reproduces the unconscious, while simultaneously taking itself as its reference (signifying itself as *fashion*, as the *mode*). So the unconscious returns to its old habits, as it is generally required to do, and psychoanalysis takes on social force, just as the code does, and is followed by an extraordinary complexification of theories of the unconscious, all commutable and basically indifferent.

Fashion has its society: dreams, phantasms, fashionable psychoses, scientific theories, fashionable schools of linguistics, not to mention art and politics – but this is only small change. Fashion haunts the *model* disciplines more profoundly, indeed to the extent that they have successfully made their axioms autonomous for their greater glory, and have moved into an *aesthetic*, almost a play-acting stage where, as in certain mathematical formulae, only the perfect specularity of the analytic models counts for anything.

The Flotation of Signs

Contemporary with political economy and like the market, fashion is a universal form. In fashion, all signs are exchanged just as, on the market, all products come into play as equivalents. It is the only universalisable sign system, which therefore takes possession of all the others, just as the market eliminates all other modes of exchange. So if in the sphere of fashion no general equivalent can be located, it is because from the outset fashion is situated in an even more formal abstraction than political economy, at a stage when there is not even any need for a perceptible general equivalent (gold or money) because there remains only the *form of general equivalence*, and that is fashion itself. Or even: a general equivalent is necessary for the *quantitative* exchange of value, whereas models are required for the exchange of differences. Models are this kind of general equivalent diffracted throughout the matrices which govern the differentiated fields of fashion. They are shifters, effectors, dispatchers, the media of fashion, and through them fashion is indefinitely reproduced. There is fashion from the moment that a form is no longer produced according to its own determinations, but *from the model itself* – that is to say, that it is never produced, but always and immediately *reproduced*. The model itself has become the only system of reference.

Fashion is not a *drifting* of signs – it is their *flotation*, in the sense in which monetary signs are floated today. This flotation in the economic order is recent: it requires that 'primitive accumulation' be everywhere finished, that an entire cycle of dead labour be completed (behind money, the whole economic order will enter into this general relativity). Now this process has been managed for a long time within the order of signs where primitive accumulation is indeed anterior, if not always already given, and fashion expresses the already acheived stage of an accelerated and limitless circulation of a fluid and recurrent combinatory of signs, which is equivalent to the instantaneous and mobile equilibrium of floating monies. All cultures, all sign systems, are exchanged and combined in fashion, they contaminate each other, bind ephemeral equilibria, where the machinery breaks down, where there is nowhere any meaning [*sens*]. Fashion is the pure speculative stage in the order of signs. There is no more constraint of either coherence or reference than there is permanent equality in the conversion of gold into floating monies – this indeterminacy implies the characteristic dimension of the cycle and recurrence in fashion (and no doubt soon in economy), whereas determinacy (of signs or of production) implies a linear and continuous order. Hence the fate of the economic begins to emerge in the form of fashion, which is further down the route of general commutations than money and the economy.

The 'Pulsion'[2] of Fashion

Were the attempt made to explain fashion by saying that it serves as a vehicle for the unconscious and desire, it would mean nothing if desire itself was 'in fashion'. In fact there is a 'pulsion' of fashion which hasn't got a great deal to do with the individual unconscious – something so violent that no prohibition has ever exhausted it, a desire to have done with meaning [*sens*] and to be submerged in pure signs, moving towards a raw, immediate sociality. In relation to mediated, economic, etc., social processes, fashion retains something of a radical sociality, not at the level of the psychical exchange of contents, but at the immediate level of the distribution of signs. As La Bruyère has already said:

> Curiosity is not a taste for the good or the beautiful, but for the rare, for what one has and others have not. It is not an affection for the perfect, but for what is current, for the fashionable. It is not an amusement, but a passion, sometimes so violent that it only yields to love and ambition through the modesty of its object. ('De la Mode 2' [in J. Benda (ed.), *Oeuvres Complètes*, Paris: Gallimard, 1951], p. 386)

For La Bruyère, the passion for fashion connects the passion for collecting with the object-passion: tulips, birds, engravings by Callot. In fact fashion draws nearer to the collection (in those terms) by means of subtle detours, 'each of which', for Oscar Wilde, 'gives man a security which not even religion has given him'.

Paying tribute to it, he finds salvation in fashion [*faire son salut dans la mode*]. A passion for collecting, passion for signs, passion for the cycle (the collection is also a cycle); one line of fashion put into circulation and distributed at dizzying speeds across the entire social body, sealing its integration and taking in all identifications (as the line in collection unifies the subject in one and the same infinitely repeated cyclic process).

This force, this enjoyment, takes root in the sign of fashion itself. The semiurgy of fashion rebels against the functionalism of the economic sphere. Against the ethics of production[3] stands the aesthetics of manipulation, of the reduplication and convergence of the single mirror of the model: 'Without content, it [fashion] then becomes the spectacle human beings grant themselves of their power to make the insignificant signify' (Barthes, *The Fashion System* [tr. Mathew Ward and Richard Howard, Berkeley: University of California Press, 1983], p. 288). The charm and fascination of fashion derives from this: the decree it proclaims with no other justification but itself. The arbitrary is enjoyed like an election, like class solidarity holding fast to the discrimination of the sign. It is in this way that it diverges radically from the economic while also being its crowning achievement. In relation to the pitiless finality of production and the market, which, however, it also stages, fashion is a festival. It epitomises everything that the regime of economic abstraction censures. It inverts every categorical imperative.

In this sense, it is spontaneously contagious, whereas economic calculation isolates people from one another. Disinvesting signs of all value, it becomes passion again – passion for the artificial. It is the utter absurdity, the formal futility of the sign of fashion, the perfection of a system where nothing is any longer exchanged against the real, it is the arbitrariness of this sign at the same time as its absolute coherence, constrained to a total relativity with other signs, that makes for its contagious virulence and, at the same time, its collective enjoyment. Beyond the rational and the irrational, beyond the beautiful and the ugly, the useful and the useless, it is this immorality in relation to all criteria, the frivolity which at times gives fashion its subversive force (in totalitarian, puritan or archaic contexts), which always, in contradistinction to the economic, makes it a *total social fact* – for which reason we are obliged to revive, as Mauss did for exchange, a total approach.

Fashion, like language, is aimed from the outset at the social (the dandy, in his provocative solitude, is the *a contrario* proof of this). But, as opposed to language, which aims for meaning [*sens*] and effaces itself before it, fashion aims for a theatrical sociality, and delights in itself. At a stroke, it becomes an intense site from which no-one is excluded – the mirror of a certain desire for its own image. In contradistinction to language, which *aims* at communication, fashion *plays* at it, turning it into the goal-less stake of a signification without a message. Hence its aesthetic pleasure, which has nothing to do with beauty or ugliness. Is it then a sort of festival, an increasing excess of communication?

It is especially fashion in dress, playing over the signs of the body, that appears 'festive', through its aspect of 'wasteful consumption', of 'potlach'. Again this is especially true of *haute couture*. This is what allows *Vogue* to make this tasty profession of faith:

> What is more anachronistic, more dream-laden than a sailing ship? *Haute couture*. It discourages the economist, takes up a stance contrary to productivity techniques, it is an affront to democratisation. With superb languor, a maximum number of highly qualified people produce a minimum number of models of complex cut, which will be repeated, again with the same languor, twenty times in the best of cases, or not at all in the worst . . . . Perhaps two million dresses. 'But why this debauchery of effort?' you say. 'Why not?' answer the creators, the craftsmen, the workers and the four thousand clients, all possessed by the same passion for seeking perfection. Couturiers are the last adventurers of the modern world. They cultivate the *acte gratuit* . . . . 'Why *haute couture*?' a few detractors may think. 'Why champagne?' Again: 'Neither practice nor logic can justify the extravagant adventure of clothes. Superfluous and therefore necessary, the world is once more the province of religion.'

Potlach, religion, indeed the ritual enchantment of expression, like that of costume and animal dances: everything is good for exalting fashion against the economic, like a transgression into a play-act sociality.

We know, however, that advertising too wants a 'feast of consumption', the media a 'feast of information', the markets a 'feast of production', etc. The art market and horse races can also be taken for potlach – 'Why not?' asks *Vogue*. We would like to see a functional squandering everywhere so as to bring about symbolic destruction. Because of the extent to which the economic, shackled to the functional, has imposed its principle of utility, anything which exceeds it quickly takes on the air of play and futility. It is hard to acknowledge that the law of value extends well beyond the economic, and that its true task today is the jurisdiction of all models. Wherever there are models, there is an imposition of the law of value, repression by signs and the repression of signs by themselves. This is why there is a radical difference between the symbolic ritual and the signs of fashion. In primitive cultures signs openly circulate over the entire range of 'things', there has not yet been any 'precipitation' of a signified, nor therefore of a reason or a truth of the sign. The real – the most beautiful of our connotations – does not exist. The sign has no 'underworld', it has no *unconscious* (which is both the last and the most subtle of connotations and rationalisations). Signs are exchanged without phantasms, with no hallucination of reality.

Hence they have nothing in common with the modern sign whose paradox Barthes has defined: 'The overwhelming tendency is to convert the perceptible into a signifier, towards ever more organised, closed systems. Simultaneously and in equal proportion, the sign and its systematic nature is disguised as such, it is rationalised, referred to a reason, to an agency in the world, to a substance, to a function' (cf. *The Fashion System*, p. 285). With simulation, signs merely disguise the real and the system of reference as a sartorial supersign. The real is dead, long live the realistic sign! This paradox of the modern sign induces a radical split between it and the magical or ritual sign, the same one as is exchanged in the mask, the tattoo or the feast.

Even if fashion is an enchantment, it remains the enchantment of the commodity, and, still further, the enchantment of simulation, the code and the law.

Sex Refashioned

There is nothing less certain than that sexuality invests dress, make-up, etc. – or rather it is a *modified* sexuality that comes into play at the level of fashion. If the condemnation of fashion takes on this puritan violence, it is not aimed at sex. The taboo bears on futility, on the passion for futility and the artificial which is perhaps more fundamental than the sexual drives. In our culture, tethered as it is to the principle of utility, futility plays the role of transgression and violence, and fashion is condemned for having within it the force of the pure sign which signifies nothing. Its sexual provocation is secondary with regard to this principle which denies the grounds of our culture.

Of course, the same taboo is also brought to bear on 'futile' and non-reproductive sexuality, but there is a danger in crystallising on sex, a danger that puritan tactics, which aim to change the stakes to sexuality, may be prolonged – whereas it is at the level of the *reality principle* itself, of the referential principle in which the unconscious and sexuality still participate, that fashion confrontationally sets up its pure play of differences. To place sexuality at the forefront of this history is once again to *neutralise the symbolic by means of sex and the unconscious*. It is according to this same logic that the analysis of fashion has traditionally been reduced to that of dress, since it allows the sexual metaphor the greatest play. Consequences of this diversion: the game is reduced to a perspective of sexual 'liberation', which is quite simply achieved in a 'liberation' of dress. And a new cycle of fashion begins again.

Fashion is certainly the most efficient neutraliser of sexuality (one never touches a woman in make-up – see 'The Body, or The Mass Grave of Signs' below) – precisely because it is a passion which is not complicitous, but in competition with sex (and, as La Bruyère has already noted, fashion is victorious over sex). Therefore the passion for fashion, in all its ambiguity, will come to play on the body confused with sex.

Fashion grows deeper as it 'stages' the body, as the body becomes the medium of fashion.[4] Formerly the repressed sanctuary, the repression rendering it undecodable, from now on it too is invested. The play of dress is effaced before the play of the body, which itself is effaced before the play of models.[5] All at once dress loses the ceremonial character (which it still had up until the eighteenth century) bound up with the usage of signs *qua* signs. Eaten away by the body's signifieds, by this 'transpearence' of the body as sexuality and nature, dress loses the fantastic exuberance it has had since the primitive societies. It loses its force as pure disguise, it is neutralised by the necessity that it must signify the body, it becomes a reason.

The body too is neutralised in this operation however. It too loses the power of disguise that it used to have in tattooing and costume. It no longer plays with anything save its proper truth, which is also its borderline: its nudity. In costumery, the signs of the body, mixed openly with the signs of the not-body, play. Thereafter, costume becomes dress, and the body becomes nature. Another game is set up – the opposition of dress and the body – designation and censure (the same fracture as between the signifier and the signified, the same play of displacement and allusion). Fashion strictly speaking begins with this partition of the body, repressed and signified in an allusive way – it also puts an end to all this in the simulation of nudity, in *nudity as the model of the simulation of the body*. For the Indian, the whole body is a face, that is, a promise and a symbolic act, as opposed to nudity, which is only sexual instrumentality.

This new reality of the body as hidden sex is from the outset merged with woman's body. The concealed body is feminine (not biologically of course; rather mythologically). The conjunction of fashion and woman, since the bourgeois, puritan era, reveals therefore a double indexation: that of fashion on a hidden body, that of woman on a repressed sex. This conjunction did not exist (or not so much) until the eighteenth century (and not at all, of course, in ceremonial societies) – and for us today it is beginning to disappear. As for us, when the destiny of a hidden sex and the forbidden truth of the body arises, when fashion itself neutralises the opposition between the body and dress, then the affinity of woman and fashion progressively diminishes[6] – fashion is generalised and becomes less and less the exclusive property of one sex or of one age. Be wary, for it is a matter neither of progress nor of liberation. The same logic still applies, and if fashion is generalised and leaves the privileged medium of woman so as to be open to all, the prohibition placed on the body is also generalised in a more subtle form than puritan repression: in the form of general desexualisation. For it was only under repression that the body had strong sexual potential: it then appeared as a captivating demand. Abandoned to the signs of fashion, the body is sexually disenchanted, it becomes a *mannequin*, a term whose lack of sexual discrimination suits its meaning well.[7] The mannequin is sex in its entirety, but sex without qualities. Fashion is its sex. Or rather, it is in fashion that sex is lost as difference but is generalised as reference (as simulation). Nothing is sexed any longer, everything is sexualised. The masculine and the feminine themselves rediscover, having once lost their particularity, the chance of an unlimited second existence. Hence, in our culture alone, sexuality impregnates all signification, and this is because signs have, for their part, invested the entire sexual sphere.

In this way the current paradox becomes clear: we simultaneously witness the 'emancipation' of woman and a fresh upsurge of fashion. This is because fashion has only to do with the feminine, and not with women. Society in its entirety is becoming feminine to the extent that discrimination against women is coming to an end (as it is for madmen, children, etc., being the normal consequence of the logic of exclusion). Hence *prendre son pied*, at once 'to find one's feet', and a familiar French expression of the female orgasm [*jouissance*], has now become generalised, while simultaneously, of course, destabilising its signification. We must also note however, that woman can only be 'liberated' and 'emancipated' as 'force of pleasure' and 'force of fashion', exactly as the proletariat is only ever liberated as the 'labour force'. The above illusion is radical. The historical definition of the feminine is formed on the basis of the destiny of the body and sex bound up with fashion. The historical liberation of the feminine can only be the realisation of this destiny writ large (which immediately becomes the liberation of the whole world, without however losing its discriminatory character). At the same moment that woman accesses a universal labour modelled on the proletariat, the whole world also accesses the emancipation of sex and fashion, modelled on women. We can immediately, and clearly, see that fashion is a labour, to which it becomes necessary to accord equal historical importance to 'material' labour. It is also of capital importance (which by the same token becomes part of capital!) to produce commodities in accordance with the market, and to produce the body in accordance with the rules of sex and fashion. The division of labour won't settle where we think, or rather there is no division of labour at all: the production of the body, the production of death, the production of signs and the production of commodities – these are only modalities of one and the same system. Doubtless it is even worse in fashion: for if the worker is divided from himself under the signs of exploitation and of the reality principle, woman is divided from herself and her body under the signs of beauty and the pleasure principle!

The Insubvertible

History says, or so the story goes, that the critique of fashion (O. Burgelin) was a product of conservative thinking in the nineteenth century, but that today, with the advent of socialism, this critique has been revived by the left. The one went with religion and the other with revolution. Fashion corrupts morals, fashion abolishes the class struggle. Although this critique of fashion may have passed over to the left, it does not necessarily signify an historical reversal: perhaps it signifies that with regard to morality and morals, the left has quite simply taken over from the right, and that, in the name of the revolution, it has adopted the moral order and its classic prejudices. Ever since the principle of revolution entered into morals, quite a categorical imperative, the whole political order, even the left, has become a moral order.

Fashion is immoral, this is what's in question, and all power (or all those who dream of it) necessarily hates it. There was a time when immorality was recognised, from Machiavelli to Stendhal, and when somebody like Mandeville could show, in the eighteenth century, that a society could only be revolutionized through its vices, that it is its immorality that gives it its dynamism. Fashion still holds to this immorality: it knows nothing of value-systems, nor of criteria of judgement: good and evil, beauty and ugliness, the rational/irrational – it plays within and beyond these, it acts therefore as the subversion of all order, including revolutionary rationality. It is power's hell, the hell of the relativity of all signs which all power is forced to crush in order to maintain its own signs. Thus fashion is taken on by contemporary youth, as a resistance to every imperative, a resistance without an ideology, without objectives.

On the other hand, there is no possible subversion of fashion since it has no system of reference to contradict (it is its own system of reference). We cannot escape fashion (since fashion itself makes the refusal of fashion into a fashion feature – blue-jeans are an historical example of this). While it is true that one can always escape the reality principle of the content, one can never escape the reality principle of the code. Even while rebelling against the content, one more and more closely obeys the logic of the code. Why so? It is the diktat of 'modernity'. Fashion leaves no room for revolution except to go back over the very genesis of the sign that constitutes it. Furthermore, the alternative to fashion does not lie in a 'liberty' or in some kind of step beyond towards a truth of the world and systems of reference. It lies in a deconstruction of both the form of the sign of fashion and the principle of signification itself, just as the alternative to political economy can only lie in the deconstruction of the commodity/form and the principle of production itself.

Notes

1. [I have translated the French noun *jouissance* and the verb *jouir*, whose admixture of libidinal and political economy is well known in contemporary French theory, variously according to context. In the main I have translated it as 'enjoyment'; sometimes as 'intense pleasure', with the French following in brackets. – tr.]

2. [*Pulsion* is the French translation of Freud's *Trieb*, which the *Standard Edition* translates as 'instinct', a move which for many reasons has been found inadequate. The current translation is 'drive', which I have sometimes used for reasons of euphony. The French *pulsion*, however, seems preferable since it confers a less mechanistically dominated energetics than does 'drive'. These are the only options used throughout the present text. – tr.]

3. But we have seen that the economic today conforms with the same indeterminacy, ethics drops out in aid of a 'finality without end' of production whereby it rejoins the vertiginous futility of fashion. We may say then of production what Barthes says of fashion: 'The system then abandons the meaning yet does so without giving up any of the *spectacle of signification*' [*The Fashion System*, p. 288, J.B's emphasis].

4. The three modalities of the 'body of fashion' cited by Barthes (cf. *The Fashion System*, pp. 258–9):

   1. It is a pure form, with no attributes of its own, tautologically defined by dress.
   2. Or: every year we decree that a certain body (a certain type of body) is in fashion. This is another way of making the two coincide.
   3. We develop dress in such a way that it transforms the real body and makes it signify the ideal body of fashion.

   These modalities more or less correspond to the historical evolution of the status of the model: from the initial, but non-professional model (the high-society woman) to the professional mannequin whose body also plays the role of a sexual model up until the latest (current) phase where everybody has become a mannequin – each is called, summoned to invest their bodies with the rules of the game of fashion – the whole world is an 'agent' of fashion, just as the whole world becomes a productive agent. General effusion of fashion to all and sundry and at every level of signification.

   It is also possible to tie these phases of fashion in with the phases of the successive concentration of capital, with the structuration of the economic sphere of fashion (variation of fixed capital, of the organic composition of capital, the speed of the rotation of commodities, of finance capital and industrial capital – cf. *Utopie*, Oct. 1971, no. 4). However, the analytic principle of this interaction of the economic and signs is never clear. More than in the direct relation with the economic, it is in a sort of movement homologous to the extension of the market that the historical extension of the sphere of fashion can be seen:

   1. In the beginning fashion is concerned only with scattered details, minimal variations, supported by marginal categories, in a system which remains essentially homogeneous and traditional (just as in the first phase of political economy only the surplus of a yield is exchanged, which in other circumstances is largely exhausted in consumption within the group – a very weak section of the free labour force and the salariat). Fashion then is what is outside culture, outside the group, the foreigner, it is the city-dweller to the country-dweller, etc.

   2. Fashion progressively and virtually integrates all the signs of culture, and regulates

the exchange of signs, just as in a second phase all material production is virtually integrated by political economy. Both systems anterior to production and exchange are effaced in the universal dimension of the market. All cultures come to play within fashion's universality. In this phase fashion's reference is the dominant cultural class, which administers the distinctive values of fashion.

3. Fashion is diffused everywhere and quite simply becomes *the way of life* [*le mode de vie*]. It invests every sphere which had so far escaped it. The whole world supports and reproduces it. It recuperates its own negativity (the fact of not being in fashion), it becomes its own signified (like production at the stage of reproduction). In a certain way, however, it is also its end.

5. For it is not true that a dress or a supple body stocking which lets the body 'play' 'frees' something or other: in the order of signs, this is a supplementary adulteration. To denude structures is not to return to the zero degree of truth, it is to wrap them in a new signification which gets added to all the others. So it will be the beginning of a new cycle of forms. So much for the cycle of formal innovation, so much for the logic of fashion, and no-one can do anything about it. To 'liberate' structures (of the body, the unconscious, the functional truth of the object in design, etc.) still amounts to clearing the way for the *universalisation of the system of fashion* (it is the only universalisable system, the only one that can control the circulation of every sign, including contradictory ones). A *bourgeois* revolution in the system of forms, with the appearance of a bourgeois political revolution; this too clears the way for the *universalisation of the system of the market*.

6. There are of course other, social and historical, reasons for this affinity: woman's (or youths') marginality or her social relegation. But this is no different: social repression and a malefic sexual aura are always brought together under the same categories.

7. [The French *mannequin* signifies a masculine, a feminine and a neuter; a man with no strength of character who is easily led, a woman employed by a large couturier to present models wearing its new collection, and an imitation human. Its gender is masculine (*le mannequin*). – tr.]

4

THE BODY, OR THE MASS GRAVE
OF SIGNS

A Sex is a mass grave of Signs
The Sign is a disembodied Sex

The Marked Body

The entire contemporary history of the body is the history of its demarcation, the network of marks and signs that have since covered it, divided it up, annihilated its difference and its radical ambivalence in order to organise it into a structural material for sign-exchange, equal to the sphere of objects, to resolve its playful virtuality and its symbolic exchange (not to be confused with sexuality) into sexuality taken as a determining agency, a *phallic* agency entirely organised around the fetishisation of the phallus as the general equivalent. In this sense, the body is, under the sign of sexuality as it is currently understood, that is, under the sign of its 'liberation', caught up in a process whose functioning and strategy themselves derive from political economics.

Fashion, advertising, nude-look, nude theatre, strip-tease: the play-script of erection and castration is everywhere. It has an absolute variety and an absolute monotony. Ankle boots and thigh boots, a short coat under a long coat, over the elbow gloves and stocking-tops on the thigh, hair over the eyes or the stripper's G-string, but also bracelets, necklaces, rings, belts, jewels and chains – the scenario is the same everywhere: a mark that takes on the force of a sign and thereby even a perverse erotic function, a boundary to figure castration which *parodies* castration as the symbolic articulation of *lack*, under the structural form of a bar articulating two *full* terms (which then on either side play the part of the signifier and the signified in the classical economy of the sign). The bar makes a zone of the body work as its corresponding terms here. This is not an erogenous zone at all, but an erotic, eroticised zone, a fragment erected into the phallic signifier of a sexuality that has become a pure and simple concept, a pure and simple signified.

In this fundamental schema, analogous to that of the linguistic sign, castration is *signified* (it passes into the state of a sign) and therefore subject to misrecognition [*méconnaissance*]. The nude and the not-nude play in a structural opposition and thus contribute to the *designation* of the fetish. The image of the stocking top on the thigh derives its erotic potential not from the proximity of the real genital and its *positive* promise (from this naïve functionalist perspective, the naked thigh would have to play the same role), but from the apprehension surrounding the genitals (the panic of recognising castration) being *arrested in a staged castration*. The innocuous mark, the line of the stocking above which, instead of lack, ambivalence and the chasm, there is nothing more than a sexual plenitude. The naked thigh and, metonymically, the entire body has become a *phallic effigy* by means of this caesura, a fetishistic object to be contemplated and manipulated, deprived of all its menace.[1] As in fetishism, desire can then be fulfilled at the cost of warding off castration and the death drive.

Eroticisation always consists in the erectility of a fragment of the barred body, in a phallic phantasmatisation of everything beyond the bar in the position of the signifier and the simultaneous reduction of sexuality to the rank of the signified (*represented* value). A reassuring structural conjuring operation enables the subject to be recovered as phallus, to identify himself with and reappropriate this fragment of the body, or the entire positivised, fetishised body in the fulfilment of a desire that will for ever misconstrue his proper loss.

We can read this operation in the slightest detail. The tight-fitting bracelet round the arm or the ankle, the belt, the necklace and the ring establish the foot, the waist, the neck or the finger as *erectile parts*. Ultimately there is no further need for a mark or a visible sign: stripped of signs, it is nevertheless on the basis of a phantasmatic separation, thus tricking and eluding castration, that the body's eroticity functions exclusively in *nudity*. Even if the body is not structuralised by some mark (a jewel, some make-up or a wound can all work to this end), even if it is not fragmented, the bar is always there as the clothes come off, signalling the emergence of the body as phallus, even if, or, rather, especially if, it is a woman's body: this is the whole art of strip-tease, which we will come back to later.

We should reinterpret so-called Freudian 'symbolism' in this sense. It is not by virtue of their protuberant form that the foot, finger, nose or some other part of the body may act as metaphors for the penis (in accordance with a schema of analogy between these diverse signifiers and the real penis): rather, their phallic value rests solely on the basis of phantasmatic cut that erects them (the 'castrated' penis is a penis *because* it is castrated). Full, phallicised terms marked out by the bar that makes them autonomous. Everything beyond this bar is the phallus, everything is resolved into a phallic equivalent, even the female genitals, or any gaping organ or object traditionally listed as a symbol of the 'feminine'. The body is not arranged into masculine or feminine symbols: at a much deeper level, it is the site of the drama and the denial of castration, illustrated by the Chinese custom (cited by Freud in 'Fetishism' [in *Standard Edition*, ed. and tr. James Strachey, London: Hogarth Press and the Institute of Psychoanalysis, Vol. 21, 1961]) where, beginning by mutilating a woman's foot, they then venerate the mutilated foot as a fetish. The entire body is susceptible to innumerable forms of marking and mutilation,[2] followed by phallic veneration (erotic exaltation). This, rather than the anamorphosis of the genital organs, is where the body's secret lies.

In this way, rouged lips are phallic (face paint and make-up are pre-eminent in the arsenal of the body's structural enhancement).

A made-up mouth no longer speaks, its beatified lips, half open, half closed, are no longer used for speaking, eating, vomiting or kissing. Beyond these always ambivalent exchange functions – introjection and rejection – and on the basis of their denegation, the perverse erotic and cultural function is established. This fascinating mouth, like an artificial sign, like cultural labour, the game and the rules of the game, neither speaks nor eats, and no-one kisses it. The painted mouth, objectified like a jewel, derives its intense erotic value not, as one might imagine, from accentuating its role as an erotogenic orifice, but conversely from its closure – paint being as it were the trace of the phallic, the mark that institutes its *phallic exchange-value*: an erectile mouth, a sexual tumescence whereby woman becomes erect and man's desire will be received in its own image.[3]

Mediated by this structural labour, desire, implacable as it is when it is based on loss, on the void between one and the other, becomes *negotiable* in terms of signs and exchanged phallic values, indexed on a general phallic equivalent where each party operates in accordance with a contract and converts its own enjoyment into cash in terms of a phallic accumulation: a perfect situation for a *political economy* of desire.

The same holds true for the gaze. The strand of hair falling over the eye (and every other ocular erotic artifact) implements the denegation of the gaze as the unending dimension of castration and, at the same time, as an amorous offering. When the eyes are metamorphosed by make-up, there is an ecstatic reduction of the threat and the gaze of the other where the subject may be reflected in his proper lack, but where he may also be vertiginously eliminated if these eyes open on him. These sophisticated eyes, these Medusa's[4] eyes, gaze at nobody, they don't open onto anything. Caught in the labour of the sign, they possess the sign's redundancy: they revel in their own fascination, and their seduction derives from this perverse onanism.

We could go on: what is true of these privileged sites of symbolic exchange (the mouth and the gaze) is also true of any part of the body whatever when it is caught in the process of erotic signification. But the most beautiful object, which always epitomises this *mise-en-scène* and seems to be the key to the vault of the political economy of the body, is the female body. The female body unveiled in the thousand variants of eroticism is obviously the emergence of the phallus, the fetish-object, an immense labour of phallic simulation at the same time as the endlessly repeated spectacle of castration. With the immense diffusion of images in the meticulous ritual of the strip-tease, the smooth and faultless potency [*puissance*] of the exhibited female body always functions as a phallic display, a potency medusified, paralysed, by a relentless phallic demand (hence the profound imaginary affinity between the escalation of the erotic and productivist growth).

The erotic privilege of the female body works for women just as much as for men. In fact, a single perverse structure works for everyone: centred on the denial of castration, it works with the female body as with the immanence of castration.[5] Thus the logical progression of the system (here once again homologous to political economy) leads to an erotic recrudescence of the female body because it best lends itself to phallic general equivalence, being deprived of a penis. The male body is not subject to the same erotic return (far from it) because it permits neither the fascinating reminder of castration, nor the spectacle of constantly overcoming it. It can never really become a smooth, closed and perfect object since it is stamped with the 'truc' *mark* (the one the general system valorises) and in consequence is less susceptible to *demarcation*, to this long task of phallic formation. Of course, it is by no means certain that one day it too may be actualised as a phallic variation. We are approaching a new order where there is no erectile advertising nor any erectile nudity: it is at this cost that there can be a controlled transfer of erectility across the entire spectrum of objects, including the female body. At the limit, the erection itself is not incompatible with the system.[6]

We must see how, in woman's erotic 'privilege', historical and social subjection operate. Not by some mechanism of 'alienation' like a double of social alienation, but by trying to see *if the same process of misrecognition* [*méconnaissance*] works towards all political discrimination as towards sexual difference in fetishism, resulting in a fetishism of class or of the dominated group, along with a sexual overvaluation so as to better stave off the crucial examination that it conducts of the order of power. If such reflections are accurate then all signifying material of the erotic order is made up of nothing but the outfits of slaves (chains, collars, whips, etc.), savages (negritude, bronzed skin, nudity, tattooing) and all the signs of the dominated classes and races. This is how it is for the woman in her body, annexed to a phallic order which, when expressed in political terms, condemns her to a non-existence.[7]

Secondary Nudity

Any body or part of the body can operate functionally in the same way, provided that it is subject to the same erotic *discipline*: it is necessary and sufficient that it be as closed and as smooth as possible, faultless, without orifice and 'lacking' nothing, every erogenous difference being conjured up by the structural bar that will *design(ate)* this body (in the double sense of 'designate' and 'design'), visible in clothing, jewellery or make-up, invisible but always present in complete nudity, since it then envelops the body like a *second skin*.

The ubiquity of phrases such as 'almost naked', 'naked without being naked, as if you were naked' and the tights in which 'you are more naked than is natural' in the discourse of advertising is characteristic of this. This is all in order to reconcile the naturalist ideal of living 'in touch with' your body with the commercial imperative of surplus-value. It is much more interesting, however, to note that in this discourse nudity is defined as secondary nudity, the nudity of tights X or Y, of the veil so transparent that 'their transparency even affects you'. Moreover, this nudity is very often relayed by the mirror – in any case, it is in this reduplication that the woman is united with 'the body of her dreams: her own'. And for once the advertising myth is absolutely right: there is no nudity other than that which is reduplicated in signs, which envelops itself in its signified truth and reconstructs, like a mirror, the fundamental rule of the body as erotic matter, the nudity of becoming, in order to be phallically celebrated, the diaphanous, smooth, depilated substance of a glorious and unsexed body.

The James Bond film *Goldfinger* provides a perfect example of this. In it, a woman is painted in gold, all her orifices are blocked up in a radical make-up, making her body a flawless phallus (that the make-up should be gold only emphasises the homology with political economy), which of course amounts to death. The nude gold-varnished playgirl will die by having incarnated to an absurd extent the phantasm of the erotic, but this is the case for every skin in functional aesthetics, in the mass culture of the body. 'Body hugging' tights, girdles, stockings, gloves, dresses and clothes, not to mention sun-tans: the *leitmotiv* of the 'second skin' and the transparent pellicle always come to vitrify the body.

The skin itself is defined not as 'nudity' but as an erogenous zone, a sensuous medium of contact and exchange, a metabolism of absorption and excretion. The body does not stop at this porous skin, full of holes and orifices; only metaphysics institutes it as the borderline of the body. This body is denied in the interests of a second, non-porous skin that neither exudes nor excretes,[8] that is, neither hot nor cold (it is 'cool' and 'warm': optimally air-conditioned), with no proper density (a clear or, in French, 'transparent' complexion), and above all without orifices (it is smooth). As functional as a cellophane wrapper. All these qualities (coolness, suppleness, transparency, one-piece) are qualities of *closure*, a zero degree resulting from the denegation of ambivalent extremes. The same goes for the 'youth' of the body, which will neutralise the old–young paradigm in an eternal youth of simulation.

The vitrification of nudity is related to the obsessional function of the protective wax or plastic coating of objects and the labour of scrubbing and cleaning intended to keep them in a constant state of propriety, of flawless abstraction. In both cases, vitrification and protection, it is a matter of blocking secretions (patina, oxidisation, dust), preventing them from collapsing and maintaining them in a sort of abstract immortality.

'Design(at)ed' nudity implies that there is nothing behind the lattice of signs that it weaves, especially not a body: neither a body of labour, nor a body of pleasure; neither an erogenous body nor a broken body. It formally exceeds all that in a simulacrum of the pacified body, just like Brigitte Bardot, who is 'beautiful because she fits her dress exactly' – a functional equation without any unknown factors. As opposed to the rent skin and torn muscles of the anatomical body, the modern body comes much more under the heading of the inflatable, a theme illustrated by a cartoon strip in *Lui* where we see a stripper, her clothes scattered on the floor around her, making one final gesture: she 'uncorks' her navel and deflates immediately, leaving only a small heap of skin on the stage.

A utopia of nudity, of the body *present* in its truth: this is at most the ideology of the body that can be *represented*. The Indian (I no longer know which one) said: 'The naked body is an expressionless mask hiding each of our true natures.' By this he meant that the body only has meaning when it is marked, covered in inscriptions. Alphonse Allais' Rajah, a fanatic for denotation and truth, translated this contrariwise: not content to have made the dancing girl undress, he flays her alive.

The body is not at all the surface of being, a virginal beach without tracks, nature. It has only taken on this 'original' value through repression: and so, *to liberate the body as such in accordance with naturalist illusions is to liberate it as repressed*. Even in nudity, the body turns back on itself, shrouding itself with an ethereal and ineluctable censorship: the second skin. For the skin, like every sign that takes on the value of a sign, is doubled through signification: it is always already the second skin, not the final skin, but always the only one.

In the redundancy of the nudity-sign, which works towards a reconstruction of the body as a phantasm of totalisation, we again find the infinite speculation of the conscious subject through its mirror-image, capturing and bringing a formal resolution to the insurmountable division of the subject in this reduplication. The signs inscribed on the body, where the death drive is also tangentially inscribed, merely repeat the metaphysical operations of the conscious subject on corporeal material. 'By beating our skins we beat metaphysics back into our brains', as Artaud said.

Closure of the mirror, phallic reduplication of the mark: in both cases the subject is seduced by itself. It seduces its own desire and conjures it up in its own body, doubled in signs. Behind the exchange of signs, behind the labour of the code which functions as a fortification of the phallic, the subject can hide away and recover its strength: shying away from the desire of the other (from its own lack), and, as it were, to see (to see oneself) without being seen. The logic of the sign meets the logic of perversion.

It is important here to make a radical distinction between the labour of inscription and the mark at the level of the body in 'primitive' societies and that which takes place in our current system. They are too easily mixed up in the category of the 'symbolic expression' of the body. As if the body had always been what it is, as if archaic tattooing had the same meaning as make-up, as if, beyond all the revolutions of the mode of production, there existed an unexchanged mode of signification at the basis of every age extending even into the sphere of political economy. In archaic society, as opposed to our own, where *signs are exchanged under the regime of the general equivalent*, where they have an exchange-value in a system of phallic abstraction and of the imaginary saturation of the subject, marking the body as a masking practice, all have the function of immediately actualising symbolic exchange, gift-exchange with the gods or within the group. Here, negotiation is not a *negotiation of identity by the subject* behind the mask, nor the manipulation of the sign: on the contrary, it *consumes the subject's identity* and, like the subject, enters the game of possession and dispossession, the entire body becoming, just like gods and women, material for symbolic exchange. Finally, within this standard schema of signification, our transcendental Signifier/Signified, our Phallus/Subjectivity, which governs our entire political economy of the body, has not yet emerged. When the Indian (perhaps the same one) says 'everything is a face to me', in response to the white man's questions as to why he is naked, he is saying that his entire body (which, as we have seen is never nude) is given over to symbolic exchange, while for us, nudity has a tendency to be reduced to a single face and a single look. For the Indian, bodies gaze at each other and exchange all their signs. These signs are consumed in an incessant relaying and refer neither to a transcendental law of value, nor to a private appropriation of the subject. For us, the body is sealed in signs, increasing its value through a calculus of signs that it exchanges under the law of equivalence and the reproduction of the subject. The subject is no longer eliminated in the exchange, it speculates. The subject, not the savage, is enmeshed in fetishism: through the investment [*faire-valoir*] of its body, it is the subject that is fetishised by the law of value.

Strip-tease

Bernardin (manager of the Crazy Horse Saloon):

> You neither strip nor tease . . . you parody . . . I am a hoaxer: you give the impression of giving the naked truth, there could not be a greater hoax.
>
> This is the opposite of life, because when she is nude, she has many more adornments than when she is dressed. Bodies are made up with extremely beautiful special foundations, leaving the skin satin smooth . . . She has gloves that cut off on her arms, which is always so beautiful, green, red or black stockings on her legs, also cut off at the thigh . . . .
>
> Dream strip-tease: the space-woman. She was dancing in the void. Because the more slowly a woman dies, the more erotic it is. So I believe that this would reach its apex with a woman in a state of weightlessness.
>
> Beach nudity has nothing to do with stage nudity. On stage the women are goddesses, they are untouchable . . . . The wave of nudity sweeping through the

theatre and elsewhere is superficial, it is limited to a mental act: I am going to take my clothes off, I am going to show nude actors and actresses. Precisely these limits make it uninteresting. Other people present reality: here, I am only suggesting the impossible.

The reality of sex which is flaunted everywhere, diminishes the subjectivity of eroticism.

Iridescent under intense lights, embellished by a voluminous orange wig, the whole thing set off with jewels, Usha Barock, an Austrian-Polish half-caste, will continue the tradition of the Crazy Horse: creating what you cannot hold in your arms.

The strip-tease is a dance, perhaps the only one, and definitely the most original in the contemporary Western world. Its secret is a woman's auto-erotic celebration of her own body, which becomes desirable in exact proportion to the intensity of this celebration. Without this narcissistic mirage that is the substance of every gesture, without this gestural repertoire of caresses that come to envelop the body, making it into an emblem as a phallic object, there would be no erotic effect. A sublime masturbation whose slow pace, as Bernardin said, is fundamental. This slow pace marks the fact that the gestures with which the girl covers herself (stripping, caressing, even as far as mimicking orgasm [*jouissance*]), come from 'the other'. Her gestures weave a phantom sexual partner around her. By the same token, however, the other is excluded, since she replaces it and appropriates its gestures for herself following a work of condensation which is not in fact far removed from dream-processes. The whole erotic secret (and labour) of the strip lies in this evocation and revocation of the other, through gestures so slow as to be poetic, as is slow motion film of explosions or falls, because something in this, before being completed, has *time to pass you by*, which, if such a thing exists, constitutes the perfection of desire.[9]

The only good strip is the one that reflects the body in the mirror of gestures and follows this rigorous narcissistic abstraction: the gestural repertoire being the mobile equivalent of the panoply of signs and marks at work in situations such as erectile stagings of the body at every level of fashion, make-up and advertising.[10] The bad strip is obviously a pure undressing, which simply restores a state of nudity, the alleged finality of the spectacle, lacking any hypnosis of the body, in order to give it directly over to the audience's lusts. It is not that the bad strip is unable to capture the audience's desire – on the contrary – but because the girl was unable to recreate her body as an object *for herself*, because she was unable to effect this transubstantiation of profane (realist, naturalist) nudity into sacred nudity, where a body describes its own contours, feels itself (but always across a kind of subtle void, a sensual distance, of a circumlocution which, once again, as in the dream, reflects the fact that gestures are like a mirror, that the body is turned back on itself by this mirror of gestures).

The bad strip is threatened by nudity or immobility (or the absence of 'rhythm', the awkward gesture): all that remains on the stage is a woman and an 'obscene' (in the strict sense of the term) body, rather than the closed sphere of a body which, by means of this aura of gestures, design(ate)s itself as a phallus and specifies itself as a *sign* of desire. To succeed is not at all to 'make love with the audience' as is generally thought, it is rather precisely the opposite. The stripper is a goddess according to Bernardin, and the prohibition cast over her, which she traces around herself, does not signify that you cannot *take* anything from her (cannot pass into sexual acting-out, this repressive situation belongs to the bad strip), but rather that you cannot *give* her anything, because she gives herself everything, hence the complete transcendence that makes her fascinating.

The slow pace of the gestures comes from the priesthood and from transubstantiation. Not bread and wine in this case, but the transubstantiation of the body into the phallus. Every piece of clothing that falls brings her no closer to nudity, to the naked 'truth' of sex (although the entire spectacle is also fuelled by the voyeuristic drive, haunted by a violent laying bare and the rape-drive, but these phantasms run counter to the spectacle). As her clothes fall, she design(ate)s what she strips down as a phallus – she unveils herself-as-other and the same game becomes profound, the body emerging more and more as a phallic effigy to the rhythm of the strip. This is not then a game of stripping signs away in order to reveal a sexual 'depth', but, on the contrary, an ascending play of the construction of signs – each mark deriving an erotic force by means of its labour as a sign, that is, by means of the reversal it effects of what has never been (loss and castration) into what it design(ate)s instead to take its place: the phallus.[11] This is why the strip-tease is slow: it ought to go as fast as possible if it is simply a matter of preparing for sex. It is slow because it is discourse, the construction of signs, the meticulous elaboration of deferred meaning. The gaze too testifies to this phallic transfiguration. A fixed gaze is an essential asset of the good stripper. This is commonly interpreted as a distantiation technique, a coolness intended to mark the limits of this erotic situation. Yes and no: the fixed gaze that merely marks a prohibition would once more turn the strip into a kind of repressive pornodrama. That is not a good strip, the mastery of the gaze has nothing to do with a willed 'cool': if it is cool, as with mannequins, it is on condition that cool is redefined as a very specific quality of the whole contemporary media and body culture, and no longer belongs to the order of the hot and the cold. This gaze is the neutralised gaze of auto-erotic fascination, of the woman-object gazing at herself with her eyes wide open, then closing her eyes on herself. This is not the effect of desire undergoing censorship, it is the peak of perfection and perversion. It is the fulfilment of the entire sexual system that has it that a woman is never more completely herself, and therefore never so seductive, as when she accepts giving *herself* pleasure first of all, taking pleasure in herself, having no other desire or transcendence than that of her own image.

The ideal body, as outlined in this statute, is that of the mannequin. The mannequin offers the model of every phallic instrumentalisation of the body. The word itself states this: *manne-ken*, 'little man', the child or the penis. The woman wraps her own body in a sophisticated manipulation, a flawless and intense narcissistic discipline, which effectively makes it the paradigm of seduction. And doubtless it is here, in this perverse process that turns her and her sacralised body into a living phallus, that we find the *real castration of woman* (also of man, but according to a model which tends to crystallise around the woman). To be castrated is to be covered with phallic substitutes. The woman is covered in them, she is summoned to produce a phallus from her body, on pain of perhaps not being desirable. And if women are not fetishists it is because they perform this labour of continual fetishisation on themselves, they become *dolls*. We know that the doll is a fetish produced in order to be continually dressed and undressed, dressed up and dressed down. It is this play of covering and uncovering that gives the doll its childhood symbolic value, it is in this play, conversely, that every object- and symbolic relation regresses when the woman *turns herself* into a doll, becomes her own fetish and the fetish of the other.[12] As Freud says: 'pieces of underclothing, which are so often chosen as a fetish, crystallise the last moment of undressing, the last moment in which the woman could still be regarded as phallic ('Fetishism', in *Standard Edition*, Vol. 21, p. 155).

Thus the fascination of the strip-tease as a spectacle of castration derives from the immanence of discovering, or rather seeking and never managing to discover, or better still searching by all available means without ever discovering, that there is nothing there. 'An aversion, which is never absent in any fetishist, to the real female genitals remains a *stigma indelibile* of the repression that has taken place' (ibid., p. 154). The experience of this unthinkable absence, which subsequently remains constitutive of every 'revelation', every 'unveiling' (and in particular the sexual status of 'truth'), the obsession with the hole is changed into the converse fascination with the phallus. From this mystery of the denied, barred, gaping void, a whole population of fetishes surges forth (objects, phantasms, body-objects). The fetishised woman's body itself comes to bar the point of absence from which it arose, it comes to bar this vertigo in all its erotic presence, a 'token of a triumph over the threat of castration and a protection against it' (ibid., p. 154).

There is nothing behind this succession of veils, there never has been, and the impulse which is always pressing forward in order to discover this is strictly speaking the process of castration; not the recognition of lack, but the fascinating vertigo of this nihilating substance. The entire march of the West, ending in a vertiginous compulsion for realism, is affected by this myopia of castration. Pretending to restore the 'ground of things', we unconsciously 'eye up' the void. Instead of a recognition of castration, we establish all kinds of phallic alibis; then, following a fascinated compulsion, we seek to dismiss these alibis one by one in order to uncover the 'truth', which is always castration, but which is in the last instance always revealed to be castration *denied*.

Planned Narcissism

All this leads us to repeat the question of narcissism in terms of social control. There is a passage in Freud that brings out everything we have been discussing up to this point:

> Women, especially if they grow up with good looks, develop a certain self-contentment which compensates them for the social restrictions that are imposed on them in their choice of object. Strictly speaking, it is only themselves that such women love with an intensity comparable to that of the man's love for them. Nor does their need lie in the direction of loving, but of being loved; and the man who fulfils this condition is the one who finds favour with them. . . . Such women have the greatest fascination for men, not only for aesthetic reasons, since as a rule they are the most beautiful, but also because of a combination of interesting psychological factors. ('On narcissism: An introduction', in *Standard Edition*, Vol. 14, 1957, pp. 88–9)

There follows a question 'of children, cats, and certain animals' which 'we env[y] . . . for maintaining . . . an unassailable libidinal position', and for the 'narcissistic consistency . . . they manage' (ibid., p. 89). In the current system of erotics, however, it is not a question of primary narcissism bound to a sort of 'polymorphous perversity'. It is rather a matter of the displacement of '[the narcissism] enjoyed in childhood by the actual ego [onto] the ego-ideal', or, more precisely, the projection of the 'narcissistic perfection of . . . childhood' (ibid., p. 94) as the ideal ego which, as we know, is bound up with repression and sublimation. The gratification the woman takes from her body and the rhetoric of beauty reflect, in fact, a fierce discipline, an ethics which parallels the one that governs the economic order. Neither can one distinguish, in the framework of this functional aesthetics of the body, the process by which the subject submits to its narcissistic ideal ego from that by which society enjoins the subject to conform to this ideal, leaving it no other alternative but to love itself, to invent itself and invest itself in accordance with socially imposed rules. This narcissism is therefore radically distinct from that of the cat or the child *in that it is placed under the sign of value*. This is a planned narcissism, a managed and functional exaltation of beauty as the exploitation and exchange of signs. Self-seduction is only apparently gratuitous; in fact its every detail is finalised by the norm of the optimal management of the body on the market of signs. Modern erotics, whatever phantasms are in play in it, is organised around a rational economy of value, differentiating it absolutely from primary or infantile narcissism.

Thus fashion and advertising sketch the auto-erotic *Carte du Tendre*[13] and plan its exploration: you are responsible for your body and must invest in it and make it yield benefits – not in accordance with the order of enjoyment – but with the *signs* reflected and mediated by mass models, and in accordance with an organisation chart of prestige, etc. A strange strategy is operative here; there is a diversion and transfer of investments from the body and the erogenous zones towards *staging the body and erotogeneity*. From now on, narcissistic seduction becomes associated with the body or with parts of the body objectified by a technique, by objects, gestures and a play of marks and signs. This *neo-narcissism* is associated with the *manipulation* of the body as value. This is a planned economy of the body based on a schema of libidinal and symbolic destructuration, an administered dismantling and restructuration of investments, a 'reappropriation' of the body according to models of management and hence under the control of meaning, transferring the fulfilment of desire onto the code.[14] All this is established as a 'synthetic' narcissism which must be distinguished from the two classical forms of narcissism:

1. Primary, fusional narcissism.

2. Secondary narcissism: the investment of the body as distinct, the mirror of the ego. Integration of the ego by specular recognition and the gaze of the other.

3. Tertiary, 'synthetic', narcissism: rewriting the body, deconstructed as a 'personalised' Eros, that is, indexed on collective functional models. The homogenised body as the site of the industrial production of signs and differences, mobilised under the sign of programmatic seduction. The interception of ambivalence in the interests of a total positivisation of the body as the schema of seduction, satisfaction and prestige. The body as a *summation* of partial objects, the subject of which is the second person plural of consumption.[15] The interception of the subject's relation to its proper lack in its body, by the body which has itself become the medium of totalisation. This was made admirably apparent in the film *Le Mépris*, with Brigitte Bardot, examining her own body in a mirror, offering each part of it to the erotic approval of the other, the finished product being a formal addition as object: 'So, d'you love every bit of me?' The body becomes a total system of signs arranged by models under the general equivalent of the phallic cult, just as capital becomes the total system of exchange-value under the general equivalent of money.

Incestuous Manipulation

The current 'liberation' of the body necessarily undergoes this narcissism. The 'liberated' body is a body where law and prohibition, which once used to censor sex and the body from the outside, are somehow interiorised as a narcissistic variable. External constraints have changed into the constituency of the sign, a closed simulation. And if, in the Name-of-the-Father, the puritan law was initially and in a violent manner brought to bear on genital sexuality, the current phase corresponds to a mutation of all these characteristics:

1. It is no longer a violent repression, it has been pacified.

2. It is no longer fundamentally oriented towards genital sexuality, but is subsequently sanctioned by morality. This infinitely more subtle and radical stage of repression and control is oriented towards the *level of symbolic exchange itself*. That is to say, that repression, overcoming secondary sexuation (genitality and the social bisexual model) reaches

primary sexuation (erogenous difference and ambivalence, the subject's relation to his own lack on which the virtuality of all symbolic exchange is based).[16]

3. It no longer takes place in the Name-of-the-Father, but in some way in the Name-of-the-Mother. Because symbolic exchange is based on incest prohibition, every abolition (censorship, repression, destructuration) at this level of symbolic exchange signifies a process of incestuous regression. We have seen that the eroticisation of the phallic manipulation of the body is characterised as fetishisation: now, fetishistic perversion is defined by the fact that it has never gotten over the desire for the mother, making the fetish the replacement for what the fetishist lacked. All the labour of the perverse subject consists in settling into the mirage of himself as the living phallus of the mother so as to find a fulfilment of desire there: this is in fact the *fulfilment of the desire for the mother* (whereas traditional genital repression signifies the *fulfilment of the word of the Father*). We can see that this creates a strictly incestuous situation: the subject is no longer divided (he no longer abandons his phallic identity) and no longer divides (he no longer relinquishes any part of himself in a relation of symbolic exchange). This is fully defined by identification with the mother's phallus. Exactly the same process as in incest, where it never leaves the family.

Today, generally speaking, the same goes for the body: if the law of the Father or puritan morality has been (relatively speaking) avoided here, it is according to a libidinal economy characterised by the destructuration of the symbolic and the raising of the incest barrier. This general model of the fulfilment of desire, circulated by the mass-media, always comes with an obsessional and anxious quality that is utterly different from the basically hysterical puritan neurosis. It is no longer a matter of an anxiety bound up with Oedipal prohibition, but of an anxiety bound up with the fact, even *at the breast* of satisfaction and multiplied phallic enjoyment, in the 'heart'[17] of the gratifying, tolerant, soothing, permissive society, of being only the living marionette of the desire for the mother. A deeper anxiety than that of genital frustration, since it entails the abolition of the symbolic and of exchange, as well as the incestuous position where the subject comes to lack even his own lack. This anxiety is translated into and betrayed everywhere today as the phobic obsession with *manipulation*.

We are all, at every level, living with this subtle form of repression and alienation: its sources are elusive, its presence insidious and total, and the forms that a struggle might take remain undiscovered and perhaps cannot be found. This is because manipulation refers to the original manipulation of the subject by the mother as much as by his own phallus. We can no longer stand against this fusional and manipulatory plenitude, this dispossession, as we could against the transcendental law of the Father. Every future revolution must take account of this fundamental condition and, between the law of the Father and the desire for the mother, between the 'cycle' of repression and transgression and the cycle of regression and manipulation, rediscover the form of the articulation of the symbolic.[18]

Models of the Body

1. For medicine, the body of reference is the *corpse*. In other words, the corpse is the ideal limit of the body in its relation to the system of medicine. The accomplished practice of the corpse produces and reproduces medicine under the sign of the preservation of life.

2. For religion, the ideal reference of the body is the *animal* (instincts and appetites of the 'flesh'). The corpse as a mass grave, and its reincarnation beyond death as a carnal metaphor.

3. For the system of political economy, the ideal type of the body is the *robot*. The robot is the accomplished model of the functional 'liberation' of the body as labour power, it is the extrapolation of absolute, asexual, rational productivity (this may be a cerebral robot: the computer is always the extrapolation of the brain and labour power).

4. For the system of the political economy of the sign, the reference model of the body is the *mannequin* (along with all its variations). Contemporary with the robot (this is the ideal pair of science fiction: *Barbarella*), the mannequin also represents a totally functionalised body under the law of value, but this time as the site of the production of the value-*sign*. It is no longer labour power, but models of signification that are produced – not only sexual models of fulfilment, but *sexuality itself as a model*.

Behind the ideality of its ends (health, resurrection, rational productivity, liberated sexuality), every system thus alternately reveals the reductive phantasm on which it is articulated, and the delirious vision of the body that provides its strategy. Corpse, animal, machine and mannequin – these are the negative ideal types of the body, the fantastic reductions under which it is produced and written into successive systems.

The strange thing is that the body is nothing other than the models in which different systems have enclosed it, and at the same time every other thing: their radical alternative, the irreducible difference that denies them. We may still call the body this inverse virtuality. For this however – for the body as material of symbolic exchange – *there is no model*, no code, no ideal type, no controlling phantasm, *since there could not be a system* of the body as anti-object.

Phallus Exchange Standard

Since the Industrial Revolution, a single immense mutation has enveloped material goods, language and sexuality (the body), in accordance with a process that marks either the progressive generalisation of political economy, or the entrenchment of the law of value.

1. Products become commodities: use-value and exchange-value. Intended on the one hand for the abstract finality of the 'needs' that they

'satisfy', and on the other hand to the structural form that governs their production and exchange.

2. Language becomes a means of communication, a field of signification. It is arranged into signifiers and signifieds. Just like the separation of the commodity into a referential finality, language as a medium has the goal of expression, and is separated into the order of signifieds and a structural form that governs the exchange of signifiers: the code of *langue*.

In both cases, the passage to a functional finality, the rational assignation of an 'objective' content (use-value or signified-referent), seals the assignation of a structural form that is the form of political economy itself. In the 'neo-capitalist' (techno- and semiocratic) framework, this form is systematised at the expense of 'objective' reference: signifieds and use-values progressively disappear to the great advantage of the operation of the code and exchange-value.

At the term of this process, a term which today remains only an outline for us, the two 'sectors' of production and signification are merging. Products and commodities are produced as signs and messages and are regulated on the basis of the abstract configuration of language: transporting contents, values, finalities (their signifieds), they circulate according to an abstract general form organised by *models*. Commodities and messages both culminate in the same sign-status. Thereby, moreover, their reference is blurred in the face of the play of signifiers which can also in this way attain structural perfection. With the acceleration and proliferation of messages, information, signs and models, it is in *fashion* as a total cycle that the linear world of the commodity will reach completion.

The body and sexuality can be analysed in terms of everything that preceded it (use-value and exchange-value; signifier and signified).

1. We can show how sexuality is reduced, *in its current mode of 'liberation'*, to use-value (the satisfaction of 'sexual needs') and exchange-value (the play and calculation of the erotic signs governed by the circulation of models). We can also show that sexuality becomes separated as a *function*: from the collective function of the reproduction of the species, it passes to the individual functions of physiological equilibrium (part of a general hygiene), mental equilibrium, 'self-expression' or the expression of subjectivity, unconscious emanations, the ethics of sexual pleasure (what else?). In any case, sexuality becomes an *element of the economy of the subject*, an objective finality of the subject itself obedient to an order of finalities (whatever they might be).

2. The more it is functionalised (the more it submits to some transcendent reference that *speaks through it*, even if it were its own idealised principle, the libido, the signified's last subterfuge), the more sexuality takes on a structural form (like the products of industry or the language of communication). It reverts to the great oppositions (male/female) in whose disjunctions it is imprisoned, and crystallises around the exercise of a particular sexual *model*, attested to by a particular sexual organ, and closes the play of the body's signifiers.

3. The Male/Female *structure* becomes confused with the privilege granted to the *genital* function (whether reproductive or erotic). The privilege of genitality over all the body's erogenous virtualities reverberates in the structure of a male dominated social order, for structure hinges on biological difference. This is not merely in order to maintain a genuine difference, but, on the contrary, to establish a *general equivalence*, the Phallus becoming the absolute signifier around which all erogenous possibilities come to be measured, arranged, abstracted, and become equivalent. The *Phallus exchange standard* governs contemporary sexuality in its entirety, including its 'revolution'.

4. The emergence of the phallus as the general equivalent of sexuality, combined with the emergence of sexuality itself as the general equivalent of the virtualities of symbolic exchange, delineates the emergence of a *political economy of the body* which is established on the ruins of the body's symbolic economy. In the context of a general liberalisation, revelling in the current sexual 'revolution' is only the expression of the accession of the body and sexuality to the stage of political economy, a sign of their integration with the law of value and general equivalence.

5. From both angles – the promotion of *sexuality as function* or the promotion of *sexuality as structural discourse* – the subject turns out to be back with the fundamental norm of political economy: it thinks itself and locates itself sexually in terms of *equilibrium* (an equilibrium of functions under the sign of the identity of the ego) and *coherence* (the structural coherence of a discourse under the sign of the infinite reproduction of the code).

Just as 'design(at)ed' objects – seized by the political economy of the sign – obey an imperative of deprivation that reflects an ascetic economy of calculated functions; just as the sign in general has a functional tendency to divest itself in order to translate, as closely as possible, the adequation (of the signifier and the signified) which is its law and its reality principle, so the body seized by political economy also tends towards a formal nudity as if towards its absolute imperative. This nudity embodies all the labour of inscription and marks, fashion and make-up at the same time as the whole idealist perspective of 'liberation' makes no 'discoveries' or 'rediscoveries' concerning the body: it translates the *logical* metamorphosis of the body in the historical process of our societies. It translates the modern status of the body in its relation to political economy. Just as the divestment of objects characterises their assignation to a function, that is to say, *their neutralisation by the function*, so the body's nudity defines its assignation to the *sex/function*, its assignment to sex as function, that is to say, the *reciprocal neutralisation of the body and sex*.

Demagogy of the Body

Under the sign of the sexual revolution, the transfiguration of the pulsion as revolutionary substance and the unconscious as the subject of history.

Liberating the primary processes as the 'poetic' principle of social reality, *liberating the unconscious as use-value*, such is the imaginary that crystallises under the slogan of the body. Sex and the body are able to bear all these hopes because, repressed under whatever order used to cover our 'historic' societies, they have become *metaphors of radical negativity*. They want to make these metaphors pass into the state of a revolutionary *fact*. Error: to take the side of the body is a trap. We cannot take the side of the primary processes, this remains a secondary illusion.[19]

At best, the body will remain, theoretically too, eternally ambivalent: object and anti-object – cutting across and annulling the disciplines that claim to unify it; site and non-site – the site of the unconscious as the non-site of the subject, and so on. Even after the partition of the body into the anatomical and the erogenous, contemporary psychoanalysis (Leclaire) continues to set down the movement of desire in its name, under the regime of the letter. Always the body, since there are no words to express the non-site: the best is doubtless still that which, throughout a long history, has designated what has no, or does not take, place: the repressed. We must, however, be aware of the risks this inherited word involves. The subversive privilege the body was given since it was always in a state of repression is now coming to an end in the process of its emancipation[20] (not entirely due to the actions of a repressive politics of desublimation; psychoanalysis too plays its part in the officialisation of sex and the body: here again we find an inextricable confusion between sex and the body as the crucial *event* of the subject, as process, labour, and also as an historical *advent* in the order of concepts and values). We must ask ourselves if this body we are 'liberating' does not forever denegate the symbolic potentialities of the old repressed body, if the body 'everybody's talking about' is not precisely the converse of the speaking body. In the current system, the body as the site of the primary processes is contrasted to the body as secondary process: erotic use- and exchange-value, a rationalisation under the sign of value. The pulsional body menaced by *desire* is contrasted to the semiurgic, structural body, theatricised in nudity, functionalised by *operational sexuality*.

The secondary body of sexual emancipation and 'repressive desublimation' is set *under the sign of Eros alone*. There is a confusion with sex and the mere principle of Eros, that is to say, a *neutralisation of one by the other with the ex-inscription of the death-drive*. The pleasure principle is thus established as the rationality of a 'liberated' subjectivity, a 'new political economy' of the subject. 'Eros redefines reason in his own terms. Reasonable is what sustains the order of gratification' (Herbert Marcuse, *Eros and Civilisation* [London: Sphere, 1970], p. 180). From now on, 'liberated' subjectivity is exhausted in inscribing itself as positivity in the exercise of Eros, the pleasure principle, which is simply the reification of the libido as the model of fulfilment. There is a new *reason* here, opening the way to an unlimited finality of the subject, and so there is no longer any difference between sexual 'escalation' and the schema of indefinite societal growth, of the 'liberation' of the forces of production; both evolve according to the same movement, both equally destined for failure in accordance with the irrevocable reflux of a death drive they thought they could conjure away.

The body organised under the sign of Eros represents a more advanced phase of political economy. Here the reabsorption of symbolic exchange is as radical as the alienation of human labour in the classical system of political economy. If Marx has described the historical phase where the alienation of labour power and the logic of the commodity necessarily resulted in a *reification of consciousness*, today we could say that the inscription of the body (and of all symbolic domains) into the logic of the sign is necessarily doubled by a *reification of the unconscious*.

Instead of being cut through by desire, nudity operates as the equivalent to and staging of desire. Instead of sex cutting through the body, it operates as the signifier and the equivalent of sex. Instead of ambivalence dividing sexuality, it operates throughout the structural combination of the 'male' and the 'female' as the equivalent of this ambivalence! The sexual duopoly operates as the scenario of difference. The libido is structurally divided into two terms and operates as the reductive equivalent of the death drive. In this way nudity, sex, the unconscious, etc., instead of opening up a more profound difference, are linked metonymically to one another as a constellation of representative equivalents in order to define, term by term, a discourse of sex as value. This is the same operation as in psycho-metaphysics, where the subject, as ideal referent, is nothing in fact but circulation, a metonymic exchange interrupted by terms of consciousness, will, representation, etc.

Apologue

> – So ultimately, why are there two sexes?
> – What are you complaining about? Do you want twelve of them or just one?
>
>   A modern novel

The margin could be wider: why not zero or an infinity of sexes? The question of the 'total' is absurd here (whereas we can *logically* ask 'why not six fingers on each hand?'). It is absurd because sexualisation is precisely the partition that cuts across every subject, making the 'one' or 'several' unthinkable. The 'two' also becomes unthinkable, however, since the 'two' is already a total (besides, the above dialogue operates on the figure of the 'two'). Now sex, understood radically, cannot accede to the stage of the sum total nor to a calculable status: it is a *difference*, and the two 'sides' of difference, which are not *terms*, cannot be added together nor become parts of a series. They cannot be calculated on the basis of *units*.

By contrast, the dialogue is logical in the context of the imposed bisexual model (Male/Female) since from the outset it sets sex up as two structurally opposed *terms*. The possibility of an absurd passage to the limit of serial numeration, to *sex as accumulation*, is implied by the bisexual structure from the moment male and female are set up as whole terms.

In this way the *ambivalence* of sex is reduced by *bivalence* (the two poles and their sexual roles). Today, when bivalence is undergoing the metamorphoses of the 'sexual revolution', and where we see, as they say, a blurring of the differences between the male and the female, the ambivalence of sex is reduced by the *ambiguity* of the unisex.

Against the metaphor of the sex principle.

Today, our way lit by Freud, we know very well, too well, how to discern the sublimation and secondary rationalisation of the pulsional processes behind any given social practice, ethics or politics. It has become a cultural cliché to decode every discourse in terms of repression and phantasmatic *determination*.

This is only right, however: they are now only *terms*, and the unconscious is merely a language to which to refer. Sexual discourse too becomes entirely phantasmatic when sex itself, the critical reduction of moral and social mystification that it used to be, becomes the mode of *rationalisation* of a problem situated at the level of the *total symbolic destruction of social relations*, an examination the sexualist discourse contributes to locking away under a security code. It is easy today to read in the Sunday papers that frigidity in so many women is due to their overbearing fixation on the father, and that they punish themselves for this by prohibiting pleasure: this psychoanalytic 'truth' now becomes a part of culture and *social* rationalisation (hence the ever increasing impasse in the analytic cure).

The sexual or analytic interpretation has no privilege. It too can become the phantasm of the definitive truth, and immediately therefore can also become the revolutionary theme. This is what is happening today – the collusion between the revolution and psychoanalysis results from the same imaginary and the same distortion as the 'bourgeois' recuperation of psychoanalysis; both result from the *inscription of sex and the unconscious as the determining* agency, that is to say, their reduction to a rationalist causality.

There is mystification from the moment there is a rationalisation in the name of some agency or other, as soon as the sexual is sublimated and rationalised into the political, the social and the moral, but equally as soon as the symbolic is censored and sublimated into a dominant sexual *parole*.

Zhuang-Zi's Butcher

'Hey!' Prince When-Hui said to him, 'how can your art reach such a level?' The butcher put his knife down and said, 'I love the Tao and so I progress in my art. At the start of my career, I saw only the ox. After three years' experience, I no longer saw the ox. Now my mind works more than my eyes do. My senses no longer act, only my mind. I knew the natural conformation of the ox and only attacked it at the interstices. If I do not damage the arteries, veins, muscles and nerves, then I shouldn't damage the major bones! A good butcher uses one knife in a year since he cuts only flesh. An ordinary butcher uses one knife in a month since he shatters bones with it. I have used the same knife for nineteen years. It has carved up many thousands of oxen and its cutting edge seems as if it has been newly sharpened. Strictly speaking, the joints of the bones have gaps in them and the cutting edge of the knife has no width. Whoever knows how to drive the extremely fine blade into the gaps manages his knife with ease because it is working in empty spaces. That is why I have used my knife for nineteen years and its cutting edge always appears newly sharpened. Every time I have cut the joints of the bones, I notice particular difficulties to be solved and I hold my breath, fix my gaze and work slowly. I wield my knife very gently and the joints separate as easily as we disturb the earth on the ground. I am taking up my knife again and getting back to work.' (Zhuang-Zi, *The Principle of Hygiene* III)

A perfect example of analysis and its prodigious operationality when it exceeds the full, substantial and opaque vision of the object ('at the start . . . I saw only the ox'), the anatomical vision of the body as a full edifice of bone, flesh and organs, unified by external representations, that can be carved up at will. This is the body on which the ordinary butcher labours, cutting by brute force, getting as far as to be able to recognise the articulation of the void and the structure of the void where the body is articulated ('[I] only attacked it at the interstices'). Zhuang-Zi's butcher-knife is not a mass passing though a mass, it is itself the void ('with ease because it is working in empty spaces'). The knife that works in line with the analytic mind does not therefore work in spaces filled by oxen to which the senses and the eyes attest, but in accordance with the internal logical organisation of the rhythm and the intervals. If it does not wear out, it is because it does not set out to conquer a substance of the density of flesh and bone – because it is pure difference operating on difference – in order to disassemble a body (a practical operation) which, as we can clearly see, rests on a symbolic economy which is neither 'objective' knowledge nor a relation of forces, but a structure of exchange: the knife and the body *are exchanged*, the knife *articulates* the body's lack and thereby deconstructs it in accordance with its own rhythm.

This knife is also Leclaire's letter. The latter comes to divide a particular site on the body erotogenically in accordance with the logic of desire. A receptive, hard wearing and 'useless' [*inusable*] symbolic inscription, when the letter, due to its extremely fine thread, disjoins the anatomical body and works in the void articulated by the body. This instead of the poor butcher's full discourse that merely cuts anatomically and according to material evidence.

The millenial brother of Lichtenberg's knife,[21] the logical paradox of which (the knife with no blade which is missing a handle) sets up the symbolic configuration of an *absent* phallus instead of the full phallus and its f(ph)antas(ma)tic evidence. This knife does not work on the body, it resolves it, circling it attentively and dreamily (free-floating attention: 'I hold my breath, fix my gaze and work slowly'), proceeding *anagrammatically*, that is to say, it does not advance from one term to another, from one

organ, juxtaposed and connected to another like words by the thread of a
functional syntax: this is how the bad butcher and the linguist of
signification proceed. Here, the thread of meaning is quite different: it
splits the manifest body and follows the body beneath the body, like the
anagram which follows the model of the dispersal and resolution of a *first*
term or corpus whose secret is another articulation than that which runs
beneath discourse and traces something (a name, a formula) whose
absence haunts the text. It is this formula of the body which defies the
anatomical body, that the knife describes and resolves. It is certain that the
efficacy of the sign, its symbolic efficacy in primitive societies, far from
being 'magical', is bound up with this extremely precise labour of
anagrammatical resolution. Hence the architecture of the erogenous body,
which is only ever the anagrammatic articulation of a formula 'lost without
ever having been', a formula whose thread of desire reforms the disjunctive synthesis that it retraces without saying: desire itself is nothing other
than the resolution of the signifier in the orphic dispersal of the body, in the
anagrammatical dispersal of the poem, according to the musical rhythm of
the knife of Zhuang-Zi's butcher.

Notes

1. The genitals themselves, the object-sex, are never fetishised, only the phallus as the
    general equivalent; just as in political economy, the product or the commodity in itself is
    never fetishised, but rather the form of exchange-value and its general equivalent.
2. There is an affinity between the ceremonial of signs surrounding the erotic body and the
    ceremonial of suffering that surrounds sado-masochistic perversion. The marks of
    'fetishism' (necklaces, bracelets, chains) always mimic and evoke the marks of sado-
    masochism (mutilation, wounds, cuts). These two perversions electively crystallise
    around this system of marks.
       Certain marks (and only these are suggestive) render the body *more nude than if it
    were really nude*. Here the body's nudity is the perverse nudity associated with the
    ceremonial. These marks may be clothes or accessories, but also gestures, music or
    technique. All perversions need effects in the widest sense of the term. In sado-
    masochism suffering becomes the emblem of the body, just as jewels or rouge may in
    fetishist passion.
       All perversions revel in something: in the erotic system we are describing, the body
    revels in indulgence, self-seduction; in sado-masochism, it revels in suffering (painful
    auto-eroticism). There is, however, an affinity between the two, since whether the other
    suffers or indulges in himself, he is radically objectified. Every perversion acts out death.
3. The sexual act is often only possible at the cost of this perversion: the other's body is
    phantasised as a mannequin, a phallus-mannequin, a phallic fetish, cherished, caressed
    and possessed as the phantasiser's own penis.
4. Against the thesis of the phallic mother who terrifies because she is phallic, Freud said
    that the paralysis produced by the *Medusa*'s head worked because the snakes that
    replaced her hair came, as many times as there were snakes, to deny castration.
    Whoever wished to annul castration was repeatedly reminded of it through this reversal
    (A. Green). The same goes for the fascination with make-up and the strip-tease: each
    fragment of the body highlighted or phallically enhanced by the mark also happens to
    deny castration, which nevertheless re-emerges everywhere in the very separation of
    these part-objects so that, like the fetish-object, they only ever appear to 'testify to and
    veil the castrated genitals' (Lacan).

5. If the line of the stocking is more erotic than the shawl covering the eye or the line of the glove on the arm, it is not due to the promiscuity of the genitals: it is simply because castration is played out and denied here *at close range*, as near as possible and in the greatest possible immanence. Thus in Freud it is the last perceived object, the closest to the discovery of the absence of the penis in women that will become the fetish-object.

6. Only the annulment of phallus-value and the irruption of the radical play of difference remain unthinkable and inadmissible.

7. That said, the fact that one of the terms of sexual binomialism, the male, although it has become the marked term and although this in turn has become the general equivalent in the system, this structure which to us appears ineluctable is in fact without biological foundation: like every great structure, its goal is precisely to break with nature (Lévi-Strauss). We can imagine a culture where the terms are reversed: a male strip-tease in a matriarchal culture. All that is required is that the female become the marked term and operate as the general equivalent. We must see, however, that even if these terms are alternated (which largely encapsulates women's 'liberation'), the structure remains unchanged as does the refusal of castration and phallic abstraction. So we can see that the real problem is not whether the system carries within it any possibility for structural alteration, but rather lies in a radical alternative, which puts into question the very abstraction of this political economy of sex, based on making one of the terms a general equivalent and on the misrecognition [*méconnaissance*] of castration and the symbolic economy.

8. Except for the noble excretion of tears, but with incredible precautions! Cf. this admirable text for a cosmetics firm called Longcil; 'when an emotion overwhelms you to the point that only looks can translate its depth, at this moment more than any other, you don't want your eye-shadow to betray you. At this moment more than any other, *Longcil* is irreplaceable . . . especially in moments like these, it takes care of your looks to protect and improve them . . . so that now you need only put on your make-up and not give it a second thought.'

9. The gestural narrative, or, technically speaking, the 'bump and grind', realises here what Bataille called the 'ruse of opposition' [*feinte du contraire*]: because it is continuously covered and concealed by the same gestures that denude it, the body here acquires its poetic meaning by force of ambivalence. On the other hand, we see how naïve nudists and others are, their 'superficial beach nudity' that Bernardin speaks of, who believe they are laying reality entirely bare and fall into the equivalence of the sign: reality is nothing more than the equivalent signifier to a natural signified. This naturalist unveiling is only ever a 'mental act', as Bernardin put it so well, it is an *ideology*. In this sense the *strip*, through its perverse play and its sophisticated ambivalence, is as opposed to 'liberation through nudity' as it is to a *liberal-rationalist ideology*. The 'escalation of the nude' is the escalation of rationalism, the rights of man, formal liberation, liberal demagogy, and petty-bourgeois free-thinking. This realistic aberration was put perfectly back into its place by a little girl's words when she was offered a doll that pisses: 'My little sister can do that too. Couldn't you give me a real one?'

10. A play of transparent veils can play the same role as this play of gestures. Advertising is of the same order when it frequently puts two or several women on stage. It is only in appearance that this is a homosexual thematic, since it is in fact a variant of the narcissistic model of self-seduction, a play of reduplications centred on the self by means of the detour of a sexual simulation (which may be homosexual besides: there are only ever men in advertising to act as a narcissistic warning, to help the woman to take pleasure in herself).

11. Even when the last piece of clothing falls away, the integral strip does not alter its logic. We know that gestures are enough to trace an enchanted line around the body, a much more subtle marker than panties. In any case, it is not a sexual organ that this structural marker (panties or gesture) bars, but the very sexualisation that crosses the body: the spectacle of the organ and, at the limit, of the orgasm do not therefore eliminate this at all.

12. The *perverse* desire is the *normal* desire imposed by the *social* model. If the woman avoids auto-erotic regression, she is no longer an object of desire, she becomes a subject of desire, and thereby resistant to the structure of the perverse desire. But she too could very well seek to fulfil her desire in the fetishistic neutralisation of the desire of the other, so that the perverse structure (that kind of division of the labour of desire between the subject and the object which is the secret of perversion and its erotic yield) remains unchanged. The only alternative is that everyone should break down this phallic fortress and open up the perverse structure which surrounds the sexual system; instead of fixing their eyes on a phallic identity, on its absence in the place of the other, leave the white magic of phallic identification in order to recognise their own perilous ambivalence, so that the play of desire as symbolic exchange becomes possible once more.

13. [In the seventeenth century a certain Mlle de Scudéry imagined a map [*carte*] of the country or kingdom she conceived and called *Tendre*, following the contemporary usage of the word *tendre* to designate the 'tender emotions' and sentiments, as opposed to the 'military virtues' of strength, toughness, coldness and cruelty, etc. (*Le Petit Robert*). – tr.]

14. If we refer to the function of the letter in Leclaire's work, an erotic function of differential inscription and the annulment of difference, we can see that the current system is characterised by the abolition of the opening function of the letter and by augmenting its closure property. The literal function has broken with the alphabet of desire (symbolic inscription disappeared to the great advantage of structural inscription) in favour of the alphabet of the code. Even in analysis, the ambivalence of the letter has been replaced by an equivalence within the system of the code, its literal function as (linguistic) value. The letter is then reduplicated and reflects itself like a full sign, it is fetishistically invested as a single line instead and in place of erogenous difference. The letter is invested as a phallus in which all differences are eliminated. The scansion of the subject by the letter in enjoyment is eliminated in favour of the fulfilment of desire in the fetishised letter alone. Thus not only the anatomical body is opposed to Leclaire's erogenous body, but also and especially the semiurgic body, made up of a lexis of full, coded signifiers, signifying models of the fulfilment of desire.

15. The subject of consumption, in particular the consumption of the body, is neither the ego, nor the unconscious subject, it is the second person plural, the 'you' of advertising, i.e. the intercepted, fragmented subject reconstituted by the dominant models, 'personalised' and brought into play in the sign-exchange. Being no more than the simulation model of the second person of exchange, the 'you' is effectively *no-one*, only a fictive term maintained by the discourse of the model. This 'you' is no longer the one that speaks, but the effect of the division of the code, a phantom that appeared in the mirror of signs.

16. We really must appreciate that the 'liberation' and 'revolution' of the body works essentially at the level of secondary sexualisation, i.e. a bisexual rationalisation of sex. They are therefore operative in a late phase, where a puritan repression used to be, while at the same time they are caught at the level of contemporary, symbolic, repression. This revolution is 'one war too late' as regards the mode of repression. Put better (or worse), there is an insidious and widespread progression of primary repression which, by the mere fact of the 'sexual revolution', disturbingly merges with the 'gentle' repression under the sign of the management of narcissism discussed above.

17. [In this passage, Baudrillard is punning on the maternal function of the breast [*sein*] and being 'in the midst' or 'at the heart of' [*au sein de*] the 'maternal' society he here claims has displaced that of the law of the Father. – tr.]

18. This presupposes a type of exchange that has remained outside the dominance of incest prohibition and the law of the Father (such as the type of economic and linguistic exchange that we are familiar with), *which is based on value* and culminates in the system of exchange-value. This type of exchange exists: it is symbolic exchange which, by contrast, is based *on the annulment of value*, and hence cancels the prohibition on which it is based and overcomes the law of the Father. Symbolic exchange is neither a

regression within the law (towards incest), nor a pure and simple transgression (always dependent on the law), it is the *revolution* of this law.

19. Cf. Jean-François Lyotard, *Discours, figure* [Paris: Klincksieck, 1971], p. 23.

20. After the history of the body's negativity comes the history of its positivity. The ambiguity of the current 'revolution' derives entirely from the fact that centuries of repression have based the body on *value*. Repressed, the body is charged with a transgressive virtuality of all values. Similarly however, we must understand that a long lasting and inextricable confusion between the body and a series of 'materialist' values (health, well-being, sexuality, liberty) has been at work in the shadows of repression. The concept of the body has grown up in the shadow of a certain transcendental materialism which has slowly matured in the shadow of idealism as its revitalising solution, even bringing about its resurrection in accordance with determinate finalities, and operates as a dynamic element in the equilibrium of the new system of values. Nudity becomes the emblem of radical subjectivity. The body becomes the standard of the pulsions. But this liberation has something of the ambiguity of every liberation, in that it is here liberated as value. Just as labour is never 'liberated' as anything other than labour power in a system of forces of production and exchange-value, subjectivity is only ever liberated as a phantasm and sign-value in the framework of planned signification, a systematics of signification whose coincidence with the systematics of production is clear enough. In the final analysis, subjectivity is only ever 'liberated' in the sense that it is once again seized by political economy.

21. And the opposite of Ockham's razor, which castrates and traces the taut thread of abstraction and reason.

5

POLITICAL ECONOMY AND DEATH

The Extradition of the Dead

As soon as savages began to call 'men' only those who were members of their tribe, the definition of the 'Human' was considerably enlarged: it became a universal concept. This is precisely what we call culture. Today all men are men. Universality is in fact based exclusively on tautology and doubling, and this is where the 'Human' takes on the force of a moral law and a principle of exclusion. This is because the 'Human' is from the outset the institution of its structural double, the 'Inhuman'. This is all it is: the progress of Humanity and Culture are simply the chain of discriminations with which to brand 'Others' with inhumanity, and therefore with nullity. For the savages who call themselves 'men', the others are something else. For us, by contrast, under the sign of the Human as a universal concept, others are nothing. In other cases, to be 'man' is, like being a gentleman, a challenge, a distinction experienced as a great struggle, not merely giving rise to an exchange of *quality* or status amongst different beings (gods, ancestors, foreigners, animals, nature . . .), but *imposing* its stakes universally, being praised and prohibited. We are happy to be promoted to the universal, to an abstract and generic value indexed on the equivalence of the species, to the exclusion of all the others. In some sense, therefore, the definition of the Human inexorably contracts in accordance with cultural developments: each 'objective' progressive step towards the universal corresponded to an ever stricter discrimination, until eventually we can glimpse the time of man's definitive universality that will coincide with the excommunication of all men – the purity of the concept alone radiant in the void.

Racism is modern. Previous races or cultures were ignored or eliminated, but never under the sign of a universal Reason. There is no criterion of man, no split from the Inhuman, there are only differences with which to oppose death. But it is our undifferentiated concept of man that gives rise to discrimination. We must read the following narrative by Jean de Léry, from the sixteenth century: *Histoire d'un voyage en la terre de Brésil* ('The History of a Journey to the Land of Brazil') to see that racism did not exist in this period when the Idea of Man does not yet cast its shadow over all the metaphysical purity of Western culture. This Reformation puritan from Geneva, landing amongst Brazilian cannibals, is not racist. It is due to the extent of our progress that we have since become racists, and not only towards Indians and cannibals: the increasing hold of rationality on our culture has meant the successive extradition of inanimate nature, animals and inferior races[1] into the Inhuman, while the cancer of the Human has invested the very society it claimed to contain within its absolute superiority. Michel Foucault has analysed the extradition of madmen at the dawn of Western modernity, but we also know of the extradition and progressive confinement of children, following the course of Reason itself, into the idealised state of infancy, the ghetto of the infantile universe and the abjection of innocence. But the old have also become inhuman, pushed to the fringes of normality. Like so many others, the mad, children and the old have only become 'categories' under the sign of the successive segregations that have marked the development of culture. The poor, the under-developed, those with subnormal IQs, perverts, transsexuals, intellectuals and women form a folklore of terror, a folklore of excommunication on the basis of an increasingly racist definition of the 'normal human'. Quintessence of normality: ultimately all these 'categories' will be excluded, segregated, exiled in a finally universal society, where the normal and the universal will at last fuse under the sign of the Human.[2]

Foucault's analysis, amongst the masterpieces of this genuine cultural history, takes the form of a genealogy of discrimination in which, at the start of the nineteenth century, labour and production occupy a decisive place. At the very core of the 'rationality' of our culture, however, is an exclusion that precedes every other, more radical than the exclusion of madmen, children or inferior races, an exclusion preceding all these and serving as their model: the exclusion of the dead and of death.

There is an irreversible evolution from savage societies to our own: little by little, *the dead cease to exist*. They are thrown out of the group's symbolic circulation. They are no longer beings with a full role to play, worthy partners in exchange, and we make this obvious by exiling them further and further away from the group of the living. In the domestic intimacy of the cemetery, the first grouping remains in the heart of the village or town, becoming the first ghetto, prefiguring every future ghetto, but are thrown further and further from the centre towards the periphery, finally having nowhere to go at all, as in the new town or the contemporary metropolis, where there are no longer any provisions for the dead, either in mental or in physical space. Even madmen, delinquents and misfits can find a welcome in the new towns, that is, in the rationality of a modern society. Only the death-function cannot be programmed and localised. Strictly speaking, we no longer know what to do with them, since, today, *it is not normal to be dead*, and this is new. To be dead is an unthinkable anomaly; nothing else is as offensive as this. Death is a delinquency, and an incurable deviancy. The dead are no longer inflicted on any place or space-time, they can find no resting place; they are thrown into a radical utopia. They are no longer even packed in and shut up, but obliterated.

But we know what these hidden places signify: the factory no longer exists because labour is everywhere; the prison no longer exists because arrests and confinements pervade social space-time; the asylum no longer exists because psychological control and therapy have been generalised and become banal; the school no longer exists because every strand of social progress is shot through with discipline and pedagogical training; capital no longer exists (nor does its Marxist critique) because the law of value has collapsed into self-managed survival in all its forms, etc., etc. The cemetery no longer exists because modern cities have entirely taken over their function: they are ghost towns, cities of death. If the great operational metropolis is the final form of an entire culture, then, quite simply, ours is a culture of death.[3]

Survival, or the Equivalent to Death

It is correct to say that the dead, hounded and separated from the living, condemn us to an *equivalent death*: for the fundamental law of symbolic obligation is at play in any case, for better or worse. Madness, then, is only ever the *dividing* line between the mad and the normal, a line which normality *shares* with madness and which is even defined by it. Every society that internalises its mad is a society invested in its depths by madness, which alone and everywhere ends up being symbolically exchanged under the legal signs of normality. Madness has for several centuries worked hard on the society which confines it, and today the asylum walls have been removed, not because of some miraculous tolerance, but because madness has *completed* its normalising labour on society: madness has become pervasive, while at the same time it is forbidden a resting place. The asylum has been reabsorbed into the core of the social field, because normality has reached the point of perfection and assumed the characteristics of the asylum, because the virus of confinement has worked its way into every fibre of 'normal' existence.

So it is with death. Death is ultimately nothing more than the social line of demarcation separating the 'dead' from the 'living': therefore, it affects both equally. Against the senseless illusion of the living of willing the living to the exclusion of the dead, against the illusion that reduces life to *an absolute surplus-value* by subtracting death from it, the indestructible logic of symbolic exchange re-establishes the equivalence of life and death in the indifferent fatality of survival. In survival, death is repressed; life itself, in accordance with that well known ebbing away, would be nothing more than a survival determined by death.

The Ghetto Beyond the Grave

The concept of immortality grew alongside the segregation of the dead. For the flip-side of death, this eminent status which is the mark of the 'soul' and 'superior' spiritualities, is only a story that conceals the real extradition of the dead and the rupturing of a symbolic exchange with them. When the dead are there, lifelike [*vivants*] but different from the living [*vivants*] whom they partner in multiple exchanges, they have no need to, and neither is it necessary that they should, be immortal, since this fantastic quality shatters all reciprocity. It is only to the extent that they are excluded by the living that they quietly become immortal, and this idealised survival is only the mark of their social exile.

We must get rid of the idea of *progress* in religions, leading from animism to polytheism and then to monotheism, in the course of which an immortal soul progressively emerges. It is to the precise extent that the dead are confined that they are conferred an immortality, just as, in a similar way, we see life expectancy grow simultaneously with the segregation of pensioners, deemed asocial, in our societies.

Immortality is progressive, and this is one of the strangest things. It progresses in time, passing from limited to eternal survival; in social space, immortality becomes democratic and passes from being the privilege of a few to being everyone's virtual right. This is relatively recent, however. In Egypt, certain members of the group (Pharoahs, then priests, chiefs, the wealthy, the initiates of the dominant class), according to the degree of their power, slowly broke away as immortals, others having only the right to death and the double. Towards the year 2000 BC, everyone accedes to immortality in a sort of social conquest, perhaps the outcome of a great struggle. Without attempting a social history or constructing a fiction, we can well imagine, in Egypt and the Great Dynasties, revolts and social movements demanding the right to immortality for all.

In the beginning, then, immortality was a matter of an emblem of power and social transcendence. Where, in primitive groups, there were no structures of political power, there was no personal immortality either. Consequently, in the least segmented societies, a 'relative' soul and a 'restricted' immortality correspond to a similarly relative transcendence of power structures. Then, with the Grand Empires, despotic societies of total transcendence of power, immortality is generalised and becomes eternal. The King or the Pharoah is the first to benefit from this advancement, but then, at a more advanced stage, issuing from God Himself who is immortality *par excellence*, immortality is democratically redistributed. But the phase of the immortal God, which coincides with the great universalist religions (and Christianity in particular), is already a phase of a huge abstraction of social power in the Roman Imperium. If the Greek gods were mortals, it is because they were bound to a specific culture and were not yet universal.

In its initial stages, Christianity was not in accord over immortality, which was a late acquisition. The Church Fathers still admitted the provisional elimination of the soul awaiting resurrection. Even when St Paul preached the idea of resurrection, the pagans mocked him for it and even the Church Fathers had a deep resistance to it. In the Old Testament (Daniel), resurrection is promised only to those who have not received retribution during their lifetime for *good or evil*. The beyond of life, *survival*, is only the settling of all accounts, existing only according to what remained unexchanged in life. Resurrection, or immortality, is a fine example of the last resort as regards the symbolic possibility of the archaic group's *immediate* regulation of all its accounts, annulling all its symbolic debt without reference to an afterlife.

Originally the distinctive emblem of power, the immortality of the soul acts, throughout Christianity, as an egalitarian myth, as a democratic beyond as opposed to worldly inequality before death. It is only a myth. Even in its most universalist Christian version, immortality only belongs to every human being *by right*: in fact, it is sparingly granted, remaining the privilege of *a* culture, and within this culture, the privilege of a specific social and political caste. Have the missionaries ever believed in the immortal soul of the natives? Has woman ever really had a soul in 'classical' Christianity? What about madmen, children and criminals? In fact it always comes down to this: only the rich and powerful have a soul. Social, political and economic inequality (life expectancy, prestigious funerals, glory and living on in men's memories) before death is only ever the effect of this fundamental discrimination: some, the only real 'human beings', have the right to immortality; others have only the right to death. Nothing has changed greatly since Egypt and the Great Dynasties.

'What does immortality matter?' the naïve materialist will say, 'It's all imaginary.' Yes, and it is exciting to see that this is where the basis of the *real* social discrimination lies, and that nowhere else are power and social transcendence so clearly marked than in the imaginary. The economic power of capital is based in the imaginary just as much as is the power of the Church: capital is only its fantastic secularisation.

We can also see that democracy changes nothing here. We used to be able to fight in order to gain immortality for the souls of all, just as generations of proletarians fought in order to gain equality in terms of goods and culture. It is the same fight, the former for survival in the beyond, and the latter for survival here. It is the same trap: the personal immortality of a few resulting, as we have seen, in the break-up of the group – so what's the point of demanding immortality for all? It is simply to generalise the imaginary. The revolution can only consist in the abolition of the separation of death, and not in equality of survival.

Immortality is only a kind of general equivalent bound to the abstraction of linear time (taking form as soon as time becomes this abstract dimension bound to the process of political-economic accumulation and, in short, to the abstraction of life).

Death Power

The emergence of survival can therefore be analysed as the fundamental operation in the birth of power. Not only because this set-up will permit the necessity of the sacrifice of this life and the threat of recompense in the next (this is exactly the priest-caste's strategy), but more profoundly by instituting the *prohibition of death* and, at the same time, the agency that oversees this prohibition of death: power. Shattering the union of the living and the dead, and slapping a prohibition on death and the dead: the primary source of social control. Power is possible only if death is no longer free, only if the dead are put under surveillance, in anticipation of the future confinement of life in its entirety. This is the fundamental Law, and power is the guardian at the gates of this Law. It is not the repression of unconscious pulsions, libido, or whatever other energy that is fundamental, and it is not anthropological; it is the repression of death, the *social* repression of death in the sense that this is what facilitates the shift towards the repressive socialisation of life.

Historically, we know that sacerdotal power is based on a monopoly over death and exclusive control over relations with the dead.[4] The dead are the first restricted area, the exchange of whom is restored by an obligatory mediation by the priests. Power is established on death's borders. It will subsequently be sustained by further separations (the soul and the body, the male and the female, good and evil, etc.) that have infinite ramifications, but the principal separation is between life and death.[5] When the French say that power 'holds the bar',[6] it is no metaphor: it is the bar between life and death, the decree that suspends exchange between life and death, the tollgate and border control between the two banks.

This is precisely the way in which power will later be instituted between the subject separated from its body, between the individual separated from its social body, between man separated from his labour: the agency of mediation and representation flourishes in this rupture. We must take note, however, that the archetype of this operation is the separation between a group and its dead, or between each of us today and our own deaths. Every form of power will have something of this smell about it, because it is on the manipulation and administration of death that power, in the final analysis, is based.

All the agencies of repression and control are installed in this divided space, in the suspense between a life and its proper end, that is, in the production of a literally fantastic and artificial temporality (since at every instant every life has its proper death there already, that is to say, in this same instant lies the finality it attains). The first abstract social time is installed in this rupture of the indivisible unity of life and death (well before abstract social labour time!). All the future forms of alienation that Marx denounces, the separations and abstractions of political economy, take root in this separation of death.

The economic operation consists in life taking death hostage. This is a *residual* life which can from now on be read in the operational terms of calculation and value. For example, in Chamisso's *The Man who Lost his Shadow*, Peter Schlemil becomes a rich and powerful capitalist once his shadow has been lost (once death is taken hostage: the pact with t.. is only ever a political-economic pact).

Life given over to death: the very operation of the symbolic.

The Exchange of Death in the Primitive Order

Savages have no biological concept of death. Or rather, the biological fact, that is, death, birth or disease, everything that comes from nature and that we accord the privilege of necessity and objectivity, quite simply has no meaning for them. This is absolute disorder, since it cannot be symbolically exchanged, and what cannot be symbolically exchanged constitutes a mortal danger for the group.[7] They are unreconciled, unexpiated, sorcerous and hostile forces that prowl around the soul and the body, that stalk the living and the dead; defunct, cosmic energies that the group was unable to bring under control through exchange.

We have de-socialised death by overturning bio-anthropological laws, by according it the immunity of science and by making it autonomous, as individual fatality. But the physical materiality of death, which paralyses us through the 'objective' credence we give it, does not stop the primitives. They have never 'naturalised' death, they know that death (like the body, like the natural event) is a *social relation*, that its definition is social. In this they are much more 'materialist' than we are, since for them the real materiality of death, like that of the commodity for Marx, lies in its *form*, which is always the form of a social relation. Instead, all our idealism converges on the illusion of a biological materiality of death: our discourse of '*reality*', which is in fact the discourse of the *imaginary*, surpasses the primitives in the intervention of the *symbolic*.

Initiation is the accented beat of the operation of the symbolic. It aims neither to conjure death away, nor to 'overcome' it, but to articulate it socially. As R. Jaulin describes in *La Mort Sara* [Paris: Plon, 1967], the ancestral group 'swallows the *koys*' (young initiation candidates), who die '*symbolically*' in order to be reborn. Above all, we must avoid understanding this according to the degraded meaning we attach to it, but in the sense that their death becomes the stakes of a reciprocal-antagonistic exchange between the ancestors and the living. Further, instead of a break, a social relation between the partners is established, a circulation of gifts and counter-gifts as intense as the circulation of precious goods and women: an incessant play of responses where death can no longer establish itself as end or agency. By offering her a piece of flesh, the brother gives his wife to a dead member of the family, in order to bring him back to life. By nourishing her, this dead man is included in the life of the group. But the exchange is reciprocal. The dead man gives his wife, the clan's land, to a living member of the family in order to come back to life by assimilating himself to her and to bring her back to life by assimilating her to himself. The important moment is when the *moh* (the grand priests) put the *koy* (the initiates) to death, so that the latter are then consumed by their ancestors, then the earth gives birth to them as their mother had given birth to them. After having been 'killed', the initiates are left in the hands of their initiatory, 'cultural' parents, who instruct them, care for them and train them (initiatory birth).

It is clear that the initiation consists in an exchange being established where there had been only a brute fact: they pass from natural, aleatory and irreversible death to a death that is *given* and *received*, and that is therefore reversible in the social exchange, 'soluble' in exchange. At the same time the opposition between birth and death disappears: they can also be *exchanged* under the form of symbolic reversibility. Initiation is the crucial moment, the social nexus, the darkroom where birth and death stop being the terms of life and twist into one another again; not towards some mystical fusion, but in this instance to turn the initiate into a real social being. The uninitiated child has only been born biologically, he has only one 'real' father and one 'real' mother; in order to become a social being he must pass through the *symbolic* event of the initiatory birth/death, he must have gone through the circuit of life and death in order to enter into the symbolic reality of exchange.

It is not, in this initiatory test, a matter of staging a second birth to eclipse death. Jaulin himself leans towards this interpretation: society 'conjured' death away, or even opposed it 'dialectically', in the initiation, to a term of his invention which it uses and 'overcomes': 'To the life and death they are given, men have added initiation, by means of which they transcend the disorder of death.' This formula is very beautiful and very ambiguous at the same time, since initiation is not 'added' to the other terms, and it doesn't play life off *against* death towards a rebirth (we are extremely suspicious of those who triumph over death!). It is the *splitting* of life and death that initiation conjures away, and with it the concomitant fatality which weighs down on life as soon as it is split in this way. For life then becomes this biological irreversibility, this absurd physical destiny, life has then been lost in advance, since it is condemned to decline with the body. Hence the idealisation of one of these terms, birth (and its doubling in resurrection) at the expense of the other, death. This, however, is simply one of our ingrained prejudices concerning the 'sense' or 'meaning of life'. For birth, as an irreversible individual event, is as traumatising as death. Psychoanalysis puts this differently: birth is a sort of death. And with baptism, Christianity has done nothing more than, through a collective ritual, to define the *mortal* event of birth. The advent of life is a *crime* of sorts, if it is not repeated and expiated by a collective simulacrum of death. Life is only a benefit in itself within the calculable order of value. In the symbolic order, life, like everything else, is a crime if it survives unilaterally, if it is not seized and destroyed, given and returned, 'returned' to death. Initiation effaces this crime by resolving the *separate* event of life and death in one and the same social act of exchange.

Symbolic/Real/Imaginary

The symbolic is neither a concept, an agency, a category, nor a 'st
but an act of exchange and *a social relation which puts an end to the real,*
which resolves the real, and, at the same time, puts an end to the
opposition between the real and the imaginary.

The initiatory act is the reverse of our reality principle. It shows that the
reality of birth derives solely from the separation of life and death. Even
the *reality* of life itself derives solely from the disjunction of life and death.
The *effect of the real* is only ever therefore the structural effect of the
disjunction between two terms, and our famous reality principle, with its
normative and repressive implications, is only a generalisation of this
disjunctive code to all levels. The reality of nature, its 'objectivity' and its
'materiality', derives solely from the separation of man and nature, of a
body and a non-body, as Octavio Paz put it. Even the reality of the body,
its material status, derives from the disjunction of a spiritual principle,
from discriminating a soul from a body.

The symbolic is what puts an end to this disjunctive code and to
separated terms. *It is the u-topia that puts an end to the topologies of the
soul and the body, man and nature, the real and the non-real, birth and
death.* In the symbolic operation, the two terms lose their reality.[8]

The reality principle is never anything other than the *imaginary* of the
other term. In the man/nature partition, nature (objective, material) is
only the imaginary of man thus conceptualised. In the sexual bipartition
masculine/feminine, an arbitrary and structural distinction on which the
sexual reality (and repression) principle is based, 'woman' thus defined is
only ever man's imaginary. Each term of the disjunction excludes the
other, which eventually becomes its imaginary.

So it is with life and death in our current system: the price we pay for the
'reality' of this life, to live it as a positive value, is the ever-present
phantasm of death. For us, defined as living beings, death is our
imaginary.[9] So, all the disjunctions on which the different structures of the
real are based (this is not in the least abstract: it is also what separates the
teacher from the taught, and on which the reality principle of their relation
is based; the same goes for all the social relations we know) have their
archetype in the fundamental disjunction of life and death. This is why, in
whatever field of 'reality', every separate term for which the other is its
imaginary is haunted by the latter as *its own death.*

Thus the symbolic everywhere puts an end to the fascination with the
real and the imaginary, to the closure of the phantasm drawn up by
psychoanalysis, but where, at the same time, psychoanalysis locks itself up
by establishing, through a considerable quantity of disjunctions (primary
and secondary processes, unconscious and conscious, etc.), a psychical
reality principle of the unconscious inseparable from psychoanalysis's own
reality principle (the unconscious as psychoanalysis's reality principle!) and
thus in which the symbolic cannot but put an end to psychoanalysis too.[10]

The Inevitable Exchange

The real event of death is imaginary. Where the imaginary creates a symbolic disorder, initiation restores symbolic order. Incest prohibition does the same thing in the domain of filiation: the group responds to the real, natural, 'asocial' event of biological filiation by a system of alliance and the exchange of women. It is essential that everything (women in this case, but otherwise birth and death) becomes available for exchange, that is, comes under the jurisdiction of the group. Incest prohibition, in this sense, is interdependent with and complementary to initiation, in that in the one case young initiates circulate amongst the living adults and the dead ancestors: they are given and returned, whereby they accede to symbolic recognition. In the other case, it is women who circulate: they too only attain real social status once given and returned, instead of being retained by the father or brothers for their own use. 'Whosoever gives nothing, whether his daughter or his sister, is dead.'[11]

Incest prohibition lies at the basis of alliances amongst the living. Initiation lies at the basis of alliances amongst the living and the dead. This is the fundamental fact that separates us from the primitives: exchange does not stop when life comes to an end. Symbolic exchange is halted neither by the living nor by the dead (nor by stones or beasts). This is an absolute law: obligation and reciprocity are insurmountable. None can withdraw from it, for whom- or whatever's sake, on pain of death. Death is nothing other than this: taken hostage by the cycle of symbolic exchanges (cf. Marcel Mauss, 'L'effet physique chez l'individu de l'idée de mort suggérée par la collectivité', in *Sociologie et Anthropologie* [4th edn, Paris: PUF, 1968]).[12]

But we could also say that this does not separate us from the primitives, and that *it is exactly the same for us*. Throughout the entire system of political economy, the law of symbolic exchange has not changed one iota: we continue to exchange with the dead, even those denied rest, those for whom rest is prohibited. We simply pay with our own death and our anxiety about death for the rupture of symbolic exchanges with them. It is profoundly similar with inanimate nature and beasts. Only an absurd theory of liberty could claim that we are quits with the dead, since the debt is universal and unceasing: we never manage to 'return' what we have taken for all this 'liberty'. This huge litigation, involving all the obligations and reciprocities that we have denounced, is properly the unconscious. No need for a libido, for desire, for an energetics or for the pulsions and their destinations to give an account of this. The unconscious is social in the sense that it is made up of all that could not be exchanged socially or symbolically. And so it is with death: it is exchanged in any case, and, at best, it *will be exchanged* in accordance with a social ritual, as with the primitives; at worst, it will be *'redeemed' by an individual labour of mourning*. The unconscious is subject in its entirety to the distortion of the death of a symbolic process (exchange, ritual) into an economic process (redemption, labour, debt, individual). This entails a considerable difference in enjoyment: we trade with our dead in a kind of melancholy, while the primitives live with their dead under the auspices of the ritual and the feast.

The Unconscious and the Primitive Order

The reciprocity of life and death, which entails their exchange in a social *cycle* instead of being cut up according to biological *linearity* or the *repetition* of the phantasm, the reabsorption of the prohibition separating the living from the dead that rebounds so violently on the living; all this puts the very hypothesis of the unconscious into question again.

In his *Oedipe africain* [Paris: Plon, 1969], Edmond Ortigues asks what it means 'to marry one's mother' and 'to kill one's father':

> The verb 'to marry' has a different meaning in different contexts, it has not got the same social and psychological content. As for the verb 'to kill', apparently so clear-cut, are we quite certain that it holds no surprises? What then is a 'dead father' in a country where the ancestors are so close to the living? . . . Everything changes, requiring us to re-examine the meaning of each term.
>
> In a society under the sway of ancestral law, it is impossible for the individual to kill the father, since, according to the customs of the Ancients, the father is always already dead and always still living. . . . To take the father's death upon oneself or to individualise the moral consciousness by reducing paternal authority to that of a mortal, a substitutable person separable from the ancestral altar and from 'custom', *would be to leave the group*, to remove oneself from the basis of tribal society.
>
> When we talk of the dissolution of the Oedipus complex, we think of an individually experienced drama. But what might this be in a tribal society where the religion of 'fertility' and the 'ancestors' proposes as the explicit basis of the collective tradition what, for us, the young Oedipus is condemned to live out in his personal phantasms?

Therefore, the 'symbolic function' in primitive societies is articulated not through the law of the Father and the individual psychical reality principle, but from the outset through a collective principle, through the collective movement of exchanges. In the initiation, we have seen how, by means of a social process, the biological figures of filiation break up in order to make way for the initiatory parents. These parents are symbolic figures who refer to the socius, that is, to all the fathers and mothers of the clan, and ultimately to the dead fathers, the ancestors, and to the clan's earth mother. The instance of the Father does not appear, it is broken down into the collectivity of rival brothers (initiates). 'Aggressivity will be displaced along a horizontal line, into fraternal rivalry, overcompensated by an extremely powerful solidarity' (Ortigues, ibid.). (Why 'will be *displaced*'? As if it were normally directed onto the Father?) Opposed to the Oedipus principle, which corresponds to the *negative* aspect of incest prohibition (prohibited with the mother and imposed by the father) is, in the *positive* sense, a principle of the exchange of sisters by brothers. It is the sister, and not the mother, who is at the centre of this apparatus, and it is at the level of brothers that the whole social act of exchange is organised. Therefore, no desocialised Oedipal triangle, no closed familial structure sanctioned by prohibition and the dominant Word of the Father, but a principle of exchange between *peers*, on the basis of the challenge and reciprocity: an autonomous principle of social organisation.

> The appearence of the concept of the gift was implemented at the core of one and the same age group in an atmosphere of equality. The sacrifice to which the child consents in the nursery to benefit another child is not of the same order as separation from the mother. (Ortigues, ibid.)

All this tells of a social principle of exchange opposed to a psychical principle of prohibition. All this tells of a symbolic process opposed to an unconscious process. Nowhere in the primitive order, since it is well ventilated and resolutely social, does there emerge the *psychically* over-determined *biological* triad of the family, with the psychical apparatus and the intertwined phantasms, as its double, the whole thing crowned by the fourth purely 'symbolic' term, the phallus. The phallus is 'strictly necessary in order to introduce a relation to the level of speech, and to make it into a reciprocal law of recognition amongst subjects'. It is here, in fact (at least in psychoanalytic theory), that the Name of the Father, the signifier of the Law, is inscribed for us, and alone introduces us into exchange. The famous ploy of the Word of the Father protects us against mortal fusion with, and absorption by, the desire for the mother. Without the phallus, there is no salvation. The necessity of this Law and of a symbolic agency barring the subject, thanks to which the primary repression at the basis of the formation of the unconsious is implemented, by the same token gives the subject access to his own desire. Without this agency to arrange exchanges, without the mediation of the phallus, the subject, incapable of repression, no longer even gains access to the symbolic and sinks into psychosis.

Because they were effectively ignorant of this Law, and the structure of repression and the unconscious which it entails, we were able to say that primitive societies were 'psychotic' societies. Of course, this is simply our fierce way of abandoning them to their gentle madness (if not to see, as begins to happen in the psychoanalytic West itself, whether psychosis might not conceal a more radical meaning, a more radical symbolicity than we have ever glimpsed under the sign of psychoanalysis). Yes, these societies have access to the symbolic.[13] No, they do not gain access to the symbolic by means of the intercession of an immutable Law, the image of which is sketched in the social order itself: the Father, the Chief, the Signifier and Power. The symbolic is not an *agency* here, so that access to it would be regulated by the mediation of a Phallus, an upper-case figure to embody all the metonymic figures of the Law. The symbolic is precisely this cycle of exchanges, the cycle of giving and returning, an order born of the very reversibility which escapes the double jurisdiction, the repressed psychical agency, and the transcendent social instance.[14]

When fathers are exchanged, given, received and transmitted from one generation of initiates to the other in the form of already dead and always living ancestors (the biological father is himself inexchangeable, no-one can stand in for him, and his symbolic figure, his word, is immutable; it too remains unexchanged, a word with no response); when the mother (the ancestral grounds put at stake with each successive initiation), is *given*, received and transmitted (this is also the tribal language, the secret language to which the initiate gains access) by the fathers, then everything – the father, the mother and the word – loses its character as a fatal and indecipherable agency, even its position in a structure controlled by prohibition (just as birth and death lose their status as fatal events, as necessity and as law, in the symbolic hyperevent of initiation).

If we can speak of a society with neither repression nor unconscious, it is not in order to rediscover some miraculous innocence where the flows of 'desire' roam freely and the primary processes are realised without prohibition. This is *an order of the dispressed* [*défoulé*], an idealism of desire and the libido such as haunts Freudo-Reichian, Freudo-Marxist and even schizo-nomadic imaginations: the phantasm of a desire or a (machined) unconscious naturalised in order to be 'liberated'. The phantasm of 'liberty' has today been transferred from the spheres of rational thought to those of the irrational, the brute, the 'primary' and the unconscious while, however, remaining a *bourgeois* problematic (namely the Cartesian and Kantian problematic of freedom and necessity).

To put the theory of the unconscious into question is also to put the theory of Desire into question, in that here, at the level of an entire civilisation, it is always simply a matter of a negative phantasm of the rational order. Hence Desire becomes an integral part of our reigning prohibition, its dreamt materiality becomes part of our imaginary. Whether it is dialectically related to the prohibition, as with Oedipus and psychoanalysis, or whether it is exalted in its brute productivity, as in Deleuze and Guattari's *Anti-Oedipus*, it remains the promise of a savage naturality, the phantasm of an *objective*, liberatory pulsional energy to be liberated – a force of desire inherited from the mobile field of revolutions: good old labour force. As we know, the effect of force is always the effect of repression, as the effect of reality is always the effect of the imaginary. We must write the 'Mirror of Desire' as we have written *The Mirror of Production*.

An example: primitive cannibalism. Apart from the question of sustenance, this is a problem of the 'oral drive' of devouring, on which there weighs a fundamental (perhaps even the most fundamental) prohibition for us, whereas certain primitives would naïvely transgress and fulfil their 'desire' through this very process. A postulate: every man would like to devour his fellow man, and when, due to necessity, a Catholic rugby team did just this after their plane crashed in the Cordillère des Andes, the whole world was astonished at this divine resurgence of a nature they thought dead and buried. Even the Pope blessed and exculpated them, so as not to make them into an example; nevertheless, this is no longer *absolutely* a crime. And why not, if only by reference to a *nature* whose consecration (unconscious and psychoanalytic), whose *libidinal* consecration is today in competition with the sanctity of the divine and the religious? Cannibals themselves do not claim to live in a state of nature, nor in accordance with their desire at all; they quite simply claim, through their cannibalism, to *live in a society*, the most interesting case being a society that eats its own dead. This is neither due to a vital necessity nor because the dead no longer count for anything, quite the contrary: it is in order to pay homage to them and thus to prevent those left to rot in accordance with the natural order, escaping from the social order, turning against the group and persecuting it. This devouring is a social act, a *symbolic* act, that aims to maintain a tissue of bonds with the dead man or the enemy they devour. In any case they don't just eat anybody, as we know; whoever is eaten is always somebody worthy, it is always a mark of respect to devour somebody since, through this, the devoured even becomes sacred. *We* scorn what we eat, we can only eat what we despise, that is, death, the inanimate, the animal or the vegetable condemned to biological assimilation. We think of anthropophagia as despicable in view of the fact that we despise what we eat, the act of eating and ultimately even our own bodies. Primitive devouring is ignorant of the abstract separation of the eater and the eaten into the active and the passive. Between the two there is a duel mode, combining honour and reciprocity, perhaps even a challenge and a duel *tout court*, which the eaten can eventually win (cf. the whole ritual of propitiation as regards nourishment). In any event, it is not a mechanical act of absorption.[15] It is not even an absorption of the 'vital forces', as ethnologists, following the natives, communally claim, merely passing from an alimentary to a magical functionalism (the psychoanalysts adhere to a psychical functionalism of the pulsion). Devouring, no longer just an act of subsistence, nor a transubstantiation of manna benefiting the eater, is a *social* act, a sacrificial process where the metabolism of the whole group is at stake. Neither the fulfilment of desire nor the assimilation of something or other, it is on the contrary an act of expenditure, consumption or consummation, and of the transmutation of the flesh into a symbolic relation, the transformation of the body in social exchange. We find the same thing in the Eucharist, but in the abstract form of the sacrament, using the general equivalence of bread and wine. The accursed share consumed here is already considerably sublimated and evangelised.

Killing no longer has the same meaning for us. The ritual murder of the king has nothing to do with the 'psychoanalytic' murder of the father. Behind the obligation to expiate the privilege the king retains through death, his murder aims to keep what threatened to accumulate and become fixed on the king's person (status, wealth, women and power) within the flow of exchanges, within the group's reciprocal movements. His death prevents this accident. This is the essence and function of sacrifice: to extinguish what threatens to fall out of the group's symbolic control and to bury it under all the weight of the dead. The king must be killed from time to time, along with the phallus which began to rule over social life. The king's murder does not therefore come from the depths of the unconscious or from the figure of the father, on the contrary, it is our unconscious and its peripeteia that result in the loss of sacrificial mechanisms. We now only conceive of murder within a closed economy, as the phantasmatic murder of the father, that is, as the balance of repression and the law, as the fulfilment of desire and as the regulation of the accounts. The stake is phallic, and it is certain that it is on the basis of repression that, with the death of the father, the phallic peripeteia of the seizure of power enters the game. This is an extremely simplified rewriting of death and murder as repressed aggression, as a violence equivalent to the violence of repression. In the primitive order, murder is neither violence nor an acting-out of the unconscious. So for those who kill the king, there is no seizure of power nor any increase in guilt, as there is in the Freudian myth. Neither does the king simply endure this. Instead, he *gives* his death, returns it in exchange, and marks it with the feast, whereas the phantasmatic murder of the father is lived as the experience of guilt and anxiety.

Thus, neither killing nor eating have the same meaning for us: they do not result in a 'murder-pulsion', in an oral sadism, nor in a structure of repression, which alone gives them the meaning they have for us today. They are social acts that rigorously follow the apparatus of symbolic obligation. Amongst other things, they never have the unilateral meaning in which all the aggression at the basis of our culture is expressed: killing–eating – I kill I eat – you are killed, you are eaten. The unconscious and all its phantasms (and their psychoanalytic theory) presuppose the acknow-ledgement of this disjunction, the repression of ambivalence, the resti-tution of which, under whatever form it may be, in the symbolic process, puts an end to the jurisdiction of the unconscious.

KILLING POSSESSING DEVOURING – the entirety of our indivi-dual unconscious is organised around these terms and the phantasmas that surround them, under the sign of repression.

GIVING RETURNING EXCHANGING – with the primitives, every-thing operates in the manifest collective exchange around these three terms, in the myths that underlie them.

Each of these 'verbs' of the unconscious presupposes a break, a rupture, the bar we find everywhere in psychoanalysis, along with the guilt it gives rise to, the play and the repetition of the prohibition. The 'verbs' of the symbolic assume on the contrary a reversibility, an indefinite cyclical transition.

Above all, however, the radical difference lies in the autonomisation of a psychical sphere: something operates collectively in primitive societies, the repression of which works for us solely on the agency of the psychical apparatus and the unconscious. The ritual is utterly different to the phantasm, as is the myth from the unconscious. All the analogies on which anthropology and psychoanalysis play are profound mystifications.

The distortion that psychoanalysis submits primitive societies to is of the same order, but in the opposite sense than what they have to endure under Marxist analysis.

1. For the anthropo-Marxists, the economic instance is also present and determinant in the type of society, it is merely hidden, latent, whereas for us it is manifest. This difference is judged to be secondary, however; the analysis does not stop and passes without meeting any opposition onto its materialist discourse.

2. For the anthropo-psychoanalysts, the agency of the unconscious is also present and determinant in this type of society; it is simply manifested, externalised, whereas for us it is latent, repressed. This difference remains inessential, however, and the analysis continues without disguising its discourse in terms of the unconscious.

On both sides there is the same misrecognition [méconnaissance] of this apparently miniscule difference: for one and the same structure, the economy or the unconscious, we pass from primitive formations to our own, now from the manifest to the hidden, now the reverse. Only our own metaphysics could neglect this detail, in the illusion that the content remains the same. But this is radically false: when the economic 'is hidden behind' other structures, it quite simply ceases to exist; it provides no account of anything, it is nothing. On the other hand, when the unconscious is 'manifest', when it becomes a manifest and articulated structure, it is no longer unconscious at all. A psychical structure and a process based on repression have no meaning in the other, ritual and non-psychical configuration of an overt resolution of signs. Everything changes when we pass from the latent to the manifest, and from the manifest to the latent.[16] This is why, against Marxist and psychoanalytic misrecognition, we must start over again *beginning from* this displacement.

We will come to see that the impossibility of locating and specifying the economic is due precisely to the symbolic. And that the possibility of overtly manifesting something unconscious, but which by this very fact ceases to be so, is also due to the symbolic.

The Double and the Split

The figure of the double, intimately bound up with figures of death and magic, poses in itself all the problems of psychological and psychoanalytic interpretation.

Shadow, spectre, reflection, image; a material spirit almost remains visible, the primitive double generally passes for the crude prefiguration of the soul and consciousness in accordance with an increasing sublimation and a spiritual 'hominisation', as in Teilhard de Chardin: towards the apogee of a single God and a universal morality. But this single God has everything to do with the form of a unified political power, and nothing to do with the primitive gods. In the same way, soul and consciousness have everything to do with a principle of the subject's unification, and nothing to do with the primitive double. On the contrary, the historical advent of the 'soul' puts an end to a proliferating exchange with spirits and doubles which, as an indirect consequence, gives rise to another figure of the double, wending its diabolical way just beneath the surface of Western reason. Once again, this figure has everything to do with the Western figure of alienation, and nothing to do with the primitive double. The telescoping of the two under the sign of psychology (conscious or unconscious) is only a misleading rewriting.

Between the primitive and its double, there is neither a mirror relation nor one of abstraction, as there is between the subject and its spiritual principle, the soul, or between the subject and its moral and psychological principle, consciousness. There is no sign of such a reason common to both the primitive and its double, no relation of ideal equivalence that structures the subject for us to the point of splitting it. The double is no longer a fantastic ectoplasm, an archaic resurgence issuing from guilt and the depths of the unconscious (we will come back to this). The double, like the dead man (the dead man is the double of the living, the double is the familiar living figure of the dead), is a *partner* with whom the primitive has a personal and concrete relationship, sometimes happy, sometimes not, a certain type of visible exchange (word, gesture and ritual) with an invisible part of himself. *We cannot speak of alienation here*, for the subject is only alienated (like we are) when he internalises an abstract agency, issuing from the 'other world', as Nietzsche said – whether psychological (the ego and the ego-ideal), religious (God and the soul) or moral (conscience and the law) – an irreconcilable agency to which everything else is subordinated. Historically then, alienation begins with the internalisation of the Master by the *emancipated* slave: there is no alienation as long as the *duel*-relation of the master and the slave lasts.

The primitive has a non-alienated duel-relation with his double. He really can trade, as we are forever forbidden to do, *with his shadow* (the real shadow, not a metaphor), as with some original, living thing, in order to converse, protect and conciliate this tutelary or hostile shadow. The shadow is precisely not the reflection of an 'original' body, it has a full part to play, and is consequently not an 'alienated' part of the subject, but one of the figures of exchange. In another context, this is precisely what poets find when they question their own body, or interpellate words in language. To speak to one's body and to speak to language in a duel mode beyond the active and the passive (my body speaks (to) me, language speaks (to) me) – to make each fragment of the body and each fragment of language autonomous, like a living being, capable of responding and exchanging – is to bring about the end of separation and the split, which is only the submissive equivalence of each part of the body to the principle of the subject, and the submissive equivalence of each fragment of language to the code of language.

The status of the double (as well as that of spirits and gods, which are also real, living and different beings, not idealised essences) in primitive society is therefore the inverse of our alienation: one being multiplies into innumerable others just as alive as the first, whereas the unified, individual subject can only confront itself in alienation and death.

With the internalisation of the soul and consciousness (the principle of identity and equivalence), the subject undergoes a real confinement, similar to the confinement of the mad in the seventeenth century as described by Foucault. It is at this point that the primitive thought of the double as continuity and exchange is lost, and the haunting double comes to the fore as the subject's discontinuity in death and madness. 'Whoever sees his double, sees his death.' A vengeful and vampiric double, an unquiet soul, the double begins to prefigure the subject's death, haunting him in the very midst of his life. This is Dostoevsky's double, or Peter Schlemihl's, the man who lost his shadow. We have always interpreted this double as a metaphor of the soul, consciousness, native soil, and so on. Without this incurable idealism and without being taken as a metaphor, the narrative is so much more extraordinary. We have all lost our *real* shadows, we no longer speak to them, and our bodies have left with them. To lose one's shadow is already to forget one's body. Conversely, when the shadow grows and becomes an autonomous power (as with the mirror-image in *The Student of Prague*, which has the effect of the Devil and dementia), it is so as to devour the subject who has lost it, it is a murderous shadow, the image of all the rejected and forgotten dead who, as is quite normal, never accept being nothing in the eyes of the living.

Our entire culture is full of this haunting of the separated double, even in its most subtle form, as Freud gave it in 'Das Unheimliche' ('The Uncanny': 'Disturbing Strangeness' or 'Disturbing Familiarity'): the anxiety that wells up around the most familiar things. Here the *vertigo of separation* builds up to its greatest intensity, since this is its simplest form. There comes a moment, in fact, when the things closest to us, such as our own bodies, the body itself, our voice and our appearance, are separated from us to the precise extent that we internalise the soul (or any other equivalent agency or abstraction) as the ideal principle of subjectivity. This is what kills off the proliferation of doubles and spirits, consigning them once again to the spectral, embryonic corridors of unconscious folklore, like the ancient gods that Christianity *verteufelt*, that is, transformed into demons.

By a final ruse of spirituality, this internalisation also *psychologises* doubles. In fact it is interpretation in terms of an archaic *psychical apparatus* that is the very last form of the *Verteufelung*, the demonic corruption and elimination of the primitive double: projection of the guilt attached to the phantasmatic murder of the other (the close relative) in accordance with the magic of the omnipotence of ideas (*Allmacht der Gedanken*), the return of the repressed, etc. In 'The Uncanny', Freud writes:

Our analysis of instances of the uncanny has led us back to the old, animistic conception of the universe. This was characterised by the idea that the world was peopled with the spirits of human beings; by the subject's narcissistic overvaluation of his own mental processes; by the belief in the omnipotence of thoughts and the technique of magic based on that belief; by the attribution to various outside persons and things of carefully graded magical powers, or '*mana*'; as well as by all the other creations with the help of which man, in the unrestricted narcissism of that stage of development, strove to fend off the manifest prohibitions of reality. It seems as if each one of us has been through a phase of individual development corresponding to the animistic stage in primitive men, that none of us has passed through it without preserving certain residues and traces of it which are still capable of manifesting themselves, and that everything which now strikes us as 'uncanny' fulfils the condition of touching those residues of animistic mental activity within us and bringing them back to expression. (*Standard Edition*, Vol. 17, 1955, pp. 240–1)

This is how psychology, our authority in the depths, our own 'next world', this omnipotence, magical narcissism, fear of the dead,[17] this animism or primitive psychical apparatus, is quietly palmed off on the savages in order then to recuperate them for ourselves as 'archaic traces'. Freud does not think this is what he said in speaking of 'narcissistic overvaluation of . . . mental processes'. If there is such an overvaluation of one's own mental processes (to the point of exporting this theory, as we have done with our morality and techniques, to the core of every culture), then it is Freud's overvaluation, along with our whole psychologistic culture. The jurisdiction of the psychological discourse over all symbolic practices (such as the dazzling practices of the savages, death, the double and magic; but also over our current symbolic practices) is even more dangerous than that of the economistic discourse: it is of the same order as the repressive jurisdiction of the soul and consciousness over the body's entire symbolic potential. Psychoanalysis's reinterpretation of the symbolic is a reductive operation. Since we live under the unconscious (but is this the case? Isn't it our own myth, marking out and even participating in repression: a repressed thought of repression?), we believe that we are justified in extending the jurisdiction of psychical history as we used to do with history itself, to every possible configuration. The unconscious, and the psychical order in general, becomes the insurmountable agency, giving the feudal right of trespass over every previous individual and social formation. This imaginary also spreads into the future, however: if the unconscious is our modern myth, and psychoanalysis its prophet, the liberation of the unconscious (Desiring-Revolution) is its millenial heresy.

The idea of the unconscious, *like the idea of consciousness*, remains an idea of discontinuity and rupture. Put simply, it substitutes the irreversibility of a lost object and a subject forever 'missing' itself, for the positivity of the object and the conscious subject. However decentred, the subject remains within the orbit of Western thought, with its successive 'topologies' (hell/heaven – subject/nature – conscious/unconscious), where the fragmented subject can only dream of a lost continuity.[18] It will never get back to, or catch up with [*rejoindre*] utopia, which is not at all the phantasm of a lost order but, contrary to all the topologies of discontinuity and repression, the idea of a duelling order, of reversibility, of a symbolic order (in the strong etymological sense of the term) where, for example, death is not a separate space; where neither the subject's own body nor its own shadow are separate spaces; where there is no death putting an end to the history of the body; where there is no bar putting an end to the ambivalence of the subject and the object; where there is neither a beyond (survival and death) nor an 'on this side' (the unconscious and the lost object); only an immediate, non-phantasmatic actualisation of symbolic reciprocity. This utopian idea is not fusional: only nostalgia engenders fusional utopias. There is no nostalgia here, nor is anything lost, separated or unconscious. Everything is already there, reversible and sacrificed.

Political Economy and Death

> We do not die because we must, we die because it is a habit,
> to which one day, not so long ago, our thoughts became bound.
>
> Raoul Vaneigem

> *Den Göttern ist der Tod immer nur ein Vorurteil*
> [To the Gods, death is only ever a prejudice.]
>
> F.W. Nietzsche

As a universal of the human condition, death exists only when *society* discriminates against the dead. The *institution* of death, like that of the afterlife and immortality, is a recent victory for the *political* rationalism of castes, priests and the Church: their power is based on the management of the imaginary sphere of death. As regards the disappearance of the religious afterlife, it is the even more recent victory for the *State's* political rationality. When the afterlife fades in the face of the advances made by 'materialist' reason, it is quite simply because it has crossed over into life itself. The power of the State is based on the management *of life as the objective afterlife*. In this, it is more powerful than the Church, since the abstract power of the State is increased not by an imaginary beyond, but by the imaginary of life itself. It relies on secularised death, the transcendence of the social, and its force derives from the mortal abstraction it embodies. Just as medicine is the management of the corpse, so the State is the management of the dead body of the socius.

From the start, the Church was established on the bipartition of survival, or the afterlife, from life, the earthly world and the Kingdom of Heaven. It kept a jealous watch over this partition, for if the distance disappeared, its power would be at an end. The Church lives in the *deferred eternity* (as the State lives in deferred society, as revolutionaries live in the deferred revolution: all are living in death) that it had so much trouble imposing. All primitive Christianity, and later popular, messianic and heretical Christianity, lived in the hope of parousia, in the necessity of the immediate realisation of the Kingdom of God (cf. W.E. Mühlmann,

Les Messianismes révolutionnaires [tr. J.B., 1968]). The mad Christians did not at first believe in a heaven and hell in the beyond: their vision implied the pure and simple resolution of death in the collective will for *immediate eternity*. The great Manichean heresies that threatened the foundations of the Church hold the same principle since they interpret this world as an antagonistic duality, a *here* and a *there*, of the principles of good and evil; impiously, they bring heaven and hell down to earth. For having effaced the glaze of the beyond they were ferociously suppressed, as were the spiritualist heretics of the St Francis of Assisi or the Joachim of Fiore type, whose radical charity amounted to establishing a total community on this earth and thus sparing the Last Judgement. The Cathars also set their sights a little too much on *achieved* perfection in the inseparability of body and soul, the immanence of salvation in collective faith, which made a joke of the Church's power of death. Throughout its history, the Church has had to dismantle the primitive community which had a tendency to seek salvation in the intense reciprocity with which it was shot through and on which it drew for its own energy. Against the abstract universality of God and the Church, sects and communities practised the 'self-management' of salvation, which then consisted in the group's symbolic exaltation, finally turning into a deadly vertigo. The Church's sole condition of possibility is the incessant elimination of this symbolic demand. This is also the State's sole condition of possibility. At this point political economy enters the arena.

To counter the dazzling sight of earthly communities, the Church imposes a *political economy of individual salvation*. First through faith (which became the soul's *personal* relation to God instead of the effervescent community), then through the accumulation of works and merits, that is, an economy in the strict sense of the term, with its final account and its equivalences. It is then, as always since the appearance of processes of accumulation,[19] that death really arose at the horizon of life. It is then that the Kingdom really passes to the other side of death, before which everyone finds themselves *alone* once again. Wherever it goes, Christianity trails with it the fascination with suffering, solitude and death involved in the destruction of archaic communities. In the completed form of the religious universal, as in the economic (capital), everyone finds themselves alone again.

With the sixteenth century, the modern figure of death was generalised. The Counter-Reformation, the funereal and obsessional games of the Baroque, and especially Protestantism, by individualising conscience before God and disinvesting collective ceremonials, brought about the progress of the individual's anguish of death. It also gave rise to the immense modern enterprise of staving off death: the ethics of accumulation and material production, sacralisation through investment, the labour and profit collectively called the 'spirit of capitalism' (Max Weber, *The Protestant Work Ethic* [tr. T. Parsons, London: Routledge, 1992]) constructed a salvation-machine from which intra-worldly ascesis is little by little withdrawn in the interests of worldly and productive accumulation, without changing the aim of protecting itself against death.

With the turn of the sixteenth century, the vision and iconography of death in the Middle Ages was still folkloric and joyous. There is a *collective theatre* of death, which was not yet buried in individual consciousness (nor, as later, in the unconscious). In the fifteenth century, death also inspired the great messianic and egalitarian festival of the Dance of Death: kings, bishops, princes, townsfolk and villagers are all equal in the face of death, by way of a challenge to the unequal order of birth, wealth and power. This was the last great movement that Death was able to appear as an offensive myth, and as collective speech, since, as we know, death has become an individual, tragic[20] thought 'of the law [*de droite*]', a 'reactionary' thought as regards revolt and social revolutionary movements.

Our death was really born in the sixteenth century. It has lost its scythe and its clock, it has lost the Apocalyptic Horsemen and the grotesque and macabre plays of the Middle Ages. Again, all this came from folklore and festival, in which death was still exchanged, not of course with the primitives' 'symbolic efficacy', but at least as the *collective* phantasm on cathedral pediments and in the divided operations of hell. We could even say that pleasure is possible insofar as there is a hell. Its disappearence from the imaginary is only the sign of its psychological interiorisation; death ceases to be the Grim Reaper, and becomes an anguish concerning death. More subtle and more scientific generations of priests and sorcerers will flourish on this psychological hell.

With the disintegration of traditional Christian and feudal communities through bourgeois Reason and the nascent system of political economy, death is no longer divided. It is cast in the image of the material goods which, as in previous exchanges, begin to circulate less between insepar-able partners (it is always more or less a community or a clan who exchange), and increasingly under the sign of a general equivalent. In the capitalist mode, everyone is alone before the general equivalent. It is no coincidence that, in the same way, everyone finds themselves alone before death, since *death is general equivalence*.

From this point on the obsession with death and the will to abolish death through accumulation become the fundamental motor of the rationality of political economy. Value, in particular time as value, is accumulated in the phantasm of death deferred, pending the term of a linear infinity of value. Even those who no longer believe in a personal eternity believe in the infinity of time as they do in a species-capital of double-compound interests. The infinity of capital passes into the infinity of time, the eternity of a productive system no longer familiar with the reversibility of gift-exchange, but instead with the irreversibility of quantitative growth. The accumulation of time imposes the idea of progress, as the accumulation of science imposes the idea of truth: in each case, what is accumulated is no longer symbolically exchanged, but becomes an *objective* dimension. Ultimately, the total objectivity of time, like total accumulation, is the total impossibility of symbolic exchange, that is, death. Hence the absolute impasse of political economy, which intends to eliminate death through accumulation: the time of accumulation is the time of death itself. We cannot hope for a dialectical revolution at the end of this process of spiralling hoarding.

We already know that the economic rationalisation of exchange (the market) is the social form which *produces* scarcity (Marshall Sahlins, 'The original affluent society', in *Stone Age Economics* [Chicago: Aldine and Atherton, 1972]). Similarly, the infinite accumulation of time as value under the sign of general equivalence entails the *absolute scarcity of time that is death*.

A contradiction in capitalism? No, communism in this instance is in solidarity with political economy, since, in accordance with the same fantastic schema of an eternal accumulation of productive forces, communism too aims for the abolition of death. Only its total ignorance of death (save perhaps as a hostile horizon to be conquered by science and technics) has protected it up to now from the worst contradictions. For nothing can will the abolition of the law of value if you want to abolish death, that is, to preserve life as absolute value, at the same time. Life itself must leave the law of value and achieve a successful exchange against death. The materialists, with their idealistic life expurgated of death, a life 'free' at last of all ambivalence, hardly trouble themselves with this.[21]

Our whole culture is just one huge effort to dissociate life and death, to ward off the ambivalence of death in the interests of life as value, and time as the general equivalent. The elimination of death is our phantasm, and ramifies in every direction: for religion, the afterlife and immortality; for science, truth; and for economics, productivity and accumulation.

No other culture had this distinctive opposition of life and death in the interests of life as positivity: life as accumulation, death as due payment.

No other culture had this impasse: as soon as the *ambivalence* of life and death and the symbolic reversibility of death comes to an end, we enter into a process of accumulation of life as *value*; but by the same token, we also enter the field of the *equivalent* production of death. So life-become-value is constantly *perverted* by the equivalent death. Death, at the same instant, becomes the object of a perverse desire. Desire invests the very separation of life and death.

This is the only way that we can speak of a death-drive. This is the only way we can speak of the unconscious, for *the unconscious is only the accumulation of equivalent death*, the death that is no longer exchanged and can only be cashed out in the phantasm. The symbolic is the inverse dream of an end of accumulation and a possible reversibility of death in exchange. *Symbolic* death, which has not undergone the *imaginary* disjunction of life and death which is at the origin of the *reality* of death, is exchanged in a social ritual of feasting. Imaginary-real death (our own) can only be redeemed through the individual work of mourning, which the subject carries out over the death of others and over himself from the start

life. This work of mourning has fuelled Western metaphysics of
:e Christianity, even in the metaphysical concept of the death

The Death Drive

With Freud we pass from philosophical death and the drama of consciousness to death as a pulsional process inscribed in the unconscious order;
from a metaphysics of anguish to a metaphysics of the pulsion. It's just as if
death, *liberated from the subject*, at last gained its status as an *objective*
finality: the pulsional energy of death or the principle of psychical
functioning.

Death, by becoming a pulsion, does not cease to be a finality (it is even
the only end from this standpoint: the proposition of the death drive
signifies an extraordinary simplification of finalities, since even Eros is
subordinate to it), but this finality sinks, and is inscribed in the unconscious. Now this sinking of death into the unconscious coincides with the
sinking of the dominant system: death becomes simultaneously a 'principle
of psychical functioning' and the 'reality principle' of our social formations,
through the immense repressive mobilisation of labour and production. In
other words, with the death drive, Freud installs the process of *repetition* at
the core of objective determinations, at the very moment when the general
system of production passes into pure and simple *reproduction*. This
coincidence is extraordinary, since we are much more interested in a
genealogy of the concept of the death drive than in its metaphysical status.
Is the death drive an anthropological 'discovery' which supplants all the
others (and which can from now on provide a universal explanatory
principle: we can imagine political economy entirely governed and engendered by the death drive), or is it *produced* at a given moment in relation to
a particular configuration of the system? In this case, its radical nature is
simply the radical nature of the system itself, and the concept merely
sanctions a culture of death by giving it the label of a trans-historical
pulsion. This operation is characteristic of all idealist thought, but we
refuse to admit this with Freud. With Freud (as with Marx), Western
reason will stop rationalising and idealising its own principles, it will even
stop idealising reality through its critical effect of 'objectivity'. Ultimately,
reality will designate unsurpassable pulsional or economic structures: thus
the death drive as the *eternal* process of desire. But how is it that this
proposition is itself not a matter of a secondary elaboration?

It is true that, at first, the death drive breaks with Western thought.
From Christianity to Marxism and existentialism: either death is openly
denied and sublimated, or it is dialecticised. In Marxist theory and
practice, death is already conquered in the being of the class, or it is
integrated as historical negativity. In more general terms, the whole
Western practice of the domination of nature and the sublimation of

aggression in production and accumulation is characterised as constructive Eros: Eros makes use of sublimated aggression for its own ends and, in the movement of becoming (this applies just as much to political economy), death is distilled as negativity into homeopathic doses. Not even the modern philosophies of 'being-towards-death' reverse this tendency: here death serves as a tragic haunting of the subject, sealing its absurd liberty.[22]

In Freud it is quite another matter. A dialectic with the death drive is no longer possible; there is no longer any sublimation, even if it is tragic. For the first time, death appeared as an indestructible *principle*, in opposition to Eros. The subject, class and history are irrelevant in this regard: the irreducible duality of the two pulsions, Eros and Thanatos, rewakens the ancient Manichean version of the world, the endless antagonism of the twin principles of good and evil. This very powerful vision comes from the ancient cults where the basic intuition of a specificity of evil and death was still strong. This was unbearable to the Church, who will take centuries to exterminate it and impose the pre-eminent principle of the Good (God), reducing evil and death to a negative principle, dialectically subordinate to the other (the Devil). But there is always the nightmare of Lucifer's autonomy, the Archangel of Evil (in all their forms, as popular heresies and superstitions that always have a tendency to take the existence of a principle of evil literally and hence to form cults around it, even including black magic and Jansenist theory, not to mention the Cathars), which will haunt the Church day and night. It opposes the dialectic as an institutional theory and as a deterrent to a radical, dualistic and Manichean concept of death. History will bring victory to the Church and the dialectic (including the 'materialist' dialectic). In this sense, Freud breaks quite profoundly with Christian and Western metaphysics.

The duality of the life and death instincts corresponds more precisely to Freud's position in *Beyond the Pleasure Principle*. In *Civilisation and its Discontents*, the duality completes itself in a cycle dominated solely by the death drive. Eros is nothing but an immense detour taken by culture towards death, which subordinates everything to its own ends. But this last version does not, however, revert to an inverted dialectic between the two terms of the duality, since dialectics can only be the constructive becoming of Eros, whose goal is 'to establish ever larger unities and to bind and regulate energies'. Two principal characteristics oppose the death drive to this:

1. It dissolves assemblages, unbinds energy and undoes Eros's organic discourse by returning things to an inorganic, *ungebunden*, state, in a certain sense, to utopia as opposed to the articulate and constructive topics of Eros. Entropy of death, negentropy of Eros.

2. This power of disintegration, disarticulation and *defection* implies a radical counter-finality in the form of an involution towards the prior, inorganic state. The compulsion to repeat (*Wiederholungszwang*), or the 'tendency to reproduce and revive even those past events that involve no satisfaction whatsoever', is primarily, for every living being, the tendency

to reproduce the non-event of a prior inorganic state of things, that is to say, death. It is thus always as a repetitive cycle that death comes to dismantle the constructive, linear or dialectical finalities of Eros. The viscosity of the death drive and the elasticity of the inorganic is everywhere victorious in its resistance to the structuration of life.

In the proposed death drive therefore, whether in its duel form or in the incessant and destructive counter-finality of repetition, there is something irreducible to all the intellectual apparatuses of Western thought. Freud's thought acts fundamentally as the death drive in the Western theoretical universe. But then, of course, it is absurd to give it the constructive status of 'truth': the 'reality' of the death instinct is indefensible; to remain faithful to the intuition of the death drive, it must remain a deconstructive hypothesis, that is, it must be adopted solely within the limits of the deconstruction that it carries out on all prior thought. As a concept, however, it too must be immediately deconstructed. We cannot think (other than as the ultimate subterfuge of reason) that the principle of deconstruction is all that escapes it.

The death drive must be defended against every attempt to redialecticise it into a new constructive edifice. Marcuse is a good example of this. Concerning repression through death, he writes: 'Theology and philosophy today compete with each other in celebrating death as an existential category. Perverting[!] a biological fact into an ontological essence, they bestow transcendental blessing on the guilt of mankind which they help to perpetuate' (*Eros and Civilisation* [London: Sphere, 1970], p. 188). Thus it is for 'surplus-repression'. As for fundamental repression:

> The brute fact of death denies once and for all the reality of a non-repressive existence. For death is the final negativity of time, but 'joy wants eternity'. . . . Time has no power over the Id, the original domain of the pleasure principle. But the Ego, through which alone pleasure becomes real, is in its entirety subject to time. The mere anticipation of the inevitable end, present in every instant, introduces a repressive element into all libidinal relations. (ibid., p. 185)

We will overlook the 'brute fact of death': it is never a brute fact, only a social relation is repressive. What is most curious is the way in which death's primal repression exchanges signs with the 'liberation' of Eros:

> The death instinct operates under the Nirvana principle: it tends towards . . . a state without want. This trend of this instinct implies that its *destructive* manifestations would be minimised as it approached such a state. If the instinct's basic objective is not the termination of life but of pain – the absence of tension – then paradoxically, in terms of the instinct, the conflict between life and death is the more reduced, the closer life approximates the state of gratification. . . . Eros, freed from surplus-repression, would be strengthened, and the strengthened Eros would, as it were, absorb the objective of the death instinct. *The instinctual value of death would have changed.* (ibid., p. 187, J.B.'s emphasis)

Thus we will be able to change the instinct and triumph over the brute fact, in accordance with good old idealist philosophy of freedom and necessity:

> Death can become a token of freedom. The necessity of death does not refute

the possibility of final liberation. Like the other necessities, it can be made rational – painless. (ibid., p. 188)

The Marcusean dialectic therefore implies the total restoration of the death drive (in *Eros and Civilisation*, however, this passage is immediately followed by the 'Critique of Neo-Freudian Revisionism'!), thus limiting the resistances this concept provokes in pious souls. Here again, it is not too much for dialectics – the 'liberation' of Eros in this instance; in others the 'liberation' of the forces of production – to bring about the end of death.

The death drive is irritating, because it does not allow of any dialectical recovery. This is where its radicalism lies. But the panic it provokes does not confer the status of truth on it: we must wonder if, in the final instance, it is not itself a rationalisation of death.

This is first of all the conviction that we hear in Freud (elsewhere he will talk of a speculative hypothesis):

The dominating tendency of mental life . . . is the effort to reduce, to keep constant or to remove internal tension due to stimuli (the 'Nirvana principle', to borrow a term from Barbara Low) . . . [which] is one of our strongest reasons for believing in the existence of death instincts. ('Beyond the pleasure principle', in *Standard Edition*, Vol. 18, 1955, pp. 55–6)

Why, then, all Freud's efforts to ground the death instinct in biological rationality (Weissmann's analysis, etc.)? This positivist effort is generally deplored, a little like Engels' attempt to dialecticise Nature that we agree to ignore out of affection for him. However:

If we are to take it as a truth that knows no exception that everything living dies for *internal* reasons – becomes inorganic once again – then we shall be compelled to say that '*the aim of all life is death*' and, looking backwards, that '*inanimate things existed before living ones*'. . . . Thus these guardians of life [instincts], too, were originally the myrmidons of death. (ibid., p. 38)

It is difficult to rid the death drive of positivism here in order to turn it into a 'speculative hypothesis' or 'purely and simply a principle of psychical functioning' (J.B. Pontalis, *L'Arc*, 34, 1968). Moreover, at this level there is no longer any real pulsional duality: death alone is finality. But it is this finality that in turn poses a crucial problem, since it inscribes death as anterior, as psychical and organic destiny, almost like programming or genetic code, in short, as a *positivity* that, unless we believe in the scientific reality of this pulsion, we can only take it as a myth. We can only set Freud against what he himself says:

The theory of the drives is so to say our mythology. Drives are mythical entities, magnificent in their indefiniteness. ('New introductory lectures', in *Standard Edition*, Vol. 22, 1964, p. 95)

If the death drive is a myth, then this is how we will interpret it. We will interpret the death drive, and the concept of the unconscious itself, as myths, and no longer take account of their effects or their efforts at 'truth'. A myth *recounts* something: not so much in the content as in the form of its discourse. Let's make a bet that, under the metaphoric species of sexuality and death, psychoanalysis tells us something concerning the fundamental organisation of our culture, that when the myth is no longer told, when it establishes its fables as axioms, it loses the 'magnificent indefiniteness' that Freud spoke of. 'The concept is only the residue of a metaphor', as Nietzsche said. Let's bet then on the *metaphor* of the unconscious, on the *metaphor* of the death drive.

Eros in the service of death, all cultural sublimation as a long detour to death, the death drive nourishing repressive violence and presiding over culture like a ferocious super-ego, the forces of life inscribed in the compulsion to repeat; all this is true, but true of *our* culture. Death undertakes to abolish death and, for this very purpose, erects death above death and is haunted by it as its own end. The term 'pulsion' or 'drive' is stated metaphorically, designating the contemporary phase of the political-economic system (does it then remain political economy?) where the law of value, in its most terroristic structural form, reaches completion in the pure and simple compulsive reproduction of the code, where the law of value appears to be a finality as irreversible as a pulsion, so that it takes on the figure of a destiny for our culture. Stage of the immanent repetition of one and the same law, insisting on its own end, caught, totally invested by death as objective finality, and total subversion by the death drive as a deconstructive process – the metaphor of the death drive says all of this simultaneously, for the death drive is at the same time the system and the system's *double*, its doubling into a radical counter-finality (see the Double, and its 'worrying strangeness', *das Unheimliche*).

This is what the myth recounts. But let's see what happens when it sets itself up as the objective discourse of the 'pulsion'. With the term 'pulsion', which has both a biological and a psychical definition, psychoanalysis settles down into categories that come straight from the imaginary of a certain Western reason: far from radically contradicting this latter, it must then interpret itself as a moment of Western thought. As for the biological, it is clear that scientific rationality produces the distinction of the living and the non-living on which biology is based. Science, producing itself as a code, on the one hand literally produces the dead, the non-living, as a conceptual object, and, on the other, produces the separation of the dead as an axiom from which science can be legitimated. The only good (scientific) object, just like the only good Indian, is a dead one. Now it is this inorganic state to which the death drive is oriented, to the non-living status that only comes about through the arbitrary decrees of science and, when all's said and done, through its own phantasm of repression and death. Ultimately, being nothing but the cyclical repetition of the non-living, the death drive contributes to biology's arbitrariness, doubling it through a psychoanalytic route. But not every culture produces a separate concept of the non-living; only our culture produces it, under the sign of biology. Thus, suspending the discrimination would be enough to invalidate the concept of the death drive, which is ultimately only a theoretical agreement between the living and the dead, with the sole result that

science loses its footing amongst all the attempts at articulation.
living is always permanently sweeping science along into the axion
a system of death (see J. Monod, *Chance and Necessity* [tr. .
Wainhouse, London: Collins, 1970]).

The problem is the same as regards the psychical, putting the whc.. of
psychoanalysis into question. We must ask ourselves when and why our
system began to produce the 'psychical'. The psychical has only recently
become autonomous, doubling biology's autonomy at a higher level. This
time the line passes between the organic, the somatic and 'something else'.
There is nothing psychical save on the basis of this distinction. Hence the
ensuing insoluble difficulty of linking the two parts together again; the
precise result of this is the concept of the pulsion, which is intended to form
a bridge betwen the two, but which merely contributes to the arbitrariness
of each. Here the metapsychology of the pulsion reverts to mind–body
metaphysics, rewriting it at a more advanced stage.

The separated order of the psychical results from our precipitate desire,
in our (conscious or unconscious) 'heart of hearts', for everything that the
system prohibits from collective and symbolic exchange: it is an order of
the repressed. It is hardly astonishing that this order is governed by the
death drive, since it is nothing but the precipitate individual of an order of
death. Psychoanalysis, like every other discipline, theorises the death drive
as such within its own order, and so merely sanctions this mortal
discrimination.

Conscious, unconscious, super-ego, guilt, repression, primary and
secondary processes, phantasm, neurosis and psychosis: yes, all this works
very well *if we consent to* the circumscription of the psychical as such,
which circumscription produces our system (not just any system) as the
immediate and fundamental form of intelligibility, that is to say, as *code*.
The omnipotence of the code is precisely the inscription of separate
spheres, which then justifies a specialised investigation and a sovereign
science; but it is undoubtedly the psychical that has the best future. All the
savage, errant, transversal and symbolic processes will be inscribed and
domesticated within it, *in the name of the unconscious itself*, which, like an
unexpected joke, is generally considered today as the leitmotiv of radical
'liberation'! Death itself will be domesticated under the sign of the death
drive!

In fact the death drive must be interpreted against Freud and psychoanalysis if we wish to retain its radicality. The death drive must be
understood as acting against the scientific positivity of the psychoanalytic
apparatus as developed by Freud. The death drive is not just the limit of
psychoanalysis's formulations nor its most radical conclusion, it is its
reversal, and those who have rejected the concept of the death drive have,
in a certain sense, a more accurate view than those who take it, as even
Freud himself did, in their psychoanalytic stride without, perhaps, understanding what he had said. The death drive effectively goes far beyond all
previous points of view and renders all previous apparatuses, whether

economic, energetic, topological or even the psychical apparatus itself, useless. All the more reason, of course, for the pulsional logic it draws on, inherited from the scientific mythology of the nineteenth century. Perhaps Lacan guessed this when he spoke of the 'irony' of the concept of the death drive, of the unheard of and insoluble paradox that it poses. Historically, psychoanalysis has taken the view that this is its strangest offspring, but death does not allow itself to be caught in the mirror of psychoanalysis. It acts as a total, radical, functional principle, and has no need of the mirror, repression, nor even a libidinal economy. It merely meanders through successive topologies and energetic calculi, ultimately forming the economics of the unconscious itself, denouncing all that *as well* as Eros's positive machinery, as the positive interpreting machine that it disrupts and dismantles like any other. A principle of counter-finality, a radical speculative hypothesis, meta-economic, metapsychical, meta-energetic, metapsychoanalytic, the death (drive) is beyond the unconscious: it must be wrested from psychoanalysis and turned against it.

Death in Bataille

Despite its radicality, the psychoanalytic vision of death remains an *insufficient vision*: the pulsions are *constrained* by repetition, its perspective bears on a final equilibrium within the inorganic continuum, eliminating differences and intensities following an involution towards the lowest point; an entropy of death, pulsional conservatism, equilibrium in the absence of Nirvana. This theory manifests certain affinities with Malthusian political economy, the objective of which is to protect oneself against death. For political economy only exists by default: death is its blind spot, the absence haunting all its calculations. And the absence of death alone permits the exchange of values and the play of equivalences. *An infinitesimal injection of death would immediately create such excess and ambivalence that the play of value would completely collapse.* Political economy is an economy of death, because it economises on death and buries it under its discourse. The death drive falls into the opposite category: it is the discourse of death as *the* insurmountable finality. This discourse is oppositional but complementary, for if political economy is indeed Nirvana (the infinite accumulation and reproduction of dead value), then the death drive denounces its truth, at the same time as subjecting it to absolute derision. It does this, however, in the terms of the system itself, by idealising death as a drive (as an objective finality). As such, the death drive is the current system's most radical negative, but even it simply holds up a mirror to the funereal imaginary of political economy.

Instead of establishing death as the regulator of tensions and an equilibrium function, as the *economy* of the pulsion, Bataille introduces it in the opposite sense, as the paroxysm of exchanges, superabundance and excess. Death as excess, always already there, proves that life is only defective when death has taken it hostage, that life only exists in bursts and in exchanges with death, if it is not condemned to the discontinuity of value and therefore to absolute deficit. 'To will that there be life only is to make sure that there is only death.' The idea that death is not at all a breakdown of life, that it is willed by life itself, and that the delirial (economic) phantasm of eliminating it is equivalent to implanting it in the heart of life itself – this time as an endless mournful nothingness. Biologically, '[t]he idea of a world where human life might be artificially prolonged has a nightmare quality about it' (G. Bataille, *Eroticism* [2nd edn, tr. M. Dalwood, London: Marion Boyars, 1987], p. 101), but symbolically above all; and here the nightmare is no longer a simple possibility, but the reality we live at every instant: death (excess, ambivalence, gift, sacrifice, expenditure and the paroxysm), and so real life is absent from it. We renounce dying and accumulate instead of losing ourselves:

> Not only do we renounce death, but also we let our desire, which is really the desire to die, lay hold of its object and we keep it while we live on. We enrich our life instead of losing it. (*Eroticism*, p. 142)

Here, luxury and prodigality predominate over functional calculation, just as death predominates over life as the unilateral finality of production and accumulation:

> On a comprehensive view, human life strives towards prodigality to the point of anguish, to the point where the anguish becomes unbearable. The rest is mere moralising chatter. . . . A febrile unrest within us asks death to wreak its havoc at our expense. (ibid., p. 60)

Death and sexuality, instead of confronting each other as antagonistic principles (Freud), are exchanged in the same cycle, in the same cyclical *revolution* of continuity. Death is not the 'price' of sexuality – the sort of equivalence one finds in every theory of complex living beings (the infusorium is itself immortal and asexual) – nor is sexuality a simple detour on the way to death, as in *Civilisation and its Discontents*: they exchange their energies and excite each other. Neither has its own specific economy: life and death only fall under the sway of a single economy if they are separated; once they are mixed, they pass beyond economics altogether, into festivity and loss (eroticism according to Bataille):

> [W]e can no longer differentiate between sexuality and death [, which] are simply the culminating points of the festival nature celebrates, with the inexhaustible multitude of living beings, both of them signifying the boundless wastage of nature's resources as opposed to the urge to live on characteristic of every living creature. (*Eroticism*, p. 61)

This festivity takes place because it reinstates the *cycle* where penury imposes the *linear* economy of duration, because it reinstates a cyclical revolution of life and death where Freud augurs no other issue than the repetitive involution of death.

In Bataille, then, there is a vision of death as a principle of excess and an anti-economy. Hence the metaphor of luxury and the luxurious character of death. Only sumptuous and useless expenditure has meaning; the economy has no meaning, it is only a residue that has been made into the law of life, whereas wealth lies in the luxurious exchange of death: sacrifice, the 'accursed share', escaping investment and equivalence, can only be annihilated. If life is only a need to survive *at any cost*, then annihilation is a *priceless* luxury. In a system where life is ruled by value and utility, death becomes a useless luxury, and the only alternative.

In Bataille, this luxurious conjunction of sex and death figures under the sign of *continuity*, in opposition to the discontinuous economy of individual existences. Finality belongs in the discontinuous order, where discontinuous beings secrete finality, all sorts of finalities, which amount to only one: their *own* death.

> We are discontinuous beings, individuals who perish in isolation in the midst of an incomprehensible adventure, but we yearn for our lost continuity. (*Eroticism*, p. 15)

Death itself is without finalities; in eroticism, the finality of the individual being is put back into question:

> What does physical eroticism signify if not a violation of the very being of its practitioners . . .? The whole business of eroticism is to destroy the self-contained character of the participants as they are in their normal lives. (ibid., p. 17)

Erotic nakedness is equal to death insofar as it inaugurates a state of communication, loss of identity and fusion. The fascination of the dissolution of constituted forms: such is Eros (*pace* Freud, for whom Eros binds energies, federates them into ever larger unities). In death, as in Eros, it is a matter of introducing all possible continuity into discontinuity, a game of complete continuity. It is in this sense that 'death, the rupture of the discontinuous individualities to which we cleave in terror, stands there before us more real than life itself' (ibid., p. 19). Freud says exactly the same thing, but by default. It is no longer a question of the same death.

What Freud missed was not seeing the curvature of life in death, he missed its vertigo and its excess, its reversal of the entire economy of life, making it, in the form of a final pulsion, into a belated equation of life. Freud stated life's final economy under the sign of repetition and missed its paroxysm. Death is neither resolution nor involution, but a reversal and a symbolic challenge.

> For once they travel down their allotted paths
> With open eyes, self-oblivious, too ready to
> Comply with what the gods have wished them,
> Only too gladly will mortal beings
> Speed back into the All by the shortest way;
> So rivers plunge – not movement, but rest they seek,
> Drawn on, pulled down against their will from
> Boulder to boulder – abandoned, helmless –
> By that mysterious yearning toward the chasm;
> Chaotic deeps attract, and whole peoples too
> May come to long for death
> [By Xanthos once, in Grecian times, there stood
> The town]

The kindness of Brutus provoked them. For
When fire broke out, most nobly he offered them
His help, although he led those troops which
Stood at their gates to besiege the township
Yet from the walls they threw all the servants down
Whom he had sent. Much livelier then at once
The fire flared up, and they rejoiced, and
Brutus extended his arms towards them,
All were beside themselves. And great crying there,
Great jubilation sounded. Then into flames
Leapt man and woman; boys came hurtling
Down from the roofs or their fathers stabbed them.
It is not wise to fight against heroes. But
Events long prepared it. Their ancestors
When they were quite encircled once and
Strongly the Persian forces pressed them,
Took rushes from the rivers and, that their foes
Might find a desert there, set ablaze the town;
And house and temple – breathed to holy
Aether – and men did the flame carry off there.
So their descendants heard . . . (Hölderlin, 'Voice of the people'
[2nd version, in *Friedrich Hölderlin: Poems and Fragments*, tr. and ed. Michael
Hamburger, London: Routledge and Kegan Paul, 1966, pp. 178–83])

The proposition according to which life and death are exchanged, and
exchanged at the highest price with death, no longer belongs to the order
of scientific truth, since it is a 'truth' that science is forever forbidden.

> If the union of two lovers comes about through love, it involves the idea of
> death, murder or suicide . . . [a] continuous violation of discontinuous individu-
> ality . . . the orifices, gulfs and abysses whereby beings are absorbed into
> continuity, somehow assimilates it to death. (Bataille, *Eroticism*, pp. 21ff)

When Bataille says this, concerning eroticism, there is no objective
relation, no law, and no natural necessity in any of this. Luxury and excess
are not functions, they are inscribed neither in the body nor in the world.
Nor on the other hand is death – sumptuous, symbolic death, which
belongs to the order of the challenge – inscribed in a body or a nature any
longer. The symbolic can never be confused with the real or with science.

But even Bataille commits the following error:

> The desire to produce at cut prices is niggardly and human. Nature, for its part,
> is boundlessly prodigious, and 'sacrifices' in good spirits. (ibid., p. 60)

Why seek the security of an ideally prodigious nature, as opposed to the
economists' ideally circulating nature? Luxury is no more 'natural' than
economics. Sacrifice and sacrificial expenditure are not of the order of
things. This error leads Bataille to confuse reproductive sexuality with
erotic expenditure:

> The excess from which reproduction springs can only be understood with the aid
> of the excess of death, and vice-versa. (ibid., p. 101)

But reproduction as such has no excess – even if it implies the individual's
death, it is still a matter of a positive economy and a functional death –
from which the species might benefit. Sacrificial death, however, is anti-

productive and anti-reproductive. It is true that it aims at continuity, as Bataille says, but not that of the species, which is only the continuity of an order of life, whereas the radical continuity in which the subject is ruined by sex and death always signifies the fabulous loss of an order. It is no more supported by the reproductive act than desire is supported by need, no more than sumptuary expenditure prolongs the satisfaction of needs: this biological functionalism is annihilated in eroticism. To look for the secret of sacrifice, sacrificial destruction, play and expenditure in the law of the species, is to reduce it all to a functionalism. There is not even a contiguity between sacrifice and the law of the species. Erotic excess and the reproductive sexual function have nothing in common. The symbolic excess of death has nothing in common with the body's biological losses.[23]

Bataille, here, labours the influence of the temptation of naturalism, if not biologism, leading him, conversely, to naturalise a tendency to discontinuity: 'The urge to live on characteristic of every living creature' (ibid., p. 61). The 'living creature' protects itself against the living energies of a debauched nature, an orgy of annihilation by means of prohibitions, resisting the excess of the death drive that comes from nature by every available means (its resistance, however, is only ever provisional: 'Men have never definitively said *no* to violence and death' – ibid., p. 62).

Thus, on the basis of a *natural* definition of expenditure (nature as the model of prodigality) and a substantial and ontological definition of economics (the subject wishes to live on in his being – but where does this basic desire come from?), Bataille sets up a kind of *subjective dialectic* of prohibition and transgression, where the initially high-spirited character of sacrifice and death is lost in the delights of Christianity and perversion;[24] a kind of *objective dialectic* between continuity and discontinuity where the challenge posed by death to economic organisation is effaced in the face of a great metaphysical alternation.

Nevertheless, something remains in Bataille's excessive and luxuriant vision of death that removes it from psychoanalysis and its individual and psychical domain. This something provides the opportunity to disturb every economy, shattering not only the objective mirror of political economy, but also the inverse psychical mirror of repression, the unconscious and libidinal economy. Beyond all mirrors, or in their fragments, shattered like those of the mirror where *The Student of Prague* rediscovered his real image at the moment of death, something appears for us today: a fantastic dispersal of the body, of being and wealth. Bataille's figure of death is the closest premonition of this.

My Death is Everywhere, my Death Dreams

Punctual Death, Biological Death

The irreversibility of biological death, its objective and punctual character, is a modern fact of science. It is specific to our culture. Every other culture says that death begins before death, that life goes on after life, and that it is impossible to distinguish life from death. Against the representation which sees in one the *term* of the other, we must try to see the radical *indeterminacy* of life and death, and the impossibility of their autonomy in the symbolic order. Death is not a due payment [*échéance*], it is a nuance of life; or, life is a nuance of death. But our modern idea of death is controlled by a very different system of representations: that of the machine and the function. A machine either works or it does not. Thus the biological machine is either dead or alive. The symbolic order is ignorant of this digital abstraction. And even biology acknowledges that we start dying at birth, but this remains with the category of a functional definition.[25] It is quite another thing to say that death articulates life, is exchanged with life and is the apogee of life: for then it becomes absurd to make life a process which expires with death, and more absurd still to make death equivalent to a deficit and an accelerated repayment. Neither life nor death can any longer be assigned a given *end*: there is therefore no punctuality nor any possible *definition* of death.

We are living entirely within evolutionist thought, which states that we go from life to death: this is the illusion of the subject that sustains both biology and metaphysics (biology wishes to reverse metaphysics, but merely prolongs it). But there is no longer even a subject who dies at a given moment. It is more real to say that whole parts of 'ourselves' (of our bodies, our language) fall from life to death, while the living are subjected to the work of mourning. In this way, a few of the living manage to forget them gradually, as God managed to forget the drowned girl who was carried away by the stream of water in Brecht's song:

Und es geschah, dass Gott sie allmählich vergass,
zuerst das Gesicht, dann die Hände, und zuletzt das Haar . . .
[It happened (very slowly) that it gently slid from God's thoughts:
First her face, then her hands, and right at the end her hair.]
['The Drowned Girl' in *Bertolt Brecht: Poems and Songs*, ed and tr. John Willett, London: Methuen, 1990, p. 14]

The subject's identity is continually falling apart, falling into God's forgetting. But this death is not at all biological. At one pole, biochemistry, asexual protozoa are not affected by death, they divide and branch out (nor is the genetic code, for its part, ever affected by death: it is transmitted unchanged beyond individual fates). At the other, symbolic, pole, death and nothingness no longer exist, since in the symbolic, life and death are reversible.

Only in the infinitesimal space of the individual conscious subject does death take on an irreversible meaning. Even here, death is not an event, but a myth experienced as anticipation. The subject needs a myth of its end, as of its origin, to form its identity. In reality, the subject is never there: like the face, the hands and the hair, and even before no doubt, it is always already somewhere else, trapped in a senseless distribution, an end-less cycle impelled by death. This death, everywhere in life, must be con-jured up and localised in a precise point of time and a precise place: the body.

In biological death, death and the body neutralise instead of stimulating each other. The mind–body duality is biology's *fundamental* presupposition. In a certain sense, this duality is death itself, since it objectifies the body as residual, as a bad object which takes its revenge by dying. It is according to the mind that the body becomes the brute, objective fact, fated for sex, anguish and death. It is according to the mind, this imaginary schizz, that the body becomes the 'reality' that exists only in being condemned to death.

Therefore the mortal body is no more 'real' than the immortal soul: both result simultaneously from the same abstraction, and with them the two great complementary metaphysics: the idealism of the soul (with all its moral metamorphoses) and the 'materialist' idealism of the body, prolonged in biology. Biology lives on as much by the separation of mind and body as from any other Christian or Cartesian metaphysics, but it no longer declares this. The mind or soul is not mentioned any more: as an ideal principle, it has entirely passed into the moral discipline of science; into the legitimating principle of technical operations on the real and on the world; into the principles of an 'objective' materialism. In the Middle Ages, those who practised the discourse of the mind or soul were closer to the 'bodily signs' (Octavio Paz, *Conjunctions and Disjunctions* [tr. Helen Lane, New York: Arcade, 1990]) than biological science, which, techniques and axioms, has passed entirely over to the side of the 'non-body'.

The Accident and the Catastrophe

There is a paradox of modern bourgeois rationality concerning death. To conceive of it as natural, profane and irreversible constitutes the sign of the 'Enlightenment' and Reason, but enters into sharp contradiction with the principles of bourgeois rationality, with its individual values, the unlimited progress of science, and its mastery of nature in all things. Death, neutralised as a 'natural fact', gradually becomes a *scandal*. Octavio Paz has analysed this brilliantly in his theory of the Accident:

> Modern science has eliminated epidemics and has given us plausible explanations of other natural catastrophes: nature has ceased to be the depository of our guilt feelings; at the same time, technology has extended and widened the notion of accident and, what is more, it has given it an absolutely different character. . . . Accidents are part of our daily life and their shadow peoples our dreams. . . . The uncertainty principle in contemporary physics and Gödel's proof in logic are the equivalent of the Accident in the historical world. . . . Axiomatic and deterministic systems have lost their consistency and revealed an inherent defect. But it is not really a defect: it is a property of the system, something that belongs to it as a system. The Accident is not an exception or a sickness of our political regimes; nor is it a correctable defect of our civilisation: it is the natural consequence of our science, our politics and our morality. The Accident is part of our idea of progress. . . . The Accident has become a paradox of necessity: it possesses the fatality of necessity and at the same time the uncertainty of freedom. The *non-body*, transformed into a materialist science, is a synonym for terror: the Accident is one of the attributes of reason that we adore. . . .

Christian morality has given its powers of repression over to it, but at the same time this superhuman power has lost any pretension to morality. It is the return of the anguish of the Aztecs, without any celestial signs or presages. Catastrophe has become banal and laughable because in the final analysis the Accident is only an accident. (*Conjunctions and Disjunctions*, pp. 111–13)

Just as society gives rise to madmen and anomalies at its peripheries in the process of normalisation so reason and the technical mastery of nature, as they become more entrenched, become surrounded by the catastrophic breakdown of the 'inorganic body of nature' they give rise to as unreason. This unreason is intolerable, since reason wants to be sovereign and can no longer even think of what escapes it; it is unresolvable since for us there are no longer any propitiating or reconciling rituals: the accident, like death, is absurd, that's all there is to it. It is a piece of *sabotage*. An evil demon is there to make this beautiful machine always break down. Hence this rationalist culture suffers, like no other, from a collective paranoia. Something or someone must have been responsible for the least accident, the slightest irregularity, the least catastrophe, an earth tremor, a house in ruins, bad weather; everything is an *assassination attempt*. Thus the new wave of sabotage, terrorism and banditism is less interesting than the fact that what happens is *interpreted* this way. Accident or not? Undecidable. Nor is it important, since the category of the Accident analysed by Octavio Paz has fallen under that of the assassination attempt. And this is normal in a rational system: since chance can only be left to a *human* will, every breakdown is interpreted as a curse, an *evil spell*, or, politically, as a breach of the social order.[26] And it is true that a natural catastrophe is a danger to the established order, not only because of the real disorder it provokes, but by the blow it strikes to every sovereign 'rationality', politics included. Hence the state of siege for the earth tremor (Nicaragua), hence the police presence at the scenes of catastrophes (which, at the time of the Ermenonville DC–10 catastrophe, is more important than at a demonstration). For no-one knows to what extent the 'death drive', primed by the accident or the catastrophe, may be unleashed on this occasion and turn against the political order.

It is remarkable that we have returned, in the heyday of the rational system and as a full logical consequence of this system, to the 'primitive' vision where we impute a hostile will to every event, and particularly to death. But it is ourselves and ourselves alone who are full primitives (which nickname we attach to the primitives in order to exorcise it). For the 'primitives' themselves, this conception corresponded to the logic of their reciprocal and ambivalent exchanges involving everything around them; even natural catastrophes and death were easily intelligible through the categories of their social structures, whereas for us it is plainly paralogical. This is arational paranoia, the axioms of which give rise to an increasingly ubiquitous and absolute unintelligibility: death as unacceptable and insoluble, the Accident as persecution, as the absurd and spiteful resistance of a matter or a nature that *will not* abide by the 'objective' laws with which we

have pursued it. Hence the ever increasing fascination with the catastrophe, the accident and the assassination attempt: reason itself is pursued
by the hope of a universal revolt against its own norms and privileges.

'Natural' Death

An ideal or standard form of death, 'natural' death, corresponds to the
biological definition of death and the rational logical will. This death is
'normal' since it comes 'at life's proper term'. Its very concept issues from
the possibility of pushing back the limits of life: living becomes a process of
accumulation, and science and technology start to play a role in this
quantitative strategy. Science and technology do not manage to fulfil an
original desire to live as long as possible; through the symbolic disintrica-
tion of death, life passes into life-capital (into a quantitative evaluation),
which alone gives rise to a biomedical science and technology of prolonging
life.

Natural death therefore signifies not the acceptance of death within 'the
order of things', but a systematic denegation of death. Natural death is
subject to science, and death's call is to be exterminated by science. This
clearly signifies that death is inhuman, irrational and senseless, like
untamed nature (the Western concept of 'nature' is always the concept of a
repressed or domesticated nature). The only good death is a death that has
been defeated and subjected to the law: this is the ideal of natural death.

It should be possible for everyone to reach the term of their biological
'capital', to enjoy life 'to the end' without violence or premature death. As
if everyone had their own little print-out of a life-plan, their 'normal
expectation' of life, basically a 'contract of life'; hence the *social* demand
for a quality of life that makes up part of a natural death. The new social
contract: society as a whole, with its science and technology, becomes
collectively responsible for the death of each individual.[27] This demand
could moreover involve calling the existing order into question, as do
quantitative (wage) demands: to demand a *just* lifespan just as one
demands just rewards for one's labour power. Essentially, this right, like
every other, conceals a repressive jurisdiction. Everyone has a right, but
also a *duty*, to a natural death, for this death is characteristic of the system
of political economy, its typical *obligation* to die:

1. As a system of maximalisation of the forces of production (in an
'extensive' system of manpower, slaves have no natural death, they are
made to work themselves to death);

2. More importantly, that everyone should have a *right* to their life
(habeas corpus – habeas vitam) extends social jurisdiction over death.
Death is socialised like everything else, and can no longer be anything but
natural, since every other death is a *social* scandal: we have not done what
is necessary. Is this social progress? No, it is rather the progress *of* the
social, which even annexes death to itself. Everyone is dispossessed of their
death, and will no longer be able to die as it is now understood. One will no

longer be free to live as long as possible. Amongst other things, this signifies the ban on consuming one's life without taking limits into account. In short, the principle of natural death is equivalent to the neutralisation of life.[28] The same goes for the question of equality in death: life must be reduced to quantity (and death therefore to nothing) in order to adjust it to democracy and the law of equivalences.

Old Age and Retirement: the 'Third Age'

Here too, science's conquest of death enters into contradiction with the system's rationality: retirement becomes a dead weight on social self-management. An entire portion of social wealth (money and moral values) is sunk into it without being able to give it a meaning. A third of society is thus segregated and placed in a situation of economic parasitism. The lands conquered on this death march are socially barren. Recently colonised, old age in modern times burdens society with the same weight as colonised native populations used to. Retirement, or the 'Third Age', says precisely what it means: it is a sort of Third World.

Old age has merely become a marginal and ultimately asocial slice of life – a ghetto, a reprieve and the slide into death. Old age is literally being eliminated. In proportion as the living live longer, as they 'win' over death, they cease to be symbolically acknowledged. Condemned to a forever receding death, this age group loses its status and its prerogatives. In other social formations, old age actually exists as the symbolic pivot of the group. In such societies, the status of the elderly, the perfected form of the ancestor, is the most prestigious. 'Years' constitute real wealth which is exchanged for authority or power, instead of the situation today, where years 'gained' are only calculable accumulated years that have no capacity to be exchanged. Prolonged life expectancy has therefore simply ended up discriminating against old age, which follows logically from discriminating against death itself. Here again, the 'social' has worked well, making old age into a 'social' territory (which in journals appears under this rubric alongside immigrants and abortions), and socialising this part of life into an enclosure over itself. Under the 'beneficent' sign of *natural death*, it has been made into an early *social death*.

> Because the individual life of civilised man, placed into an infinite 'progress' according to its own immanent meaning should never come to an end; for there is a further step ahead of one who stands in the march of progress. And no man who comes to die stands upon the peak which lies in infinity. Abraham, or some peasants of the past, died 'old and satiated with life' because he stood in the organic cycle of life; because his life, in terms of its meaning and on the eve of his days, had given to him what life had to offer; because for him there remained no puzzles he might wish to solve; and therefore he could have had 'enough' of life. Whereas civilised man, placed in the midst of the continuous enrichment of culture by ideas, knowledge and problems, may become 'tired of life' but not 'satiated by life' . . . And because death is meaningless, civilised life as such is meaningless. (Max Weber, 'Science as a Vocation' [in *From Max Weber: Essays*

in Sociology, tr. and ed. H.H. Gerth and C. Wright Mills, London: Routledge and Kegan Paul, 1970], pp. 139–40)

Natural Death and Sacrificial Death

Why is it that today there are no expected and foreseen deaths from old age, a death in the family, the only death that had full meaning for the traditional collectivity, from Abraham to our grandfathers? It is no longer even touching, it is almost ridiculous, and socially insignificant in any case. Why on the other hand is it that violent, accidental, and chance death, which previous communities could not make any sense of (it was dreaded and cursed as vehemently as we curse suicide), has so much meaning for us: it is the only one that is generally talked about; it is fascinating and touches the imagination. Once again, ours is the culture of the Accident, as Octavio Paz says.

Death is not abjectly exploited by the Media since they are happy to gamble on the fact that the only events of immediate, unmanipulated and straightforward significance for all are those which in one way or another bring death onto the scene. In this sense the most despicable media are also the most objective. And again, to interpret this in terms of repressed individual pulsions or unconscious sadism is trivial and uninteresting, since it is a matter of a *collective* passion. Violent or catastrophic death does not satisfy the little individual unconscious, manipulated by the vile mass-media (this is a secondary revision, and is already *morally* weighted); this death moves us so profoundly only because it works on the group itself, and because in one way or another it transfigures and redeems in its own eyes.

'Natural' death is devoid of meaning because the group has no longer any role to play in it. It is banal because it is bound to the policed and commonplace [*banalisé*] individual subject, to the policed and commonplace nuclear family, and because it is no longer a collective mourning and joy. Each buries his own dead. With the primitives, there is no 'natural' death: every death is social, public and collective, and it is always the effect of an adversarial *will* that the group must absorb (no biology). This absorption takes place in feasting and rites. Feasting is the exchange of wills (we don't see how feasting would reabsorb a *biological* event). Evil wills and expiation rites are exchanged over the death's head. Death deceives and symbolically gains esteem; here death gains status, and the group is enriched by a partner.

To us, the dead have just passed away and no longer have anything to exchange. The dead are residual even before dying. At the end of a lifetime of accumulation, the dead are subtracted from the total in an economic operation. They do not become effigies: they serve entirely as alibis for the living and to their obvious superiority over the dead. This is a flat, one-dimensional death, the end of the biological journey, settling a credit: 'giving in one's soul', like a tyre, a container emptied of its contents. What banality!

All passion then takes refuge in violent death, which is the sole manifestation of something like the sacrifice, that is to say, like a real transmutation *through the will of the group*. And in this sense, it matters little whether death is accidental, criminal or catastrophic: from the moment it escapes 'natural' reason, and becomes a challenge to nature, it once again becomes the business of the group, demanding a collective and symbolic response; in a word, it arouses the *passion for the artificial*, which is at the same time sacrificial passion. Nature is uninteresting and meaningless, but we need only 'return' one death to 'nature', we need only exchange it in accordance with strict conventional rites, for its energy (both the dead person's energy and that of death itself) to affect the group, to be reabsorbed and expended by the group, instead of simply leaving it as a natural 'residue'. We, for our part, no longer have an effective rite for reabsorbing death and its rupturing energies; there remains the phantasm of sacrifice, the violent artifice of death. Hence the intense and profoundly *collective* satisfaction of the automobile death. In the fatal accident, the artificiality of death fascinates us. Technical, non-natural and therefore *willed* (ultimately by the victim him- or herself), death becomes interesting once again since *willed* death has a meaning. This artificiality of death facilitates, on a par with the sacrifice, its *aesthetic* doubling in the imagination, and the enjoyment that follows from it. Obviously 'aesthetics' only has a value for us since we are condemned to contemplation. The sacrifice is not 'aesthetic' for the primitives, but it always marks a refusal of natural and biological succession, an intervention of an initiatory order, a controlled and socially governed violence. These days, we can only rediscover this anti-natural violence in the chance accident or catastrophe, which we therefore experience as *socially* symbolic events of the highest importance, as sacrifices. Finally, the Accident is only accidental, that is to say, absurd, for official reason; for the symbolic demand, which we have never been without, the accident has always been something else altogether.

Hostage-taking is always a matter of the same scenario. Unanimously condemned, it inspires profound terror and joy. It is also on the verge of becoming a political ritual of the first order at a time when politics is collapsing into indifference. The hostage has a symbolic yield a hundred times superior to that of the automobile death, which is itself a hundred times superior to natural death. This is because we rediscover here a *time* of the sacrifice, of the ritual of execution, in the immanence of the collectively expected death. This death, totally undeserved, therefore totally artificial, is therefore perfect from the sacrificial point of view, for which the officiating priest or 'criminal' is expected to die in return, according to the rules of a symbolic exchange to which we adhere so much more profoundly than we do to the economic order.

The workplace accident is the concern of the economic order and has no symbolic yield whatsoever. Since it is a machinic breakdown rather than a sacrifice, it is as indifferent to the collective imagination as it is to the capitalist entrepreneur. It is the object of a mechanical refusal, of a mechanical revolt, based on the right to life and to security, and is neither the object nor the cause of a *ludic* terror.[29] Only the worker, as is well known, *plays* too freely with his security, at the whim of the unions and bosses who understand nothing of this challenge.

We are all hostages, and that's the secret of hostage-taking, and we are all dreaming, instead of dying stupidly working oneself to the ground, of *receiving* death and of *giving* death. Giving and receiving constitute one symbolic act (the symbolic act *par excellence*), which rids death of all the indifferent negativity it holds for us in the 'natural' order of capital. In the same way, our relations to objects are no longer living and mortal, but instrumental (we no longer know how to destroy them, and we no longer expect our own death), which is why they are really dead objects that end up killing us, in the same fashion as the workplace accident, however, just as one object crushes another. Only the automobile accident re-establishes some kind of sacrificial equilibrium. For death is something that is shared out, and we must know how to share it out amongst objects just as much as amongst other men. Death has only given and received meaning, that is to say, it is socialised through exchange. In the primitive order, everything is done so that death is that way. In our culture, on the contrary, everything is done so that death is never done to anybody by *someone* else, but only by 'nature', as an impersonal expiry of the body. We experience our death as the 'real' fatality inscribed in our bodies only because we no longer know how to inscribe it into a ritual of symbolic exchange. The order of the 'real', of the 'objectivity' of the body as elsewhere the order of political economy, are always the results of the rupture of this exchange. It is from this point that even our bodies came into existence as the place in which our inexchangeable death is confined, and we end up believing in the biological essence of the body, watched over by death which in turn is watched over by science. Biology is pregnant with death, and the body taking shape within it is itself pregnant with death, and there are no more myths to come and free it. The myth and the ritual that used to free the body from science's supremacy has been lost, or has not yet been found.

We try to circumscribe the others, our objects and our own body within a destiny of instrumentality so as no longer to receive death from them but there is nothing we can do about this – the same goes for death as for everything else: no longer willing to give or receive it, death encircles us in the biological simulacrum of our own body.

The Death Penalty

> Until the eighteenth century, we hanged guilty animals, after a formal condemnation, for causing a man's death. We even hanged horses.

> Author unknown

There had to be a very specific reason for the revulsion inspired in us by punishing these animals, since it ought to have been more serious to judge a man than an animal, and more odious to make him suffer. But, in one way or another, hanging a horse or a pig, like hanging a madman or a child, seems more odious to us, since they are 'not responsible'. This secret equality of consciousness in law, so that the condemned always retain the privilege of denying the right of the other to judge, this possible challenge which is quite different from the right to a defence and which re-establishes a minimum of symbolic opposition, no longer exists at all in the case of the animal or the madman. It is precisely the application of a symbolic ritual to a situation which prohibits the possibility of a symbolic response and gives this type of punishment its particularly odious character.

As opposed to physical elimination, justice is a social, moral and ritual act. The odious character of punishing a child or a madman comes from the *moral* aspect of justice: if the 'other' must be convinced of their guilt and condemned as such, punishment looses all meaning, since neither consciousness of the wrong nor even humiliation are possible with these 'criminals'. It is therefore as stupid as crucifying lions. But there is something else in the punishment of an animal, which this time derives from the *ritual* character of justice. It is the application of a *human* ceremonial to a beast, rather than just the *infliction* of death, that gives the scene its extraordinary atrocity. Every attempt to dress an animal, every disguise and attempt to tame an animal to the human comedy is sinister and unhealthy. By dying, it would become frankly unbearable.

But why this revulsion at seeing an animal treated like a human being? Because then man changes into a beast. In the hanged animal there is, by way of the sign and the ritual, a hanged man, but a man changed into a beast as if by black magic. A 'reflex' signification results from the ubiquitous action of the deep reciprocity, whatever we are dealing with, between man and animal or the executioner and his victim, mingled with the visual representation in a terrible confusion, and this malific ambiguity (as in Kafka's 'Metamorphosis') gives rise to disgust. The end of culture, of the social, the end of the rules of the game. Killing a beast in this fundamentally human manner unleashes an equivalent monstrosity in the man, who thus becomes the victim of his own ritual. The institution of justice, by which man claims to draw a line between himself and 'brutality', turns against him. Of course, such brutality is a myth – a caesura that implies the absolute privilege of the human, the expulsion of the animal into the 'brutal'. This discrimination is justified, however, when at the same time as the privilege, it implies all the risks and responsibilities of the human, in particular that of justice and *social* death, which by contrast, according to the same logic, does not concern the animal at all. For man to impose this form on the animal is to erase the limit between the two, and at the same time to eliminate the human. Man is then only the squalid caricature of the myth of animality that he himself has instituted.

We do not need psychoanalysis, the 'Father-Figure', sadistic eroticism and guilt to explain the nausea attendant upon the torture of animals. Everything here is social, everything relates to the *social* line of demarcation that man traces around himself in accordance with a mythical code of differences, and to the contortions that shatter this line, in accordance with the law that states that *reciprocity never ends*: every discrimination is only ever imaginary and is forever cut across by symbolic reciprocity, for better or worse.

Of course, this nausea, bound up with the loss of the privilege of the human, is also therefore proper to a social order, where the break with the animal, and therefore the abstraction of the human, is definitive. This revulsion distinguishes us: it signifies that human Reason has made progress, allowing us to consign all this 'medieval' torture of humans and animals to 'barbarism'. 'As late as 1906 in Switzerland, a dog was tried and executed for participating in theft and murder.' We are so reassured when we read that 'we are no longer like that', the subtext of which is 'today we are "humane" to animals, we respect them'. But the opposite is the case: disgust is inspired in us by the execution of an animal *in exact proportion to the contempt in which we hold it*. It is insofar, as is proper to our culture, as we relegate the animal to a non-human state of irresponsibility that the animal becomes unworthy of the human ritual. All we need then do is apply this ritual to the animal to make us nauseous, not because of some moral progress, but because of the deepening of human racism.

Those who, in times past, used to ritually sacrifice animals did not take them to be beasts. Even medieval society, which condemned and punished animals in accordance with its own norms, was far closer than we are to those who are horrified by this practice. By holding animals culpable, these societies paid them tribute. The innocence to which we consign animals (along with madmen, the sick and children) is significant of the radical distance separating us from them, and of the racial exclusion by which we rigorously maintain the definition of the Human. In a context where every living being is a partner in exchange, the animal has the 'right' to sacrifice and to ritual expiation. The primitive sacrifice of the animal is bound up with its exceptional and sacred status as a divinity, as a totem.[30] We no longer sacrifice them, we no longer even punish them, and we take pride in this; but this is simply because we have domesticated them and because we have turned them into a racially inferior world, no longer even worthy of our justice; they are barely even exterminable as butcher meat. Or perhaps rational liberal thought takes those it excommunicates into their charge, such as animals, madmen and children who 'know not what they do', and who therefore do not deserve punishment and death as much as they do public charity: protectionism of every kind, the RSPCA, 'open' psychiatry, modern pedagogy; all the definitive but gentle forms of inferiorisation in which Liberal Reason takes refuge. A racial compensation whereby humanism increases its privilege over 'inferior beings'.[31]

In the light of all this, the question of the death penalty is posed, which is also the question of the naïvety or hypocrisy of every liberal humanism on this question.

With the primitives, the 'criminal' is not an inferior, abnormal or irresponsible being. On him, like the 'mad' or the 'sick', a great number of the symbolic cycles are articulated. Some of this can still be detected in Marx's formulation of the criminal as an essential function of the bourgeois order. It is onto the king that responsibility for *the* crime *par excellence* devolves: breaking the incest taboo (which is why he is king, and why he will be put to death). His expiation confers on him the highest status, since it is also what relaunches the cycle of exchanges. There is a whole philosophy of cruelty (in Artaud's sense) here, which we are no longer familiar with, and which excludes social infamy as it does the death penalty: the death of the criminal-king is not a sanction, it neither separates nor removes something rotten on the social body; on the contrary, it is a festival and an elevation in which solidarity is renewed and separations undone. The madman, the fool, the bandit, the hero and many other characters from traditional societies have all played, relatively speaking, the same role as agents of symbolic ferment. Society was articulated on their *difference*. The dead were the first to play this role. Still untouched by social Reason, traditional societies coped with the criminal extremely well, even if it was by collective ritual death,[32] just like peasant societies with their village idiots, even if it was as objects of ritual derision.

The end of the culture of cruelty where difference is glorified and expiated in one and the same sacrificial act. We no longer know any other way of dealing with deviants but extermination or therapy. We now only know how to cut, expurgate and repel them into society's dark regions. And this only to the extent of our 'tolerance', our sovereign conception of freedom.

> If contemporary societies have progressed to the moral level, this does not rule out their regression to mood shifts. (*Encyclopaedia Universalis*)

By being normalised, that is to say, by extending the logic of equivalences to everyone, society, socialised at last, excludes every antibody. It then creates, in the same movement, specific institutions to receive them, and so, throughout successive centuries, prisons, asylums, hospitals and schools have flourished, not to forget the factories, which also began to flourish with the Rights of Man (this is how labour must be understood). *Socialisation* is nothing but the immense passage from the symbolic exchange of difference to the social logic of equivalence. Every 'social' or socialist 'ideal' merely doubles the process of socialisation. Even liberal thought, which wants to abolish the death penalty, simply perpetuates it. As regards the death penalty, the thought of the right (hysterical reaction) and the thought of the left (rational humanism) are both equally removed from the symbolic configuration where crime, madness and death are modalities of exchange, the 'accursed share' around which all exchange gravitates. Why do we reintegrate the criminal into society? To make him into the equivalent of a normal man? But exactly the opposite is true. As Gentis says: 'It is not a question of returning the madman to the truth of society, but of returning society to the truth of madness' (*Les Murs de l'asile*). All humanist thought grows faint in the face of this demand, which was openly realised in previous societies, and is always present, but hidden and violently repressed, in our own (crime and death always provoke the same secret jubilation; it is however debased and obscene).

If the bourgeois order first got rid of crime and madness by elimination or confinement, then secondly it neutralised all this on a therapeutic basis. This is the phase of the progressive absolution of the criminal and his reform into a social being, by every devious means of medicine and psychology. We must see, however, that this liberal change of policy takes place on the basis of a wholly repressive social space whose *normal* mechanisms have absorbed the repressive function that hitherto devolved onto special institutions.[33]

Liberal thinking believes this cannot be put better than its claim that 'penal law is called upon to develop in the direction of a preventative social medicine and a curative social service' (*Encyclopaedia Universalis*). Does this imply the disappearance of the *penal* aspect of the law? Not at all: the penalty is called upon to be realised in its purest form in great therapeutic, psychological and psychiatric reform programmes. Penal violence finds its most subtle equivalent in re-socialisation and re-education (also in the form of self-criticism or repentance, according to the dominant social system), and from this point we are all summoned to it in normal life itself: we are all madmen and criminals.[34]

It is not just that penal violence and the death penalty *might* disappear in this society, but that they *must*, and the abolitionists, totally contradicting themselves, merely follow the tendency of the system. They want to abolish the death penalty without abolishing responsibility (since without responsibility, there would be no human conscience or dignity, and therefore no liberal thought!). This is illogical, and above all futile, since responsibility has been dead for a long time. As a vestigial individual trait from the Enlightenment, it has been eliminated by the system itself as the latter becomes *more rational*. When capitalism rested on merit, initiative, individual enterprise and competition, it needed an ideal of responsibility, and therefore its repressive equivalent: for better or worse, everyone, whether entrepreneur or criminal, received his penalty or his credit. In a system that rests on bureaucratic programming and the execution of a plan, *irresponsible* executants are required, and so the entire system of values based on responsibility collapses into itself, since it is no longer viable. It is a matter of indifference whether you struggle for abolition or not: the death penalty is useless. Justice also collapses: generally irresponsible, the individual becomes, whatever happens to him, a pretext for bureaucratic structures, and will no longer accept being tried by just anyone, nor even by society as a whole. Even the problem of collective responsibility is a red herring: responsibility has quite simply disappeared.

Hence the secondary benefit of the elimination of humanist values and the dismantling of the repressive apparatus, based on the possibility of being able to distinguish 'in one's conscience', between good and evil, and on this criterion to be able to try and to condemn. But this order has had every opportunity to renounce the death penalty. It is still making gains in this respect, and hence open prisons become possible. For death and the prison were the truth of the social jurisdiction of a society that remained heterogeneous and divided. Therapy and reform are the truth of the social jurisdiction of a homogeneous and normalised society. The thought of the right still refers to the first, while the thought of the left refers to the second; both, however, obey the same system of values.

In other contexts, both speak the same medical language: remove a diseased member, says the right; cure a sick organ, says the left. On either side death acts at the level of equivalences. The primitive procedure is only aware of reciprocities: clan *contra* clan, death *contra* death (gift *contra* gift). We know only a system of equivalences (a death *for* a death) between two terms as abstract as in economic exchange: society and the individual under the jurisdiction of a 'universal' and legal morality.

A death for a death, says the right, fair's fair, you have killed so you must die, that's the law of the contract. Intolerable, says the left, the criminal must be spared: *he is not really responsible.* The principle of equivalence is intact: basically one of the terms (responsibility) tends towards zero, while the other (penalty) also tends in this direction. The environment, childhood, the unconscious,[35] social conditions, outline a new equation of responsibility, but still in terms of causality and the contract. In the terms of this new contract, the criminal merits no more than (Christian) pity or social security. Here again, the thought of the left merely invents more subtle neo-capitalist formations, where repression becomes diffuse, as surplus-value did in another context. In the psychiatric and ergonomic cures, however, it is very much a matter of an *equivalent* to death. Here the individual is treated as a functional survivor, as an object to be retrained: we surround him with care and solicitude, so many traits of his anomaly, and we *invest* in him. The tolerance he enjoys is of the same order as that we have seen being exercised over the beasts: it is an operation by means of which the social order exorcises and controls its own hauntings. Does the system make us all irresponsible? We can only accept this if we delimit a category of *notorious* examples of irresponsibility, that we will care for as such. By the effect of contrast, it will return the illusion of responsibility to us. Delinquents, criminals, children and madmen will suffer the effects of this clinical operation.

A simple examination of the evolution of the death penalty in 'materialist' terms (of profit and class) should leave those who wish to abolish it in perplexity. It is always through the discovery of more profitable economic substitutes, subsequently rationalised as 'more humane', that the death penalty is curbed: hence prisoners of war are spared in order to be made slaves; hence, in Rome, criminals were sent to the salt mines; hence the prohibition of duels in the seventeenth century, the institution of forced labour as a corrective solution, the variable extortion of the labour force and the ergo-therapeutic retraining of the Nazi camps. There are no miracles anywhere: death disappears or subsides when the system, for one reason or another, has an interest in it (1830: the first extenuating circumstances in a trial involving a bourgeois). Neither social conquest nor the progress of Reason: just the logic of profit or privilege.[36]

But this analysis remains totally insufficient, since it merely substitutes an economic for a moral rationality. Something else is in operation here, a 'heavy' hypothesis with respect to which the materialist interpretation appears to be a 'light' hypothesis. Profit may be an effect of capital, but it is never the fundamental law of the social order. It's fundamental law is the progressive control of life and death. Its objective is equally therefore to snatch death away from radical difference in order to submit it to the law of equivalence. And the naïvety of humanist thought (liberal or revolutionary) consists in not seeing that its rejection of death is necessarily the same as that of the system, that is, the rejection of something that escapes the law of value. It is only in this sense that death is an evil. But humanist thought turns it into an *absolute* evil, and it is from this point that it becomes enmeshed in the worst contradictions.[37] Claude Glayman (discussing the execution of Buffet and Bontemps):

> The irremediably human feeling that no man has the right to deal out death at will ('irremediably' is a kind of *lapsus*: the humanist does not appear to be totally convinced of this evidence). Life is sacred. But even without religious faith we are completely persuaded. . . . In a consumer society that tends to banish scarcity, death, we might say, is still more intolerable (life as a consumer good, death as scarcity: what an incredible platitude! But communism, and even Marx himself, are in agreement over this equation.) . . . Here too, the impression of a sort of permanence of the Middle Ages remains. . . . What society do we live in? What shores are we drifting towards? For we must not turn our backs on life, whatever it may be. (*Le Monde*)

This is precisely the 'rear' entry to life, the basic principle of pious souls, who are also those who enter the revolution backwards and turn their backs on life. These unbelievable acrobatics are, however, typical of thought bending over backwards to satisfy its rejection of death.

We can clearly see that the humanist debate starts from the individualist system of values of which it is the crown: 'The social and individual instinct of conservation', says Camus, 'requires the postulate of individual responsibility.' But precisely these postulates define the platitude of life and death in our equivalence-dominated systems. Beyond this point, man need only cultivate the instinct of conservation or responsibility (two complementary prejudices in the abstract and rationalist view of the subject). Death resumes its meaning as a sacrificial exchange, a collective moment and an intense deliverance of the subject. 'There is no passion . . . so weak but it mates and masters the fear of death', said Bacon (*Essays* [London: Dent, 1906], Vol. II, p. 6). But this is too little: *death is itself a passion.* And at this level the difference between self and others is effaced: 'The desire to kill often coincides with the desire to die oneself or to eliminate oneself'; 'Man desires to live, but he also desires to be nothing, he wants what cannot be undone, he wants death for its own sake. In this case, not only will the possibility of being put to death not stop the criminal, it is rather probable that it will add to the vertigo in which he is lost.' We know that suicide and murder can often be substitutes for one another, with a strong predilection for suicide.

This passionate, sacrificial death overtly accepts the *spectacle of death*, which, as with all organic functions, we have made into a *moral* and therefore clandestine and shameful function. The good souls heavily insist on the shameful character of *public* executions, but they do not see that odiousness of this type of execution stems from its *contemplative* attitude in which the death of the other is savoured as a spectacle at a distance. This is not sacrificial violence, which not only demands the presence of the whole community, but *is* one of the forms of its self-presence [*présence à elle-même*]. We rediscover something of this contagious festivity in an episode in England in 1807, when the 40,000 people who came to attend an execution were seized by delirium upon seeing a hundred dead bodies lying on the ground. This collective act has nothing in common with the spectacle of extermination. By confusing the two in the same abstract reprobation of violence and death, one merges with the thought of the State, that is, the pacification of life. Now, if the right prefers to use repressive blackmail, the left, for its part, is distinguished by imagining and setting up future models of pacified socialisation.

A civilisation's progress is thus measured only by its respect for life as absolute value. What a difference from public, celebrated death by torture (the Black from the Upper Volta laughing in the face of the guns that hit him, cannibalism in the Tupinamba), and even murder and vengeance, passion for death and suicide! When society kills in a totally premeditated fashion, we do it a great honour when we accuse it of a barbaric vengeance worthy of the Dark Ages, because vengeance is still a *fatal* reciprocity. It is neither 'primitive' nor 'purely the way of nature'; nothing could be more false. It has nothing to do with our calculable and statistical abstract death, which is the by-product of an agency both moral and bureaucratic (our capital punishment and concentration camps), and thus has everything to do with the system of political economy. This system is similarly abstract, but never in the way that a revenge, a murder or a sacrificial spectacle is abstract. We have produced a judicial, ethnocidal and concentration camp death, to which our society has adjusted. Today, everything and nothing has changed: under the sign of the values of life and tolerance, the same system of extermination, only gentler, governs everyday life, and it has no need of death to accomplish its objectives.

The same objective that is inscribed in the monopoly of institutional violence is accomplished as easily by forced survival as it is by death: a forced 'life for life's sake' (kidney machines, malformed children on life-support machines, agony prolonged at all costs, organ transplants, etc.). All these procedures are equivalent to disposing of death and imposing life, but according to what ends? Those of science and medicine? Surely this is just scientific paranoia, unrelated to any human objective. Is profit the aim? No: society swallows huge amounts of profit. This 'therapeutic heroism' is characterised by soaring costs and 'decreasing benefits': they manufacture unproductive survivors. Even if social security can still be analysed as 'compensation for the labour force in the interests of capital', this argument has no purchase here. Nevertheless, the system is facing the same contradiction here as with the death penalty: it overspends on the prolongation of life because this system of values is essential to the strategic equilibrium of the whole; economically, however, this overspending unbalances the whole. What is to be done? An economic choice becomes necessary, where we can see the outline of euthanasia as a semi-official doctrine or practice. We choose to keep 30 per cent of the uraemics in France alive (36 per cent in the USA!). Euthanasia is already everywhere, and the ambiguity of making a humanist demand for it (as with the 'freedom' to abortion) is striking: it is inscribed in the middle to long term logic of the system. All this tends in the direction of an increase in social control. For there is a clear objective behind all these apparent contradictions: to ensure control over the entire range of life and death. From birth control to death control, whether we execute people or compel their survival (the prohibition of dying is the caricature, but also the logical form of progressive tolerance), the essential thing is that the decision is withdrawn from them, that their life and their death are never freely theirs, but that they live or die according to a social visa. It is even intolerable that their life and death remain open to biological chance, since this is still a type of freedom. Just as morality commanded: 'You shall not kill', today it commands: 'You shall not die', not in any old way, anyhow, and only if the law and medicine permit. And if your death is conceded you, it will still be by order. In short, death proper has been abolished to make room for death control and euthanasia: strictly speaking, it is no longer even death, but something completely neutralised that comes to be inscribed in the rules and calculations of equivalence: rewriting–planning–programming–system. It must be possible to *operate* death as a social service, integrate it like health and disease under the sign of the Plan and Social Security. This is the story of 'motel-suicides' in the USA, where, for a comfortable sum, one can purchase one's death under the most agreeable conditions (like any other consumer good); perfect service, everything has been foreseen, even trainers who give you back your appetite for life, after which they kindly and conscientiously send the gas into your room, without torment and without meeting any opposition. A *service* operates these motel-suicides, quite rightly paid (eventually reimbursed?). Why did death not become a social service when, like everything else, it is functionalised as individual and computable consumption in social input and output?

In order that the system consents to such economic sacrifices in the artificial resurrection of its living losses, it must have a fundamental interest in withdrawing even the biological chance of death from people. 'You die, we'll do the rest' is already just an old advertising slogan used for funeral homes. Today, *dying is already part of the rest*, and the Thanatos centres charge for death just as the Eros centres charge for sex. The witch hunt continues.

A transcendent, 'objective' agency requires a delegation of justice, death and vengeance. Death and expiation must be wrested from the circuit, monopolised at the summit and redistributed. A bureaucracy of death and punishment is necessary, in the same way as there must be an abstraction of economic, political and sexual exchanges: if not, the entire structure of social control collapses.

This is why every death and all violence that escapes the State monopoly is subversive; it is a prefiguration of the abolition of power. Hence the fascination wielded by great murderers, bandits or outlaws, which is in fact closely akin to that associated with works of art: a piece of death and violence is snatched from the State monopoly in order to be put back into the savage, direct and symbolic reciprocity of death, just as something in feasting and expenditure is retrieved from the economic in order to be put back into useless and sacrificial exchange, and just as something in the poem or the artwork is retrieved from the terrorist economy of signification in order to be put back into the consumption of signs. This alone is what is fascinating in our system. Only what is not exchanged as values, that is, sex, death, madness and violence, is fascinating, and for this reason is universally repressed. Millions of war dead are exchanged as values in accordance with a general equivalence: 'dying for the fatherland'; we might say they can be converted into gold, the world has not lost them altogether. Murder, death and violation are legalised everywhere, if not legal, provided that they can be reconverted into value in accordance with the same process that mediatises labour. Only certain deaths, certain practices, escape this convertibility; they alone are subversive, but do not often make the headlines.

Amongst these is suicide, which in our societies has taken on a different extension and definition, to the point of becoming, in the context of the offensive reversibility of death, the form of subversion itself. While there are fewer and fewer executions, more and more commit suicide in prison, an act of *subverting* [*détournement*] institutional death and turning it against the system that imposes it: through suicide, the individual tries and condemns society in accordance with its own norms, by inverting the authorities and reinstating reversibility where it had completely disappeared, while at the same time regaining the advantage. Even suicides outside prison become political in this sense (*hari-kiri* by fire is only the most spectacular form of this): they make an infinitesimal but inexpiable breach, since it is total defeat for a system not to be able to attain total perfection. All that is needed is that the slightest thing escapes its rationality.

The prohibition of suicide coincides with the advent of the law of value. Whether religious, moral or economic, the same law states 'no-one has the right to remove any capital or value'. Yet each individual is a parcel of capital (just as every Christian is a soul to be saved), and therefore has no right to destroy himself. It is against this orthodoxy of value that the suicide revolts by destroying the parcel of capital he has at his disposal. This is unpardonable: we will go so far as to hang the suicide for having succeeded. It is therefore symptomatic that suicide increases in a society saturated by the law of value, as a challenge to its fundamental rule. But we must also take another look at its definition: if every suicide becomes subversive in a highly integrated system, all subversion of and resistance to this system is reciprocally, by its very nature, suicidal. Those actions at least that strike at its vitals. For the majority of so-called 'political' or 'revolutionary' practices are content to exchange their survival with the system, that is, to convert their death into cash. There are rarely suicides that stand against the controlled production and exchange of death, against the *exchange-value of death*; not its use-value (for death is perhaps the only thing that has no use-value, which can never be referred back to need, and so can unquestionably be turned into a weapon) but its value as rupture, contagious dissolution and negation.

The Palestinians or the rebellious Blacks setting fire to their own district become suicidal, as is resistance to the security forces in all its forms, as are the neurotic behaviour and multiple breakdowns by which we challenge the system's capacity to ever fully integrate us. Also suicidal are all political practices (demos, disorder, provocation, etc.) whose objective is to arouse repression, the 'repressive nature of the system', not as a secondary consequence, but as the immediacy of death: the game of death unmasks the system's own function of death. The order has possession of death, but it cannot *play* it out – only those who set death *playing* against itself win.

The property system is so absurd that it leads people to demand their death as their own good – the private appropriation of death. The mental devastation of this appropriation is so great that it leads to investment in the 'immovable' [*immobilier*] property of death, not only as a preoccupation with the 'third home', such as the tomb or the burial ground have become (many people buy a concession in the village cemetery at the same time as they buy their country house), but as the demand for a 'quality of death'. A comfortable, personalised, 'designer' death, a 'natural' death: this is the inalienable right constituting the perfected form of bourgeois individual law. Besides, immortality is only ever the projection of this natural and personal right into infinity – the subject's appropriation of the afterlife and eternity; her body and her death are equally inalienable. What despair is hidden by this absurd demand, analogous to that which fuels our delirious accumulation of the objects and signs from which we manically assemble our own private universe: death must once again become the final object in this collection and, instead of going through this inertia as the only possible event, it must itself re-enter the game of accumulating and administering things.

Contrary to the twists the subject stamps on his own demise, dispossession occurs only in violent, unexpected death, which reinstates the possibility of escaping the neurotic control of the subject.[38]

Everywhere, a stubborn and fierce resistance springs up to the principle of the accumulation, production and conservation of the subject in which he can read his own programmed death. Everywhere death is played off against death. In a system which adds up living and capitalises life, the death drive is the only alternative. In a meticulously regulated universe, the only temptation is to normalise everything by destruction.

Security as Blackmail

Security is another form of social control, in the form of life blackmailed with the afterlife. It is universally present for us today, and 'security forces' range from life assurance and social security to the car seatbelt by way of the state security police force.[39] 'Belt up' says an advertising slogan for seatbelts. Of course, security, like ecology, is an industrial business extending its cover up to the level of the species: a convertibility of accident, disease and pollution into capitalist surplus profit is operative everywhere. But this is above all a question of the worst repression, which consists in dispossessing you of your own death, which everybody dreams of, as the darkness beneath their instinct of conservation. It is necessary to rob everyone of the last possibility of *giving* themselves their own death as the last 'great escape' from a life laid down by the system. Again, in this symbolic short-circuit, the *gift-exchange* is the challenge to oneself and one's own life, and is carried out through death. Not because it expresses the individual's asocial rebellion (the defection of one or millions of individuals does not infringe the law of the system at all), but because it carries in it a principle of sociality that is radically antagonistic to our own social repressive principle. To bury death beneath the contrary myth of security, it is necessary to exhaust the gift-exchange.

Is it so that men might live that the demand for death must be exhausted? No, but in order that they die the only death the system authorises: the living are separated from their dead, who no longer exchange anything but the form of their afterlife, under the sign of comprehensive insurance. Thus car safety: mummified in his helmet, his seatbelt, all the paraphernalia of security, wrapped up in the security myth, the driver is nothing but a corpse, closed up in another, non-mythic, death, as neutral and objective as technology, noiseless and expertly crafted. Riveted to his machine, glued to the spot in it, he no longer runs the risk of dying, since he is *already* dead. This is the secret of security, like a steak under cellophane: *to surround you with a sarcophagus in order to prevent you from dying*.[40]

Our whole technical culture creates an artificial milieu of death. It is not only armaments that remain the general archetype of material production, but the simplest machine around us constitutes a horizon of death, a death that will never be resolved because it has crystallised beyond reach: fixed capital of death, where the living labour of death has frozen over, as the labour force is frozen in fixed capital and dead labour. In other words, all material production is merely a gigantic 'character armour' by means of which the species means to keep death at a respectful distance. Of course, death itself overshadows the species and seals it into the armour the species thought to protect itself with. Here again, commensurate with an entire civilisation, we find the image of the automobile-sarcophagus: the protective armour is just death miniaturised and become a technical extension of your own body. The biologisation of the body and the technicisation of the environment go hand in hand in the same obsessional neurosis. The technical environment is our over-production of pollutant, fragile and obsolescent objects. For production lives, its entire logic and strategy are articulated on fragility and obsolescence. An economy of stable products and good objects is indispensable: the economy develops only by exuding danger, pollution, usury, deception and haunting. The economy lives only on the suspension of death that it maintains *throughout material production*, and through renewing the *available death stocks*, even if it means conjuring it up by a security build up: blackmail and repression. Death is definitively secularised in material production, where it is reproduced on a large scale as capital. Even our bodies, which have become biological machinery, are modelled on this inorganic body, and therefore become, at the same time, a *bad object*, condemned to disease, accident and death.

Living by the production of death, capital has an easy time producing security: it's the same thing. *Security is the industrial prolongation of death*, just as ecology is the industrial prolongation of pollution. A few more bandages on the sarcophagus. This is also true of the great institutions that are the glory of our democracy: Social Security is the social prosthesis of a dead society ('Social Security is death!' – May '68), that is to say, a society already exterminated in all its symbolic wheels, in its deep system of reciprocities and obligations, which means that *neither the concept of security nor that of the 'social' ever had any meaning*. The 'social' begins by taking charge of death. It's the same story as regards cultures that have been destroyed then revived and protected as folklore (cf. M. de Certeau, 'La beauté du mort' [in *La culture au pluriel*, Paris: UGE, 1974]). The same goes for life assurance, which is the domestic variant of a system which everywhere presupposes death as an axiom. The social translation of the death of the group – each materialising for the other only as social capital indexed on death.

Death is dissuaded at the price of a continual mortification: such is the paradoxical logic of security. In a Christian context, ascesis played the same role. The accumulation of suffering and penitence was able to play the same role as character armour, as a protective sarcophagus against hell. And our obsessional compulsion for security can be interpreted as a gigantic collective ascesis, an anticipation of death in life itself: from protection into protection, from defence to defence, crossing all jurisdictions, institutions and modern material apparatuses, life is no longer anything but a doleful, defensive book-keeping, locking every risk into its sarcophagus.

Keeping the accounts on survival, instead of the radical compatibility of life and death.

Our system lives off the production of death and pretends to manufacture security. An about-face? Not at all, just a simple twist in the cycle whose two ends meet. That an automobile firm remodels itself on the basis of security (like industry on anti-pollution measures) without altering its range, objectives or products shows that security is only a question of exchanging terms. Security is only an internal condition of the reproduction of the system when it reaches a certain level of expansion, just as feedback is only an internal regulating procedure for systems that have reached a certain point of complexity.

After having exalted production, today we must therefore make security heroic. 'At a time when anybody at all can be killed driving any car whatsoever, at whatever speed, the true hero is he who refuses to die' (a Porsche hoarding: 'Let's put an end to a certain glorification of death'). But this is difficult, *since people are indifferent to security*: they did not want it when Ford and General Motors proposed it between 1955 and 1960. *It had to be imposed in every instance.* Irresponsible and blind? No, this resistance must be added to that which traditional groups throughout have opposed to 'rational' social progress: vaccination, medicine, job security, a school education, hygiene, birth control and many other things. Always these resistances have been broken, and today we can produce a 'natural', 'eternal' and 'spontaneous' state based on the need for security and all the good things that our civilisation has produced. We have successfully infected people with the virus of conservation and security, even though they will have to fight to the death to get it. In fact, it is more complicated, since they are fighting for the *right* to security, which is of a profoundly different order. As regards security itself, no-one gives a damn. They had to be infected over generations for them to end up believing that they 'needed' it, and this success is an essential aspect of 'social' domestication and colonisation. That entire groups would have preferred to die out rather than see their own structures annihilated by the terrorist intervention of medicine, reason, science and centralised power – this has been forgotten, swept away under the universal moral law of the 'instinct' of conservation. However, this resistance always reappears, even if only in the form of the workers' refusal to apply safety standards in the factories; what do they want out of this, if not to salvage a little bit of control over their lives, even if they put themselves at risk, or if its price is increasing exploitation (since they produce at ever greater speed)? These are not 'rational' proletarians. But they struggle in their own way, and they know that .economic exploitation is not as serious as the 'accursed share', the accursed fragment that above all they must not allow to be taken from them, the share of symbolic challenge, which is at the same time a challenge to security and to their own lives. The boss can exploit them to death, but he will only really dominate them if he manages to make each identify with their own individual interests and become the accountant and the capitalist of their own lives. He would then genuinely be the Master, and the worker the slave. As long as the exploited retain the choice of life and death through this small resistance to security and the moral order, they win on their own, symbolic, ground.

The car driver's resistance to security is of the same order and must be eliminated as immoral: thus suicide has been prohibited or condemned everywhere because primarily it signifies a challenge that society cannot reply to, and which therefore ensures the pre-eminence of a single suicide over the whole social order. Always the accursed share (the fragment that everyone takes from their own lives so as to challenge the social order; the fragment that everyone takes from their own body so as to give it; this may even be their own death, on condition that everyone *gives* it away), the fragment which is the whole secret of symbolic exchange, because it is given, received and returned, and cannot therefore *be breached* by the dominant exchange, remaining irreducible to its law and fatal to it: its only real adversary, the only one it must exterminate.

Funeral Homes and Catacombs

> By dint of washing, soaping, furbishing, brushing, painting, sponging, polishing, cleaning and scouring, the grime from the things washed rubs off onto living things.
>
> Victor Hugo

The same goes for death: by dint of being washed and sponged, cleaned and scoured, denied and warded off, death rubs off onto every aspect of life. Our whole culture is hygienic, and aims to expurgate life from death. The detergents in the weakest washing powder are intended for death. To sterilise death at all costs, to varnish it, cryogenically freeze it, air-condition it, put make-up on it, 'design' it, to pursue it with the same relentlessness as grime, sex, bacteriological or radioactive waste. The make-up of death: Hugo's formula makes us think of those American funeral homes where death is immediately shielded from mourning and the promiscuity of the living in order to be 'designed' according to the purest laws of standing, smiling and international marketing.

It is not so worrying that the dead man is made beautiful and given the appearance of a representation. Every society has always done this. They have always staved off the abjection of natural death, the *social* abjection of decomposition which voids the corpse of its signs and its social force of signification, leaving it as nothing more than a substance, and by the same token, precipitating the group into the terror of its own symbolic decomposition. It is necessary to ward off death, to smother it in artificiality in order to evade the unbearable moment when flesh becomes nothing but flesh, and ceases to be a sign. The skeleton, with its stripped bones, already seals the possible reconciliation of the group, for it regains the force of the mask and the sign. But between the two, there is the abject passage through nature and the biological that must be warded off at all costs by sarcophagic practices (the devouring of flesh), which are in fact semiurguic practices. Therefore, every thanatopraxis, even in contemporary societies, is analysed as the will to ward off this sudden loss of signs that befalls the dead, to prevent there remaining, in the *asocial* flesh of the dead, something which signifies nothing.[41]

In short, every society has its sarcophagic rituals; embalming, the artificial preservation of the flesh, is one of its variants. The practices of the funeral homes, which appear so ridiculous and misplaced to us, idealists of natural death that we are, therefore remain faithful to the most remote traditions. The point at which they become absurd is their connotation of *naturalness*. When the primitive showers the dead with signs, it is in order to make the transition towards the state of death as quick as possible, beyond the ambiguity between the living and the dead which is precisely what the disintegrating flesh testifies to. It is not a question of making the dead play the role of the living: the primitive concedes the dead their difference, for it is at this cost that they will be able to become partners and exchange their signs. The funeral home scenario goes the other way. Here, it becomes a question of the dead retaining the appearance of life, the *naturalness* of life: he still smiles at you, the same colours, the same skin, he seems himself even after death, he is even a little fresher than when he was alive, and lacks only speech (but we can still hear this in stereo). A faked death, idealised in the colours of life: the secret idea is that life is natural and death is against nature. Death must therefore be *naturalised* in a stuffed simulacrum of life. In all of this there is on the one hand a refusal to let death signify, take on the force of a sign, and, behind this sentimental nature-fetishism on the other, a great ferocity as regards the dead himself: rotting and change are forbidden, and instead of being carried over to death and thus the symbolic recognition of the living, he is maintained as a puppet within the orbit of the living in order to serve as an alibi and a simulacrum of their own lives. Consigned to the natural, he loses his right to difference along with every chance of a *social* status.

This is what separates those societies that are afraid neither of the sign nor of death, since they make it signify overtly, from our 'ideological' societies where everything is buried under the natural, where signs have become nothing but designs, entertaining the illusion of a natural reason. Death is the first victim of this ideologisation: rigidly set in the banal simulacrum of life, it becomes shameful and obscene.

There is an enormous difference between these sanctuaries and drug-stores of smiling, sterilised death and the corridors of the Capuchin convent in Palermo, where three centuries of disinterred corpses, meticulously fossilised in the clay of the cemetery, with skin, hair and nails, lie flat or suspended by the shoulders in close ranks, along the length of reserved corridors (the corridor of the religious, the corridor of the intellectuals, the corridors of women, children, etc.), still dressed either in a crude wrap or, on the contrary, in costume with gloves and powdered muslin. In the pale half light from the barred windows, 8,000 corpses in an incredible multiplicity of attitudes – sardonic, languid, heads bent, fierce or timid: a dance of death which was for a long time, before becoming the Grevin Museum for the tourists, a place for dominical walks for the relatives and friends who used to come to see their dead, to acknowledge them, show them to their children with the familiarity of the living, a 'dominicality' of death similar to those of the Mass or the theatre. A Baroque of death (the first unburied corpses date from the sixteenth century and the Counter-Reformation). The solidity of a society capable of exhuming its dead, of opening a route to them, half-way between intimacy and the spectacle, of bearing without fright or obscene curiosity, that is, without the effects of sublimation and seriousness to which we are accustomed, the theatre of death, where cruelty is still a sign, even if this is no longer in the bloody rites of the Tarahumaras. What a contrast with the fragility of *our* societies, which are incapable of confronting death without wan humour or perverse fascination. What a contrast with the anxious warding off in the funeral homes.

The Dereliction of Death

The cult of the dead is on the wane. An order has been placed over the tombs, no longer a perpetual concession. The dead become socially mobile. The devotion to death remains, particularly in the working or middle classes, but today this is much more as a variable of status (a second home) than as tribal piety. We speak less and less of the dead, we cut ourselves short and fall silent: death is discredited. End of a solemn and detailed 'death in the family': we die in hospital, death has become extraterritorial. The dying lose their rights, including the right to know when they are going to die. Death, like mourning, has become obscene and awkward, and it is good taste to hide it, since it can offend the well-being of others. Etiquette forbids any reference to the dead. Cremation is the limit point of this discrete elimination, since it minimalises the remains. No more vertigo of death, only dereliction [*désaffecté*]. And the immense funeral cortège is no longer of a pious order, it is the sign of dereliction itself, of the consumption of death. In consequence, it grows in proportion to the disinvestment of death.

We no longer have the experience that others had of death. Spectacular and televised experience has nothing to do with this. The majority no longer have the opportunity to see somebody die. In any other type of society, this is something unthinkable. The hospital and medicine take charge of you; the technical Extreme Unction has replaced every other sacrament. Man disappears from his nearest and dearest before being dead. He dies somewhere else.

Roos, a Swiss woman, had the idea of going to speak to the dying about their own death, of making them speak. This is an obscene idea, a general denegation: no-one dies in the service of any hospital (it is the staff that have a problem). She was taken to be a madwoman, a provocatrice, and so she discharged herself from hospital. When she found a dying man to speak to, she went to find her students, but on her return she found him dead (here, she perceived that the problem was hers and her students'). She has subsequently succeeded: soon there will be a staff of psychologists to watch over the dying and give speech back to them. The neo-spiritualism of the human and psycho-social sciences.

The priest and the extreme unction still bore a trace of the community where death was discussed. Today, blackout. In any case, if the priest was nothing but a vulture, today this function is largely fulfilled by the doctor, who shuts speech off by overwhelming the dying with care and technical concern. An *infantile* death that no longer speaks, an inarticulate death, kept out of sight. Serums, laboratories and healing are only the alibi of the prohibition of speech.

The Exchange of Disease

In any case, we no longer die at home, we die in hospital – for many good 'material' reasons (medical, urbane, etc.), but especially because the sick or dying or man, as *biological* body, no longer has any place but within a *technical* milieu. On the pretext of being cared for, he is then deported to a functional space-time which is charged with neutralising the symbolic difference of death and disease.

Precisely where the goal is the elimination of death, the hospital (and medicine in general) takes charge of the sick as the virtually dead. Therapeutic scientificity and efficiency presuppose the radical objectification of the body, the social discrimination of the sick, and hence a process of mortification. The logical conclusion to the medical genealogy of the body:

> Medicine becomes modern with the corpse. . . . It will no doubt remain a decisive fact about our culture that its first scientific discourse concerning the individual had to pass through this stage of death. (Michel Foucault, *The Birth of the Clinic* [tr. A.M.S. Smith, London: Routledge, 1990], p. 197)

Mortified, the patient is also deadly, taking his revenge as he can: by means of its functions, its specialisations and its hierarchies, the clinical institution as a whole seeks to preserve itself from contamination from the already-dead. The patient is dangerous because he is expected to die the death to which he has been condemned, and because of the neutrality in which he is enclosed at the term of his cure. From now on, the dead body can only act its incidental nature and its cure, it radiates the total difference between itself and the sick man, and, as dead, all its potential malificence. Neither the technical manipulation, the 'humane environment', nor even the occasion of his death in reality will be too much to ensure his silence.

The most serious danger the sick man represents, and by reason of which he is genuinely asocial and like a dangerous madman, is his profound demand to be recognised as such and to *exchange his disease*. It is an aberrant and inadmissible demand from the sick (and the dying) to base an exchange on this difference, not in order to be cared for and recover, but to *give* his disease so that it might be *received*, and therefore symbolically recognised and exchanged, instead of being neutralised in the techniques of clinical death and the strictly functional survival called health and curing.

The human or therapeutic relation to the hospital cannot be perfected; the general practice of medicine cannot change anything as concerns the blackout or the symbolic lock-out. Summoned to cure the sick, devoted to healing, the doctor and his helpers, exclusively equipped to cure the entire institution, including its walls, its surgical machinery and its psychological apparatuses (alternating between coldness and solicitude, and today the 'humanisation' of the hospital): none of this breaks the fundamental prohibition of a different status for disease and death. At best, the sick will be left the possibility of 'self-expression', of speaking about his disease, and recontextualising his life, in short the possibility of not experiencing this temporary anomaly so negatively. As regards recognising the madness of disease as difference, as meaning, a wealth of meaning, as material *from which to restructure* an exchange, without trying in any way to 'return the sick to their normal lives', this presupposes the total elimination of medicine and the hospital, the entire system of enclosing the body in its 'functional' truth; ultimately even the social order in its entirety, for which the mere demand that disease be treated as a *structure of exchange* is an absolute danger.[42]

Sexualised Death and Deadly Sex

Speaking of death makes us laugh in a strained and obscene manner. Speaking of sex no longer provokes the same reaction: sex is legal, only death is pornographic. Society, having 'liberated' sexuality, progressively replaces it with death which functions as a secret rite and fundamental prohibition. In a previous, religious phase, death was revealed, recognised, while sexuality was prohibited. Today the opposite is true. But all 'historical' societies are arranged so as to dissociate sex and death in every possible way, and play the liberation of one off against the other – which is a way of neutralising them both.

Is everything evenly balanced in this strategy, or is there a priority of one term over the other? For the phase which concerns us, everything happens as if the indexation of death were the principal objective, bound up with the exaltation of sexuality: the 'sexual revolution' was entirely oriented in this direction, under the sign of the one-dimensional Eros and the *function* of pleasure. In other places, this is precisely what gave it its naïvety, its pathos, its sentimentality, and, at the same time, its 'political' terrorism (the categorical imperative of desire). The slogan of sexuality is in solidarity with political economy, in that it too aims at abolishing death. We will only have exchanged prohibitions. Perhaps, by means of this 'revolution', we will even have set up the fundamental prohibition against death. In so doing, the sexual revolution devours itself, since death is the real sexualisation of life.

My Death is Everywhere, my Death Dreams

Pursued and censured everywhere, death springs up everywhere again. No longer as apocalyptic folklore, such as might have haunted the *living* imagination in certain epochs; but voided precisely of any imaginary substance, it passes into the most banal reality, and for us takes on the mask *of the very principle of rationality* that dominates our lives. Death is when everything functions and serves something else, it is the absolute, signing, cybernetic functionality of the urban environment as in Jacques Tati's film *Play-Time*. Man is absolutely indexed on his function, as in Kafka: the age of the civil servant is the age of a culture of death. This is the phantasm of total programming, increased predictability and accuracy, finality not only in material things, but in fulfilling desires. In a word, *death is confused with the law of value* – and strangely with the structural law of value by which everything is arrested as a coded difference in a universal nexus of relations. This is the true face of ultra-modern death, made up of the faultless, objective, ultra-rapid connection of all the terms in a system. Our true necropolises are no longer the cemeteries, hospitals, wars, hecatombs; death is no longer where we think it is, it is no longer biological, psychological, metaphysical, it is no longer even murder: our societies' true necropolises are the computer banks or the foyers, blank spaces from which all human noise has been expunged, glass coffins where the world's sterilised memories are frozen. Only the dead remember *everything* in something like an immediate eternity of knowledge, a quintessence of the world that today we dream of burying in the form of microfilm and archives, making the entire world into an archive in order that it be discovered by some future civilisation. The cryogenic freezing of all knowledge so that it can be resurrected; knowledge passes into immortality as sign-value. Against our dream of losing and forgetting everything, we set up an opposing great wall of relations, connections and information, a dense and inextricable artificial memory, and we bury ourselves alive in the fossilised hope of one day being rediscovered.

Computers are the transistorised death to which we submit in the hope of survival. Museums are already there to survive all civilisations, in order to bear testimony. But to what? It is of little importance. The mere fact that they exist testifies that we are in a culture which no longer possesses any meaning for itself and which can now only dream of having meaning for someone else from a later time. Thus everything becomes an environment of death as soon as it is no longer a sign that can be transistorised in a gigantic whole, just as money reaches the point of no return when it is nothing more than a system of writing.

Basically, political economy is only constructed (at the cost of untold sacrifices) or designed so as to be recognised as immortal by a future civilisation, or as an instance of truth. As for religion, this is unimaginable other than in the Last Judgement, where God recognises his own. But the Last Judgement is there already, realised: it is the definitive spectacle of our crystallised death. The spectacle is, it must be said, grandiose. From the hieroglyphic schemes of the Defense Department or the World Trade Center to the great informational schemes of the media, from siderurgical complexes to grand political apparatuses, from the megapolises with their senseless control of the slightest and most everyday acts: humanity, as Benjamin says, has everywhere become an object of contemplation to itself.

> Its self-alienation has reached such a degree that it can experience its own destruction as an aesthetic pleasure of the first order. ('The Work of Art in the Age of Mechanical Reproduction', in *Illuminations* [tr. Harry Zohn, ed. Hannah Arendt, London: Jonathan Cape, 1970], p. 244)

For Benjamin, this was the very form of fascism, that is to say, a certain exacerbated form of ideology, an aesthetic perversion of politics, pushing the acceptance of a culture of death to the point of jubilation. And it is true that today the whole system of political economy has become the finality without end and the aesthetic vertigo of productivity to us, and this is only the contrasting vertigo of death. This is exactly why art is dead: at the point of saturation and sophistication, all this jubilation has passed into the spectacle of complexity itself, and all aesthetic fascination has been monopolised by the system as it grows into its own double (what else would it do with its gigantic towers, its satellites, its giant computers, if not double itself as signs?). We are all victims of production become spectacle, of the aesthetic enjoyment [*jouissance*], of delirious production and reproduction, and we are not about to turn our backs on it, for in every spectacle there is the immanence of the catastrophe. Today, we have made the vertigo of politics that Benjamin denounces in fascism, its perverse aesthetic enjoyment, into the experience of production at the level of the general system. We produce the experience of a de-politicised, de-ideologised vertigo of the rational administration of things, of endlessly exploding finalities. Death is immanent to political economy, which is why the latter sees itself as immortal. The revolution too fixes its sights on an immortal objective, in the name of which it demands the suspension of death, in the interests of accumulation. But immortality is always the monotonous immortality of a social paradise. The revolution will never rediscover death unless it demands it immediately. Its impasse is to be hooked on the end of political economy as a *progressive* expiry, whereas the demand for the end of political economy is posed right now, in the demand for immediate life and death. In any case, death and *enjoyment*, highly prized and priced, will have to be paid for throughout political economy, and will emerge as insoluble problems on the 'day after' the revolution. The revolution only opens the way to the problem of death, without the least chance of resolving it. In fact, there is no 'day after', only days for the administration of things. Death itself demands to be experienced immediately, in total blindness and total ambivalence. But is it revolutionary? If political economy is the most rigorous attempt to put an end to death, it is clear that only death can put an end to political economy.

Notes

1. Racism *was founded*, and from the universal point of view we claim to have overcome it in accordance with the egalitarian morality of humanism. Neither the soul, in times past, nor today the biological characteristics of the species, on which this egalitarian morality is based, offer a more objective or less arbitrary argument than, for example, the colour of one's skin, since they too are *distinctive* criteria. On the basis of such criteria (soul or sex), we effectively obtain a Black = White equivalence. This equivalence, however, excludes everything that has not a 'human' soul or sex even more radically. Even the savages, who hypostatise neither the soul nor the species, recognise the earth, the animal and the dead as the socius. On the basis of our universal principles, we have rejected them from our egalitarian metahumanism. By integrating Blacks on the basis of white criteria, this metahumanism merely extends the boundaries of abstract sociability, *de jure* sociality. The same white magic of racism continues to function, merely whitening the Black under the sign of the universal.

2. The more we stress the human character of the divine essence, and the more we see the distance that separates God from man increase, the more we see reflection on religion or theology nullify the identity and unity of the divine essence and the human essence, the more we see the debasement of all that is human, in the sense that human consciousness becomes its object. The reason for this is that if everything positive in the conception we have of the divine being is reduced to the human, then man, the object of consciousness, could only become a negative and inhuman conception. To enrich God, man must become poor (Ludwig Feuerbach, *The Essence of Christianity* [I.H.G. translation; available tr. George Eliot, New York: Harper and Row, 1957]).
   This text clearly describes an 'abduction' into the universal. The universalisation of God is always bound up with an exclusion and reduction of the human in its originality. When God starts to resemble man, man no longer resembles anything. What Feuerbach does not say, because he is still too wrapped up in religion, is that the universalisation of man also takes place at the cost of the exclusion of all others (madmen, children, etc.) in their difference. When Man starts to resemble Man, others no longer resemble anything. Defined as universality and as an ideal reference, the Human, just like God, is properly inhuman and extravagant. Feuerbach has equally nothing to say concerning the act of abduction, by which God captures the human for his own ends, in such a way that man is nothing more than the anaemic negative of God, which, backfiring, killed God himself. Even Man is dying from the various 'inhumanities' (madness, infancy, savagery) he has instituted.

3. At a time when public sector housing is taking on the appearance of a cemetery, cemeteries normally adopt the form of real estate (as in Nice, etc.). On the other hand, it is remarkable that in the American metropolis, and often in the French, traditional cemeteries constitute the only green, or empty, spaces in the urban ghetto. That the space of the dead became the only district in the city where living is tolerable says a great deal about the inversion of values in the modern necropolis. In Chicago children play in cemeteries, cyclists ride there and lovers kiss. What architect would dare to draw inspiration from the truth of the contemporary urban set-up and form a conception of a city on the basis of cemeteries, waste ground and 'accursed' spaces? This would truly be the death of architecture.

4. Heresies always put this 'Kingdom of the Beyond' in question to establish the Kingdom of God *hic et nunc*. To deny the doubling of life and sur-vival, to deny the next world, is also to deny the rupture with the dead and therefore the necessity of crossing over via an

intermediary agency to establish trade with them. This is the end of the Church and its power.

5. God keeps the signifier and the signified, good and evil, apart, He also separates man and woman, the living and the dead, the body and the mind, the Other and the Same, etc. More generally, it is He who maintains the split between the poles of every distinct opposition, and therefore between the inferior and the superior, Black and White. As soon as reason becomes political, that is to say, as soon as the distinct opposition is resolved as power and leans in the interests of one of these terms, God is already on this side.

6. [*tient la barre*: 'at the helm' – tr.]

7. For us, by contrast, everything which is symbolically exchanged constitutes a mortal danger for the dominant order.

8. There is therefore no distinction on the symbolic plane between the living and the dead. The dead have a different status, that is all, which requires certain ritual precautions. But visible and invisible do not exclude each other since they are two possible states of a person. Death is an aspect of life. The Canaque arriving in Sydney for the first time, stupefied by the crowds, soon explains the thing by the fact that in this country the dead walk amongst the living, which is nothing strange. 'Do Kamo', for the Canaques (Maurice Leenhardt, *Do Kamo: Person and Myth in the Melanesian World* [tr. Basia Miller Gulati, Chicago: University of Chicago Press, 1979]), is that 'which lives', and everyone may belong to this category. There again the living/non-living is a distinctive opposition that we alone make, and we base all our 'science' and our operational violence on it. Science, technics and production assume this rupture of the living and the non-living, privileging the living on which alone science in all its rigour is based (cf. J. Monod, *Chance and Necessity*). Even the 'reality' of science and technics is also the separation of the living and the dead. The very finality of science as a pulsion, as the death drive (the desire to know), is inscribed in this disjunction, so that an object is only real insofar as it is dead, that is, relegated to inert and indifferent objectivity, as were initially, above everything else, the dead and the living.

    By contrast, the primitives were not plunged, as we like to say so much, into 'animism', that is, into the idealism of the living, into the irrational magic of forces: they privilege *neither one term nor the other*, for the simple reason that they do not make this distinction.

9. This rule also applies in the political sphere. Thus the peoples of the Third World (Arabs, Blacks and Indians) act as Western culture's imaginary (as much an object or support of racism as the support of revolutionary aspirations). On the other hand, we, the technological and industrial West, are their imaginary, what they dream of in their separation. This is the basis of the *reality* of global domination.

10. Of course, the psychoanalytic (Lacanian) real is no longer given as substance, nor as a positive reference: it is the always lost object that cannot be located, and of which there is nothing ultimately to say. A delimited absence in the network of the 'symbolic order', this real retains however the charm of a game of hide-and-seek with the signifier which traces after it. From the representation to the trace, the real is effaced – not entirely, however. There is all the difference between an unconscious topology and utopia. Utopia *puts an end to the real*, even as absence or lack.

    At least in Lacan there is something other than the idealist misinterpretation of Lévi-Strauss, for whom, in his *Structural Anthropology* [2 vols, tr. M. Layton, Harmondsworth, Penguin, 1977–9]), 'the function of the symbolic universe is to resolve on the ideal plane what is experienced as contradictory on the real plane'. Here (not too far from its most degraded sense), the symbolic appears as a sort of ideal compensation function, mediating between the *separation* of the real and ideal. In fact, the symbolic is quite simply reduced to the imaginary.

11. On the other hand, whoever cannot be *given* also dies, or falls to the necessity of *selling* themselves. This is where prostitution takes hold, as the residue of gift-exchange and the first form of economic exchange. Even though the prostitute's wages were initially, in

the ancient context, a 'sacrificial wage', it inaugurates the possibility of another type of exchange.

12. Cf. also M. Leenhardt: There is no idea of nothingness in death. The Canaque does not mistake the idea of death for that of nothingness. Perhaps we may find in their term *sèri* an idea similar to our 'nothingness'. *Sèri* indicates the situation of the bewitched or cursed man who has been abandoned by his ancestors, the *baos*, a man in perdition, out of society. He feels himself non-existent and suffers a veritable ruin. For him 'nothingness' is, at most, a social negation and is not a part of the idea he has of death. (*Do Kamo*, p. 35)

13. Such societies are consequently less psychotic than our modern societies (for which we politely reserve the qualification 'neurotic', but which are in fact in the process of becoming 'psychotic' according to our own definition, that is, they are in the process of a total loss of access to the symbolic).

14. Because the 'social' itself does not exist in 'primitive societies'. The term 'primitive' has been eliminated today, but we must also eliminate the equally ethnocentric term 'society'.

15. Cf. the cannibalism scene in Jean de Lhéry's *Les Indiens de la Renaissance*.

16. On this point see René Girard, *Violence and the Sacred* [tr. Patrick Gregory, Baltimore: Johns Hopkins, 1979].

17. Just like Jaulin (*La Mort Sara*) on the primitive fear of the dead: 'By lending anti-social intentions to the forces of death, the Sara have merely logically extended some very broad observations and, at the same time, several unconscious givens.' It is not at all certain that these unconscious 'givens' have much to do with this. The haunting and the negativity of the forces of death might well be explained as the menacing agency and the immanence of these wandering forces as soon as they escape from the group, where they can no longer be exchanged. 'The dead man', in fact, 'avenges himself.' But the hostile double, the hostile dead man, is repeatedly incarnated in the group's failure to preserve his material in symbolic exchange, to repatriate, through an appropriate ritual, this 'nature' that escapes with the dead man and which then cyrstallises into a malefic instance. This nevertheless leaves his relation with the group intact: he exercises it in the form of persecution (the dead labour frozen within capital plays the same role for us). This has nothing to do with a superegoic projection or an unconscious apparatus issuing from the depths of the species . . .

18. The neo-millennialism of the liberation of the unconscious should not be analysed as a distortion of psychoanalysis: it follows logically from the imaginary resurrection of the lost object (*objet petit 'a'*) that psychoanalysis buried at the core of its theory: the always unlocatable real which allows it to guard the gates to the symbolic. The *objet petit 'a'* is in fact the true mirror of Desire, and, at the same time, the mirror of psychoanalysis.

19. Science itself is cumulative only because it is half bound up with death, because it heaps death upon death.

20. In times past, however, there had already existed another individual and pessimistic thought of death: the Stoics' aristocratic, pre-Christian thought was also bound up with the conception of a personal solitude in death in a culture where collective myths were collapsing. The same emphases are also found in Montaigne and Pascal, in the feudal lord or the Jansenist of *noblesse de robe* (the ennobled bourgeoisie), in humanist resignation or desperate Christianity. This, however, marks the beginning of the modern anguish of death.

21. In this respect, there is no difference between atheist materialism and Christian idealism, for they part company only on the question of the afterlife (but whether or not there is anything after death has no importance: 'that is not the question' [in English in the original – tr.]), they agree on the basic principle: life is life, and death is always death; that is, they share the will to keep them scrupulously at a distance from each other.

22. The Christian dialectic of death epitomises and puts an end to Pascal's formula: 'It is important for all life to know whether the soul is mortal or immortal', is succeeded by

humanist thinking, a rationalist mastery over death. In the West, this has been drawn on from the Stoics and the Epicureans (Montaigne – the denegation of death – benign or cold serenity), up to the eighteenth century and Feuerbach: 'Death is a phantom, a chimera, since it exists only when it does not exist.' The staging of reason never results in an excess of life, nor in an enthusiastic sense of death: humanism seeks a *natural* reason for death, a wisdom backed up by science and the Enlightenment thinkers.

Dialectical reason – death as negativity and the movement of becoming – succeeds this formal and rationalist overcoming of death. The beautiful dialectic follows the upward mobility of political economy.

The dialectic then breaks down to make room for the irreducibility of death and its insurmountable immanence (Kierkegaard). With Heidegger, dialectical reason falls into ruin, taking a subjective and irrational turn towards a metaphysics of despair and the absurd which, however, does not prevent it from continuing to be the dialectic of a conscious subject finding a paradoxical freedom in it: 'Everything is permitted, since death is insurmountable' (quia absurdum: Pascal was not so far from the modern pathos of death). Camus: 'The absurd man fixes death with an impassioned stare; this fascination liberates him.'

The anguish of death as a test of truth. Human life as being-towards-death. Heidegger: 'Authentic being-towards-death – that is to say, the finitude of temporality – is the hidden basis of Dasein's historicality' (*Being and Time* [tr. J. Macquarrie and E. Robinson, Oxford: Blackwell, 1978], §74, p. 438). Death as 'authenticity': there is in this, in relation to a system that is itself mortifying, a vertiginous escalation, a challenge which is in fact a profound obedience.

The terrorism of authenticity through death remains a secondary process in that, by means of dialectical acrobatics, consciousness recuperates its 'finitude' as destiny. Anxiety as the reality principle and as 'freedom' remains the imaginary which, in its contemporary phase, has substituted the mirror of death for that of immortality. But all this remains extremely Christian and is moreover constantly mixed up with 'existential' Christianity.

Revolutionary thought, for its part, oscillates between the *dialecticisation* of death as negativity, and the *rationalist* objective of the abolition of death: to put an end to it as a 'reactionary' obstacle in solidarity with capital, with the help of science and technics, *en route* to the immortality of generic man, beyond history, in communism. Death, like so many other things, is only a superstructure, whose exit will be governed by the revolution of the infrastructure.

23.   There is a great risk of confusion here, for if we acknowledge that death and sexuality are biologically intertwined in the organic destiny of complex beings, this has *nothing to do* with the *symbolic* relation of death and sex. The first is inscribed in the positivity of the genetic code, the second in the destruction of social codes. Or rather, the second has no biological equivalent *inscribed* anywhere, whether in a code or in language. It is play, challenge and intense pleasure [*jouissance*] as it mockingly thwarts the former. Between the two, between the *real* relation of death and sexuality and their symbolic relation, there passes the caesura of exchange, a social destiny where everything plays.

Weissman: soma is mortal, plasma germinative and immortal. Protozoa are virtually immortal, death arising only with differentiated metazoa for whom death becomes possible and even *rational* (the unlimited duration of an individual life becomes a useless luxury. For Bataille, death on the contrary becomes an 'irrational' luxury). *Death is only a late acquisition of living beings.* In the history of the species of living creatures, it appears along with sexuality.

So also Tournier in *Friday or the Other Island* ([tr. Norman Denny, Harmondsworth: Penguin, 1984], pp. 106–7):

Sex and death. Their close association . . . he insisted that this was a sacrifice of the individual to the species, since in the act of procreation the individual loses something of his substance. Thus sexuality is the living presence, ominous and mortal, of the species in the essence of the individual. To procreate is to bring forth a new generation which innocently and inexorably will thrust its predecessor towards extinction. . . . The instinct which brings the sexes together is then an instinct of death. But Nature has thought it prudent to disguise her stratagem, transparent though it is, and what appears to be the self-indulgence of lovers is in reality a course of mad self-abnegation.

This fable is accurate, but demonstrates only the correlation between *biological* sex and death: in fact, death's decree appears along with sexuality, since the latter is already the inscription of a *functional* distribution, and therefore is immediately of a repressive order. But this functional distribution is not of the order of the pulsion; it is *social*. It appeared in a certain type of social relation. Savages do not make sexuality autonomous like we do; they are closer to what Bataille describes: 'Through the activity of organs in a flow of coalescence and renewal, like the ebb and flow of waves . . . , the self is dispossessed' (*Eroticism* [2nd edn, tr. M. Dalwood, London: Marion Boyars, 1987], p. 18).

24. In fact, Bataille's vision 'of excess' often falls into the trap of transgression, a fundamentally Christian dialectics or mysticism (but shared by contemporary psychoanalysis and by every 'libertarian' ideology of the festival and release [*défoulement*]) of the prohibition and transgression. *We* have made the festival into an aesthetics of *transgression*, because our entire culture is one of prohibition. Repression still marks the idea of the festival, which by the same token may be accused of reactivating the prohibition and reinforcing the social order. We treat the primitive feast to the same analysis since we are basically incapable of imagining anything other than the bar, its on-this-side and its beyond, which again issues from our fundamental schema of an uninterrupted linear order (the 'good form' which culture excludes is always that of the end, of a final fulfilment). Like the sacrifice, the primitive feast is not a transgression but a reversal, a cyclical revolution. This is the only form that puts an end to the bar and its prohibitions. The inverse order of the transgression or 'liberation' of repressed energies simply ends up in a compulsion to repeat the prohibition. Thus only reversibility and the cycle are in excess; transgression remains by default. 'In the economic order, all production is reproduction; in the symbolic order, all reproduction is production.'

25. It is, moreover, curious to see how, technically, death becomes increasingly undecidable for science itself: heart failure, then a level encephalogram; but then what? There is no longer any objective progress here: something of the indeterminacy and undecidability of death in the heart of science itself is reflected on the symbolic plane.

26. To the point that it is sufficient that certain political groups *demand* some accident or assassination attempt of unknown origin: this is their only 'practice', transforming chance into subversion.

27. Since today this contractual demand is addressed to social authorities, whereas before one signed pacts with the Devil to prolong, enrich and enjoy one's life. The same contract, and the same trap: the Devil always wins.

28. This is more important than the maximal exploitation of the labour force. This can clearly be seen in the case of the elderly: they are no longer exploited (if they are allowed to live on the fruits of society) if they are forced to live, since they are the living example of the accumulation of life (as opposed to its consumption). Society supports them as models of the use-value of life, *accumulation* and saving. This is precisely why they no longer have any symbolic presence in our society.

29. It only becomes the object of a passion again if it can be imputed to a person (a particular capitalist or a particular business personified), and is therefore experienced once again as crime and sacrifice.

30. Contrary to what is generally thought, human sacrifices *succeeded* animal sacrifice to the extent that the animal lost its magical pre-eminence, and the man-king succeeded the animal-totem as worthy of the sacrificial function. The more recent substitutive sacrifice of the animal has a very different meaning.

31. Hence in the past prisoners of war were spared in order to be used as slaves. No longer worthy of potlach and sacrifice, they were condemned to the lowliest role and to a slow death from labour.

32. But when and why did this death cease to be a sacrifice and become a torture? When did it cease to be a form of torture to become an execution, as it is for us? There is no history of death and the death penalty: there is only a genealogy of the social configurations to provide death with meaning.

33. The same liberal policy change took place, at another level, in England in 1830, where they wanted to replace the executioner with a preventative regular police force. The English prefer the executioner to the regular police force. And in fact the police, established in order to reduce the violence being wrought on the citizens, quite simply took over from crime in wreaking this violence against the citizen. In time, it revealed itself to be much more repressive and dangerous for the citizen than crime itself. Here again, overt and selective repression metamorphoses into generalised preventative repression.

34. Hence the meaning of the famous formula, 'We are all German Jews' (but also, 'we are all Indians, Blacks, Palestinians, women or homosexuals'). From the moment that the repression of difference was no longer carried out by extermination, but by absorption into the repressive equivalence and universality of the social, we are all different and repressed. There are no more detainees in a society that has invented 'open' prisons, just as there are no more survivors in a society that claims to abolish death. In this retaliatory contamination, the omnipotence of the symbolic order can be read: the unreal basis of the separations and the lines traced by power. Hence the power of this particular formula – We are all German Jews – in that rather than expressing an abstract solidarity (of the type 'all *together* for . . . we are all *united behind* this or that . . . forward *with* the proletariat', etc.), it expresses the inexorable fact of the symbolic reciprocity between a society and those it excludes. In a single movement it falls into line with them as radical difference. This is how it captured something fundamental in May '68, whereas other slogans were mere political cant.

35. For in this will to abolish death, which is the project of political economy, the unconscious, by a curious reversal ('that which knows no death' is the death drive), starts to play an important role. It becomes the referential discourse of the thesis of the criminal's irresponsibility (crime as acting out). It is well versed in the defence dossier as an explanatory system. *The unconscious plays a decisive role today in rationalist progressivist and humanist thought*: it has indeed fallen on hard times. And in this way, psychoanalysis also enters (without willing it?) ideology. The unconscious, however, would have had many other things to say about death if it had not learnt to speak the system's language: quite simply, it used to say that death did not exist, or, rather, that to abolish death was a phantasm that itself originates from the depths and repression of death. Instead of this, today it serves only as evidence, to our social idealists, of irresponsibility and justifies their *moral* discourse: life is a good, and death is an evil.

   In its violent classical phase, which even today coincides with conservative thought, capital plays on the discourse of conscious psychology and responsibility, and therefore repression: this is the terrorist discourse of capitalism. In its more advanced phase, which coincides with progressive, even revolutionary thought, neo-capitalism plays on the discourse of psychoanalysis: unconscious, irresponsibility, tolerance and reform. Consciousness and responsibility are the normative discourse of capital. The unconscious is the liberal discourse of neo-capitalism.

36. In 1819, under pressure from even the entrepreneurs and proprietors, and because the penal machine was jammed by the courts being too severe with the death penalty (jurors had the stark choice between the death penalty and acquittal), the death penalty was abolished in a hundred or so cases (England). Its abolition therefore corresponds to a rational adaptation, to an increasing efficiency of the penal system. Koestler:

   Our capital punishment is not the inheritance of the butchery of the Dark Ages. It has its own history. It is the residue of a jurisdiction which is contemporary with the development of political economy, and whose fiercest period – the Bloody Code in nineteenth century England – coincides with the industrial revolution. Medieval custom reserved death for a few particularly serious offences. Bound to the increasingly imperious defence of the right to private property, the curve began to rise through the height of the nineteenth and up to the twentieth centuries. ('The "bloody code" ', in *Reflections on Hanging* [London: Gollancz, 1956], pp. 13ff. [Baudrillard has paraphrased and summarised rather than cited Koestler here. – tr.])

This curve, then, also charts the ascendancy of the capitalist bourgeois class. And its recession after 1850 is the effect not of absolute human progress, but that of the capitalist system.

37. Of the type: 'The state is led to multiply very real murders in order to avoid an unknown murder. It will never know if whether this murder has any chance of being perpetrated' (Camus, *Sur la peine capitale*). This play on logic, seeking to place the system in contradiction with itself, leads liberal humanism directly to abject compromise: 'The abolition of the death penalty must be demanded both for reasons of logic and realism(!)' (ibid.). 'In the last resort, the death penalty is bad because, by its very nature, it rules out any possibility of making punishment and responsibility proportionate' (Koestler, 'The "bloody code" '); this was already the reason that the English capitalists had demanded its abolition in 1820! The liberal argument is: terror goes against its own ends; a scale of well administered penalties, of 'minimal punishment', is both 'more humane and more effective(!)' The equivalence of the human and the effective has a long history in humanist thought.

38. It's not so simple however, since the subject can still invoke violent death, death 'from the outside' – an accident, suicide or a bomb – to avoid putting his 'natural' immortality into question. The ultimate subterfuge, the ultimate ruse of the ego that may lead the subject to the opposite extreme, to seek an 'absurd' death in order to better safeguard his immortal principle.

39. [CRS – Compagnies Républicaines de Sécurité: the French riot police – tr.]

40. Cryogenic freezing, or being sealed in a gel so as to be resurrected, is the limit-form of this practice.

41. Just as much by simply devouring the body: in this sense, cannibalising the dead is itself a semiurgic activity (the idea that is always put forward is that through cannibalism 'one assimilates the forces of the dead': this is a secondary magical discourse for both the primitive and the ethnologist. It is not a question of force, that is to say, of a *natural* surplus or potential; on the contrary, it is a question of signs, that is to say, of preserving the sign's potential *against* every natural process, against the devastations of nature).

42. For the Dangaleat (Jean Pouillon, *Nouvelle Revue de Psychoanalyse*, no. 1, 1967), disease had an initiatory value. One must have been sick in order to become part of the group. One only becomes a doctor if one has been sick, and by the very fact of having been so. Disease comes from the *margaï*, each has their own *margaï* or *margaïs*, which they inherit from father to son. Every social position is acquired thanks to disease, which is a sign of election. Disease is a mark, a meaning – the normal man goes his own way, he is1insignificant. Disease is culture, the source of value and the principle of social organisation. Even where disease does not have this determinant social function, it is always a social matter, a social crisis, socially and publically resolved, by reactivating the whole social metabolism through the extraordinary relation between the doctor and the sick man, and setting it to work. This is radically different from contemporary medical practice, where the illness is individually borne and therapy individually applied. The reciprocity and exchange of the illness is preponderant in primitive societies. Illness is a social relation, like labour, etc. Organic causality can be recognised and treated by all sorts of means; the illness itself is never conceived as an organic lesion, but in the last instance as the rupture and breakdown of social exchange. The organic is a metaphor: it will therefore be treated 'metaphorically' by the symbolic operation of social exchange

through the two protagonists in the cure. The two are always three in other contexts: the group is immanent to the cure, at once the operator and the stakes of 'symbolic efficacy'. In short, the doctor and the sick are redistributed around the illness as social relation, instead, as is the case for us, of making the illness autonomous as an organic relation with its objective causality, doctor and patient each becoming objectified as passive and active, patient or specialist.

6

THE EXTERMINATION OF THE NAME OF GOD

The Anagram

The model of a symbolic exchange also exists within the field of language, something like the core of a political anti-economy, a site of the extermination of value and the law: poetic language. In the field of an anti-discourse, a beyond of the political economy of language, Saussure's *Anagrams* constitute the fundamental discovery. The same discovery that will later lend its conceptual arms to linguistic science had previously, in his *Cahiers d'anagrammes*, brought out the antagonistic character of a non-expressive language, beyond the laws, axioms and finalities assigned it by linguistics, in the form of a *symbolic* operation of language, that is to say, not a structural operation of representation by signs, but exactly the opposite, the deconstruction of the sign and representation.

The principle of poetic functioning proclaimed by Saussure does not claim to be revolutionary. Only the passion he puts into establishing this principle as the recognised and conscious structure of remote, Vedic, Germanic and saturnine texts, and establishing its *proof*, is proportionate to the incredible scope of his hypothesis. He himself draws no radical or critical consequences from it, he does not care for one moment to generalise it on a speculative level, and when he failed to find this proof, he abandoned this revolutionary intuition and went on to the edification of linguistic science. It is perhaps only today, at the term of half a century of uninterrupted development in this science, that we can draw out the consequences of the hypothesis Saussure abandoned,[1] and investigate to what extent it lays the advance foundations for a decentring of all linguistics.

The rules of the poetic proclaimed by Saussure are the following.[2]

The Law of the Coupling

1. 'A vowel has no right to figure within the Saturnine unless it has its *counter-vowel* in some other place in the verse (to ascertain the identical vowel, without attention to quantity). The result of this is that if the verse has an even number of syllables, the vowels couple up exactly, and must always have a remainder of zero, with an even total for each type of vowel.'

2. The law of consonants is identical, and no less strict: there is always an even number of any consonant whatever.
3. He goes so far as to say that if there is an irreducible remainder either of vowels (unpaired verse) or consonants, then, contrary to what we might think, this does not escape condemnation even if it is a matter of a simple 'e': we will then see it reappear in the following verse, as a new remainder corresponding to the overspill from the preceding one.

The Law of the Theme-word

In the composition of the verse, the poet sets the phonemic material provided by the theme-word to work. One (or several) verse(s) contain(s) anagrams of a single word (in general a proper name, of a god or a hero) by being constrained to reproduce itself, especially in a vocal rendition. 'on hearing one or two Latin Saturnine verses, F. de Saussure heard the principal phonemes of a proper name become clearer and clearer' (Starobinski, *Les mots*, p. 28). Saussure writes:

> In the hypogram, it is a matter of emphasising a name or a word, striving to repeat its syllables and thus giving it a second, artificial way of being, added, so to speak, to the original being of the word.

TAURA*SIA CI*SAUNA SAMN*IO* CEP*IT* (*SCIPIO*)

*A*ASE*N* A*R*GALE*ON* A*NEMON* A*MEGA*RTOS AUT*ME* (*AGAMEMNON*)

These simple rules are repeated untiringly in multiple variants. As regards alliteration, the rule to which it used to be thought we were able to submit all ancient poetry, Saussure says that it is only one aspect 'of an otherwise vast and important phenomenon', given that '*all* syllables alliterate, or assonate, or are combined in some other phonemic harmony'. Phonemic groups 'become echoes',

> entire verses to be anagrams of other preceding verses, however far off, in the text. . . . [P]olyphonies visually reproduce, when the occasion arises, the syllables of an important word or name, whether they figure in the text or present themselves naturally to the mind through the context. . . . [P]oetry analyses the phonemic substances of words, whether to turn them into accoustic series or signifying [*significative*] series when one alludes to a certain name [the anagrammatised word – J.B.]. [In short,] everything is answered, in one way or another, within the verse . . .

whether the signifiers or the phonemes answer one another throughout the verse, or the hidden signified, the theme-word, is echoed from one polyphony to the other, 'beneath' the 'manifest' text. Moreover, both rules can co-exist:

> Sometimes conjointly with anaphony, sometimes beyond every word we imitate, there is a correspondence of all the elements, translating into an exact 'coupling', that is to say, a repetition as a pair of even numbers.

Saussure will hesitate between the terms of 'anagram', 'antigram', 'hypogram', 'paragram' and 'paratext' to designate 'the elaborate variation that allows the perspicacious reader to perceive the evident but dispersed presence of conducting phonemes' (Starobinski, *Les mots*, p. 33). We could, as an extension of Saussure's work, propose the term 'ANATH-EMA', which is originally the equivalent of an ex-voto, of a votive offering: the divine name running beneath the text, and to whom the text is consecrated, the name of he who consecrates and to whom it is consecrated.[3]

These two laws appear to say extremely little as regards what we could say about the 'essence' of the poetic. Furthermore, they take no account of the poetic 'effect', of the enjoyment [*jouissance*] proper to texts, or of their aesthetic 'value' Saussure has only considered the poet's 'inspiration', not the reader's ecstasy. Perhaps he would never even have claimed that there was any relation whatsoever between the rules he clarifies (he thought he observed them, and that's all there is to it) and the exceptional intensity it has always been agreed that we find in poetry. By limiting his perspective to a formal logic of the signifier, he seems to leave the concern with looking for poetic enjoyment of the wealth of the *signified* and the profundity of *expression* to others who, with one accord, have always done so (psychologists, linguists and the poets themselves). Saussure, however, and Saussure alone, tells us that the enjoyment derived from the poetic is enjoyment in that it shatters 'the fundamental laws of the human word'.

Linguists become refugees in the face of this subversion of their discipline, in an untenable paradox. They acknowledge, with Roman Jakobson, that

> the poetic anagram cuts across the two laws of the human word as proclaimed by Saussure, that of the codified bond between the signifier and its signified, and that of the linearity of signifiers. . . . (The means employed by poetic language are such that they make us take leave of the linear order . . .) ['F. de Saussure sur les anagrammes', in *Selected Writings*, Vol. 7, Berlin: Mouton, 1985, p. 247]

(or, as Starobinski summarizes it, 'we leave the consecutive temporality proper to common language' [*Les mots*, p. 47]), and simultaneously affirm that 'Saussure's researches open up unprecedented perspectives in the *linguistic* study of poetry' [Jakobson, *Selected Writings*, Vol. 7, p. 246].

An elegant manner to recuperate the poetic as a particular field of discourse, on which linguistics retains the monopoly. What does it matter if the poetic denies the laws of signification, since we will neutralise it by giving it the keys to the city of linguistics, and by requiring it to obey the same reality principle? But what is a signified or a signifier if it is no longer governed by the code of equivalence? What is a signifier if it is no longer governed by the law of linearity? And what is linguistics without all this? Nothing (but we will see the contortions it goes through in order to make amends for this violence).

Linguistics gets out of Saussure's first law (the coupling) by putting forward the redundancy of the signifier, or indeed the frequency with which a particular phoneme or polyphony occurs, which is greater than the average in ordinary language, etc.; it gets out of the second (properly anagrammatic) law by invoking the 'latent' name (Agamemnon) as the secondary signified of a text that inevitably 'expresses' or 'represents' it, conjointly with the 'manifest' signified ('one and the same signifier splits into two signifieds', says Jakobson [*Selected Writings*, Vol. 7, p. 247]) – a desperate attempt to save, even if it was through a more complex operation, the law of linguistic value and the essential categories of the mode of signification (signifier, signified, expression, representation, equivalence). The linguistic imaginary seeks to annex the poetic to itself and even claims to enrich poetics' economy of the *term* and *value*. But against it, and giving full scope to Saussure's discovery, it must be said that, on the contrary, the poetic is a process of *the extermination of value*.

The law of the poem is in fact to make sure, following a rigorous proceedure, that *nothing remains of it*. This is why it contrasts sharply with the discourse of linguistics, which, for its part, is a process of the accumulation, production and distribution of language as value. The poetic is irreducible to the mode of signification, which is nothing other than the mode of production of the values of language. This is why it is irreducible to the linguistic, which is the science of this mode of production.

The poetic is the insurrection of language against its own laws. Saussure himself never formulated this subversive consequence. Others, however, have accurately assessed the danger inherent in the simple formulation of another possible formulation of language. This is why they have all made to conceal this in accordance with their code (calculating the signifier as a term, and the signified as value).

The Poetic as the Extermination of Value

1. Saussure's first law, that of the coupling, is in no way, as he himself insists, that of the unlimited expressive alliteration or redundancy of some phoneme or other.

> *Pour qui sont ces serpents qui sifflent sur nos têtes?*
> [For whom are these snakes whistling over our heads?]

These *serpents* are the rattlesnakes of a linguistics of the recurrence and accumulation of the signified: s-s-s-s- '*ÇA*' [*ID*] also whistles in the signifier, and the more 's's there are, the more *ça* whistles, the more menacing it is and the better it 'expresses'. Thus again:

> . . . the faint fresh flame of the young year flushes
> from leaf to flower and flower to fruit . . .

'In Swinburne's lines', says Ivan Fonagy, 'we feel the breeze passing, without the poem expressly mentioning it' ('Form and Function in Poetic Language', *Diogène*, 51, 1965, p. 90). Saussure's coupling is a calculated, conscious and rigorous duplication which refers to another *status of repetition*, not as the accumulation of terms, as the accumulative or alliterative (com)pulsion, but as the *cyclical cancellation of terms, two by two, the extermination of doubling by the cycle.*

> Vowels always couple up exactly, AND MUST ALWAYS GIVE A REMAINDER OF ZERO. (Saussure cited in Starobinski, *Les mots*, p. 21)

And in the emblematic citation that he gives this law – NUMERO DEUS PARI GAUDET ('God rejoices in even numbers') – it is said that in one way or another, enjoyment is inseparable not from amassing the Same, reinforcing meaning by the addition of the Same, but quite the contrary, from its cancellation by the *double*, by the cycle of the anti-vowel or the anti-gram where the phonematic character comes to be cancelled as if in a mirror.

2. Saussure's second law, which concerns the theme-word or the 'anathema' that runs through the text, must be analysed in the same way. It must be seen that it is not at all a matter of repeating the original signifier or reproducing its phonematic components throughout a text.

'*Aasen argaleôn anemôn amegartos autmè*' does not 'reproduce' Agamemnon even though Saussure is ambiguous on this point. He says:

> In the hypogram, it is a question of emphasising a name, a word, striving to repeat its syllables and thus giving it a second, artificial way of being added, so to speak, to the original being of the word.

In fact, the theme-word is *diffracted* throughout the text. In a way, it is 'analysed' by the verse or the poem, reduced to its simple elements, decomposed like the light spectrum, whose diffracted rays then sweep across the text. In other words then, the original corpus is dispersed into 'partial objects'. It is therefore a matter not of another manner of being the Same, of reiteration or paraphrase, of a clandestine avatar of the original name of God, but rather of an explosion, a dispersion, a dismembering where this name is annihilated. Not an 'artificial double' (what use is this unless it is in order to be reduced to the same thing?), but a dismembered double, a body torn limb from limb like Osiris and Orpheus. Far from reinforcing the signifier in its being, repeating it positively, this metamorphosis of its scattered members is equivalent to its death as such, to its annihilation. To sum it up, this is, *on the level of the signifier, of the name it incarnates, the equivalent of putting God or a hero to death in the sacrifice.* Following this, the animal totem, the god or the hero circulate, disarticulated, disintegrated by its death in the sacrifice (eventually torn limb from limb and eaten), as the symbolic material of the group's integration. The name of God, torn limb from limb, dispersed into its phonemic elements as the signifier, is put to death, haunts the poem and rearticulates it in the rhythm of its fragments, without ever being reconstituted in it as such.

The symbolic act never consists in the reconstitution of the name of God after a detour and analytic breakdown within the poem; the symbolic act never consists of the resurrection of the signifier. Starobinski is wrong when he says:

It will be a matter of reassembling the principal syllables, as Isis reunited Orpheus' dismembered body.

Lacan gets his theory of symbolism wrong when he says:

> If man finds himself open to desiring as many others within himself as his members have names other than his, if he is to recognise as many disjointed members, lost without ever having been a unity, as there are beings that are metaphors of these members, we can also see that the question of ascertaining the epistemological value of these symbols has been resolved, since these are the very members that return to him after wandering through the world in an alienated fashion. (*La psychanalyse,* Vol. V, 1960, p. 15)

The symbolic act is never in this 'return', in this retotalisation that follows alienation, in this resurrection of an identity; on the contrary, it is always in the volatilisation of the name, the signifier, in the *extermination of the term*, disappearance with no return. This is what makes possible the intense circulation on the interior of the poem (also in the primitive group on the occasion of feasting and sacrifice), this is what gives enjoyment a language, and, again, one from which *nothing results nor remains*. The entire pack of linguistic categories cannot do too much to efface the scandal of the loss and death of the signifer in this feverish agitation of language which, as Bataille says concerning life, 'demands that death exert its ravages at its expense'.

Here, of course, the limits Saussure imposes on himself explode. This poetic principle is not only applicable to Vedic, Germanic or Latin poetry, and it is pointless to seek, as he did, for a hypothetical generalisation of the *proof* of this. It is obvious that modern poets have never made use of the generative theme-word, if ever the ancient poets did. But this is not an objection since it is clear that, for all languages and all epochs, the *form* Saussure distinguished is sovereign. It is clear to all – enjoyment bears witness to this – that *a good poem is one where nothing is left over*, where all the phonemic material in use is consumed; and that, on the other hand, a bad poem (or 'not-poetry-at-all') is one where there is a remainder, where not every significant phoneme, diphoneme, syllable or term has been seized by its double, where not every term has been volatilised and consumed in a rigorous reciprocity (or antagonism), as in primitive gift-exchange, where we feel the weight of the remainder that has not found its corresponding term, nor therefore its death and absolution, which has not *been* successfully *exchanged* in the very operation of the text: it is in proportion to this residue that we know that a poem is bad, that it is the slag of discourse, something which has not exploded, which has been neither lost nor consumed in the festival of reversible speech.

Value is residue. It is the discourse of signification, our language governed by linguistics. The *economy* of signification and communication, where we produce and exchange terms and meaning-values, under the law of the code, rests on everything that has not been seized by the symbolic operation of language, by symbolic extermination.

The economic process is inaugurated in the same way: what re-enters the circuits of accumulation and value is what *remains* from sacrificial consumption, what has not been exhausted in the incessant cycle of the gift and the counter-gift. It is this remainder that we accumulate, we speculate on the rest, and here the birth of the economic begins.

We can distinguish a third dimension of our mode of signification from the notion of the remainder. We know that the poetic operation 'shatters the fundamental laws of language':

1. The signifier–signified equivalence.
2. The linearity of the signifier (Saussure: 'In linguistics, we should not, due to its being obvious, lightly disregard the truth that the elements of a word *follow each other*, since, on the contrary, it provides in advance the central principle of all useful reflection on words.')
3. The third dimension, never really taken into account, and strictly interdependent with the two others, is that of *the boundlessness, the limitless production of signifying material.* Just as equivalence defines a dimension of the economic (that of unlimited productivity, the infinite reproduction of value), so the signifier–signified equivalence defines an unlimited field of *discursivity*.

We no longer even see this proliferation of our discursive customs, it becomes so 'natural' to us, but it is what distinguishes us from all other cultures. We use and abuse words, phonemes and signifiers with no ritual, religious or poetic restriction of any kind, in total 'freedom', with no responsibility as regards the immense 'material' that we produce as we please. Everyone is free to endlessly use and endlessly draw on phonemic material in the name of what they want to 'express' and with the sole consideration of what they have to say. This 'freedom' of discourse, the possibility of *taking* it and using it without ever *returning* it, answering to it, nor sacrificing even a share of one's goods to it, as the primitives used to in order to ensure its symbolic reproduction; *the idea of language as an all purpose medium* of an inexhaustible nature, like a place where the utopia of political economy would be realised: 'to each according to his needs'; this phantasm of an unprecedented stock, a raw material that would be magically reproduced in exact proportion to its use (no need even for primitive accumulation), and therefore the freedom of a fantastic wastage, is the exact status of our discursive communication, a staggering availability of signifying material. All this is thinkable only in a general configuration where the same principles govern the reproduction of both material goods and the species itself. A mutation runs simultaneously through social formations where material goods, the number of individuals and the proliferation of words are, in a more or less rigorous fashion, distributed, limited and controlled inside a symbolic cycle, and our 'modern' social formations, which are distinguished by an infinite productivity, as economic as it is linguistic and demographic. These societies are caught in an endless escalation at every level: material accumulation, linguistic expression, and the proliferation of the species.[4]

This model of productivity (exponential growth, galloping demographics, unlimited discursivity) must be simultaneously analysed everywhere. On the plane of language, which is alone in question here, it is clear that the unrestrained freedom to use phonemes in unlimited number for purposes of expression, without the reverse processes of cancellation, expiation, reabsorption or destruction (it does not matter which term), is radically opposed by the simple law announced by Saussure, that in poetry a vowel, a consonant or a syllable cannot be uttered without being doubled, that is to say, somehow exorcised, without fulfilling itself in the repetition that cancels it.

From that point on, there is no question of unlimited use. The poetic, like symbolic exchange, brings into play a strictly limited and distributed corpus, but it undertakes *to reach the end of it*, whereas our economy of discourse implements an unlimited corpus that cares nothing for resolution.

What becomes of words and phonemes in our discursive system? We should not think that they graciously disappear as soon as they have served their purpose, nor that they return somewhere, like the characters on a Linotype matrix, and wait until the next time they are used. Again, this is part of our idealist conception of language. Every term or phoneme not taken back, not *returned*, not volatilised by poetic doubling, not exterminated as a term and as a value (in its equivalence to what it 'meant' or 'wanted to say'), *remains*. It is a residue. It will return to a fantastic sedimentation of waste, of opaque discursive material. (We begin to perceive that the essential problem of a productive civilisation may be that of its waste, *which is nothing other than the problem of its own death*: giving way under its own remains. Industrial leftovers are nothing, however, in relation to the remains of language.) Such as it is, our culture is haunted and jammed by this gigantic, petrified, residual instance: by means of an escalation of language it attempts to reduce a tendential decline in the rate of 'communication'. Nothing happens. Just as every commodity, that is to say, everything produced under the sign of the law of value and equivalence, is an *irreducible residue* that comes to bar social relations, so every word, every term and every phoneme produced and not symbolically destroyed accumulates like the repressed, weighs down on us with all the abstraction of dead language.

An economy of profusion and wastage rules over our language: the affluent utopia. But although 'affluence' and wastage are recent characteristics of the material economy, an *historical* trait, they appear to be a natural dimension, always already given, of spoken or written language. There is and will always be, at every instant, a utopia, insofar as we will want it for the whole world – the utopia of an unlimited *capital* of language as use- and exchange-value. In order to signify, everyone proceeds by the accumulation and cumulative exchange of signifiers whose truth lies elsewhere, in the equivalence to what they want to say (one can say it in fewer words: concision is a *moral* virtue, but this is only ever an economy of *means*). This discursive 'consumption', over which the spectre of penury never hangs, this wasteful manipulation, sustained by the imaginary of profusion, results in a prodigious inflation that leaves, in the image of our societies of uncontrolled growth, an equally prodigious residue, a non-degradable waste of consummated, but never entirely consumed, signi-fiers. For used words are not volatilised, they accumulate like waste – a sign pollution as fantastic as, and contemporary with, industrial pollution.

Linguistics seized the stage of the *waste product* [*déchet*], the stage of a functional language that it universalises as the natural state of all language. It imagines no other:

> Just as the Romans and the Etruscans divided the sky by rigid mathematical lines, and in this way delimited space as a *templum* and conjured up a God, so every people has above them such a sky divided up by mathematical concepts and, under the demand for truth, it intends that from now on every conceptual God should be sought nowhere other than within this sphere. (Nietzsche, *The Philosopher's Book*)

This is what linguistics does: it *forces* language into an autonomous sphere in its own image, and feigns to have found it there 'objectively', when, from start to finish, it invented and rationalised it. It is incapable of imagining a state of language other than that of the combinatory abstrac-tion of the code [*langue*] accompanied with an infinite manipulation of speech [*parole*]; in other words, speculation (in the double sense of the term) on the basis of general equivalence and free circulation, everyone using words as they please and exchanging them in accordance with the law of the code.

But *let's suppose* a stage where the signs of language were deliberately distributed (like money is for the Are-Are): restricted distribution, no formal 'freedom' of production, circulation or use. Or rather a double circuit:

- the circuit of 'liberated' words, gratuitously useable, circulating as exchange-value; a zone of meaning 'commerce', analogous to the sphere of the gimwali in economic exchange;
- the controlled circuit of a non-'liberated' zone, of a material restricted to symbolic use where words have neither use- nor exchange-value, and where they cannot be gratuitously multiplied nor uttered, analogous to the sphere of the kula for 'precious' goods.

The general principle of equivalence does not operate in this sphere, nor therefore does the logical and rational articulation of the sign with which semio-linguistic 'science' is preoccupied.

The poetic recreates the situation of primitive societies in linguistic material: a restricted corpus of objects whose uninterrupted circulation in the gift-exchange creates an inexhaustible wealth, a feast of exchange. Assessed by their volume or their value, primitive goods end up in an almost absolute penury. Tirelessly consumed in feasting and exchange, they recount, through their 'minimal volume and number', the 'maximal energy of signs' of which Nietzsche spoke, or the first and only genuine affluent society of which Marshall Sahlins spoke (*Les temps modernes*, Oct. 1968).

Words here have the same status as objects or goods: they are not freely available to everybody, language has no 'affluence'. In these magical and ritual formulations there reigns a restriction which alone preserves the symbolic efficacity of signs. The shaman and the prophet (*Vates*) act on considered, coded and limited phonemes or formulae, exhausting them in a maximal configuration of meaning. So the formula is pronounced, in its literal and rhythmic exactitude, so it binds the future, but not because it signifies.[5]

The same goes for the poetic, which is defined by the fact of operating on a *restricted* corpus of the signifier, and by aiming to resolve it completely. And it is precisely because the poetic (or the primitive ritual of language) aims not at the production of signifieds, but at the exact consumption and cyclical resolution of a signifying material, that it takes on a limited corpus. *Limitation* is neither restrictive nor penurious in this context: *it is the fundamental rule of the symbolic.* Conversely, the inexhaustible character of our discourse is bound to the rule of equivalence and linearity, just as the infinite character of our material production is inseparable from the change to equivalence in exchange-value (it is this linear infinity which simultaneously breeds, at every moment of capital, the fact of poverty and the phantasm of a final wealth).

The signifier, doubling up and returning to cancel itself out, follows the same movement as the gift and the counter-gift, giving and returning; it is a reciprocity where the use-value and the exchange-value of an object cancel each other out, and the same complete cycle results in the nothingness of value, on which the intensity of the social relation or the enjoyment of the poem acts.

This is a question of *revolution*. What the poetic accomplishes with the phoneme-value at a microscopic level, every social revolution accomplishes over the entire flanks of the code of value – use-value, exchange-value, rules of equivalence, axioms, value-systems, coded discourses, rational finalities, etc. – when the death drive is linked to it in order to volatilise them. This same process of completion does not stop short of the analytic operation: in contrast to science as a process of accumulation, the real *analytic* operation *eliminates its object*, which comes to an end in it. The term of the analysis – not its 'constructive' finality, but its real *end* – is this volatilisation of the object and its own concepts; or again, these are the processes of the subject who, far from attempting to master its object, accepts being analysed by it in turn, in which movement the respective positions of each are irremediably dismantled. It is only from this point that the subject and the object *are exchanged*, whereas in their respective positivity (in science for example) they merely draw themselves erect and face each other off for an indefinite period. Science is bound to the construction of its object and to its repetition as a phantasm (as much as to the phantasmatic reproduction of the subject of knowledge). A perverse pleasure is attached to this phantasm, the pleasure of continually reconstructing a faltering object, whereas it is proper to analysis, and to enjoyment, *to bring its object to an end.*[6]

The poetic is the restitution of symbolic exchange in the very heart of words. Where words, in the discourse of signification, finalised by meaning, do not respond to each other, do not speak to each other (and neither, within words themselves, do consonants, vowels and syllables), in the poetic, on the contrary, once the authority of meaning has been broken, all the constitutive elements enter into exchange with, and start to respond to, each other. They are not 'liberated', nor is any deep or 'unconscious' content 'set free' through them: they are simply returned to exchange, and this very process is enjoyment. It is futile to look for the secret in an energetics, a libidinal economy or a fluid dynamics: enjoyment is not bound up with the effectuation of a force, but with the actualisation of an exchange – an exchange without traces, where no force casts a shadow, since every force, and the law behind it, has been resolved. For it is the operation of the symbolic to be its own definitive end.

The mere possibility of this is a revolution in relation to an order where nothing and no-one, neither words, men, their bodies nor their gazes, are given access to direct communication, but instead pass in transit as values through the models that engender or reproduce them in total 'estrangement' to each other . . . The revolution is everywhere where an exchange crops up – be it the infinitesimal exchange of phonemes or syllables in a poetic text, or of millions of men speaking to each other in an insurgent city – that shatters the finality of the models, the mediation of the code and the consecutive cycle of value. For the secret of a social *parole*, of a revolution, is also the anagrammatic dispersal of the instance of power, the rigorous volatilisation of every transcendent social instance. The fragmented body of power is then exchanged as social *parole* in the poetry of rebellion. Nothing remains of this *parole*, nor is any of it accumulated anywhere. Power is reborn from what is not consumed in it, for power is the residue of *parole*. In social rebellion the same anagrammatical dispersal is at work as that of the body in eroticism, as that of knowledge and its object in the analytic operation: the revolution is symbolic or it is not a revolution at all.

The End of the Anathema

The whole science of linguistics can be analysed as resistance to the operation of dissemination and literal resolution. Everywhere there is the same attempt to reduce the poetic to a meaning, a 'wanting-to-say' [*vouloir-dire*], to bring it back under the shadow of a meaning, to shatter the *utopia* of language and to bring it back to the topic of discourse. Linguistics opposes the discursive order (*equivalence and accumulation*) to the literal order (*reversibility and dissemination*). We can see this counteroffensive unfolding in the interpretations of the poetic given here and there

(Jakobson, Fonagy, Umberto Eco – see 'The Linguistic Imaginary', below). Psychoanalytic interpretation, to which we will return, also arises from this resistance. For the radicality of the symbolic is such that all the sciences or disciplines that labour to neutralise it come to be analysed by it in their turn, and returned to their ignorance [*méconnaissance*].

These, then, are the principles of linguistics and psychoanalysis that will be at stake as regards Saussure's anagrammatic hypothesis. Although he made this hypothesis in connection with a precise point and subject to assessment, there is nothing to prevent us developing it and drawing out its ultimate consequences. In any case, *the radicalisation of hypotheses is the only possible method* – theoretical violence being the equivalent, in the analytic order, of the 'poetic violence which replaces the order of all the atoms of a phrase' of which Nietzsche speaks.

We will begin with Starobinski's commentary on Saussure [*Les mots*, pp. 33ff.]. Two aspects of his commentary are especially in question here: the theme-word (whether or not it exists); and the specificity of the poetic (and thus Saussure's discovery).

Saussure's whole argument seems to draw its support from the *real* existence of the key-word, the latent signifier, the 'matrix' and the 'corpus princeps':

> This versification seems to be dominated by a *phonemic* preoccupation, some-times internal and free (the mutual correspondence of elements by couplets or rhymes), sometimes external, that is to say, drawing inspiration for phonemic composition from a name like Scipio, Jovei, etc.

And we know that after having had this intuition, all his efforts were brought to bear on establishing its proof. Here, it is true, Saussure falls into the trap of scientific validation, into the superstition of the fact. Fortuna-tely, he fails to establish this proof (of knowing whether the practices of the ancient poets were governed scientifically by the anagram of the theme-word), and this failure preserves the scope of his hypothesis, which would in fact, once delimited by a proof, be restricted to a certain type of ancient poetry and, more seriously, it would have restrained the poetic act to the formal gymnastics of the cryptogram, a game of hide-and-seek with the key-word, playing for the reconstitution of a term that had been voluntarily buried and dislocated. This is how Starobinski interprets it:

> Poetic discourse will therefore only ever be the second manner of being of a name: an elaborate variation that would allow the perspicacious reader to see the obvious but dispersed presence of the principal phonemes . . . The hypogram slides from a simple name into the complex spread of the syllables in a line; it will be a question of recognising and reassembling of the principal syllables, as Isis reunites the dismembered body of Osiris.

From the outset, Starobinski eliminates both the emanationist or mystical theory (the germinal diffusion of the theme-word through the line) and the productive theory (the theme-word used by the poet as a framework for the labour of composition). The theme-word is neither an original cell, nor a model: Saussure never tries to establish a relation of semantic privilege between the two levels (nominal and anagrammatised) of the word. Mannequin, sketch, miniature scene, theme or anathema: what status can we give it? This is important, since the whole schema of signification, of 'making a sign', is at stake: it is certain at least that we cannot turn the theme-word into the signified of the poem as signifier; and no less certain that there exists, if not a *reference*, then at least a *coherence* between the two. Starobinski seems to be sticking as close as possible to Saussure when he proposes:

> The latent theme-word differs only from the manifest line by its compression. It is *a* word like the *many* words deployed in the line: they differ only therefore in the way that the one differs from the multiple. Developed before the total text, hidden behind the text, or rather in it, the theme-word shows no qualitative difference: it is neither of a superior essence, nor of a more humble nature. It offers its substance to an inventive interpretation, causing it to survive in an extended echo.

But, if it is a word *like* other words, why is it necessary that it is hidden or latent? On the other hand, the 'manifest' text is something other than the 'development, multiplication, prolongation' and 'echo' of the theme-word (in itself, the echo is not poetic): this something else is dissemination, dismemberment and deconstruction. Starobinski overlooks this aspect of the operation until his most nuanced interpretation:

> The diction of the theme-word seemed to be dislocated, subjected to a rhythm other than that of the vocables through which the manifest discourse unfolds; the theme-word becomes looser, in the manner in which the subject of a fugue is stated, when it is treated as imitation by augmentation. There can be no question of recognising it, the theme-word never having been the object of an exposition; it must be divined in a reading attentive to the possible links between disparate phonemes. This reading is developed according to another tempo (and in another tense): ultimately, we leave the time of the 'continuity' proper to customary language.

This interpretation, more subtle in that it is allied to the analytic process (floating attention to a free discourse), also seems however to fall into the trap of presupposing a generative formula, whose scattered presence in the poem would in some sense be merely a secondary state, whose identity it would nevertheless always be possible (it is even the necessary condition of reading) to locate. Simultaneous double presence at two levels: Osiris dismembered is the same in another form, his finality is to become Osiris again following the phase of dispersion. The identity remains latent, and the process of reading is a process of identification.

This is the trap, this is the linguistic *defence*: as complex as they are, these interpretations only ever turn the poetic into a *supplementary* operation, a detour in a process of recognition (of a word, a term, a subject). It is always the same that is given to read. But then why this laborious reduction; and what makes all this 'poetic'? If it is in order to repeat the same term, if the line is only the phonemic dissimulation of the key-word, then all this is futile complication and subtlety. And enjoyment remains unexplained. Poetic intensity never consists in the repetition of an identity, but in the *destruction* of an identity. It is ignorance [*méconnaissance*] of this that produces the linguistic reduction, this is where it subtly distorts the poetic in the direction of its own axioms: identity, equivalence, refraction of the same, 'imitation by augmentation', etc. It especially never recognises the mad distortion, the perdition of the signifier and death in the anagram, as the symbolic form of lanuage, remaining within the linguistic game, where poetry is only a code, a 'key', in the way we speak of a key to dreams.

This is what societies' games do, and this is all they do. This is what bad poetry, allegory and figurative music do, when they refer in too facile a fashion to what they 'signify', or endlessly metaphorise into other terms. These are charades, riddles and spoonerisms, in which, with the discovery of the key-word, everything is complete. And of course there is pleasure in this detour, as there is removing the mask from what is hidden, and whose secret presence attracts you. But this pleasure has nothing to do with poetic enjoyment, which is radical in another way, *and not perverse*: nothing is discovered in it, nothing expressed in it, and nothing shows through it. No riddles or 'divinations', no secret terms, no abutment of meaning. The poetic destroys every cleared path towards a final term, every key, it resolves the *anathema,* the law weighing down upon language.

We could offer the hypothesis that enjoyment is a direct function of the resolution of every positive reference. It is at its minimum where the signified is immediately produced as value: in 'normal' communicative discourse – linear and steady speech, exhausted in decoding. Beyond this discourse – the zero degree of enjoyment – all sorts of combinations are possible where a game of hide-and-seek is set up with the signified, a deciphering, and no longer a pure and simple decoding. This latter is the traditional anagram or the text with keys, the 'Yamamoto Kakpoté' or the texts from the *Fliegende Blätter* (interpreted by Freud and analysed by Lyotard in 'The Dreamwork Does Not Think', *Oxford Literary Review*, 6 (1) 1983), where, behind a coherent or incoherent manifest text, there lies a latent text to be found. In both cases, there is a disengagement, a distantiation of the signified, of the last word of history, a detour by way of the signifier, *différance* as Derrida says. But in any case, it is possible, by whatever developments, to seize hold of the last word, the formula that controls the text. This formula may be subconscious (in the joke, the *mot d'esprit*, to which we shall return) or unconscious (in the dream), but it is always coherent and discursive. With the dawning of this formula, the cycle of meaning is exhausted. And enjoyment, in every case, is proportionate to the detour, the delay, the loss of the statement, to the *time lost* in rediscovering it. It is therefore extremely restrained in society's games, more intense in the *mot d'esprit,* where the decoding is suspended and where we laugh in proportion to the destruction of meaning. *In the poetic text, it is infinite*, because no code whatsoever can be found there, no deciphering is possible, and because there is never a signified to put an end to the cycle. Here, the formula is not even unconscious (this is the limit of all psychoanalytic interpretations), *it does not exist.* The key is definitively lost. This is the difference between simple cryptogrammatic pleasure (the entire category of the brainwave, where the operation always ends up with a positive residue) and the symbolic radiation of the poem. In other words, if the poem refers to something, it is always to NOTHING, to the term of nothingness, to the signified zero. Poetic intensity consists in the vertigo of this perfect resolution, which leaves the place of the signified or the referent perfectly empty.[7]

'Aboli bibelot d'inanité sonore': a perfect line where the anagrammatic form is taken up again. 'ABOLI' is the generative theme-word running throughout the line, and referring to nothing. The anagrammatic form and its content seal an extraordinary union here.

Several other things can be advanced concerning the theme-word, even within the limits of Saussure's hypothesis. The hypogram, being a god's or a hero's name, is not just any 'signified', and not even a signified at all. We know that the literal invocation of God is dangerous because of the forces it unleashes. For this reason, the anagram is necessary to veil the incantation by rigorously, but obliquely, spelling out the name of God. This allusive mode differs radically from the mode of signification, for the signifier stands for the absence, dispersal and putting to death of the signified. The name of God appeared in the eclipse of its own destruction, in the sacrificial mode, exterminated in the literal sense of the term.

From this point, it is clear that the make or break question Saussure puts to himself, and on which Starobinski's objection entirely rests, concerning the *positive* existence of the theme-word, is beside the point, since the name of God exists only in order to be annihilated.

We endlessly create the identity of the name of God, with which no kind of enjoyment is associated, since enjoyment proceeds from the death of God and his name, and more generally from the fact that where something used to be – a name, a signifier, an agency – *nothing remains*. In this there is an agonising overhaul of our anthropological conceptions. It is said that poetry was always the exaltation, the positive celebration of a god or a hero (or a great many other things since), but we must see, on the contrary, that it is only beautiful and intense because it returns the god to death, because poetry is the site of its volatilisation and his sacrifice, because in it all the 'cruelty' (in Artaud's sense) and ambivalence of the relation to the gods is played out in a precise manner. You must be as naïve as a Westerner to think that the 'savages' prostrated themselves before their gods as we do before ours. On the contrary, in their rites they have always been able to actualise their ambivalence towards the gods, *perhaps they only ever roused them in order to put them to death*. This is still alive in the poetic. In the poetic, God is not invoked in any other form, the poem does not keep trotting out His name 'in extension' (once again, what interest would there be in this? A prayer wheel is quite enough to repeat his name), he is resolved, dismembered and sacrificed *in His name*. We could say, following Bataille, that the discontinuity (discursivity) of the name is abolished in the radical continuity of the poem. The ecstasy of death.

In the poem, God is not even the hidden subject of the utterance, nor is the poet the subject of enunciation. Language itself adopts speech so as to disappear in it. And the name of God is equally the name of the Father: the law (of repression, of the signifier, of castration) that it brings to bear on the subject and, at the same time, language is exterminated in the anagram. The poetic text is the example, realised at last, of reabsorption without residue, without trace, without the merest atom of a signifier (the name of God) and, through this, of the agency of language itself and, through this reabsorption, the *resolution of the law*.

The poem is the fatal declension of the name of God. For us, who no longer have a god, but for whom language has become God (the full and phallic value of the name of God is diffused for us throughout the extent of discourse), the poetic is the site of our ambivalence as regards language, of our death drive as regards language, of the force proper to the extermination of the code.

The Nine Billion Names of God

In a science-fiction story (Arthur C. Clarke, 'The nine billion names of God' [in *Of Time and Stars*, Harmondsworth: Penguin, 1981, pp. 15–32]), a brotherhood of lamas, lost in the foothills of Tibet, devote their whole lives to the recitation of the names of God. There are a great many of these names – nine billion. When they have all been stated and declined, the world will come to an end, an entire cycle of the world. Bringing the world to an end, step by step, word by word, by exhausting the total corpus of the signifiers of God: this is their religious delirium – or the truth of their death drive.

But the lamas read slowly, their difficult task lasting many centuries. They then hear talk of mysterious Western machines that can record and decode at an incredible speed. One of them sets about ordering a powerful computer from IBM to hasten their task. The American technicians arrive in the Tibetan mountains to set up and programme the machine. According to them it will take only three months to get to the last of the nine billion names.[8] They themselves do not believe a word of the prophesied consequences of this enumeration, and, shortly before the expiry of the operation, afraid that the monks might turn against them when faced with the failure of their prophecy, they flee the monastery. Then, climbing down into the civilised world, they see the stars go out one by one . . .

The poem, too, is the total resolution of the world, as soon as the scattered phonemes of the name of God are consumed in it. When the anagram has been completely declined, nothing remains, the world has turned once again, and the intense enjoyment running through it has nowhere else to come from.

The second point on which Starobinski's commentary bears is the specificity of the poetic. Basically, he says, the rules Saussure evokes and imputes to a deliberate and calculated act may be reduced to the basic givens of all language. On the first rule (of the coupling):

> The total phonemic opportunities language offers at every instant to whoever wants to make use of them . . . are sufficiently numerous not to demand a laborious combination, requiring instead an *attentive* combination.

Ultimately no more chance: pure probability is sufficient. Again:

> The facts of phonemic symmetry [the term 'symmetry' is already a reductive term, that sees a specular redundancy in the doubling of phonemes – J.B.] noted here are striking: but are they the effect of an observed rule (of which no testimony has survived)? Could we not invoke, to justify the multiplicity of internal correspondences, an only barely conscious and half instinctive *taste for the echo*?

'An instinctive taste for the echo': the poet would be basically nothing other than a linguistic particle accelerator who merely increases the rate of the redundancy of customary language. That's what 'inspiration' is, and there is no need to calculate for it: a little 'attention' and 'instinct' is all we need:

> Must the Ancients' poetic practices resemble the obsessional ritual more than the surge of inspired speech?

Of course we can acknowledge formal constraints:

> It is true that traditional scansion subjects the *vates*' diction to a regularity that we must indeed qualify as *obsessional*. Nothing prevents us from imagining, since the facts go along with this, an increasing formal requirement that would oblige the poet to use every phonetic element twice in the same line.

But whether the poet is an inspired resonator or a calculating obsessional, it is always the same type of interpretation: the coupling and the anagram are the effects of a resonance, a redundancy, an 'imitation by augmentation', etc. – in short, the poetic is a play of combinations, and since all language is combinatory, the poetic becomes once more a particular case of language:

> Why do we not turn our attention to an aspect of the *process* of speech in the anagram, a process which is neither fortuitous, nor fully conscious? Why should there not exist an iteration, a generative and involuntary repetition that would double and project the materials of a primary speech within discourse, unpronounced and at the same time non-evanescent? Due to the lack of a conscious *rule*, the anagram can nevertheless be considered as a *regularity* (or a law) where the arbitrary theme-word submits to the necessity of a process.

The hypothesis of the theme-word, and its rigorous dispersal

> uncovers the extremely simple truth that language is an unending resource, and that dissimulated behind every phrase is the increasing clamour of the multitude from which it was taken in order to be isolated in front of us in its originality.

But what then did Saussure uncover? Nothing. Was this a 'staggering error'? Worse: a platitude. Generalised in this way, his hypothesis is annihilated. This is how, in all linguistic 'good faith', the radical difference of the poetic is denied. Saussure was at least seized by the intoxication of the poetic – the intoxication of the rigour with which he saw language turn back on itself, operating on its own material, instead of unfolding in a linear manner, idiotically following on from itself, as in customary discourse. This is no longer the case with Starobinski: rigour has become an 'obsession', a psychopathological category; total dispersion has become a probabilistic occurrence/recurrence; anagrammatic dispersion has become the 'clamouring multitude of language', a harmonic contextuality where a particular meaning is specified in turn:

> Every discourse is a set that facilitates the subtraction of a subset . . . moreover, every text is itself the subset of another text . . . every text incorporates and is incorporated. Every text is a productive product.

Onwards to the Russian dolls, to the 'abyssal' [*en abyme*] textuality dear to *Tel Quel*.

Starobinski's whole argument amounts to saying either the poet is just an obsessive formalist (if we follow Saussure's hypothesis), or his operation is exactly the same as that of all language, and so it is Saussure who is the obsessive: everything he believed he had discovered is nothing but the researcher's retrospective illusion, since:

> Every complex structure provides the observer with sufficient elements for him to select a subset apparently endowed with meaning, which nothing prevents us according an a priori logical or chronological antecedence.

Poor Saussure, who saw the anagram everywhere, and attributed his phantoms to the poets!

Starobinski and the linguists do not dream: by verifying Saussure's hypothesis *ad infinitum*, they reduce it to zero. To do this it was enough to stick to its *content* (the inference of the theme-word, its positive role, its metamorphoses) instead of judging it on its *form*. The stakes of the poetic are not the production of, nor even the combinatory variations on, a theme, nor an identifiable 'subset'. In this case, in fact, it is clearly part of a universal mode of discourse (except we cannot then see the *necessity* of the poetic, its different status, nor the enjoyment proper to this mode as opposed to that of discourse). Its stake is, precisely through the labour of the anagram, *the point of no return* in whatever term or theme. At this point, whether the theme-word's existence is recognised or not is a false problem. This is not because, according to Starobinski, every language is, at bottom, articulated on a sort of code or formula – but because, in any case, it is the *annihilation* of this code that is the form of the poetic. As Saussure describes it, this form holds for all poetry, the most modern and the most ancient. The principle of the annihilation of the code retains all its intelligibility even if the existence of this formula cannot be verified.[9] The only thing is that this code, which in ancient poetry could have taken the form of a word-theme, might, in modern poetry, be no more than signifying constellation that can no longer be located as such, even a letter or a formula of the Leclairian type, lost forever, or unconscious, or even the 'differential signifier' that *Tel Quel* talks about. What is essential, whatever the formula is, is to consider the poetic not as the mode of the formula's appearance, but as its *mode of disappearance*. In this sense, so much the better that Saussure failed to find proof of the formula: by verifying the content, he would have taken away the radicality of the form. Saussure's failure and intoxication, since they at least maintain the urgency of the poetic, are better than all the banalities that accept the poetic as a fact of universal language.

The Linguistic Imaginary

We must now leave Saussure and look at how the linguists dealt with the poetic and the questions it brought to bear on their 'science'. All things considered, the defence they put up in the face of this danger is the same as that mounted by the adherents of political economy (and its Marxist critics) in the face of the symbolic alternative in previous societies and in our own. All of them chose to differentiate and modulate their categories while not changing their principle of rationality in any way, that is, without changing the arbitrariness and the imaginary that made them hypostatise the order of discourse and the order of production as universals. As scientists, they have good reason to believe in this order, since they are agents of order.

Thus the linguists concede that the arbitrary character of the sign is a bit shaken by the poetic; but certainly not the signifier/signified distinction, nor therefore the law of equivalence and the function of representation. Indeed, in a certain way, the signifier in this instance represents the signified far better, since it 'expresses' it directly following a *necessary* correlation between each element of the substance of the signifier and what it is supposed to express, instead of referring to it arbitrarily, as in discourse. The signifier's autonomy is conceded:

> The conceptual messages transmitted through the intermediary of sound neces-sarily differ from the pre-conceptual contents in the sound sequences and rhythms themselves. They either happen to converge or diverge. (I. Fonagy, *Diogène*, 51)

However, this is basically so that the signifier better embodies, not merely by convention, but in its materiality and its flesh, what it has to say: 'In Swinburne's lines, we feel the breeze passing . . .'. Instead of it being, as in conceptual language, the unit of primary articulation, *the phoneme, the unit of secondary articulation. becomes representative*, while, however, the form of the representation has not itself changed. It is always a question of *referring*, no longer to the concept by means of the terms of the *langue* nor syntax, but by means of vowels and syllables, the atoms of language, and their combination in rhythm, to an elementary presence, to an original instance of things (the 'breeze' as primary process!). Between the substance of language and the substance of the world (wind, water, feelings, passions, the unconscious; everything 'pre-conceptual', which is in fact already conceptualised, without appearing to be, by a whole code of perception), there is always a positive correlation at play, a play of equivalence amongst *values*.

In this way, muted vowels would stand for the dark and obscure, etc., and there would no longer be an *arbitrary* conceptual equivalence in this case, but a *necessary* phonemic equivalence. Thus Rimbaud's vowel-sonnet, and Fonagy's entire exposition of the 'symbolism' of linguistic sounds (*Diogène*, 51, p. 78): everyone would agree to recognise that '*i*' is lighter, faster and thinner than '*u*'; that '*k*' and '*r*' are harder than '*l*', etc.

> The feeling of thinness associated with the vowel '*i*' may be the result of a subconscious kinaesthetic perception of the position of the tongue in the emission of this sound. The '*r*' appears masculine [!] by reason of the greater muscular effort required to emit it in comparison with the alveolar '*l*' or the labial '*m*'.

A real metaphysics of an original *langue*, a desperate attempt to rediscover a *natural deposit* of the poetic, an expressive genius of language, that would only have to be captured and transcribed.

In fact, all this is coded, and it is just as arbitrary to correlate the repetition of the phoneme '*f*' with the passing breeze as it is to correlate the word 'table' with the concept of table. There is nothing more in common between them than there is between a piece of music and what it 'evokes' (landscape or passion), other than cultural convention, or a *code*. That this code claims to be anthropological ('naturally' soft vowels) takes nothing away from its arbitrary character. Conversely moreover, we can clearly maintain, with Benveniste, that the very strong cultural convention that binds the word 'table' to the concept of 'table' imposes genuine *necessity*, and that at bottom the sign is never arbitrary. This is correct: the fundamental arbitrariness lies not in the internal organisation of the sign, but in the imposition of the sign as *value*, that is to say, in the presupposition of two instances and their equivalence in accordance with the law: the sign acting as a stand-in, as emanating from a reality that makes signs to you. Such is linguistics' metaphysics, and such is its imaginary. Its interpretation of the poetic is still haunted by this presupposition.

By contrast, when Harpo Marx waves a real sturgeon instead of pronouncing the password 'sturgeon', then indeed, by substituting the referent of the term and by abolishing their separation, he really explodes the arbitrariness at the same time as the system of representation, in a poetic act *par excellence:* putting the signifier 'sturgeon' to death by its own referent.

Whether conceptual or pre-conceptual, it is always the 'message' and the 'aim of the message as such', by which Jakobson defines the poetic function, which by autonomising the operation of the signifying material merely refers it to a *supplementary* effect of signification. Something other

than the concept comes through, but it is still some *thing*; another v
realised through the very play of the signifier, but it remains a *value*; t
signifying material functions at another level, its own, but it continues to
function: moreover, Jakobson makes the poetic function supplementary
rather than alternative, just one linguistic function out of many – a surplus-
value of signification due to which the signifier itself is taken into account
as an autonomous value. The poetic gives you more!

The 'self-presence' [*présence à lui-même*] of the signifier is analysed in
terms of redundancy, as an internal echo, as resonance, phonetic recurrence, etc. (Hopkins: 'The verse is a discourse that repeats, either wholly
or partially, the same phonemic figure'). Or again:

> It is acknowledged that poets worthy of the name possess a delicate and
> penetrating sensibility as regards the impressive *value* of the words and sounds
> with which they compose; to communicate this value to their readers, they are
> often moved to *represent*, around the principal word, the phonemes that
> characterise it, in such a way that, in short, this word becomes the generator of
> the entire line in which it appears. (M. Grammont, *Traité de phonétique* [Paris:
> Delagrave], 1933)

In all this, the 'labour' of the signifier always appears as a positive
assemblage, concurrent with that of the signified, which sometimes
coincide, and sometimes diverge, to cite Fonagy again, but in any case the
outcome is merely '*a subjacent current of signification*' – no question of
escaping the being of discourse. And it could not be otherwise from a
perspective that conceives the poetic as the autonomisation of one of the
functional categories of the order of discourse.

The other Jakobsonian formula maintains this illusion: the poetic
function projects the principle of equivalence from the axis of selection to
the axis of combination. Equivalence is promoted to the rank of the
constitutive process of the sequence.

> In poetry, one syllable is equalized with any other syllable of the same sequence;
> word stress is assumed to equal word stress, as unstress equals unstress, long is
> matched with long, short is matched with short . . . [Jakobson, 'Linguistics and
> Poetics' in *Language in Literature*, ed. K. Pomorska and
> S. Rudy, Cambridge, Mass: Harvard, 1987, p. 71]

Of course, articulation is no longer that of customary syntax, it is always
rather a question of a *constructive* architecture; that anything other than a
scansion of equivalence could start to play a role in prosody is never
envisaged. Jakobson is content to substitute the *ambiguity* of the signified
for the *ambivalence* of the signifier.

Ambiguity is what characterises the poetic and distinguishes it from the
discursive: 'Ambiguity is an intrinsic, inalienable character of any self-
focussed message briefly, a corollary feature of poetry' (Jakobson,
'Linguistics and Poetics', p. 85). 'The machinations of ambiguity are
among the very roots of poetry' (Empson, *Seven Types of Ambiguity*
[London: Chatto & Windus, 1963]). Jakobson again:

> the poetic function over the referential function does not
> rence but makes it ambiguous. The double-sensed message
> nce in a split addresser, a split addressee, as well as in a split
> ـuistics and Poetics', p. 85]

ıl the categories of discursive communication 'work loose'
ıll, curiously, except the code, of which Jakobson does not
ـఎes the code become? Does it too become ambiguous? But it
wouلⴷ be the end of *langue* and linguistics). Ambiguity is not
dangerous ın itself. It does not change the *principles* of identity and
equivalence in the slightest, nor does it change the principle of meaning as
value; it merely produces floating values, renders identities diffuse, and
makes the rules of the referential game more complex, without abolishing
anything. Thus, for Jakobson, the ambiguous sender and addressee merely
signifies the uncoupling of the I/YOU relation, internal to the message,
from the author/reader relation: the positions of the respective subjects
have not been lost, in some sense they expand indefinitely – subjects
become unsettled *in their subject-positions*. Thus the message becomes
unsettled, ambiguous, in its definition; all categories (sender, addressee,
message, referent) move, work loose in their respective positions, but the
structural grid of discourse remains the same.

'The machinations of ambiguity' do not therefore make a great deal of
difference to the form of discourse. Jakobson has this bold formula:

> Poetry does not consist in adding rhetorical ornament to discourse: it involves a
> total revaluation of discourse and all its components, whatever they may be.

Bold and ambiguous, since the components (sender/addressee, message/
code, etc.) maintain their separate existences, they are simply 'revalued'.
The general economy remains the same – the political economy of
discourse. At no point does this thought advance to the point of the
abolition of separate functions: the abolition of the subject of communication (and therefore the sender/addressee distinction); the abolition of the
message as such (and therefore of all the code's structural autonomy). All
this work, in which the radical character of the poetic act consists, is
swamped by 'ambiguity' and by a certain hesitation as regards linguistic
categories. A 'discourse within a discourse', a 'message centred on itself':
all this merely defines a *rhetoric of ambiguity*. But the ambiguous
discourse, squinting at itself (a strabismus of signs), remains the discourse
of positivity, *the discourse of the sign as value*.

In the poetic, by contrast, language turns back on itself to be abolished.
It is not 'centred' on itself, it *decentres* itself. It undoes the entire process of
the constructive logic of the sign, resolving all the internal specularity that
makes a sign a sign: something full, reflected, centred on itself, and, as
such, effectively ambiguous. The poetic is the loss of the spectacular
closure of the sign and the message.

At bottom, this is the same metaphysics that has governed the theory of
artistic form since romanticism: the bourgeois metaphysics of totality. Art

should properly evoke 'this quality of being a whole and of belonging to larger, all-inclusive, whole which is the universe in which we live' (Jo Dewey, *Art as Experience*, pp. 194–5; quoted in Umberto Eco, *The Ope Work* [tr. Anna Cancogni, London: Hutchinson Radius, 1989], p. 26). Eco appropriates this cosmology for himself, and retranscribes it in linguistic terms. The totalisation of meaning takes place by means of a 'chain reaction' and the infinite subdivision of signifieds:

> All this is attained by means of an identification between signifier and signified . . . the aesthetic sign . . . is not confined to a given denotatum, but rather expands every time the structure within which it is inevitably *embodied*, is duly appreciated – a sign whose signified, resounding relentlessly against its signifier, keeps acquiring new echoes. (ibid., p. 36)

This, then, is a schema of a first (denotative) phase of reference, followed by a second phase of 'harmonic' reference, where a 'theoretically unlimited' chain reaction is operative – hence the evocation of the cosmic.

This theory serves as the basic ideology of everything we have been able to say about the poetic (nor does psychoanalysis escape this) – ambiguity, polysemia, polyvalence, polyphony of meaning: it is always a matter of the *radiation of the signified*, of a simultaneity of significations.

> The linear character of discourse hides an harmonious concert of different messages. (Fonagy, *Diogène*, 51, p. 104)

The semantic density of language, the wealth of information, etc.: the poet 'liberates' all sorts of virtualities (with, as a corollary, a differential hermeneutics of the role played by the reader: every interpretation 'enriches' the text with that reader's personal harmonies). This whole myth plays on a 'savage' pre-conceptual anteriority and a 'virginity' of meaning:

> The poet rejects the usual and appropriate term for the concept, which is a skeletal reduction of all previous experiences, when he finds himself in front of an untamed, virginal, reality . . . The word must be recreated each time from an intense personal experience; the skeleton of the thing in itself must be attired in living flesh so as to give it the concrete reality the thing has for me. (ibid., p. 97)

We are no longer sure whether to undress the concept or dress it up in order to rediscover the virginity of the poetic! In any case, it is a question of uncovering 'the secret correspondences that might exist between things'.

This romantic theory, with its conception of 'genius', paradoxically turns out to be rewritten today in terms of information theory. This polyphonic 'wealth' can be put in terms of 'additional information'. At the level of the signified: Petrarch's poetry constitutes a 'large capital of information' on love (Eco, *The Open Work*, p. 54). At the level of the signifier a certain type of disorder, rupture and negation of the customary and predictable linguistic order increases the rate of information of the message. There would be a 'dialectical tension' between the elements of order and disorder that can serve as a base-rate within the poetic. Whereas the most probable use of the linguistic system would yield nothing, the unexpectedness of the poetic, its relative improbability, determines a minimum rate of information. Here again, the poetic gives you more.

Thus the semiological imaginary easily reconciles romantic polyphony and quantitative description:

> The structure of poetry can most rigorously be described and interpreted in terms of a chain of possibilities. . . . A superior accumulation at mid-range frequencies of a certain class of phonemes, or the contrasting assemblage of two opposed classes in the phonemic texture of a line, a strophe, or a poem, plays the role of a *subjacent current of signification*. (Fonagy, *Diogène*, 51)

'In language, form has a manifestly granular structure, which is open to a quantitative description' (Jakobson). With this we can confront Kristeva:

> Words are not non-decomposable entities held together by their meaning, but assemblages of signifying, phonemic and scriptural atoms leaping from word to word, thus creating unsuspected and unconscious relations between the elements of the discourse: this putting into relation of signifying elements constitutes a *signifying infrastructure of the langue*. (Julia Kristeva, 'Poésie et négativité', in *Séméiotikè* [Paris: Seuil, 1969], p. 185)

All these formulas converge on the idea of a 'Brownian' stage of language, an emulsional stage of the signifier, homologous to the molecular stage of physical matter, that liberates 'harmonies' of meaning just as fission or fusion liberate new molecular affinities. The whole conceived as an 'infrastructure', a 'subjacent current', that is to say, as a logically prior, or structurally more elementary, stage of discourse, just like matter. This is a scientistic, 'materialist' view of discourse, where the atom and the molecule are properly assimilated to the secondary articulation of language, as the molecular stage – an original stage, prior to the differentiating organisation of meaning – is to the poetic, Besides, Kristeva is not afraid of her own metaphor: she says that modern science has broken the body down into simple elements in the same way as (poetic) linguistics has disarticulated signification into signifying atoms.

There, concurrently with the metaphysics of primary articulation (the metaphysics of signifieds, bound to the play of signifying units), what we might call the *metaphysics of secondary articulation* takes shape, in which the effect of infrastructural signification is bound up with the play of distinct units, the minimal entities of discourse, where they are once again taken as positive valencies (just as atoms and molecules have an elementary valency), as phonemic materiality whose assemblage takes place in terms of linkages and probabilities.

But the poetic is no more based on the autonomous articulation of the phonemic levy than on that of words or syntax. *It does not play secondary articulation off against the primary*.[10] It is the abolition of the analytic distinction of the articulations on which language's capacity for discourse and its operational autonomy rests, as the means of expression (and as the object of linguistics). In any case, why should the phonemic level be more 'materialist' than that of the lexical concept or the sentence? As soon as we turn the phonemic into minimal substances, the phoneme, like the atom, becomes an idealist reference. With the physics of the atom, science relentlessly entrenches its positivist rationality. It has not brought the phonemic any closer to another mode, which would presuppose the respective extermination of the object and subject of science. Perhaps today it is reaching its borders, at the same time as materialism is in total theoretical crisis, without meanwhile being able to step beyond its shadow: there is no 'dialectical' transition between science, even at the apogee of its crisis, and something perhaps beyond it and irremediably separated from it, since science is founded on the basis of the denegation (not dialectical negation, but *de*negation) of dialectics. The most rigorous materialism will never lead beyond the principle of the rationality of value.

Tel Quel have taken the deconstruction of the sign furthest, up to the total 'liberation' of the signifier. End of the mortgage of the signified and the message, there is no 'polysemia', it is the signifier that is plural. No more 'ambiguity' of the message, just the intertextuality of the signifier, which is linked with and is produced by its pure 'material' logic. The endless text of the paragram, *significance* is the real level of the productivity of language, a productivity beyond value, opposed to the signification of the sign-product.

Julia Kristeva, in 'Poésie et négativité' (pp.185ff.) comes closest to acknowledging a poetic form, even if the superstition of a 'materialist production' of meaning leads her nevertheless, by returning the poetic to the semiotic order, to censoriously describe it as a radical alternative.

She posits the *ambivalence* of the poetic signified (and not its mere ambiguity): it is concrete and general at the same time, it includes both (logical) affirmation and negation, it announces the simultaneity of the possible and the impossible; far from postulating the 'concrete versus the general', it explodes this conceptual break: bivalent logic (0/1) is abolished by ambivalent logic. Hence the very particular negativity of the poetic. The bivalent logic of discourse rests on the negation internal to the judgement, it founds the concept and its self-equivalence (the signified is what it is). The negativity of the poetic is a radical negativity *bearing on the logic of judgement itself*. Something 'is' and is not what it is: a utopia (in the literal sense) of the signified. The thing's self-equivalence (and, of course, the subject's) is volatilised. Thus the poetic signified is the space where 'Non-Being intertwines with Being in a thoroughly disconcerting manner'. But there is a danger (which can be seen in outline in Kristeva's work) of taking this 'space' as a *topic* again, and taking the 'intertwining' as, once again, the dialectic. There is a danger of *filling* this space up with every figure of substitution: 'Metaphor, metonymy, and all the tropes are inscribed in space surrounded by this double semantic structure.' The danger of the metaphor, of an economy of metaphor that remains positive. In Kristeva's chosen example, Baudelaire's *meubles voluptueux* ('voluptuous furniture'), the poetic effect does not stem from an added erotic value, a play of additional phantasms nor from a metaphorical or metonymic 'value'. It stems from the short-circuit of the two, the furniture being no longer furniture and the voluptuous pleasure no longer being voluptuous pleasure – the furniture *(meubles)* becomes voluptuous, and the voluptuous pleasure becomes mobile – nothing remains of the two separated fields of value. Neither of the two terms is poetic in itself, no more than their synthesis is: they are poetic in that the one is volatilised in the other. There is no relation between (poetic) enjoyment and the voluptuous pleasure as such. In love, there is only voluptuous pleasure – but it becomes enjoyment when it is volatilised into furniture. And the furniture is cancelled by the voluptuous pleasure in the same way: the same reversal sweeps away the proper position of each term. It is in this sense that Rimbaud's formula stands: 'It is true literally, in every sense.'

Metaphor is simply the *transfer of value from one field to the other,* to the point of the 'absorption of a multiplicity of texts (meanings) in the message' (Kristeva, 'Poésie et négativité', p. 194). The poetic implies the *reversibility of one field onto the other,* and thus the annulment of their respective values. Whereas values are combined, implicated and inter-textualised in the metaphor according to a play of 'harmonies' (the 'secret accord of language'), in poetic enjoyment they are annulled: radical ambivalence is non-valence.

Kristeva, then, reduces the radical theory of ambivalence to a theory of intertextuality and the 'plurality of codes'. The poetic can no longer be distinguished from discourse save by 'the infinite nature of its code' ; it is a plural discourse, the other only being the limit case of a monological discourse, a discourse with only one code. There is therefore a place for both types of discourse in a *general semiotics*: 'The semiotic practice of speech [discourse] is only one possible semiotic practice' (ibid., p. 215). Semanalysis has a duty to take them all into account, without exclusion, that is to say, without neglecting the irreducibility of the poetic, but equally without reducing it to the logic of the sign. Semanalysis has a duty to constitute a 'non-reductive typology of the plurality of semiotic practices'. There is an increasing intricacy of the different logics of meaning:

> The functioning of speech [*la parole*] is impregnated with paragrammatism, just as the functioning of poetic language is circumscribed by the laws of speech. (ibid., p. 214)

Once again Starobinski's doubts about Saussure come to the surface: the latter's tolerance of both the poetic and the discursive in the name of universal rules of language (here in the name of a 'genuinely materialist' science called semiotics). In fact, this is a reductive and repressive position. For from the poetic to the discursive there is no difference in their respective articulation of meaning, there is a radical antagonism. Neither of them is an 'infrastructure of signification' (would the logical discourse on it be its 'superstructure'?). Further, discourse, logos, is not a particular case in the infinity of codes: it is *the* code that puts an end to infinity, it is the discourse of closure that puts an end to the poetic, to the para- and the ana-grammatic. Conversely, it is on the basis of its dismantling, its destruction, that language revives the possibility of 'infinity'. In fact, 'infinity of codes' is a bad term, since it permits the amalgam of the one and the 'infinite' in the 'mathematics' of the text, and their distribution along a single chain. It must be said, in terms of radical incompatabilty and antagonism, that it is on the basis of the destruction of the discourse of *value* that language revives the possibility of *ambivalence*: this is the poetic revolution in relation to discourse, where the one can only be the death of the other.

The semiotic project is only a more subtle way of neutralising the radicality of the poetic and saving the hegemony of linguistics (re-baptised 'semiotics'), no longer by pure and simple annexation, but under cover of the ideology of 'plurality' .

The subversion of linguistics by the poetic does not stop here: it leads one to wonder whether the rules of language even hold good for the field of language over which they prevail, that is to say, in the dominant sphere of communication (similarly, the failure of political economy to give an account of anterior societies leads one, as an after-effect, to wonder if these principles have any value for us). Now it is true that the immediate practice of language is somewhat resistant to the rational abstraction of linguistics. O. Mannoni puts this well in 'The ellipsis and the bar':

> Linguistics originates from the bar it has installed between the signifier and the signified, and their reunion spells its death – which brings us back *to conversation in everyday life*. ('L'ellipse et la barre', in *Clefs pour l'imaginaire*, p. 35)

The Saussurian bar has facilitated the renewal of linguistic theory from top to bottom. In the same way, Marxism, by means of the concept of a material infrastructure opposed to the 'superstructure', has established something like an 'objective' and revolutionary analysis of society. Science is based on rupture. In exactly the same way, a 'science', a rationalist practice (organisation), originates from the distinction between theory and practice. Every science and every rationality lasts as long as this rupture lasts. Dialectics makes endless formal adjustments to this rupture, it never resolves it. To dialecticise the infra- and the superstructure, theory and practice, or even signifier and signified, *langue* and *parole*, is merely a vain effort at totalisation. Science lives and dies with the rupture.

This is indeed why current non-scientific practice, both linguistic and social, is revolutionary in some way, *because it does not make these kinds of distinctions*. Just as it has *never made a distinction between mind and body*, whereas every dominant religion and philosophy survives only on the basis of this distinction, so our, everybody's, immediate and 'savage' social practices do not make a distinction between theory and practice, infra- and superstructure: of itself and without debating the issue, it is transversal, beyond rationality, whether bourgeois or Marxist. Theory, 'good' Marxist theory, never analyses *real* social practice, it analyses the object that it produces for itself through separating this practice into an infra- and a superstructure, or, in other words, it analyses the social field that it produces for itself through the dissociation between theory and practice. Theory will never lead back to 'practice' since it only exists through having vivisected it: fortunately this practice is beginning to return to and even overcome it. But this brings with it the end of dialectical and historical materialism.

In the same way, the immediate, everyday linguistic practice of speech and the 'speaking subject' pays no attention to the distinction between the sign and the world (nor that between signifier and signified, the arbitrary character of the sign, etc.). Benveniste says and acknowledges this, but only as regards memory, since this is precisely the stage that science overcomes it and leaves it far behind: it interests only the linguistic subject, the subject of the *langue*, which is at the same time the subject of knowledge: Benveniste himself. Somewhere, however, the other is right, speaking in advance [*en deçà*] of the distinction between sign and world, in total 'superstition' – the other (along with ourselves and even Benveniste) knows more, it is true, about the essentials than Benveniste the linguist. For the methodology of the separation of signifier and signified holds no better than the methodology of the separation of the mind and the body. The same imaginary in both cases. In the one case, psychoanalysis[11] came to say what this was, as, in the other, did poetics. But there has basically never been any need for psychoanalysis nor for poetics: no-one has ever believed in them apart from the scholars and linguists themselves (just as, in the final analysis, no-one has ever believed in economic determinism other than economic scientists and their Marxist critics).

Virtually, and literally, speaking, *there has never been a linguistic subject*; it is not even true of we who speak that we purely and simply reflect the code of linguistics. Likewise, there has never been an *economic subject*, a *homo oeconomicus* – this fiction has never been inscribed anywhere other than in a code – there has never been *a subject of consciousness*, and there has never been *a subject of the unconscious*. In the simplest practice, there is always something that cuts across these simulation models, which are all rational models; there has always been a radicality absent from every code, every 'objective' rationalisation, that has basically only ever given rise to a single great subject: *the subject of knowledge*, whose form is shattered from today, from now, by undivided speech.[12] Basically we have all known this for much longer than Descartes, Saussure, Marx and Freud.

The *Witz*, or The Phantasm of the Economic in Freud

Is there an affinity between the poetic and the psychoanalytic? If it is clear that poetic form (dissemination, reversibility, strict delimitation of the corpus) cannot be reconciled with linguistic form (the signifier–signified equivalence, linearity of the signifier, undefined corpus), it seems, on the contrary, that it intersects with psychoanalytic form (primary processes:

displacement, condensation, etc.). In the dream, the lapsus, the symptom, and the joke, or *mot d'esprit*, everywhere the unconscious works, we can, with Freud, read the distortions of the signifier–signified relation, the linearity of the signifier, the discrete sign. *This distortion of discourse, excess and transgression of language, where the phantasm operates, marks enjoyment.* But what of desire and the unconsious in the poetic, and up to what point does libidinal economy account for it?

The poetic and the psychoanalytic do not mix. *The symbolic mode is not that of the labour of the unconscious.* To question the poetic as Freud does is therefore to question psychoanalysis from the standpoint of the symbolic: the analysis in reverse is always the only one that, by means of this very reversal, allows us to escape theory, which is purely and simply the exercise of power.

Freud's analysis of the joke, the *mot d'esprit*, can serve as our guiding thread, for otherwise there is no *theorised* difference in Freud between the properly symptomatic field and that of the work of art and 'artistic creation' (the concept of 'sublimation', as we know, suffers from a lack of rigour and an hereditary idealism). This is a point of considerable importance: if the poem is neither a *lapsus* nor a *mot d'esprit*, there is nothing to account for it in the theory of the unconscious.

Contrary to Saussure, who is not concerned with poetic pleasure nor even with any cause or finality whatever of what he describes, Freud's analysis is *functional*, it is a theory of enjoyment [*jouissance*] in which work on the signifier is always related to the fulfilment of a desire. Moreover, this is an *economic* theory of enjoyment. The *Witz*, the *mot d'esprit* or joke moves more rapidly, by way of short-cuts and short-circuits, towards what it means to say, and it says things, it 'liberates' significations that would never have existed without it, other than at the cost of considerable conscious intellectual effort. It is this ellipsis of psychical distance that is the source of enjoyment. In other words, the joke lifts the censorship, and the subversion this bring about 'liberates' the energies bound to the super ego and the process of repression. The 'liberation' of affects: the disinvestment of unconscious or preconscious representations; the disinvestment of the repressing psychical agency. In any case, enjoyment emerges from a residue, an excess or a differential quantum of energy made available by the operation of the *Witz*.

In this sense, concision, or the multiple use of the same material in different modalities, is a fundamental characteristic of the *mot d'esprit*. Always economising on effort: a single signifier may signify at multiple levels; we draw a maximum of (sometimes contradictory) significations from a minimum of signifiers. It is futile to insist on analogies with the poetic mode: the multiple use of the same material evokes Saussure's anagram, coupling the necessary delimitation of the corpus and the 'maximal energy in signs' of which Nietzsche speaks. Freud too says of the poet that 'polyphonic orchestration allows him to emit messages on the threefold levels of clear consciousness, the subconscious and the unconscious' . In every instance so much energy is 'economised' in relation to the ordinary system of distributing investments. In the polygon of forces that is the psychical apparatus, enjoyment is like the result of a sort of short-cut, or rather of the transversality of the *Witz*, which, cutting a diagonal across the diverse layers of the psychical apparatus catches up with its objective with less expenditure, even effortlessly attaining unforeseen objectives, yielding a kind of energetic surplus value, the enjoyment 'premium', the 'yield of pleasure'.

This energetic calculus has something of the whiff of capital about it, the capital of a saving of energy (Freud continually employs this term) where enjoyment never comes about save by the subtraction, by default, of a residue or a *surplus* from an investment (but never an excess) – or even from nothing at all: from an inverse process of expenditure, the abolition of energies and finalities. We are not speaking primarily about 'labour', or even the 'signifier', because this level is never primary for Freud. His libidinal economy is based on the existence of unconscious *contents* (affects and representations), of a repression and a pro-duction of the repressed, a calculated investment that steers this production towards an equilibrium (the resolution of tension) of bound and unbound energies. Freudian enjoyment takes place and is spoken of in terms of forces and quanta of energy. In the *Witz* or the dream, the play of signifiers is never in itself the articulation of enjoyment: it only opens roads to phantasmatic or repressed contents. The unconscious is a 'medium' which is never a 'message' in itself, since something like desire – strictly understood in terms of the topological or the economic theory – is necessary in order that it, the 'Id' that speaks, speaks in its own voice. The play of the signifier is only ever the tracery of desire. Here, around the unconscious 'mode of production' (and its mode of representation), is where the entire problem of libidinal economy and the critique of libidinal economy is posed, in the perspective of an *enjoyment that never had anything to do with the economic*.

In *The Psychopathology of Everyday Life*, Freud says of the slip of the tongue, the *lapsus*:

> The reader's preparedness alters the text and reads into it something which he is expecting or with which he is occupied. The only contribution towards a misreading which the text itself need make is that of affording some resemblance in the verbal image, which the reader can alter in the sense he requires. (*Standard Edition*, Vol. 6, 1960, pp. 112–13)

It is of course a matter of a latent, repressed content, waiting to leap up and 'profit' from the fantasies, the interstices and the weak points of logical discourse in order to cause an explosion. This, at the level of discourse, is what happens to the body in the concept of anaclisis: desire 'profits' from the satisfaction of a physiological need in order to invest libidinally in a particular zone of the body, diverting the pure and simple function (organic logic) towards the fulfilment of desire. While this is true, it is not entirely true, since the articulation of the need and the desire has never been clarified. Between the two terms, so thoughtlessly formulated, on the one hand as the determinate completion of a function, and on the other as the indeterminate fulfilment of a desire, the concept of anaclisis is only a bridging concept that articulates nothing at all. Here libidinal economy suffers from the same 'layering' of the concept of need as does the economy in general: between the subject and the object, there is 'need'; between the need and the desire, there is 'anaclisis' (the same as in linguistic economy: between the signifier and the signified, or between the sign and the world, there is, or is not, a 'motivation'). All these layerings have the discrete charm of an insoluble science: if the articulation is impossible, it is because the terms have been badly formulated, because their very position is untenable. Somewhere, doubtless, the autonomisation of desire in the face of need, of the signifier in the face of the signified, and of the subject in the face of the object, is only an effect of science. But the economies that follow from all this have a hard time, since they do not want to renounce the regular oppositions by which they live: desire–need, unconscious–conscious, primary–secondary process, and so on. Is the pleasure principle itself anything other than the psychoanalytic reality principle?

It is certain, however, that psychoanalysis has given the signifier–signified relation an almost poetic slant. The signifier, instead of manifesting the signified in its presence, is in an inverse relation with it: it signifies the signified in its absence and its repression, in accordance with a negativity that never used to appear in linguistic economy. The signifier is in a necessary (not an arbitrary) relation with the signified, but only as the presence of something is with its absence. It signifies the lost object and takes the place of this loss.

> The concept of representation could hardly, in psychoanalysis, be situated between an objective reality on the one hand and its signifying figuration on the other, but rather between an hallucinated reality, a mnemic image of a lost object of satisfaction, on the one hand, and a substitute-object on the other, whether it is a formula-object like that constituted by the phantasm, or an instrumental contraption such as the fetish may be. (S. Leclaire, *Psychanalyser* [Paris: Seuil, 1968], p. 65)

Linguistic equivalence is lost, since the signifier is instead of and in the place of something else which no longer is, nor has it ever been. It is always therefore what it no longer is. The fetish-object, in its vacillating identity, is the endless metaphoric series of what is permanently denied: the absence of the phallus in the mother, sexual difference.

The removal of identifying marks from psychoanalytic signification in relation to linguistics is well formulated by Mannoni:

> By introducing the signifier, we make meaning lose its balance. This is not because the signifier brings with it a collection of signifieds of the sort that a semantics of the traditional type might locate them, but because we interpret Saussure's ellipsis *as if it kept the place of the signified empty*, a place which can only become full again in the different discourses in which a single signifier is then the common element . . . If we also uncouple the signifier from the weight

of the signified, it is not in order to give it over to the laws which linguistics discovers in every manifest discourse, but in order that it may be said to obey the law of the *primary process*, by means of which it escapes, if only for a hesitant moment, the apparent constraints of a discourse that always tends towards the univocal, even though it exploits the equivocal. ('L'ellipse et la barre', p. 46)

A remarkable passage. But what is this 'blank' signified that successive discourses will fill? What is a signifier 'liberated' so as to be given over to another order? Can we take this 'play' from the linguistic categories of the signifier and the signified without shattering the bar which separates them?

The bar is the strategic element which establishes both the principle of non-contradiction in the sign, and its components, as values. This is a coherent structure, so we cannot inject just anything into it (such as ambivalence, contradiction, or the primary process). Benveniste puts things clearly into focus in his critique of Freud's *Gegensinn der Urworte* ('On the antithetical meaning of primal words', 1910, *Standard Edition*, Vol. 11, 1957, pp. 155ff.):

> It is thus improbable a priori that . . . languages, however archaic they are assumed to be, escape the 'principle of contradiction'. Let us suppose that a language exists in which 'large' and 'small' are expressed identically, then the distinction between 'large' and 'small' literally has no meaning. For it is indeed contradictoriness to impute to a language both a knowledge of two notions as opposite while, at the same time, the expression of these notions as identical. (E. Benveniste, *Problems in General Linguistics* [tr. Mary Elizabeth Meek, Miami: University of Miami Press, 1971], p. 71)

And this is correct: ambivalence is never part of linguistic signification. 'It being proper to language to express only what it is possible to express', it is as absurd to imagine a meaning that would not be conveyed by some distinction, as it is on the other hand, to imagine a signifier that would mean everything:

> To imagine a state of language . . . in which a certain object would be *denominated* as being itself and, at the same time, something else, and in which the relation *expressed* would be a relation of permanent contradiction, in which everything would be itself and something else, and hence neither self nor the other, is to imagine a pure chimera. (ibid., pp. 71–2)

Benveniste knows what he is talking about, since all linguistic rationalisation is there in order to prevent precisely this. There is no risk of the ambivalence of the repressed rising to the surface of linguistic science, since the latter is in its entirety a part of the repressing agency. But within its own order, linguistic science is right: nothing will ever participate in language that does not obey the principles of non-contradiction, identity and equivalence.

It is not a matter of saving linguistics, it is a matter of seeing that Benveniste is clear-sighted concerning the choice to be made here (moreover, he is only clear-sighted here because it is a matter of protecting his field from incursions from other fields – he tolerates the existence of a 'symbolic area' somewhere else, but this area 'is discourse, not language' –

stay at home and language will be well protected!): *we cannot be content to 'interpret' the Saussurian ellipsis and bar in order to return the sign to the primary process*, to bring it under analysis. The entire architecture of the sign must be demolished, even its equation must be broken, and it is not enough merely to multiply the unknown factors. Alternatively, then, we must assume that psychoanalysis still makes room somewhere for a certain mode of signification and representation, a certain mode of value and expression: this is in fact precisely what Mannoni's 'empty' signified stands for – the place of the signified remains marked as that of the mobile contents of the unconscious.

If therefore we are, with the psychoanalytic signifier, beyond all logical equivalence, we are not, for all that, outside nor beyond value. For in its 'hesitation' [*trébuchement*], it always designates what it represents as *value* in absentia, under the sign of repression. Value is no longer logically conveyed by the signifier, it haunts it phantasmatically. The bar separating them has changed its meaning, but it remains nevertheless: there indeed remains a potential signified (a repressed signifier with an unresolved value content) on the one hand, and a signifier, itself an instance established as such by repression, on the other.

In fact, there is no longer any equivalence, but equally, there is no more ambivalence, that is, dissolution of value. Here lies the difference with the poetic, where the loss of value is radical. There is no more value in the poetic, not even absent or repressed, to nourish a residual signifier in the form of a symptom, a phantasm, or a fetish. The fetish-object *is not poetic*, precisely because it is opaque, more saturated with value than any other, because the signifier is not disintegrated in it but, on the contrary, is fixed, crystallised by a value that is for ever buried and for ever hallucinated as a lost reality. There is no longer a means of unblocking the system, forever *caught fast in the obsession with meaning*, in the fulfilment of a perverse desire that comes to fill the empty form of the object with meaning. In the poetic (the symbolic) the signifier *disintegrates* absolutely, whereas in psychoanalysis it endlessly *shifts* under the effect of the primary processes and is distorted following the folds of repressed values. Whether distorted, transversal or in '*points de capiton*' (as Lacan says), the psychoanalytic signifier remains a surface indexed on the turbulent reality of the unconscious, whereas in the poetic it diffracts and radiates in the anagram-matic process; it no longer falls under the blows of the law that erects it, nor under the blows of the repressed which binds it, it no longer has anything to designate, not even the ambivalence of a repressed signified. It is nothing more than the dissemination and the absolution of value, experienced, however, without the shadow of anxiety, in total enjoyment. The illumination of the work of art or the symbolic act comes from the point of the non-repressed, the point of no return, where the repression and the incessant repetition of meaning in the phantasm or the fetish, the incessant repetition of the prohibition and value, are lifted, where death and the dissolution of meaning play without hindrance.

'Grasp in what has been written a symptom of what has been silenced' (Nietzsche, *Beyond Good and Evil* [tr. R.J. Hollingdale, Harmondsworth: Penguin, 1990]). A psychoanalytic proposition *par excellence:* everything that 'means' something (particularly scientific discourse in its 'transparency') has the function of *silencing*. And what it silences comes back to haunt it in an easy-going but irreversible subversion of its discourse. This is the place of the psychoanalytic, in the non-place relative to every logical discourse.

The poetic, however, silences nothing, and does not come back to haunt it. For it is always death that is repressed and silenced. It is actualised here in the sacrifice of meaning. The nothing, death, absence, is overtly stated and resolved: death is manifest at last, and is at last *symbolised*, whereas it is only *symptomatic* in all other formations of discourse. This, of course, signals the decline of all linguistics, which thrives on the bar of equivalence between what is said and what is meant, but it is also the end of psychoanalysis which, for its part, lives off the bar of repression between what is said and what is silenced, repressed, denied, phantasmatic and infinitely repeated in the mode of denial or de-negation: death. When, in a social formation or a formation of discourse, death speaks, is spoken and exchanged in a symbolic apparatus, psychonalysis no longer has anything more to say. When Rimbaud says, of his *Saison en enfer*, 'it is true literally, and in every sense', this also means that there is no *hidden*, latent, meaning, that nothing is repressed, that there is nothing behind it, that there is nothing for psychoanalysis. It is at this price that every meaning is possible.

> Linguistics originates from the bar it has installed between the signifier and the signified, and their reunion spells its death. (Mannoni, 'L'ellipse et la barre', p. 35)

Psychoanalysis too, originates from the bar it has installed, under the law of castration and repression, between what is said and what is silenced (or 'between an hallucinated reality . . . and a substitute-object' – Leclaire, *Psychanalyser*, p. 65), and for it, too, their reunion spells death.

That there is no residue signifies that there is no longer a signifier and a signified, no signified *behind* the signifier, no structural bar distributing them on either side; it also signifies that there is no longer a repressed agency *beneath* a repressing agency (as there is in psychoanalysis), no longer a latent beneath a manifest, nor the primary processes playing hide-and-seek with the secondary processes. There is no signified, of whatever sort, produced by the poem, no more there is a 'dream thought' behind the poetic text, nor a signifying formula (Leclaire), nor any kind of libido or potential energy which somehow threads its way through the primary processes and would still testify to a *productive* economy of the unconscious. *There is no more a libidinal than there is a political economy*, nor of course than there is a linguistic economy, that is to say, a political economy of language. Because the economic, wherever it is, *is based on the remainder* (only the remainder permits production and reproduction),[13] whether this remainder is that which is symbolically non-distributed and which re-enters commercial exchange and the circuit of commodity equivalence; whether this remainder is what is not exhausted in the anagrammatic circulation of the poem and enters the circuit of significa-tion; or whether this remainder is quite simply the phantasm, that is to say, that which could not be resolved in the ambivalent exchange and death, and which, for this reason, is resolved as the precipitate of unconscious individual *value*, the repressed stock of scenes or representations which is produced and reproduced in accordance with the incessant compulsion to repeat.

Market value, signified value and unconscious/repressed value are all produced from what remains, from the residual precipitate of the symbolic operation. It is always this remainder that is accumulated and that fuels the diverse economies that govern our lives. To pass beyond economics (and if 'to change life' has any meaning, it can only be this) is to exterminate this remainder in all domains. The poetic is the model of this, since it operates without equivalence, accumulation, or residue.

To come back to the *Witz*: can we not assume that enjoyment is the effect of 'economising', of gaining potential due to the 'ellipsis of psychical distance', or the irruption of the primary process into the order of discourse, the irruption of a meaning *beneath a meaning*, or the deeper reality imposed by the presumed duality of the psychical agencies? Can we not assume that the finality of the 'other scene' to come is produced by twisting this latter around, the finality of the return of the repressed as the psychical value of the very separation of the agencies (topographical hypothesis), and the corollary of a binding and an unbinding of energies from which, at a given moment, there would result the libidinal surplus value called enjoyment (economic hypothesis)?

Can we not assume that enjoyment happens on the contrary at the end of the separation of the separate fields, that it arises out of the very discrimination of the agencies, and therefore from the differential play of investments, and therefore from within the logical order of psychoanalysis?

Is this the effect of the conflagration, the short-circuit (*Kurzschluss*) telescoping between separate fields (phonemes, words, roles, institutions) that until then had meaning *only due to their separation*, and that *lose* their meaning in this brutal reconciliation that causes them to be exchanged? Is this not the *Witz*, the effect of enjoyment where the separated subject is also lost, not only in the reflexive distance of consciousness, but also as regards the agency of the unconscious? The abolition of the super-ego at this moment, of the effort to maintain the discipline of the reality principle and the rationality of meaning, does not merely signify the effacement of the repressing agency to the advantage of the repressed agency, it signifies the simultaneous effacement of both. This is where we find something of the poetic in the *Witz* and the comical, something beyond the compulsive resurrection of the phantasm and the fulfilment of desire.

Freud cites Kant saying 'Das Komische ist eine in nichts zergangene

Erwartung' ('[The comic is] a tense expectation that suddenly vanished, [transformed] into nothing').[14] In other words: *where there used to be something, now there is nothing* – not even the unconscious. Where there used to be some kind of finality (albeit unconscious), or even a value (albeit repressed), now there is nothing. *Enjoyment is the haemorrhage of value*, the disintegration of the code, the repressive *logos*. In the comic, the moral imperative of institutional codes (situations, roles, social characters) is lifted; in the *Witz*, the moral imperative of the identity principle of words themselves, and even the subject, is eliminated – for nothing, and certainly not in order to 'express' the 'unconscious'. Lichtenberg's definition of the knife (or the non-knife: an inspired and radically poetic witticism) retraces this explosion of meaning with no ulterior motive. A knife exists insofar as a blade and a handle exist and can be named separately. If the separation between the two is removed (and the blade and handle can only be reunited in their disappearance, as in Lichtenberg's joke), then, strictly speaking, there is no longer anything but enjoyment. The 'expectation' of the knife, Kant said, the practical expectation, as well as the phantasmatic expectation (we know what the knife can 'mean-to-say' [*vouloir-dire*]) is resolved into nothing. And this is not a primary process (displacement, condensation); there is no irruption of something from behind the blade and the handle, there is nothing behind this nothing. End of separation, end of the unconscious. Total resolution, total enjoyment.

The example of Lichtenberg is not an exceptional case. If we take a good look at them, all the examples of absurd logic (which is the limit of the *Witz*, and the point at which enjoyment is at its most acute) chosen by Freud – the cauldron, the cake, the salmon mayonnaise, cats that have two holes cut in their skin precisely at the place where their eyes are, the child that, as soon as it comes into the world, is fortunate to find a mother to take care of it – all these examples can be analysed in the same way, as the reduplication of an identity or a rationality that turns back on itself in order to disintegrate and be eliminated, as the reabsorption of a signifier into itself without a trace of meaning.

'Eifersucht ist eine Leidenschaft, die mit Eifer sucht, was Leiden schafft' (an untranslatable *Witz*: 'jealousy is a passion that with eagerness seeks what causes pain'). Multiple use of the same material, thus pleasure from the deduction of energy? But Freud himself admits that the multiple use of the same material is also the most difficult to accomplish – the simplest still being saying two different things with the aid of different signifiers. What changes is that the two things are said *simultaneously*. But the essential thing then is the abolition of the time the signifier takes to unfold, its successivity: pleasure derives not from the addition of signifieds under the same signifier (economistic interpretation), but from the elimination of the logical time of enunciation, which amounts to the cancellation of the signifier itself (anti-economistic interpretation). Moreover, the 'Eifersucht' *Witz* constitutes a proper Saussurian coupling: it realises, at the level of a phrase and its 'anti-phrase', what Saussure said of every vowel and its counter-vowel in a line. Here the rule operates at the level of an entire syntagma, whereas in Saussure it operates only on non-signifying elements (phonemes or diphones), but the spark of pleasure, the *Witz* or the poem, always derives from the same rule of the signifier's revolution around itself. Meaning, the 'wealth' of meaning or of multiple meanings does not matter. Quite the opposite: the signified often makes the pleasure of the *Witz* relatively slight, and signifieds come to end the game to safeguard meaning. Whereas, in the infinitesimal lapse of time as the signifier turns back on itself, in the time of this cancellation, there is an infinity of meaning, a virtuality of infinite substitution, a crazy and ultra-fast expenditure, an instantaneous short-circuit of all messages, but always non-signified. Meaning has not 'taken': it remains in a state of centrifugal circulation, 'revolution'; incessantly given and returned like goods in symbolic exchange, they never fall under the authority of value.

Freud often speaks of 'joke-technique', which he distinguishes from the basic process in this way:

> [The joke-technique consists in] the use of the same name twice, once as a whole and again divided up into separate syllables . . . in the manner of a riddle. (*Standard Edition*, Vol. 8, 1960, p. 31)

But this is nothing but 'technique'. The same goes for the multiple use of the same material: all these techniques can be summarised under a single category, that is, condensation:

> The multiple use of the same material is . . . a special case of condensation; play upon words is nothing other than a condensation *without* substitute-formation; condensation remains the wider category. All these techniques are dominated by a tendency to compression, or rather to saving. It all seems to be a question of economy. In Hamlet's words: 'Thrift, thrift, Horatio!' (ibid., p. 42)

What Freud neglects here is that the 'techniques' of the *Witz* are *by themselves* sources of pleasure. He affirms this, but only, however, in order to add, as quickly as possible:

> We now see that what we have described as the techniques of jokes . . . are rather the sources from which jokes provide pleasure . . . The technique which is characteristic of jokes and peculiar to them, however, consists in their procedure for safeguarding the use of these methods for providing pleasure against the objections raised by criticism, which would put an end to the pleasure . . . Their function consists from the first in lifting internal inhibitions and in making sources of pleasure fertile which have been rendered inaccessible by those inhibitions. (ibid., p. 130)

Thus everything that might have arisen from the procedure of the *Witz* itself is referred back to an original 'source' for which the *Witz* is no longer anything other than a technical medium.

The same schema applies to the pleasure of recognising and remembering:

> This rediscovery of what is familiar is pleasurable, and once more it is not difficult for us to recognise this pleasure as a pleasure in economy and to relate it to economy in psychical expenditure . . . recognition is pleasurable in itself –

i.e., through relieving psychical expenditure . . . Rhymes, alliterations, refrains, and other forms of repeating similar verbal sounds which occur in verse, make use of the same source of pleasure – the rediscovery of something familiar. (ibid., pp. 121–2)

Again, these techniques, 'which show so much similarity to that of "multiple use" in the case of jokes' (ibid., p. 122), have no meaning in themselves: they are subordinated to the resurgence of a mnemic content (conscious or unconscious: amongst other things, it may be an originary or childhood phantasm), of which these techniques are only the means of expression.[15]

Like the poetic, every interpretation of the *Witz* in terms of the 'liberation' of phantasms or psychical energy is false. When the signified begins to erupt and circulate in every sense (the simultaneity of signifieds from different levels of the psychical apparatus, the transversality of the signifier under the pressure of the primary processes), we do not laugh and we do not enjoy: there is only anguish, hallucination and madness. Ambiguity and polysemia produce anguish, because the obsession with meaning (the moral law of signification) remains in its entirety, whereas a single, clear meaning no longer responds. Enjoyment, on the contrary, comes from what every imperative, every reference to meaning (manifest or latent) has swept aside, and this is only possible in an exact reversibility of all meaning – not in the proliferation, but in the meticulous reversal of all meaning. The same goes for energy: neither its 'explosive' liberation, its unbinding, its solitary drift, nor its intensity is enjoyment. Reversibility is the only source of enjoyment.[16]

When we laugh or enjoy, it is because, in one way or another, a twisting or distortion of the signifier or energy has managed to create a void. Thus the story of someone who loses his key in a dark alley and is looking for it under the street light, because this is the only chance he has of finding it. The lost key can be given every hidden meaning (mother, death, phallus castration, etc.), all undecidable for that matter, but this is unimportant: the void of logical reason is reduplicated exactly in order to be destroyed, and it is in the void thus created that the laugh and enjoyment burst out (not, however, in order that this void 'emerges from its subsoil and establishes itself' – Lyotard). Freud puts this extremely well: *Entfesselung des Unsinns* – the unleashing of nonsense. But nonsense is not the hidden hell of meaning [*sens*], nor the emulsion of all the repressed and contradictory meanings. It is the meticulous reversibility of every term – *subversion* through *reversal*.

It is by means of the internal logic of the *Witz* that one of its 'external' characteristics must be interpreted: it shares itself out, it does not consume itself alone, it is meaningful only in exchange. The flash of wit or the funny story are like symbolic goods, like champagne, presents, rare goods, or women in primitive societies. The *Witz* provokes laughter, or the reciprocity of another funny story, or even a veritable potlach of stories in succession. We know the symbolic network of complicity that bind certain stories or jokes, that go from one to the other as poetry used to. Here, everything answers to the symbolic *obligation*. To keep a funny story to oneself is absurd, not to laugh is offensive, but to laugh first at one's own story also shatters the subtle laws of exchange in its own way.[17]

The *Witz* is necessarily inscribed in a symbolic exchange because it is bound to a symbolic (rather than an economic) mode of enjoyment. If this was a matter of 'psychical saving', we fail to see why everyone does not laugh alone, or is not the first to laugh with all this 'liberated' psychical energy. There must, therefore, have been something other than unconscious economic mechanisms to compel reciprocity. This something else is precisely the symbolic cancellation of value. It is because terms are symbolically exchanged, that is to say become reversible and are cancelled in their own operations, that the poetic and the *Witz* institute a social relation of the same type. Only subjects dispossessed of their identity, like words, are devoted to social reciprocity in laughter and enjoyment.

An Anti-Materialist Theory of Language

We see the outline, in the psychoanalytic interpretation of the dream, of the *Witz*, of neuroses and, by extension, of poetry, of a 'materialist' theory of language. The work of the primary process is possible because the unconscious treats *words as things*. The signifier, escaping the horizon and the finality of the signified, becomes pure material once more, available for another labour, an 'elementary' material available for the foldings, transports and telescopings of the primary process. The phonemic substance of language takes on the immanence of the material thing, lapsing back into (if these formulae have any meaning at all) primary articulation (signifying units), perhaps even into secondary articulation (distinct units). Sounds (or even letters) are then conceived as the atoms of a substance no different from that of the body.

It may seem that there was an unsurpassable radicality of language here. To treat words 'as things' would be in principle the fundamental operation of language, since it seems that we have the last word when we finally draw out a 'materialist' base. But the same goes for materialism as it does for everything else. The philosophical destiny of this theory is to operate a simple overturning of idealism, without surpassing endless speculation, by simply alternating between the two. Hence the concepts of 'thing' and of 'matter', negatively forged by idealism as its own hell, its negative phantasm, have passed silently into a positively real phase, indeed into a revolutionary explanatory principle, while losing none of the abstraction that they inherit from their origins. Idealism has created, in *repression*, the phantasm of a certain 'matter' which, laden with all the stigmata of idealist repression, re-emerges as materialism. Let's undertake a thorough examination of the concept of the 'thing' by means of which we would like to delimit a beyond of representation. Having evacuated all transcendence, there remains a crude, opaque and 'objective' matter, a substantial entity, a molar or molecular base of rocks or of language. But do we not see that idealism's last and most subtle resort is to have locked what it denied into this irreducible substantiality, to legitimate it as an adverse referent, as an alibi, and thus to disarm it as an 'effect' of reality which becomes the best support for idealist thought. The 'thing', 'substance', 'infrastructure' and 'matter' have never had any other meaning. Even the 'materialist' theory of language falls into the same trap of idealist interdependence. It is not true that words, when they cease to be representations and lose the sign's rationale, become 'things', thus incarnating a more fundamental status of objectivity, a surplus reality, a rediscovered stage of final appeal. There is no worse miscomprehension.

To treat words 'as things' . . . in order to express THE thing – the Unconscious – in order to materialise a latent energy. Expression always falls into the trap, unless it is the repressed, the unsaid (perhaps the unsayable that here becomes a positive reference), of assuming the force of an authority, an agency, rather than a substance. Western thought cannot bear, and has at bottom never been able to bear, a void of signification, a *non-place* and a non-value. *It requires a topography and an economics.* The radical reabsorption of the sign inaugurated in the poetic (and doubtless in the *Witz* as well) has to become the decipherable sign of an unsaid, of something that perhaps will never give up its code, but that thereby merely augments its value. Of course, I understand that psychoanalysis is not a 'vulgar' hermeneutics: it is a more subtle hermeneutics in that something else – another world, another scene – is always going on behind the operation of the material signifier, whose twists and turns can always be captured by a specialist discourse. Enjoyment is never purely and simply consumption or consummation. The libido always becomes metabolic in this operation, it always speaks from the depths of phantasm it always releases affects. In short, linguistic material is already finalised by a positive transformation (here a transcription), it always warrants an interpretation, which envelops it as its analytic reason.[18] The 'Thing' hides itself and hides something else. To look for the force is to look for the signifier.

A profound motivation of the sign-symptom, a consubstantiality of word and thing, of the fate of language and the fate of the pulsion, the figure and the force. A libidinal economy whose principle is always to metaphorise (or metonymise) the unconscious, the body, the libido and the phantasm in a linguistic *disorder*. In linguistic motivation, it is always the arbitrary character of the sign that yields to the *positive* analogy of the signifier and the thing signified. In psychoanalytic motivation, it is a *reverse* necessity that binds the deconstructed signifier to a primary energetic potential. Here motivation appears as the *transgression* of a form by an insurrectional content. The blind surreality of the libido punctures language's reality principle and its transparency. This is how, in the best cases, the poetic is interpreted: Luciano Berio's organic sound, Artaud's theatre of cruelty, groans, screams and gasps, the incantation and irruption of the body into the repressive interiorised space of language. The irruption of the partial pulsions constitutes a partial surface *under the seal of repression*, simultaneously transgressive and regressive, for this is precisely only the revolution of a repressed content, marked as such by the hegemony of form.

This is better than Swinburne's breeze, but it still has to do with motivation and metaphor: a vitalist, energetic, corporealist metaphor of the theatre of cruelty. Therefore, in the final analysis, it is a finalist metaphor, even if it is a matter of a savage finality. The magic of a 'liberation' of an original force (we know Artaud's often shocking affinity with magic and exorcism, and even, in *Héliogabale*, with orgiastic mysticism). Metaphysics is always at the crossroads, as it is at the crossroads of the economic-energetic view of the unconscious processes (put simply, that is, the concept of the unconscious): the metaphysical temptation to make the unconscious as substantial as a *body*, and thus the finality of its liberation. The contemporary illusion of the repression that forms the unconscious as a content, as a force. Form triumphs by circumscribing what it denies as content, and delimiting it within a finality of the expression of content or the resurrection of forces.

On this point, there is not so much difference between linguistics and psychoanalysis, since in both there is always the same attempt to base the poetic in the connaturality of the discourse and its object:

> The distance from words to things is altered by the use made of the 'thing' in the word, by the mediation of its flesh and the echoes its flesh might make, in the caverns of sensibility, of the rumbling created by the thing. (J.-F. Lyotard, *Discours, figure* [Paris: Klincksieck, 1971], p. 77)

Thus the linguists try – at best – to preserve the 'symbolic' value of sound against the thesis of the arbitrary. Further on, Lyotard writes:

> The thing is not 'introduced into' language, but its linguisic arrangement spreads it out over words, and between them, the rhythms consonant with those that the thing discussed in the discourse sets up in our body. (ibid., pp. 77–8)

What miracle makes the 'thing' consonant with the word through the medium of the body? Not rhythm, but metaphor. In effect, this is a matter of a *positive economy of the metaphor*: the idea of a reconciliation between the 'thing' and the word given back its materiality. But this is false. If it is true that logical discourse denies the materiality of the word (the *Wortkörper*), the poetic is not, by means of a simple inversion, the resurrection of the word as thing. Far from making the thing appear, it aims to destroy language itself as a thing. The poetic is precisely the *mutual* volatilisation of the status of thing and discourse. That is to say that it aims at the extermination of language as discourse, but also as materiality; not by repressing it as discourse does, but by taking it to task to the point of annihilating it.

This is how even Kristeva, following Heraclitus and Lucretius, states a materialist theory of the signifier: words do not *express* the (movement of the) real, they *are* it. Not by means of the mediation of ideas, but through the consubstantiality (which is more than a 'correspondence') between the material thing and the phonemic substance of language. Homologous to psychoanalysis: if language makes the unconscious visible, it is not because it expresses it, but because it is of the same structure, and because it is articulated and speaks in the same way. The same cut, the same scene, the same 'way', and the same work. Where the Ancients used to say 'fire', we say 'language, the unconscious, the body'.

But to say that language makes fire, air, water and earth (or the work of the unconscious) visible because it is itself an element, an elementary substance in direct affinity with all the others, is at once more radical than all the psycho-naturalists' 'motivation', and also very far from the truth. The whole thing needs to be reversed: it is on condition that we see that fire, water, earth and air are neither values nor *positive* elements, that they are metaphors of the continual dissolution of value, of the symbolic exchange of the world – on condition that we see that they are not substances but *anti-substances*, anti-matter – this is the sense in which language may be said to reunite them, as soon as it has been torn from the logic of the sign and value. This is what the ancient myths (and the Heraclitean and Nietzschean myth of becoming) used to say about the elements, and it is in this sense that they are poetic, and even superior to every analytic interpretation that transposes this dissolution into the hidden instance of the unsaid, 'transpearing' in a no-saying or a saying-other.

There is no materialist reference in the symbolic operation, not even an 'unconscious' one; rather there is the operation of an 'anti-matter'. We are wary of science-fiction, but it is true that there is some analogy between a particle and an anti-particle, whose encounter would result in their mutual annihilation (along with, moreover, a fabulous energy), and the principle of the vowel and its counter-vowel in Saussure, or, in more general terms, between any given signifier and the anagrammatic double that eliminates it: here again, nothing remains but a fabulous enjoyment. Kristeva writes:

> In this *other* space, where logical laws of speech have been weakened, the subject dissolves and, in place of the sign, the clash of signifiers eliminating each other is instituted. An operation of generalised negativity, which has nothing to do with the constitutive negativity of the judgement (*Aufhebung*), nor with the negativity internal to the judgement (binary logic: 0–1), an annihilating negativity (Sunyavada Buddhism). A zerological subject, a non-subject who comes to assume the thought that cancels itself. ('Poésie et négativité', p. 212)

Beyond the Unconscious

The question is this: is there room to offer an hypothesis of the unconscious – this energy and affective potential which, in its repression and in its labour, lies at the basis of the 'expressive' disturbance and dislocation of the order of discourse, and opposes its primary to its secondary processes – an hypothesis in terms of the poetic process? Evidently everything hangs together: if the unconscious is this irreversible agency, then the duality of the primary and the secondary processes is also irreducible, and the work of meaning can only consist in the return of the repressed, in its transpearance in the repressing agency of discourse. In this regard, there is no difference between the poetic and the neurotic, between the poem and the *lapsus*. We take note of psychoanalysis's radicalism: if the primary processes 'exist', they are at work everywhere, and are determinant everywhere. Conversely, however, the mere hypothesis of a different order, a symbolic order that provided the economy of the unconscious, prohibition and repression and which basically resolved the distinction between the primary and the secondary processes, is enough to relativise the whole psychoanalytic perspective, and not only on those marginal territories over which it imperialistically encroaches (anthropology, poetics, politics, etc.), but on its own terrain, in the analysis of the psyche, neurosis and the cure. To turn to Mannoni again, it cannot be ruled out that psychoanalysis, which originates from the distinction between the primary and the secondary processes, will one day die when this distinction is abolished. The symbolic is already *beyond the psychoanalytic unconscious*, beyond libidinal economy, just as it is beyond value and political economy.

We must see that the symbolic processes (reversibility, anagrammatic dispersal, reabsorption without residue) are not at all mixed up with the primary processes (displacement, condensation, repression). They are mutually opposed, even if together they are opposed to the logical discourse of meaning. This singular difference (also as regards enjoyment) means that a dream, a *lapsus*, or a joke is not a work of art or a poem. The difference between the symbolic and the libidinal unconscious, today largely effaced by the privilege of psychoanalysis, must be re-established to prohibit psychoanalysis from encroaching where it has nothing to say. Concerning the poetic (the work of art), the symbolic and (primitive) anthropology neither Marx nor Freud has been able to say anything unless either has reduced it to the mode of production on the one hand, and to repression and castration on the other. Where psychoanalysis and Marxism come to grief, we must not want to have them fall like angels (or like beasts), they must be pitilessly analysed according to their failures and omissions. Today, the limits of each are the strategic points of every revolutionary analysis.

Marx believed that *in* economics and its dialectical procedure he rediscovered the fundamental agency. In fact, he discovered, *throughout* many economic convulsions, what systematically haunted it: *the very separation of economics as an agency*. Running through the economic, breeding conflict and making it the site of contradictions is the fantastic autonomisation of the economy raised to the level of the reality principle, which these contradictions, however violent, rationalise in their own way.

But this is also true of psychoanalysis: here too, in the term of the unconscious and the labour of the unconscious, Freud gained possession of what, in the form of the individual psychical apparatus, resulted from the fracture of the symbolic as a fundamental agency. The conflictual relation of the conscious to the unconscious relentlessly translates the haunting of this very separation of the psychical as such. Freudian topography (unconscious, preconscious, conscious) merely formalises, and theorises as an original given, what results from a destructuration.

This analysis of Marx and Freud is critical. But neither are critical in relation to the respective separation of their domains. They are not conscious of the rupture that founds them. They are critical symptomatologies that subtly turn their respective symptomatological fields into the determining field. Primary processes, modes of production: 'radical' words, irreducible schemata of determination. It is as such that they imperialistically export their concepts.

Today, Marxism and psychoanalysis try to mix and exchange their concepts. Logically, in fact, if both fell within the province of 'radical' critique, they ought to be able to do this. This is not the case, as the failure of the Freudo-Marxian phantasm in all its forms testifies. But the basic reason for the incessant failure of this conceptual transfer, and why both remain desperate metaphors, is precisely due to the fact that Marxism and psychoanalysis retain their coherence only within their partial definitions (in their ignorance), and cannot therefore be generalised as analytic schemata.

A radical theory can be based neither on their 'synthesis' nor on their contamination, but only on their respective ex-termination. Marxism and psychoanalysis are in crisis. Rather than supporting one another, their respective crises must be telescoped and speeded up. They may yet do each other great collateral damage. We must not be deprived of this spectacle: they are only critical fields.

Notes

1. But 'forgotten' and covered over by all linguistics with especial care: it was only at this cost that it could be established as a 'science' and ensure its structural monopoly in all directions.
2. For what follows concerning the anagrammatic material we refer to Jean Starobinski, *Les mots sous les mots* [Paris: Gallimard, 1971]. For the basic rules, see 'Le souci de la répétition', pp. 12ff.
3. The term 'anathema' which can just as easily be an immolated victim as it can a consecrated object, having drifted in the direction of an accursed object or person, should retain all its importance for the rest of this analysis.
4. The same goes for our perception of space and time, which are unthinkable for us in any other way than infinity – a proliferation that corresponds both to their objectification as value and, here too, to the phantasm of an inexhaustible extension or succession.
5. There is a critique to be made here of what Lévi-Strauss, in his *Structural Anthropology* [2 vols, tr. M. Layton, Harmondsworth: Penguin, 1977–9], calls 'symbolic efficacity' since for him it remains bound (as is the vulgar representation of magic) to the operation of a myth on the body (or on nature) by means of a 'symbolic' exchange or correspondence of signifieds. For example, the difficult birth: mythic speech remobilises the blocked body along its signified, its content. Instead, the efficacity of the sign must be understood as the resolution of a formula. It is by making the elements of a formula

exchange and resolve themselves within this exchange that you induce the same resolution in the sick person's body: the elements of the body (or of nature) enter once again into exchanges with each other. The impact of signs on the body (or on nature, as in the legend of Orpheus), their operating force, derives precisely from not being 'value'. There is no rationalisation of the sign in primitive societies, that is to say, there is no separation between its *actual* operation and a referential signified, no 'reservoir of meaning' where analogies would be conveyed. The symbolic operation is not analogical, it resolves, it is revolutionary, and it concerns the materiality of the sign, which it exterminates as value. There being no more value, the sign actualises the ambivalence, therefore the total exchange and total reversibility of meaning. Hence its efficacy, since conflicts, including disease, are only ever resolved in the exchange.

Actualising ambivalence, the primitive sign, the 'effective' sign, *has no unconscious*. It is clear, and equal to its manifest operation. It does not operate indirectly, or by analogy, on the repressed or unconscious representation (Lévi-Strauss very clearly leans in this direction, in his comparison with psychoanalysis – 'The sorcerer and his magic' – as indeed does all psychoanalytic anthropology). It is its own operation, with no residue, and this is how it operates on the world, this is why it is the direct operation of the world.

6.   There again the *residue* of the analysis fuels the field of 'knowledge', the constructive Eros of 'science', in exactly the same way as the residues of the poetic become enmeshed in the field of communication. Science and discourse speculate on this residue in their imaginary, where they produce their 'surplus-value' and establish their power. What is not analysed and radically resolved in the symbolic operation is what is frozen under the death-mask of value – the beginning of the culture of death and accumulation.

7.   But the disappearence of every coherent signified is not sufficient to produce the poetic. If this were the case, then a lexical madness would be sufficient, or an aleatory automatic writing. It is also necessary that the signifier is eliminated in a rigorous, entirely non-aleatory, operation, without which it remains 'residual', and its mere absurdity will not save it. In automatic writing, for example, the signified is indeed eliminated ('it means nothing' – *ça ne veut rien dire*) – even though it lives entirely on the nostalgia for the signified, and its pleasure consists in leaving every possible signified to chance – in any case, the signifier is produced here without any control, unresolved, instantaneous waste: the third rule of customary discourse (see above), that of the signifier's absolute availability, has been neither shattered nor overcome. But the poetic mode involves both *the liquidation of the signified, and the anagrammatic resolution of the signifier*.

8.   The humour in this story is so successful because, if there is one thing on which the inscription of death has not taken, where the death drive is barred, it is cybernetic systems.

9.   The same goes, in a certain way, for Freud's hypothesis of the death drive – its process and its content remain, in accordance with his avowed wishes, ultimately unverifiable on the clinical level, but its form, as the principle of mental functioning and the anti-*logos*, is revolutionary.

10. This is the illusion of being able to separate the two articulations, and eventually extract the one from the other. It is the illusion of being able to rediscover, by splitting the primary, 'significative' articulation, the equivalent of non-linguistic signs in language (gestures, sounds, colours). This illusion leads J.-F. Lyotard, in *Discours, figure* [Paris: Klincksieck, 1971] to grant the level of the visual or the cry an absolute privilege as spontaneous transgression, always already beyond the discursive and closer to the figural. This illusion remains trapped by the very concept of double articulation, whereby the linguistic order again finds a means to establish itself in the interpretation of what escapes it.

11. Careful here: this all holds for psychoanalysis itself, which also thrives on the rupture between primary and secondary processes, and will die at the end of this separation. And it is true that psychoanalysis is 'revolutionary' and 'scientific' when it explores the

entire field of channels from the standpoint of this rupture (in the unconscious). But perhaps we will one day see that real, total and immediate practice does not obey this postulate, or that analytic simulation model; that *symbolic* practice is from the very first beyond the distinction between primary and secondary processes. To this day, the unconscious and the subject of the unconscious, psychoanalysis and the subject of (psychoanalytic) knowledge, has lived – the analytic field will have disappeared as such into the separation that it instituted itself – for the benefit of the symbolic field. We can already see many signs that this has already taken place.

12. This speech has nothing to do with linguistic sense of the word '*parole*', since the latter is trapped with the *langue–parole* opposition and is subject to the *langue*. Undivided (symbolic) speech itself denies the *langue–parole* distinction, just as undivided social practice denies the theory–practice distinction. Only 'linguistic' *parole* says only what it says. But such speech has never existed, unless in the dialogue of the dead. Concrete, actual speech says what it says, *along with everything else at the same time*. It does not observe the law of the discrete sign and the separation of agencies, it speaks at every level at the same time, or better, it undoes the level of the *langue*, and thus linguistics itself. The latter, by contrast, seeks to impose a *parole* which would be nothing but the execution of the *langue*, that is to say, the discourse of power.

13. Cf. Charles Malamoud, 'Sur la notion de reste dans le brahmanisme', *Wiener Zeitschrift für die Kunde Südasiens*, Vol. XVI, 1972.

14. [In *Jokes and their Relation to the Unconscious*, Freud cites Kant in the following manner: 'the comic is "an expectation that has turned to nothing" ' (*Standard Edition*, ed. and tr. James Strachey, London: Hogarth Press and the Institute of Psychoanalysis, Vol. 8, 1960, p. 199), which he takes from Kant's *Critique of Judgement*, tr. Werner Pluhar, Indianapolis, IN: Hackett, 1987, p. 204, from which I have taken the quotation – tr.]

15. It is on the reduction to and the primacy of the *economy* of the unconscious that the impossiblity of ever really theorising the difference between the phantasm and the work of art rests for Freud. He was able to say that the poets had had the intuition of everything he analysed before him, or even (in *Gradiva*), that psychiatry has no privilege over the poet and that the latter can very well express, 'without taking anything away from beauty and its works' (!) an unconscious problem in all its profundity. The poetic act remains supplementary, sublime but supplementary. J.-F. Lyotard attempts to take Freud up on this point, granting all importance to his distinction between the phantasm and the work of art, while seeking to articulate them rigorously. He first denounces every interpretation in terms of the 'liberation' of the phantasm. To liberate the phantasm is absurd, since the latter is a prohibition of desire, and is of the order of repetition (this is in fact what is currently being produced with the 'liberation' of the unconscious: they liberate it insofar as it is repressed and forbidden, a liberation, that is to say, under the sign of value, of an inverted surplus-value – but perhaps this is the 'Revolution'?). Lyotard writes: 'The artist . . . struggles to free *from* the phantasm, *from* the matrix of figures whose heir and whose locus he is, what really belongs to primary process, and is not a repetition' ('Notes on the critical function of the work of art', in *Driftworks* [New York: Semiotext(e), 1984], p. 74 [translation modified – tr.]). 'For Freud, art must be situated by reference to the phantasm . . . only the artist *does not hide* his phantasms, he gives them the form of effectively real objects, and furthermore [!] the presentation he makes of them is a source of aesthetic pleasure' (*Dérive à partir de Marx et Freud* [Paris: UGE, 1973], p. 56). In Lyotard, this theory takes on 'inverted' ways: *the artist's phantasm* is not produced in reality as the play, the reconciliation, or the fulfilment of desire, *it is produced in reality as a counter-reality*, it intervenes only in the lack of reality, hollowing out this lack. 'The function of art is not to offer a real simulacrum of the fulfilment of desire, it is to show, by way of the play of its figures, what deconstruction of the linguistic and perceptual order must be engaged

in, in order that a figure of the unconscious order allows itself to be discerned through its very evasiveness (presentation of the primary process)' (ibid., pp. 57–8).

Being the prohibition of desire, however, how can the phantasm suddenly play this subversive role? The same goes for the primary processes: 'The work of art differs from the dream and the symptom in that in it, the same operations of condensation, displacement and figuration that, in the dream and the symptom, have the goal of *disguising* desire because it is intolerable, are, in expression, used to push back the *bonne forme* of secondary process and exhibit the "unform", the unconscious disorder' (ibid., p. 58). How are we to understand that the primary processes can be reversed in this way? Are they not themselves bound to *repressed* desire, or are they then the mode of existence of a *'pur et dur'* unconscious, an unsurpassable, infrastructural unconscious? So Lyotard, who correctly says that 'one cannot write on the side of the primary processes. Taking the side of the primary process is still an effect of the secondary processes', would condemn himself.

But this is exactly what the artist does: 'The [artist's] labour may be assimilated to that of the dream and to the operations of the primary process in general, but the artist repeats them and, in so doing, reverses them, because he applies them to the work of this process itself, that is to say, to the figures that arise from the phantasm' (ibid., p. 65).

And, more radically still: 'The artist is someone who, in the desire to see death, even at the price of his own death, lends it the upper hand over the desire to produce.' 'Disease is not the irruption of the unconscious, it is this irruption *and* the furious struggle against it. The genius advances as far as the same figure of depth as the sick, but rather than defending himself against it, he desires it' (ibid., p. 60–1). But where does this acquiescence to the 'cruelty' of the unconscious come from, if not a reversal of the 'will' from an elusive 'actual grace'? And where does the enjoyment that emanates from this act come from, which must somehow, of course, stem from the *form*, and not from the content. Form, for Lyotard, is not far removed from the mystics' void. The artist will contrive 'a deconstructed space', a void, a structure receptive to phantasmatic irruption: 'meaning comes about through the violation of discourse, it is a force or a gesture in the field of significations, it remains *silent*. And in this hole the repressed word merges from its subsoil and establishes itself'. This void, this silence – the calming before the irruption – constitutes a dangerous analogy with mystical processes. But where, above all, do they proceed from? What is the process of 'deconstruction'? We soon see that it has nothing to do with the primary process – on which we here impose an incomprehensible double role: *it is both sides of the reversal.* Would we not do better here, frankly, to leave repression and repetition to one side, and to clear the poetic act of all psychoanalytic counter-dependence?

16. Pleasure, satisfaction and the fulfilment of desire belong to the economic order; enjoyment belongs to the symbolic order. We must make a radical distinction between the two. No doubt saving, recognition, psychical ellipsis and compulsive repetition are sources of a certain (somehow entropic, involutive) pleasure, simultaneously *heimlich* and *unheimlich*, familiar and disturbing, an endless source of anguish, since it is bound to the repetition of the phantasm. The economic is always accumulative and repetitive. The symbolic is the reversal, the resolution of accumulation and repetition; the resolution of the phantasm.

17. Freud thinks, remaining within the logic of economic interpretation, that if one is not the first to laugh, it is because the initiative for the *Witz* requires a certain psychical expenditure, and is therefore, moreover, unavailable for pleasure. He himself admits that this is not very satisfactory.

18. All matter is *raw* material. That is to say, that its concept only appears dependent on the appearance of the order of *production*. All those who would like to be 'materialists' (scientific, semiotic, historical, dialectical, etc.) ought to remember this. Even the sensationalist materialism of the eighteenth century is the first step towards a 'liberation'

of the body in accordance with the *pleasure-function*, as *raw material in the production of pleasure*.

Matter is only ever a force of production. But production itself is hardly 'materialist' at all – nor, moreover, is it idealist. It is an order and a code, and that's all there is to it. The same goes for science: it is an order and a code, no more or less 'materialist' than magic or anything else.

BIBLIOGRAPHY OF WORKS
BY JEAN BAUDRILLARD

This is a bibliography of Baudrillard's works in French and English only. It does not include other language translations and interviews. It has been compiled by Mike Gane for the present volume.

(1962–3a) Uwe Johnson: La frontière. *Les temps modernes*, pp. 1094–107.

(1962–3b) Les romans d'Italo Calvino. *Les temps modernes*, pp. 1728–34.

(1962–3c) La proie des flammes. *Les temps modernes*, pp. 1928–37.

(1967a) Compte rendu de Marshall McLuhan: *Understanding Media. L'homme et la société*, 5, pp. 227–30.

(1967b) L'Éphémère est sans doubt. *Utopie*, 1, pp. 95–7.

(1968a) *Le système des objets*. Paris: Denoël.

(1968b) Compte rendu de Henri Lefebvre, *Position: Contre les Technocrates. Cahiers internationaux de sociologie*, Jan–June, pp. 176–8.

(1969a) Le ludique et le policier. *Utopie*, 2–3, pp. 3–15.

(1969b) La pratique sociale de la technique. *Utopie*, 2–3, pp. 147–55.

(1969c) La morale des objets: Fonction-signe et logique de classe. *Communications*, 13, pp. 23–50. (Included in 1972a and translated in 1981b.)

(1969d) La genèse idéologique des besoins. *Cahiers internationaux de sociologie*, July–Dec., pp. 45–68. (Included in 1972a and translated in 1981b.)

(1970) *La société de consommation*. Paris: Gallimard.

(1971a) Conte de grève 2. *Utopie*, 4, Oct., pp. 24–7.

(1971b) Requiem pour les media. *Utopie*, 4, Oct., pp. 35–51.

(1971c) L'ADN ou la métaphysique du code. *Utopie*, 4, Oct., pp. 57–61.

(1972a) *Pour une critique de l'économie du Signe*. Paris, Gallimard. (In translation, 1981b.)

(1972b) Le miroir de la production. *Utopie*, 5, May, pp. 43–57.

(1973a) *Le miroir de la production*. Tournail: Casterman. (In translation, 1975a.)

(1973b) Le marxisme et le système de l'économie politique. *Utopie*, 6, Feb. pp. 5–44.

(1973c) Conte de grève 3. *Utopie*, 7, Aug., pp. 26–43.

(1974a) La dramatisation de l'économique. *Utopie*, 8, Feb., pp. 6–17.

(1974b) La campagne BNP. *Utopie*, 8, pp. 45–8.

(1974c) Les animaux malades de la plus-value. *Utopie*, 8, pp. 14–17.

(1974d) Les animaux malades de la plus-value 2. *Utopie*, 9, Apr.–May, pp. 14–17.

(1974e) Trompe-la-mort. *Utopie*, 9, Apr.–May, pp. 18–23.

(1974f) Les élections '74. *Utopie*, 10, June–July, pp. 7–17.

(1975a) *The Mirror of Production*, tr. Mark Poster. St Louis, MO: Telos. (Translation of 1973a.)

(1975b) Langages de masse. *Encyclopaedia Universalis*, Vol. 17, Organum. Paris. pp. 394–7.

(1976a) *L'échange symbolique et la mort*. Paris: Gallimard.

(1976b) Conversations à bâtons (in-)interrompus avec Jean Baudrillard. *Dérive*, 5–6, pp. 70–97.

(1976c) La réalité dépasse l'hyperréalisme. *Revue d'esthétique*, 1, pp. 139–48.

(1976d) L'économie politique des signes. *Traverses*, 1.

(1976e) Le crépuscule des signes. *Traverses*, 2.

(1976f) La mode ou la féerie du code. *Traverses*, 3.

(1976g) Crash. *Traverses*, 4, May, pp. 24–9.

(1976h) La prise d'otage 1. *Utopie*, 13, Mar.–Apr., pp. 5–9.

(1976i) Dies irae. *Utopie*, 13, Mar.–Apr., pp. 34–7.

(1976j) Porno stereo. *Utopie*, 13, Mar.–Apr., pp. 87–95.

(1976k) Le cadavre en spirale. *Utopie*, 14, May–June, pp. 10–15.

(1976l) Conte de travail 3. *Utopie*, 14, May–June, pp. 19–24.

(1976m) Quand Bataille attaquait le principe métaphysique de l'économie. *La Quinzaine Littéraire*, 234, June, pp. 4–5.

(1977a) *L'effet Beaubourg: Implosion et dissuasion*. Paris: Galilée. (In translation, 1982c.)

(1977b) *Oublier Foucault*. Paris: Galilée. (In translation, 1987c.)

(1977c) La lutte enchantée ou le flute finale. *Utopie*, 16, Apr., pp. 6–9.

(1977–8a) Castrée le veille de son mariage. *Utopie*, 17, Dec.–Jan., pp. 2–10.

(1977–8b) Notre théâtre de la cruauté (sur le terrorisme – Mogadiscio). *Utopie*, 17, Dec.–Jan., pp. 17–24.

(1978a) Territoire et métamorphoses. *Traverses*, 8.

(1978b) La précéssion de simulacres. *Traverses*, 10, pp. 3–37.

(1978c) Quand on enlève tout, il ne reste rien. *Traverses*, 11, pp. 12–15.

(1978d) *L'ange de stuc*. Paris: Galilée.

(1978e) *À l'ombre des majorités silencieuses, ou la fin du social*. Fontenay-sous-Bois: Cahiers d'Utopie. (In translation, 1983a.)

(1979a) *De la séduction*. Paris: Denoël-Gonthier. (In translation, 1990a.)

(1979b) Rituel – loi – code. In M. Maffesoli and A. Bruston (eds), *Violence et transgression*. Paris: Anthropos.

(1979c) Clone story ou L'enfant prothèse. *Traverses*, 14–15, Apr., pp. 143–8.

(1979d) Holocaust. *Cahiers du cinéma*, 302, July–Aug., p. 72.

(1979e) L'ecliptique du sexe. *Traverses*, 17, Nov., pp. 2–30.

(1980a) La fin de la modernité ou l'ère de la simulation. *Encyclopaedia Universalis*, Supplement, pp. 8–17.

(1980b) Desert for ever. *Traverses*, 19, pp. 54–8. (Translated in 1987o.)

(1981a) *Simulacres et simulation*. Paris: Galilée. (Part translation as 1983f.)

(1981b) *For a Critique of the Political Economy of the Sign*, tr. Charles Levin. St Louis, MO: Telos. (Translation of 1972a.)

(1981c) Beyond the unconscious: The symbolic. *Discourse*, 3, pp. 60–87. (Part translation of 1976a.)

(1981d) La cérémonie du monde. *Traverses*, 21–2, May, pp. 27–36.

(1981e) Le fatal ou l'imminence reversible. *Traverses*, 23, Nov., pp. 24–40. (In translation, 1981f.)

(1981f) Fatality or reversible imminence: Beyond the uncertainty principle. *Social Research*, 49 (2), pp. 272–93. (Translation of 1981e.)

(1982a) Histoires de voir: Jean Baudrillard. [Interview.] *Cinématographe*, July–Aug., pp. 39–46. (Translation in 1993a.)

(1982b) Otage et terreur: L'échange impossible. *Traverses*, 25, June, pp. 2–13.

(1982c) The Beaubourg effect: Implosion and deterrence. *October*, 20, Spring, pp. 3–13. (Translation of 1977a.)

(1983a) *In the Shadow of the Silent Majorities: Or, the End of the Social and Other Essays*, tr. Paul Foss, Paul Patton and John Johnston. New York: Semiotext(e). (Translation of 1978e.)

(1983b) *Les stratégies fatales*. Paris: Grasset. (In translation, 1990h.)

(1983c) What are you doing after the orgy? *Traverses*, 29, Oct. pp. 2–15.

(1983d) Les séductions de Baudrillard. [Interview.] *Magazine littéraire*, 193, Mar., pp. 80–5. (Translation in 1993a.)

(1983e) *Please Follow Me* (with Sophie Calle: *Suite Venitienne*). Paris: Éditions de L'Étoile. (In translation, 1988e.)

(1983f) *Simulations*, tr. P. Foss et al. New York: Semiotext(e), (Part translation of 1981a.)

(1983g) De la croissance à l'excroissance. *Débat*, 23, Jan.

(1983h) What are you doing after the orgy? *Artforum*, Oct., pp. 42–6.

(1983i) Is pop an art of consumption? *Tension*, 2, pp. 33–5.

(1983j) The ecstasy of communication. In H. Foster (ed.), *The Anti-Aesthetic*. Port Townsend: Bay Press.

(1983k) Le crystal se venge: Une interview avec Jean Baudrillard. *Parachute*, June–Aug., pp. 126–33. (Translation in 1990e and 1993a.)

(1983l) Nuclear implosion. *Impulse*, Spring–Summer, pp. 9–13.

(1983m) Sur le 'Look Generation': Interview. *Nouvel observateur*, Feb. 18, p. 50. (Translation in 1993a.)

(1983n) Interview. *Psychologie*, May, pp. 65–8. (Translation in 1993a.)

(1984a) Interview. *Cinéma 84*, January, pp. 16–18 (Translation in 1993a.)

(1984b) Astral America. *Artforum*, Sept., pp. 70–4.

(1984c) Interview: Game with vestiges. *On the Beach*, 5, Winter, pp. 19–25. (Included in 1993a.)

(1984d) L'enfant-bulle. *Traverses*, 32, Sept., pp. 15–17.

(1984–5a) Intellectuals, commitment, and political power. *Thesis Eleven*, 10–11, pp. 166–73. (Included in 1993a.)

(1984–5b) Une conversation avec Jean Baudrillard. *UCLA French Studies*, 2–3, pp. 1–22.

(1985a) *La gauche divine*. Paris: Grasset.

(1985b) The masses: The implosion of the social in the media. *New Literary History*, 16 (3), pp. 577–89.

(1985c) The child in the bubble. *Impulse*, 11 (4), p. 13.

(1985d) L'an 2000 ne passera pas. *Traverses*, 33–4, pp. 8–16.

(1985e) Modernité. *Encyclopaedia Universalis*, Vol. 10, pp. 139–41.

(1986a) *Amérique*. Paris: Grasset. (In translation, 1988a.)

(1986b) *Passage* (text: Marite Bonnal; photos: JB). Paris: Galilée.

(1986c) Clone boy. *Z/G*, 11, pp. 12–13.

(1986d) The realised utopia, America. *French Review*, 60, pp. 2–6.

(1986e) Le puissance du dégoût. *Traverses*, 37, Apr. pp. 4–13.

(1986f) L'Amérique comme fiction. [Interview with J. Heric and Guy Scarpetta.] *Art Press*, 103, May, pp. 40–2. (Translation in 1988k and 1993a.)

(1987a) *L'Autre par lui-même*. Paris: Galilée. (In translation, 1988c.)

(1987b) *Cool Memories*. Paris: Galilée. (In translation, 1990c.)

(1987c) *Forget Foucault*, tr. H. Beitchmann and M. Polizzoti. New York: Semiotext(e). (Translation of 1977b and includes interview 'Forget Baudrillard', also reprinted in 1993a.)

(1987d) *The Evil Demon of Images*, tr. Paul Patton and Paul Foss. Annandale: Power Institute. (Includes 'An interview with Jean Baudrillard', tr. Philippe Tanguy, also reprinted in 1993a.)

(1987e) When Bataille attacked the metaphysical principle of economy. *Canadian Journal of Political and Social Theory*, 11 (3), pp. 57–62. (Translation of 1976m.)

(1987f) Modernity. *Canadian Journal of Political and Social Theory*, 11 (3), pp. 63–73. (Translation of 1985e.)

(1987g) The year 2000 has already happened. In A. and M. Kroker (eds), *Body Invaders*. London: Macmillan. pp. 35–44. (Translation of 1985d.)

(1987h) Le Xerox et l'infinie. *Traverses*, 44–5, pp. 18–22. (In translation, 1988f.)

(1987i) Nous sommes tous des transsexuals. *Libération*, 14 Oct., p. 4.

(1987j) Au-delà du vrai et du faux, ou le malin génie de l'image. *Cahiers internationaux de sociologie*, 82, pp. 139–45.

(1987k) A perverse logic and drugs as exorcism. *UNESCO Courier*, 7, pp. 7–9.

(1987l) Amérique. *Literary Review*, 30 (3), pp. 475–82.

(1987m) Softly, softly. *New Statesman*, 6 March, p. 44.

(1987n) USA 80s. In *Semiotext(e) USA*. New York: Autonomedia. pp. 47–60.

(1987o) Desert for ever. In *Semiotext(e) USA*. New York: Autonomedia. pp. 135–7. (Translation of 1980b.)

(1988a) *America*, tr. C. Turner. London: Verso. (Translation of 1986a.)

(1988b) *Jean Baudrillard: Selected Writings*, ed. Mark Poster, tr. J. Mourrain. Cambridge: Polity.

(1988c) *The Ecstasy of Communication*, ed. Sylvère Lotringer, tr. B. and C. Schutze, New York: Semiotext(e). (Translation of 1987a.)

(1988d) Interview: Jean Baudrillard. *Block*, 14, pp. 8–10. (Included in 1993a.)

(1988e) *Please Follow Me* (with Sophie Calle: *Suite Venitienne*). Seattle: Bay Press. (Translation of 1983e.)

(1988f) *Xerox to Infinity*. London: Touchepas. (Translation of 1987h.)

(1988g) Necrospective autour de Martin Heidegger. *Libération*, 27 Jan. p. 2.

(1988h) Éloge d'un Krach virtuel. *Libération*, 2 March, p. 6.

(1988i) L'économie virale. *Libération*, 9 Nov., p. 6.

(1988j) Hunting nazis and losing reality. *New Statesman*. 19 Feb., pp. 16–17.

(1988k) Interview: America as fiction. *Eyeline*, 5, June, pp. 24–5. (Translation of 1986f, reprinted in 1993a.)

(1989a) The anorexic ruins, tr. David Antal. In D. Kamper and C. Wulf (eds), *Looking Back at the End of the World*. New York: Semiotext(e), pp. 29–45.

(1989b) The end of production. *Polygraph*, 2–3, pp. 5–29. (Part translation of 1976a.)

(1989c) Politics of seduction: Interview with Baudrillard. *Marxism Today*, January, pp. 54–5. (Included in 1993a.)

(1989d) Panic crash! In A. Kroker, M. Kroker and D. Cook (eds), *Panic Encyclopaedia*. London: Macmillan. pp. 64–7.

(1989e) An interview with Jean Baudrillard (Judith Williamson). *Block*, 15, pp. 16–19.

(1989f) La dépressurisation de L'Occident. *Libération*, 14 March, p. 10.

(1989g) Décongélation de l'Est et fin de l'histoire. *Libération*, 15 Dec. p. 5.

(1989i) Interview with John Johnston. *Art Papers*. Jan.–Feb., pp. 4–7. (Included in 1993a.)

(1990a) *Seduction*, tr. B. Singer. London: Macmillan. (Translation of 1979a.)

(1990b) *La transparence du mal: Essai sur les phénomènes extrêmes*. Paris: Galilée. (In translation, 1993b.)

(1990c) *Cool Memories*, tr. C. Turner. London: Verso. (Translation of 1987b.)

(1990d) *Cool Memories II*. Paris; Galilée.

(1990e) *Revenge of the Crystal: Selected Writings on the Modern Object and its Destiny, 1968–1983*, ed. and tr. Paul Foss and Julian Pefanis. London: Pluto.

(1990f) Le snobisme machinal. *Les cahiers du Musée National d'art Moderne*, Winter, pp. 35–43.

(1990g) L'hystéresie du millenium. *Débat*, 60, May–Aug., pp. 65–73.

(1990h) *Fatal Strategies*, tr. Philip Beitchman and W.G.J. Niesluchowski. London: Pluto. (Translation of 1983b.)

(1990i) L'ère de facticité. In L. Sfez and G. Coutlee (eds), *Technologies et symboliques de la communication*. Grenoble: Presses Universitaires de Grenoble.

(1990j) Fractal theory: Baudrillard and the contemporary arts. [Interview with N. Zurbrugg.] *Eyeline*, 11, June, pp. 4–7. (Included in 1993a.)

(1991a) La guerre du golfe n'aura pas lieu. *Libération*, 4 January, p. 5.

(1991b) The reality gulf. *Guardian*, 11 January, p. 25. (Translation of 1991a.)

(1991c) Le guerre du golfe a-t-elle vraiment lieu? *Libération*, 6 February, p. 10.

(1991d) Le guerre du golfe n'a pas eu lieu. *Libération*, 29 March, p. 6.

(1991e) *La guerre du golfe n'a pas eu lieu*. Paris: Galilée.

(1991f) Interview with Brigitte Lièvre. *Le journal des psychologues*. (Translation in 1993a.)

(1991g) [Interview with Anne Laurent.] 'Cette bière n'est pas une bière'. *Théâtre/Publique, Révue du Théâtre de Gennevilliers*, 100, July–Aug., pp. 56–61. (Translation in 1993a.)

(1991h) [Interview with Nicole Czechowski.] Paysage sublunaire et atonal. *Le pardon*. Paris: Éditions Autrement. (Translation in 1993a.)

(1991i) Simulacra and Science Fiction, tr. by A.H. Evans. *Science-Fiction Studies*, 18, November, p. 309–13. (Translation of part of 1981a.)

(1991j) Ballard's *Crash*, tr. by A.H. Evans. *Science-Fiction Studies*, 18, November, pp. 313–20. (Translation of 1976g.)

(1992a)*L'illusion de la fin ou la grève des événements*. Paris: Galilée.

(1992b) (with M. Guillam) *Figures de l'alterité*. Paris: Éditions Descartes.

(1992c) Transpolitics, transsexuality, transaesthetics. In W. Stearns and W. Chaloupka (eds), *Jean Baudrillard*. London: Macmillan. pp. 9–26.

(1992d) Revolution and the end of utopia. In W. Stearns and W. Chaloupka (eds), *Jean Baudrillard*. London: Macmillan. pp. 233–42.

(1992e) Baudrillard shrugs: A seminar on terrorism and the media with Sylvère Lotringer and Jean Baudrillard. In W. Stearns and W. Chaloupka (eds), *Jean Baudrillard*. London: Macmillan. pp. 238–302.

(1992f) La dictature démocratique est en bonne voie. *L'autre journal*, 30 December, pp. 40–1.

(1993a) *Baudrillard Live: Selected Interviews*, ed. M. Gane. London: Routledge.

(1993b) *Transparency of Evil: Essays on Extreme Phenomena*, tr. J. Benedict. London: Verso. (Translation of 1990b.)

(1993c) Hyperreal America. *Economy and Society*, 22 May, pp. 243–52.

(in press) Conversation with Jean Baudrillard. In Florian Rotzer (ed.), *Conversations with French Philosophers*. Atlantic Highlands, NJ: Humanities Press International.

INDEX